Ernie O'Malley

Ernie O'Malley

IRA Intellectual

Richard English

OXFORD
UNIVERSITY PRESS

Great Clarendon Street, Oxford OX2 6DP

Oxford University Press is a department of the University of Oxford
It furthers the University's objective of excellence in research, scholarship,
and education by publishing worldwide in

Oxford New York

Athens Auckland Bangkok Bogotá Buenos Aires Calcutta
Cape Town Chennai Dar es Salaam Delhi Florence Hong Kong Istanbul
Karachi Kuala Lumpur Madrid Melbourne Mexico City Mumbai
Nairobi Paris São Paulo Singapore Taipei Tokyo Toronto Warsaw
and associated companies in Berlin Ibadan

Oxford is a registered trade mark of Oxford University Press
in the UK and in certain other countries

Published in the United States
by Oxford University Press Inc., New York

British Library Cataloguing in Publication Data

Data available

Library of Congress Cataloging in Publication Data

Data applied for

ISBN 0-19-820595-3
ISBN 0-19-820807-3 (Pbk.)

1 3 5 7 9 10 8 6 4 2

Printed in Great Britain
on acid-free paper by
Bookcraft Ltd, Midsomer Norton,
Nr Bath, Somerset

For Max

Preface

This book has a number of aims. The first is to bring to life one of modern Ireland's most exciting, distinctive, and talented intellectuals. A wide range of rich sources—oral and visual as well as documentary and published—has made it possible to construct an unusually detailed biographical account. Most of this source material has not previously been explored by historians; this novelty, together with the dramatic and arresting quality of Ernie O'Malley's experience, provide reason enough for this biography. Second, the book represents a major case study in modern Irish nationalism and, more particularly, in the militant Republican strand within the Irish nationalist tradition. O'Malley was a Revolutionary Irish Republican, an exponent of that physical force tradition which has formed so significant a part of Irish and Anglo-Irish history in the modern period. Much of his historical significance lies in his having been so important a practitioner and so shrewd a chronicler of this aggressive version of Irish nationalism. As such, his ideas deserve to be treated very seriously. Whatever one's perspective on this militant Republican tradition, it is undeniable that it has been of great political importance. It has cast influence well beyond its committed adherents and, for this reason, it must be understood if one is to gain a firm grasp on Irish and Anglo-Irish politics and history. In addition to exploring the Irish physical force tradition the biography has a third ambition: to examine the changing patterns of broader Irish experience in the wake of the 1916–23 Revolution in which O'Malley influentially participated. An active and well-connected intellectual in the new Ireland, O'Malley also had experience of living in the United States during the late 1920s and early 1930s. He provides an excellent opportunity for close consideration of key themes in modern Irish experience: literary, intellectual, artistic, and social, both in Ireland and abroad. This is, then, a book about modern Ireland, one which aims to illuminate our reading of the wider Irish setting by means of the consideration of one charismatic and significant individual. It is also an attempt to go beyond that, and to reflect on the ways in which the specific experience of this particular Irish nationalist can illuminate our reading of nationalism more generally. The issues central to O'Malley's Irish Revolution are crucial elsewhere also: the definition of the authentic political nation, the tension between liberal democratic principles and ethno-religious sentiment, the galvanizing power of intertwined religious and political faith, the causes and effects of political violence. These are, indeed, some of the most important issues in modern history and it will be suggested here that close-focused case studies offer unique opportunities for their full appreciation. The book, then, has these main aims: to understand the individual, to explore the Irish Revolution, to consider key questions within modern Irish historical development, and to reflect on our approach to the broader phenomenon of nationalism.

What of its structure? This deviates from orthodox biographical practice and requires, perhaps, some comment. Chapter 1 presents 'The Life': an outline of O'Malley's experience which will introduce the man in detail. This provides a biographical foundation on which readers will be able to build during the subsequent chapters. Chapter 2 examines 'The Revolutionary'. The causes, nature, and political effects of O'Malley's 1916–24 involvement in Revolutionary Republicanism are addressed. Chapter 3 studies 'The Intellectual': O'Malley's experience as an intellectual in post-Revolutionary Ireland; his connections with leading intellectuals in various exciting worlds — in Ireland, the rest of Europe, and the United States; his writings, political and non-political; and his diverse interests in artistic and cultural development. Chapter 4 looks at 'The Companion' — at O'Malley's complex personality, at his friendships, and at his turbulent experience of family life. Chapter 5 explores 'The Legacies', political, intellectual, and cultural. This structure is essentially thematic. But it is also sensitive to O'Malley's gradual development and is in this sense chronological. Each chapter concentrates on material which follows on from the last in terms of O'Malley's chronology: the 1916–24 Revolutionary is followed by the post-Revolutionary Intellectual of the 1920s, 1930s, and beyond; the Companion chapter focuses primarily on the sources available for the years after his marriage in 1935, while the Legacies plainly concern the period after his death in 1957. The book's structure is thus both thematic and chronological, and is chosen in order both to analyse the salient themes of his life and to detail sensitively the ways in which he changed over time.

Irish history and Irish politics are rarely far apart, and the task of the scholar who writes about so contentious a figure as a leading IRA (Irish Republican Army) hero is far from easy. My approach as biographer has been neither primarily to praise nor to bury my subject, but rather to attempt to explain him within his changing contexts. The most serious attitude to take towards a figure of historical importance is to treat them as a fully rounded person rather than merely as hero or villain. In Ernie O'Malley's case the extraordinary richness and variety of the original sources make this possible. The book is intended to be respectful but not hagiographical, critical but not denigratory. O'Malley deserves a serious, rigorous biography which brings out fully the interwoven personal, political, and intellectual complexities of his life. Sophisticated, dynamic, repeatedly ambiguous; austere, demanding, instinctively dissident; determined, impressively focused, and restlessly intellectual—O'Malley is, according to the argument of this book, as personally compelling as he is historically and politically significant. He is a world-historical witness to modern Irish history.

Acknowledgements

I am indebted to a large number of people and institutions for the help which they have provided in relation to this book. Roy Foster first suggested that I work on an Ernie O'Malley biography; for this, as for his support and advice, I am lastingly grateful. David Eastwood, Charles Townshend, and George Boyce have profoundly influenced my approach to the writing of history. Colleagues at Queen's University, Belfast, have provided an enjoyable mixture of friendship and intellectual stimulation; in particular Martin Stokes, Alvin Jackson, Michael Kenny, Graham Walker, Mark Burnett, Harvey Whitehouse, Vincent Geoghegan, Bob Eccleshall, David Hempton, Paul Bew, and Patrick Maume have in various ways enriched my time at the University. A number of the above read and discussed sections of the book in manuscript, as did Brian S. Murphy, and I have benefited greatly from the resulting comments.

Many people gave their time as interviewees, correspondents, or advisers on important points, or helped in other ways with the project: Nuala Aylward, Deirdre Bair, Anthony Behan, Ronnie Buchanan, J. G. Corr, Raymond Davys, Terence Donohue, Michael J. Egan, Donald and Bertha English, Paul and Carol English, Garret FitzGerald, Jennifer FitzGerald, John Fleetwood, Tony Jordan, Angeline Kelly, Ludovic Kennedy, James Knowlson, Caitriona Lawlor, Louis le Brocquy, N. J. McGahon, Jean McGrail, Francis McKay, Deirdre McMahon, Ulick O'Connor, Michael O'Duffy, Maureen O'Hara Blair, Vivian Perlis, John Regan, Susan Schreibman, Joe Skelly, Bob and Marcia Skelly, Wendy Smith, Francis Stuart, Sean Sweeney, and Anne Yeats. Eithne Sax, who (as Eithne Golden) knew Ernie O'Malley in New Mexico, was fascinating and invaluably helpful regarding many aspects of this period of his life.

Many institutions helped make the research possible. Queen's University, Belfast, was repeatedly generous in providing time and funding for research visits. In particular, I am grateful to Bob Eccleshall and John Spencer for their support. Moreover, the University's Institute of Irish Studies and, since 1990, its Department of Politics provided me with ideal settings in which to work on the book. The British Academy and the Economic and Social Research Council both provided funding for periods of research. Other important institutions were: Ampleforth College (York), the Archives Department of

University College, Dublin (in particular, Seamus Helferty), the BBC Written Archives Centre (especially Armand De Filippo), the British Library (London), the Centre for Creative Photography (the University of Arizona, Tucson; especially Amy Rule and Dianne Nilsen), Columbia University Libraries (New York), the General Register Office (Dublin), the Library of Congress in Washington, DC (especially Wayne Shirley), the National Archives (Dublin), the National Library of Ireland (Dublin), New York Public Library, the Public Record Office (Kew), Queen's University Library (Belfast), Reading University Library, Sotheby's (London), Trinity College Library (Dublin), the University of Ulster Library (Jordanstown), Westminster Register Office (London), the Yaddo Corporation (Saratoga Springs, NY). Tony Morris and Jane Williams at OUP have been tremendously helpful.

Throughout my research the O'Malley family have been unremittingly generous, helpful, hospitable, and supportive. Quite simply, the project would have been impossible without their enthusiasm. I have greatly enjoyed, and have benefited hugely from, conversations with Ernie O'Malley's widow (the late Helen Hooker O'Malley Roelofs) and with his three children (Cahal Hooker O'Malley, Etáin O'Malley, and Cormac O'Malley). Cahal was profoundly courteous and helpful in our numerous conversations about his father and cast light on many matters. Etáin generously spent many hours with me discussing her father, and was illuminating in her observations. She also helped me greatly through her generous provision of access to papers from her mother's estate. These interviews and these archives were invaluable. Both Etáin and Cahal kindly read and commented upon a draft of the biography. Cormac and Moira O'Malley were extraordinarily hospitable towards the biographer who intruded upon their lives, first in London and then in New York and Connecticut. Their generosity and friendship have been richly appreciated. Moreover, Cormac O'Malley has—more than anyone else—made possible the writing of this biography of his father. His devoted and skilled accumulation over many years of an enormous and astonishingly full archive; his expertise and understanding regarding so many areas of his father's life; his honesty and generosity in providing access to materials and in spending many hours in discussion and interview—without such work, the biography would not have been possible. He has read and helpfully commented upon drafts of the book. While no serious biographer can expect full family endorsement of all views expressed in such a book, I do hope that the portait here presented of their father will go some way towards repaying the generosity which Cahal, Etáin, and especially Cormac O'Malley have shown to its author.

R.E.

Belfast
December 1996

Contents

List of Plates

between pp. 144–145

Abbreviations

ADUCD	Archives Department, University College, Dublin
CBS	Christian Brothers' School
CO	Colonial Office
HLRO	House of Lords Record Office, London
IHS	*Irish Historical Studies*
IPP	Irish Parliamentary Party
IRA	Irish Republican Army
NA	National Archives, Dublin
NLI	National Library of Ireland, Dublin
NYPL	New York Public Library
PP	Private Possession
PRO	Public Record Office, Kew
RIC	Royal Irish Constabulary
TCD	Trinity College, Dublin
TD	Teachta Dála [Dáil Deputy]
UCD	University College, Dublin

1

The Life

'As a youngster . . . I had the inborn hate of things English, which I
expect all Irishmen inherit.' Irish Revolutionary, Ernie O'Malley
wrote these typically arresting words in a Dublin prison shortly after
ending a forty-one day hunger strike in 1923. His letter continued with
telling autobiographical snapshots of his experiences to date. As a
child he had 'hated' the British King 'and blamed him for everything.
I had great daydreams of myself playing the part of a soldier charging at
the head of men, and reforming the dream until I was satisfied.' Educated at a Christian Brothers' School and then at Medical School in
Dublin, O'Malley had become absorbed in Irish Republicanism and
had been powerfully jolted in that direction by the 1916 Easter Rising.
He had been drawn gradually into Revolutionary activity—he used to
'kick up a row generally at the Masses . . . carrying a large Republican
flag and a small revolver'—and eventually left home in 1918 to become
a full-time Republican activist. During the ensuing war between Irish
Republicans and the forces of the British Crown, IRA man Ernie
O'Malley played a leading role as a peripatetic rebel. It could be a
lonely campaign: 'I made few friends. I grew careless about religious
matters, never went to Mass, as strangers in country districts are too
conspicuous, seldom said my prayers, and generally led my solitary life
without help from God or man.' The struggle entered a new phase

when Irish Republicans split into two factions and contested the 1922–3 Civil War; it was within this conflict that O'Malley's 1923 hunger strike and his autobiographical letter were situated. The epistle hints at many important themes from O'Malley's life: patriotic soldier-ship, Anglophobia, a self-conscious desire to record one's experience, and a combination of relentless enthusiasm, stoicism, bookishness, disciplined auto-didacticism, nationalist commitment, and religion:

At the University I learned how to waste time but developed a love of books, for literature and art, but was too lazy to read anything difficult. My years on active service [in the IRA] have taught me 'to grin and bear it', to suffer without com-plaining, to endure beyond bodily strength, not to be a coward; to play the game by your enemies, your own, and most of all yourself; to think and ponder over problems, to write memos, orders, articles, and books on military subjects, to saturate myself with my self-instructed subject so that I could lecture at ran-dom; to be more emotionally attached to books; lastly, but only of late, to know my God and to put him before my country.[1]

I

1897–1922
Reared in an Imperialistic setting I became an Irish separatist, and fought there.

(Ernie O'Malley)[2]

Of all the people I met and knew . . . [Ernie O'Malley] was the only one whom I would judge worthy of a full biography on a scale which would command uni-versal rather than merely Irish interest.

(Todd Andrews)[3]

On 29 October 1894 Luke Malley (b. 1861) and Marion Kearney (b. 1873) were married in Fairview Roman Catholic Chapel in Dublin. The daughter of Bernard and Mary Anne Kearney, Marion had been born in Clooncouse, near Castlerea in County Roscommon. Prior to her marriage she had been studying nursing in Dublin. Luke, the son of Luke and Mary Ellen Malley, had been born in Ballyglass, between Claremorris and Castlebar in County Mayo. At the time of the marriage he was working in Castlebar as managing clerk for Malachy Kelly, Crown Solicitor for County Mayo. After the marriage the Malleys settled in Ellison Street in Castlebar. On 19 October 1895 Marion gave birth to their first child, Francis Luke, in a nursing home in Gardiner Place, Dublin. The second child, Ernest Bernard,[4] was born on 26 May 1897 at home in Ellison Street. Nine other children followed: Marion Mary Nellie (b. 16 June 1898), Albert Patrick Victor (b. 9 April 1899), Cecil Patrick (b. 5 April 1902), Charles (b. 11 February 1904), John Patrick (b. 3 June 1905), Luke Kevin (b. 12 January 1907), Kathleen Mary (b. 11 May 1910), Brendan (b. 28 March 1912), Desmond Francis (b. 12 March 1918).

The west of Ireland—in particular, County Mayo—was to play a major role in Ernie O'Malley's story. While the Malleys were based in Castlebar they rented, during the summers, a spacious house near Rosbeg, Westport, County Mayo. With beautiful views of Clew Bay and Croagh Patrick, this setting provided the young O'Malley with the stuff of imaginative attachment, later celebrated in his brilliant Revolutionary memoir, *On Another Man's Wound*: 'On Clew Bay, where we went each summer, we learned to row punts and boats, to blister our hands sitting side by side tugging at the one long sweep with the fishermen. They carved small boats for us, models of schooners, frigates, ships, full-rigged boats in glass bottles. . . . We learned to love the sea, to be unafraid of it.' The rapture of the sea and the lyrical depiction of Irish countryside were to be important themes in O'Malley's world, and their roots lay in these childhood experiences.

Now we knew the country on either side of the Bay, from grey hungry Connemara to Mulranny. The bare, once ice-covered drumlins gave the land a gloomy look when the sky was clouded or when rain-winds tufted black clouds. But sun made the cold land and the dark green glint and become lush; it shone on the crowded islands, lifting them out of the water, making the cliffs recede. . . . In rain or sun we loved this country; its haunting impersonal bareness, its austerity, aloofness, small lakes, the disproportionate bulking of the mountains, smells of shrivelled seaweed rotting in grey dirt-spume, brine, storm-wood, tarred rope and riggings, sea-wrack, and mud after an ebb tide. . . . Our life was ringed by the Bay; it was a huge world to us.[5]

Similarly recreated in O'Malley's recollections of these years was the lore passed on by their nurse ('Nannie'). The two eldest children, Frank and Ernie, were told stories and legends, were treated to renditions of patriotic songs and ballads, were introduced to figures from Irish mythology such as Cuchulain, and were repeatedly enthralled and frightened by their nurse's ghost stories. In all of this, sensitive imagination is the key theme, and one which was worked and reworked by O'Malley throughout his life. His massive reading was repeatedly to take him into worlds of the imagination; and his imaginative writing left a rich legacy of recreated, reinvented experience.

In 1905 Malachy Kelly moved to Dublin to become Chief Crown Solicitor for Ireland. Luke Malley followed in 1906, but was not in fact employed under Malachy's aegis. Instead he began work in Dublin as a clerk with the Congested Districts Board. Ernie attended the Christian Brothers' School (CBS), North Richmond Street, Dublin—the O'Connell School. In his view this had been a 'fairly good school where we rubbed shoulders with all classes and conditions'.[6] The school had achieved a highly impressive academic record; along with the North Monastery, Cork, it was one of the most successful of the CBS institutions. In particular, it prided itself on the number of university entrance scholarships which were won by its boys. The foundation stone of the school had been laid in June 1828 by the great nineteenth-century Irish political leader Daniel O'Connell, and the school—which opened in August 1831—derived its name from this O'Connellite connection and from the interest which the Liberator took in its progress and success. CBS education played a significant role in shaping O'Malley's Revolutionary generation; at the very least, it is important to note the striking number of leaders and participants in the 1916 Easter Rising who had attended Christian Brothers' Schools (including a notable number from the O'Connell School itself). O'Malley was himself to be moved by the Easter rebellion, but prior to that two further and key developments should be noted. Early in the First World War his older brother Frank, who had also been educated at the O'Connell School, joined the British Army and became an officer in the Royal Dublin Fusiliers. Frank and Ernie were very close, and it is clear that Ernie intended to follow his elder brother's career path. When the 1914–18 war began, his sympathies lay with the British—'though not enthusiastically pro-British, yet I was somewhat so'[7]—and the idea of soldiership appealed to him.

For the moment, however, soldiership was eclipsed by medicine, and this is the second important point to note from this period. Although his school record shows that he performed rather better at English, History, French, and Geography than at Arithmetic, Algebra, Geometry, Science (or, incidentally, Irish), O'Malley began to pursue a medical career. In August 1915 it was announced that he was one of twenty-four successful candidates to be awarded Dublin Corporation Scholarships to the National University of Ireland. The report of the

Scholarships Committee stated that O'Malley had been placed eight-eenth out of the forty-five who had been examined in July. Thus in the autumn of 1915 he began a medical degree at Cecilia Street, Dublin. Cecilia Street Medical School had been opened in November 1855 as the Catholic University School of Medicine and had in 1909 become the Medical Faculty of University College, Dublin (a constituent college of the newly formed National University of Ireland). The religious and the social atmosphere are important here: the National was a Catholic university, and Catholic as well as Protestant medical professionals had played a significant role in the social world of Dublin's élite during the late nineteenth and early twentieth centuries. Both the religious and the social complexion of this Catholic social élite were to be telling in relation to O'Malley's Revolutionary development.

O'Malley's medical studies were, however, to be jolted—and the course of his life profoundly affected—as a result of the dramatic events of 1916. The Easter Rising of that year, recently described by one authority as 'reckless, bloody, sacrificial, and unsuccessful',[8] was yet a significant force in redirecting modern Irish politics and history, and it left an indelible mark on this particular young student. His own words testify with a characteristic sense of drama to a Damascus Road experience: 'Then came like a thunderclap the 1916 Rising.'[9] The Rising itself was the work of a small group of militant Irish nationalists— 'poets, conspirators, and socialists'[10]—who were intent on redeeming their nation through the bloodshed of a military gesture against British rule in Ireland. The rebellion began on 24 April 1916 and ended within a week: militarily defeated, the rebels managed none the less to play a major part in Ireland's subsequent history. Though not sparking off the desired national uprising, the rebels' gesture did lead to an intensification of Irish nationalist emotion. Britain's sharp wartime response, including the execution of a number of the rebel leaders, helped to create sympathy among some and to deepen it among others on behalf of the crushed Irish rebels. A British Cabinet memorandum dated 15 May 1916 observed that a significant change of mood had already been effected: 'Throughout Leinster popular sympathy for the rebels is growing'; in Connaught 'among all sections of nationalists hopes are generally expressed that the dupes of the revolution will be dealt with leniently'; in Munster 'general sympathy among all nationalists is becoming intensified in favour of the rebels arrested or sentenced'. Portentously for Irish nationalists, the memorandum also observed that 'public opinion generally throughout Ulster remains opposed to the rebellion' and noted the Ulster unionist view that the Rising would demonstrate to English people the dangers lurking within Home Rule.[11]

The aim of the 1916 rebels such as Patrick Pearse, however, was to demonstrate the inadequacy of Home Rule and of the Irish Parliamentary Party which espoused it. In place of constitutional nationalism with its project of achieving a significant measure of self-government for Ireland, the Pearsean rebels offered instead a more militant approach in pursuit of a more ambitious separatist objective. Much debate has raged about the nature and merits of the Rising's impact on Irish history.[12] The effect on the 18-year-old Ernie O'Malley was indisputably powerful and lasting. His family and setting had hardly offered encouragement towards Pearsean sympathies. 'Father and Mother', O'Malley was to write in 1923, 'did not possess any national faith, knew nothing of a national tradition, and all my life at home, so far as my country was concerned, I might as well have been living in Wales.'[13] In his first volume of autobiography, *On Another Man's Wound*, O'Malley was to recall that he and his family had adopted a sceptical, mocking attitude towards the Irish Volunteers and that his family's social environment was anything but Pearsean: 'Around us the people were mostly Imperialists or believed in the Parliamentary Party.'[14]

O'Malley was, in time, to become a rebel as much against this family world as against British rule in Ireland. But on holiday Monday, Easter 1916, he browsed the central part of Dublin. In Sackville Street (now O'Connell Street) he noticed large groups of people knotted together, and observed the tricolour flag flying from the top of the General Post Office building. Posted up in public was the rebel Proclamation through which the self-appointed Provisional Government of the Irish Republic addressed the Irish people: 'Irishmen and Irishwomen: in the name of God and of the dead generations from which she receives her old tradition of nationhood, Ireland, through us, summons her children to her flag and strikes for her freedom.' The 1916 rebellion was in progress. The names of the signatories to this epochal document— Clarke, MacDiarmada, MacDonagh, Pearse, Ceannt, Connolly, Plunkett—meant comparatively little to O'Malley at this stage. Of the pre-Rising period he later asserted that he had had no politics 'save to laugh at other people's opinions'.[15] The rebellion did indeed help to bring about a dramatic change in this outlook. 'Previous to this I had heard a little of the Irish Volunteers, but at home we always laughed at them as toy soldiers. Before [Easter] Week was finished I had changed.' As with many people, O'Malley responded particularly sharply to the post-Rising execution of rebel leaders ('When I heard of the executions I was furious'),[16] but it is clear that his imagination had been set alight, at least partially, by the ongoing rebellion itself.

In his later autobiography—though, interestingly, not in his lengthy memoir written during the Revolution itself—O'Malley tells of how he and a fellow schoolboy engaged in some sniping during Easter Week. According to this account, therefore, O'Malley shifted during the 1916 rebellion from the position of disinterested observer to that of tentatively committed participant. This episode would thus mark the first stage of a transformation which he was later to depict as the move-ment 'of a sheltered individual drawn from the secure seclusion of Irish life to responsibility of action'.[17] The attractions of being part of a meaningful, distinctive, and purposeful group; the excitement of action; the ignition of imaginative patriotism—one can begin here to trace the development of the youthful Revolutionary:

Distant sounds of firing had new sounds that echoed in my head. They meant something personal; they made me angry. The men down there were right, that I felt sure of. They had a purpose which I did not share. But no one had a right to Ireland except the Irish. In the city Irishmen were fighting British troops against long odds. I was going to help them in some way.[18]

O'Malley's reflections rarely offer a simple record—that is one of their lasting attractions to the historian—and his attitude towards the Easter Rising is a case in point. During the late 1920s, while in the United States helping to raise funds for the establishment of the nationalist *Irish Press* newspaper, O'Malley cringed when he was intro-duced to a gathering as having 'fired the first shot in 1916';[19] but during his time in America he was himself to write the autobiography which, as we have just seen, laid great stress on his 1916 involvement. As with other Irish Revolutionaries of the 1916–23 period, O'Malley beheld the rebellion as an epic, epoch-making event. Moreover, one of the most significant aspects of the Easter episode was precisely that it did exer-cise such a powerful influence over the imagination of those who led the militant Republicanism of 1919–23. The Irish people as a whole responded then, as later, in a complex variety of ways to the Easter Rising; but the Revolutionaries of O'Malley's stamp were crucially stirred, defined, and moulded by Pearse's dramatic wartime gesture.

Patrick Pearse indeed provides an illuminating point of comparison when introducing O'Malley's post-1916 enthusiasm. Pearse's rebellion had helped initiate O'Malley's rebellious career, and O'Malley was to read and strongly to identify with the 1916 leader. Poet and patriot, Pearse had offered a spiritual reading of the nation. O'Malley, as Republican neophyte, flung himself into this interwoven spiritual and literary culture. Writing in December 1923 he suggested with regret that 'it will take a big length of time to make up for the personal loss of the 1916 group. Pearse and his group set out to minister to the spiritual side of the nation.'[20] In an earlier letter O'Malley had referred to his keenness for a monthly paper 'to deal with articles such as Pearse might write, current European and Imperial events as seen through the eyes of the "underdog", literary and art criticism, book reviews, short stories, [a] little history, economics, geography—a paper for the man of average intelligence, but which would deal primarily . . . with the inculcation of a spiritual doctrine'.[21] Similarly, in his post-Rising life at university O'Malley and his Volunteer comrades exhibited a Pearsean literary nationalism: 'We subscribed to Irish papers, learned the latest songs, wrote very bad verse, and read books on Anglo-Irish poetry.'[22] Another Republican of these years—Charles Dalton— recalled O'Malley leading a crowd in rebel songs during this post-rebellion period, outside a Dublin church where a Mass had been offered for the dead patriots of the Rising.

In the afterglow of the rebellion O'Malley joined the Volunteers, the organization which was later to become known as the Irish Republican Army (IRA). He became a member of F Company, First Battalion, Dublin Brigade; 'a few of us met every week at Parnell Square for a little drill, the reading of orders or parade etc.—very minor activity'.[23] Indeed, it would be wrong to exaggerate the rapidity of O'Malley's ascent into Revolution: he remained a student after the Easter rebellion, living at home with his parents, and was not to leave home (to become a Republican rebel) until March 1918, after having twice failed his second-year medical examination at university.[24] Moreover, there were traces in his post-Rising enthusiasm of pre-1916 influences. While he picked up on the eighteenth-century United Irishman Theobald Wolfe Tone after the Rising, he had certainly known something of the 1916 leaders before it, having read Joseph Plunkett's *Irish Review* and having heard James Connolly speak at meetings prior to the Easter Rising. For O'Malley, the 1916 rebellion was an accelerator within a longer-term gathering of speed.

The Anglo-Irish War is often depicted as extending from 1919 to 1921 and, militarily, this makes a certain sense. But a wider-angle focus is also important for this period. As noted, the Easter rebellion helped to alter the outlook of many Irish nationalists, and it significantly undermined the politics of Parliamentary Party constitutionalism. Where the Irish Parliamentary Party leader John Redmond had pledged support for the British war effort, in the hope that loyalty would guarantee Home Rule for Ireland, the 1916 rebels seized the Revolutionary day by attacking Britain in pursuit of a more ambitious separatism. Rhetorically and symbolically, Irish politics was to be transformed by this gesture. For while it would be absurd to claim that Irish nationalists were all converted to Pearseanism by the 1916 Rising, it is less fanciful to suggest that the terms of debate and expectation had indeed been dramatically altered. The separatist Republic as an ideal, and insurrectionary violence as a method, received powerful sanction from the Easter martyrs. O'Malley's later Republican colleague Erskine Childers had one of his fictional characters observe that 'to feel oneself a martyr, as everybody knows, is a pleasurable thing'[25] and Pearse and his colleagues would certainly have taken some pleasure from the fact that their martyrdom was to change the terrain of Irish politics. There was much continuity during the pre- and post-Rising years—in terms of political personnel as well as political beliefs, practices, and assumptions—but post-Rising politicians could not afford to ignore the 1916 rebels. Indeed, public veneration became a standard feature of Irish nationalist politics in the post-1916 years.

The 1916 Rising was very much a First World War event. Its very occurrence owed much to wartime conditions, and the severe British response was determined by the extreme circumstances of war. Just as this response tended to intensify Irish nationalist opinion, so too the 1918 conscription crisis—when the imposition of conscription in Ireland was considered by the British authorities—helped to focus and mobilize Irish nationalist sentiment. Sinn Féin—the Irish nationalist organization whose origins lay in a 1905 initiative by Arthur Griffith (1871–1922)[26]—inherited much of the political capital of the 1916 Rising, and they also helped gather opposition to the unpopular prospect of conscription in 1918. By the time of the December 1918 United Kingdom general election, Sinn Féin were in a very powerful position indeed. Although the voting itself reflected a diversity of opinion (under half of the votes cast were votes for Sinn Féin), the emphatic Sinn Féin victory in terms of seats—73 out of 105 across

Ireland as a whole — undeniably underlined that party's emergence into political prominence in Ireland. Ominously for nationalists, however, 26 of the seats which did not go to Sinn Féin were won by unionists. In particular, the concentration of unionist sympathies in the north-east of the island was to prove a lasting obstacle to nationalist ambitions.

But this difficulty was largely overlooked at the time. In January 1919 Dáil Éireann was established in Dublin as an alternative parliament and a symbol of the Sinn Féiners' conception of alternative political legitimacy. Coinciding with this political development there occurred in the same month a significant incident in Soloheadbeg, County Tipperary. There had been attacks on the Royal Irish Constabulary (RIC) during 1918, but the Soloheadbeg ambush — in which two RIC men were killed by Irish Volunteers — is often presented as the beginning of the military campaign against the forces of the British Crown in Ireland. Republicans hold 1916 as the initiation of the Revolution and there is good reason for doing so. But the tactics of the 1916 rebels were certainly not to be repeated. What emerged instead was a revitalized Sinn Féin movement pursuing an augmented degree of independence and backed up, between 1919 and 1921, by militant Republicans and their deployment of physical force. The Anglo-Irish War, therefore, witnessed a combination of alternative politics and alternative militarism: Sinn Féin set up their own government to rival British legitimacy in Ireland, while the IRA engaged in a determined campaign to undermine British rule by military means. The two approaches did not fit together neatly; tension between Republican soldiers and Sinn Féin politicians was a persistent and telling theme during this period. Nor is it true that those who claimed the mantle of 1916 necessarily espoused, or even agreed with, Pearsean principles. In O'Malley's case, however, there is good reason to hold that if his IRA means marked a departure from the 1916 model, then his spiritual, sacrificial brand of nationalism was distinctly Pearsean.

O'Malley became an IRA activist in pursuit of the ideal of a completely independent Ireland. During the 1916–18 period he was first a Volunteer and then a Non-Commissioned Officer. Still living at home, he became immersed in Republican culture.

Ceilidhes, Irish dances, were always crowded. There, one met only people who were all right, meaning separatists. . . . I got to dances by climbing out of the back window by a ladder or the drain pipe when all were in bed. Often I took a chance. I went over the back wall before father had gone upstairs. At dawn I was in my bed. . . . I lived on a mountain top where there was no need for speech, even. I felt an understanding, a sharing of something bigger than ourselves, and a heightening of life. People could be more expressive, natural, and affectionate. They were direct, and immediate contact was not difficult. Older people had no conscious outthrust of age or experience; we all shared the adventure.[27]

Early in 1918 O'Malley left home.

It had been increasingly difficult to avoid suspicion at home. I had to listen to my comrades being laughed at and their motives questioned. . . . Often I flared up and said what I thought about the situation, then again I would sit quiet, listening whilst I boiled inside. I had to invent too many excuses. Already it was like a guerrilla war. . . . Some day or other an explanation would be demanded; I would be given a choice of paths, or police interference might decide. I would disappoint their hopes of a profession and be a black sheep. I carefully oiled and greased my rifle, wrapped it in oily rags and made my brothers promise take care of it. Then I left home in March of 1918.[28]

He began to work as a full-time IRA organizer at the rank of Second Lieutenant, initially under the instruction of Richard Mulcahy, IRA Chief of Staff from 1918. O'Malley's transition from one kind of professional career (medicine) to another (soldiership) is intriguing and complex. Certainly his medical studies had lost their way. Having passed the first medical examination at UCD in 1916, O'Malley failed his second medical in 1917 and then again in 1918, thereby forfeiting his scholarship. Having shifted towards IRA soldiership, he worked during 1918 in a number of counties (Tyrone, Offaly, Roscommon, and Donegal) reorganizing Volunteer groups or establishing new ones. While there was no orchestrated fighting with the forces of the British Crown at this point, there were several minor clashes with police as O'Malley attempted to activate the Volunteers in each locality. In August 1918 he was sent to London by Michael Collins, the IRA's boisterous Director of Organization and Adjutant General. The mission was to buy arms and O'Malley stayed in the English capital for a month, posing as a British Army officer. The following year saw O'Malley organizing and training the Volunteers in Clare, Tipperary, and County Dublin. During this year he also served as a Staff Captain attached to GHQ in Dublin, though he grew tired of this paperwork and was glad soon to be able to return to the field.

In 1920 the Anglo-Irish conflict really began to ignite, for O'Malley as for the IRA more generally; during 1920 and 1921 there was widespread unrest and violence. Arriving with the South Tipperary Brigade of the IRA, 'For the first time I had officers with me who were really interested in their work and who understood it: Sean Treacy and Seamus Robinson.'[29] The IRA's campaign involved the driving out from their posts of Crown forces and O'Malley played a significant role in this undertaking. He was a leading figure in such attacks as those on Hollyford Barracks in County Tipperary (May 1920), Drangan Barracks in County Kilkenny (June 1920), and Rearcross Barracks in County Tipperary (July 1920). The Hollyford episode gives a flavour of O'Malley's Revolutionary experience. An IRA Staff Captain at the time, and therefore responsible only to GHQ in Dublin, O'Malley had charge of the attack on the barracks. In the south to assist in IRA organization, to hold classes for officers, and to stir up trouble against the British, O'Malley was accompanied in the 12 May attack by leading IRA men Dan Breen, Seamus Robinson, and Sean Treacy. According to the authorities the attack was made 'by a large armed party who used bombs, rifles, and shot-guns and succeeded in setting fire to one end of the building with petrol. The defenders, though called upon three times to surrender and almost blinded with smoke and the intense heat, held out and the attackers withdrew after four and a quarter hours fight.'[30] O'Malley and Breen both offered written accounts of the episode which, in differing ways, reflect the drama and harshness of such encounters. O'Malley portrayed the attack on the barracks in typical colours:

Seamus and I had two revolvers each, grenades, bursting charges, supplies of fuse, detonators and hammers to smash the slates. On our backs a tin of petrol was tied, sods of turf which had been soaked in oil hung around our necks from cords. The oil sopped into our clothes. . . . The ladders were placed in position. . . . We crawled on to the roof, smashed slates with hammers, poured in petrol from our tins. We lighted sods of turf and threw them through gaps. Flames came with a yellow roar. We crawled further along the roof banging with hammers. I lighted the fuzes of two bursting charges. We lay flat on the roof. Then came two loud explosions, bits of slates flew; a piece hit me on the head. Police fired rifles and revolvers. We poured in more petrol. Flames flaunted out of the darkness. . . . My hands and face were burning hot, my hair caught fire; I rubbed my hands through it. My coat was alight. . . . This looks like the end, I thought, as I lay flat on the chimney whilst the flames waved and thrust forward with the wind.[31]

Stirred by the 1916 Rising, O'Malley had therefore moved gradually towards the position of full-time Revolutionary: sympathetic student living at home; participant in post-Rising cultural and gestural nationalism; Volunteer member, organizer, and then leader—O'Malley was drawn progressively into the inner circle of the IRA, the momentum of each step accelerating his movement towards the next. In late 1920 he was appointed Commandant General of the IRA's Second Southern Division, which covered territory in Limerick, Tipperary, and Kilkenny. He was to build up his own staff, but first was instructed to capture the headquarters of the British Auxiliaries in Inistioge, County Kilkenny. This attempt backfired dramatically. In December 1920 he was captured by Crown forces, in County Kilkenny, in an episode which was subsequently to generate much dispute. O'Malley's recorded view of Kilkenny was that the IRA there had done little fighting and that they were not particularly impressive.[32] His rather unflattering account of the Kilkenny episode was disputed by local Republicans, who suggested that O'Malley's reckless insouciance had led to his capture. O'Malley had with him at his capture a notebook detailing names of local IRA men, some of whom were consequently arrested and jailed.[33]

O'Malley himself was taken, via Dublin Castle, to imprisonment in Kilmainham Jail, Dublin. His later view of jail—'a testing ground in which qualities were severely tried in a vacuum, to fruit or to wither'[34]—reflected his Revolutionary experiences. Badly treated while in custody,[35] O'Malley—using the alias Bernard Stewart to shield his true identity—managed to escape from Kilmainham in February 1921, along with fellow IRA men Frank Teeling and Simon Donnelly. Teeling had been convicted and sentenced to death in relation to one of the Bloody Sunday murders of 21 November 1920; Patrick Moran, also imprisoned in connection with the IRA killings of Bloody Sunday, turned down the opportunity to escape with O'Malley, thinking that the case against him would not prevail. In the event he was sentenced to death on the day after the escape and was hanged a month later. After his Kilmainham escape, O'Malley took command of the IRA's Second Southern Division. Republicans had by this stage built up considerable momentum in their campaign to undermine the existing British order. Certainly, the authorities were anxious about the position across much of the south. This was evident, for example, in the RIC's view in January 1921 (Tipperary: 'in a very unsatisfactory condition during the month'; Cork: 'in a most disturbed condition'; Clare: 'continued in a disturbed state during the month'; Kerry: 'the general condition of the county was not satisfactory during January').[36]

July 1921, however, brought a truce between the British and the Republicans. O'Malley was suspicious that compromise was afoot and responded with typical impatience. Compromise ill-suited O'Malley's purist approach to politics. Referring in August to his own Republican side in the conflict, he observed that 'some would compromise, I'm sure, if they got half a chance — however, they know we have still some stuff left and are only too anxious to use it on them. Truce is much worse than war; I'm anxiously looking forward to war for a slight rest in the line of active service.'[37] In O'Malley's case the months of the truce period were spent training the brigade officers in his Divisional area in preparation for the possibility of renewed campaigning. To the same end he went to London, in late 1921, in order to buy surplus British arms. Once purchased, he had them shipped back to Limerick without being detected.

O'Malley's fears of compromise were realized with the achievement of the Anglo-Irish Treaty in December 1921. According to this pragmatic, complicated compromise there was to be established an Irish Free State comprising twenty-six of Ireland's thirty-two counties. This state was to have substantial but incomplete independence. There were links still to Britain. Members of the Free State Dáil (or Parliament) were, for example, to be required to take an oath of allegiance to the British Crown; there was to be a British Governor-General; Britain would retain access to certain key ports in the Free State. These and other features of the 1921 Treaty represented an unacceptable compromise for some, O'Malley conspicuous among them. In reality, however, the Treaty offered more than most Irish people had expected to see in their lifetime. Its defenders argued that it represented a realistic deal, that it offered substantial Irish autonomy from Britain, and that while it did not embody the full freedom sought by Irish Republicans it none the less offered the basis upon which further freedom could be achieved. This argument should not be dismissed lightly. Indeed, Eamon de Valera — a leading opponent of the Treaty in the early 1920s — was to go some way, when he came to power in the 1930s, to demonstrate that the Treaty did represent a foundation upon which more and more Irish independence could be built.

But this irony was some years away yet, and in the early 1920s many who had been involved in the 1919–21 movement found the Anglo-Irish Treaty an unacceptable compromise of their principles and ambitions. IRA man George Gilmore later informed O'Malley that 'At the split [over the Treaty] some of the [IRA] officers came around and they asked us what we were going to do. Were we going to be loyal to GHQ, or not? And I said I'd be loyal to them until I saw that they were going to subvert the Republic.'[38] In Republican Mary MacSwiney's characteristically uncomplicated opinion the issue was 'between right and wrong'.[39] Such views were held by a significant group within the Revolutionary movement and reflected their sincere attachment to an ideal of sovereign Irish independence. Those like MacSwiney who had lost people in the Anglo-Irish conflict—her brother Terence had died on hunger strike in 1920—felt the 1921 compromise to be particularly treacherous, a betrayal of the sacrifices made in pursuit of the Republic. O'Malley too exhibited this approach, his dismissive response to the Treaty being that of the furious purist: 'I cursed loud and long. So this was what we had been fighting for.'[40] His indignant response to the Treaty reflected his difficulty in moving from the exalted romance of the uncompromised Republic to the messy pragmatism of political compromise. (Refusal, or incapacity, to make such transitions was also to define much of his post-Revolutionary life.) The Dáil, however, voted in favour of the Treaty (on 7 January 1922 by the narrow margin of sixty-four to fifty-seven). More significantly, the wider Irish nationalist population favoured the Anglo-Irish agreement by a much clearer margin. In the June 1922 General Election, for example, anti-Treaty candidates won on average only 3,372 votes, while their pro-Treaty rivals averaged 5,174; in contested constituencies the pro-Treatyites won 41 seats and anti-Treatyites only 19; not one anti-Treaty candidate headed the poll in any constituency. The August 1923 General Election saw the Republicans gain a significant 27 per cent of the vote. But this too reflected the firmly minority status of the anti-Treaty position.[41]

The differing interpretations of this Civil War division between pro- and anti-Treatyites are crucially important, reflecting as they do the essence of the rival Irish political philosophies in this period. One of the most talented exponents of the pro-Treaty view, Kevin O'Higgins, argued that the conflict was of fundamental, democratic importance:

The Treaty, in my opinion, confers very great benefits, very great advantages, and very great opportunities on the Irish people and I would not declare off-hand that it is not worth Civil War. But if Civil War occurs in Ireland it will not be for the Treaty. It will not be for a Free State versus anything else. It will be for a vital, fundamental, democratic principle—for the right of the people of Ireland to decide any issue, great or small, that arises in the politics of this country.[42]

The people should be able to decide upon their political preferences; those who opposed such preferences by force stood in the way of democracy. If O'Higgins — who was to become one of the key political leaders in independent Ireland — was an articulate and principled exponent of the Free State argument, then O'Malley may be seen as just such an exponent of the anti-Free State view. In his opinion democracy had been thwarted not by the Republican anti-Treatyites, but by the British who had pressurized people into accepting the 1921 Treaty by raising the alternative of all-out war should they refuse. Again, he stressed the role of leading British politicians in pushing the Free State authorities towards an attack on the Republicans at the start of the Civil War in 1922. In O'Malley's Republican opinion, Irish democracy had been blocked by the British (a view crucial to Irish Republican thinking in more recent times too).

Defiantly opposed to the 1921 Anglo-Irish compromise, O'Malley adopted a typically belligerent attitude. Committed still to an absolutely independent Ireland, rather than to the partially independent twenty-six county state envisaged by the Treaty, O'Malley in the spring of 1922 precipitated several incidents in Tipperary and Limerick which almost sparked Civil War between the pro- and anti-Treaty factions of the splintering IRA. He and his anti-Treaty IRA men raided several barracks which the British forces were evacuating, taking possession of them before the Free State troops could do so. In the spring he attempted to take the city of Limerick, but the tense situation was defused by mediation between the two sides, pro- and anti-Treaty. Central to O'Malley's anti-Treaty response was his conviction that the IRA could have continued their struggle for the Republic had a resumption of violence been necessary. This point was debated at the time and has generated much subsequent discussion by scholars. O'Malley's own view of the period leading up to the July 1921 truce with the British is recorded in the second volume of his striking autobiographical memoirs, *The Singing Flame*: 'Our area was improving daily, the people were becoming more staunch in their allegiance to the Republic, and the British as a government no longer functioned.' The British were, he said, 'a garrison which held the cities and towns and made their influence felt in the countryside by force of arms only'.[43]

II

I am not beaten in my heart as yet.

(Ernie O'Malley)[44]

O'Malley had broken away from the (pro-Treaty) IRA GHQ early in 1922; other Divisions followed suit and a new (anti-Treaty) IRA Executive was elected. O'Malley was a member of this body, being appointed Director of Organization for the Republican forces. From an early stage, therefore, O'Malley was a leading figure in the battle against the 1921 Treaty. Of the Headquarters Staff of the IRA the majority favoured the Treaty: Michael Collins (Director of Intelligence), Richard Mulcahy (Chief of Staff), Eoin O'Duffy and J. J. O'Connell (Assistant Chiefs of Staff), Gearoid O'Sullivan (Adjutant General), Sean MacMahon (Quartermaster General), Emmet Dalton (Director of Training), Diarmuid O'Hegarty (Director of Organization), Piaras Béaslaí (Director of Publicity). Other leading IRA figures, it is true, opposed the 1921 compromise—among them Liam Mellows, Rory O'Connor, Sean Russell, Liam Lynch, and O'Malley himself. As we have seen, there was little doubt in the summer of 1922 about popular sympathy for the Treaty, and the pro-Treaty Provisional Government (which had taken over power from the British in the preceding January) were emphatic in stressing these democratic credentials.

By the summer the momentum towards Civil War had gained pace. In April 1922 Dublin's Four Courts buildings, situated by the River Liffey at the centre of the city, had been taken over by the anti-Treaty IRA to be used as a Republican headquarters; 'The uncompromising presence of Rory O'Connor, Liam Mellows, and Ernie O'Malley dominated the Four Courts occupation, and they issued intransigent press statements from there.'[45] O'Malley's reconstruction of this period was characteristically style-conscious and sensitive in portraiture; he observed that Rory O'Connor 'looked in the dimmed light more than ever like a Byzantine portrait, the dark blue-black shadows on his face recessing the lines', and noted the kind of leather jackets in which he, O'Connor, and Mellows were all clad.[46] By the period which O'Malley is here describing (June 1922) the political temperature had risen considerably, and again he had played a significant role. When Free Staters arrested a leading Republican (Leo Henderson), O'Malley suggested that Republicans respond by the capture of an equivalent figure from the government's forces. On 26 June he duly kidnapped a senior Free State army officer, Lieutenant General J. J. 'Ginger' O'Connell (Assistant Chief of Staff of the pro-Treaty government's forces), the intention being to hold him prisoner in the Four Courts until Henderson was released. O'Connell's capture enraged and provoked the government, who were already under pressure from the British to act decisively in regard to Republican defiance. The incident helped push the authorities towards decisive action against the Republicans. Thus, on 28 June 1922 the Republican stronghold in the Four Courts was bombarded. Two days later, with the Courts in ruins, the Republican forces were surrendered by O'Malley who had been in command of the garrison there. Then, in the chaos which ensued, O'Malley managed to escape:

Sean Lemass came over to me in a hurry. Normally he was very calm, but now he was excited, trying hard to keep his breath as he spoke. 'I think there's a chance of escape. The small gate here,' pointing towards the front corner of the yard, 'leads into the next house, the manager's house, and we can walk right through.' 'Let's go now,' I said. . . . We opened the small gate. There were two Staters standing near by but they did not seem to notice. We opened the back door of the house and walked through the kitchen into the hall. A man and a woman were standing at the front door looking into the street, evidently the manager and his wife. I said: 'Good-day. Please excuse us passing through your house, it's rather urgent,' and walked past into the crowd.[47]

O'Malley had, therefore, played a leading role in the precipitation of the Civil War. He recognized the difficulties facing the Republicans in this new phase of struggle. He acknowledged, for example, the problems which faced Dublin's Republican Active Service Unit in the setting of August 1922: 'They had to operate against people who knew them, against troops, many of whom knew them, and in a hostile background.'[48] But, the battle having once started, he threw himself into it with typical enthusiasm. He proceeded to organize Republican forces in Wexford, Carlow, Wicklow, and South Dublin. In September 1922, he was appointed Assistant Chief of Staff of the IRA with command of the areas of the Northern (Ulster) and Eastern (Leinster) Commands. Much of Ulster had, of course, always been beyond Republican influence; in the autumn of 1922 the picture was bleak enough in Leinster. Significantly, O'Malley himself acknowledged the low level of support for the Republicans, though he also held that with better organization, good leadership, and a strong military showing it would have been possible to stir many of the people in the right direction. Such views should not be dismissed too lightly, coming as they did from one of the IRA's leading figures. O'Malley was a thoroughly inner circle Irish Republican: having commanded the important IRA Second Southern Division, been Director of Organization on Headquarters Staff, Officer Commanding the HQ section in the Four Courts (and later Officer Commanding the Four Courts garrison itself), he had then become Assistant Chief of Staff of the IRA and Officer Commanding its Northern and Eastern Command. On 16 October 1922 the IRA Army Executive, of which O'Malley was also a member, selected a five-man Army Council: Liam Lynch, Liam Deasy, Frank Aiken, Tom Derrig, and O'Malley.

But although O'Malley was arguably well placed to make his observations about the possibilities for Republican revival in this period, the degree of popular sympathy for the pro-Treaty position should also be stressed. The electorate clearly endorsed the Treaty settlement in 1922 and 1923 in the General Elections.[49] Certainly the forces arrayed against the Republicans were formidable, and they included the Catholic authorities. In October 1922 the Catholic hierarchy declared decisively in favour of the pro-Treaty side in the Civil War and ordered the general excommunication of any IRA people who continued their struggle against the legitimate authorities:

Now Republicans who continued to carry and use arms against the state were deprived of the Sacraments. This had little or no effect on the men but it undoubtedly affected public opinion. Those people who supported the Republican movement resented the abuse of clerical power to suit political ends, but Republicans already had their minds made up, and despite the clergy, the press, and the Provisional Government, their views remained unchanged.[50]

The Irish Civil War of 1922–3 carried with it many tragedies and the O'Malley family was to experience its share. Ernie's brother Charlie was killed in July 1922 in Dublin during the fighting in the early stages of the war; other brothers were also involved in the conflict, Cecil and Patrick Malley being arrested and interned by the Free State authorities in 1922. Early on the morning of Saturday 4 November 1922, O'Malley himself was captured and very badly wounded during a raid on 36 Ailesbury Road, Dublin. He had been staying there, in the very comfortable surroundings of Ellen Humphreys's house, since September and had made it his headquarters as acting IRA Assistant Chief of

Staff: 'The neighbourhood was sedate, leisurely, respectable, and Imperial, removed from fighting, arrest, and sudden death.'[51] As a family with Republican sympathies, however, the Humphreys were likely to be suspect in the eyes of the Free State authorities. As Sheila (Ellen Humphreys's daughter) later suggested, it was 'almost certain . . . that, in a house such as ours, he would be tracked down sooner or later'.[52] At the time of the raid O'Malley was in a concealed room, which had been built by one of Michael Collins's devotees, Batt O'Connor, for use during the Anglo-Irish War. O'Connor himself had opted for the pro-Treaty side in the Civil War split and, though Sheila Humphreys retained a conviction that O'Connor would not have informed on the secret room,[53] it appears that the Free Staters who came to the house on 4 November knew in advance of the hideout. A Lieutenant Keegan led the raiding party of eight, accompanied by an Intelligence Officer, Lieutenant Byrne. Having deployed men to surround the house, Keegan and Byrne proceeded thoroughly to search it. The concealed room lay behind a wardrobe door; having knocked in the latter, Keegan found himself 'looking into the barrel of a .45 revolver'.[54] O'Malley fired, missed Keegan, and in doing so wounded Áine O'Rahilly (Ellen Humphreys's sister) in the face. Firing a second time O'Malley wounded Keegan in the hand; a finger had later to be amputated. The Lieutenant dashed outside to gather his troops. Upon returning, they were fired upon by O'Malley and 23-year-old Private McCartney was fatally wounded.

Keegan now rang Wellington Barracks for reinforcements which were promised him immediately. Coming back from the telephone he was fired upon by Sheila Humphreys and returned the gesture, though neither combatant was hit. O'Malley, however, had been badly wounded. Having shouted 'no surrender' as he shot Private McCartney, O'Malley had then sought a way out of the house in order to fight in the open. Running out from the back of the house, he came upon three soldiers taking cover at the side of the house and opened fire, putting holes through the cap of one of the three and putting the men to flight. In the open, however, O'Malley was effectively surrounded. Shot numerous times, he was severely wounded, as is evident from his evocative description:

A heavy rock struck me full force in the back. . . . I was hit again, in the right shoulder with a sledge hammer, and I fell on the grass. The pain was great. . . . I was hit again in the back. I found myself on my knees; my legs were very shaky when I stood up. My back felt wet. Blood was glueing my right hand to the rifle stock. All my bodily movements were slowed down . . . I tried to run for the back door through a burst of fire. Something struck the rifle and my back at the same time.[55]

O'Malley was taken away, first to Wellington Barracks and subsequently to the hospital in the Free State Headquarters at Portobello Barracks, Dublin. Áine O'Rahilly, Ellen Humphreys and her daughter (Sheila) and son (Dick) were also taken away, as was a find of revolvers, bombs, ammunition, and Republican documents all discovered at the Ailesbury Road house.

The *Irish Times* commented on O'Malley's dramatic capture that 'in many respects the affair was worthy of the cinema'.[56] This might yet prove prophetic. But the horror of the episode must accompany, if not outweigh, its drama. One dead and several seriously injured— O'Malley himself in a critical condition from which he was never absolutely to recover—the Ailesbury Road capture surely exemplifies the vicious and lasting tragedy of the Irish Civil War. Also significant is the gloss placed on this dramatic episode by Republicans. For the Republican news-sheet *Poblacht na h-Eireann*, it exemplified both the triumphant courage of the defiant Republican and also the puppet quality of the Free State authorities. In practice, the paper argued, the Free State forces which captured O'Malley were operating on behalf of England. 'Outnumbered forty to one he opened fire on them and fought his way from the room and down the stairs to the hall where he fell riddled by English bullets, supplied by the English for the purpose.' But if the Free State forces were agents of English interests they would also, so the Republican paper asserted, prove unsuccessful: 'Before the spirit of such men as Ernie O'Malley, the sword arm of the enemy is paralysed. The Free State is dead.'[57]

This argument about Republican continuity was a crucial one for the Civil War anti-Treatyites. According to this view, which O'Malley shared, the forces fighting against the Free State government were entirely consistent with the preceding fight against Britain during the 1916–21 period. *Poblacht na h-Eireann* made the point by referring to Kevin Barry, another IRA man with UCD medical experience, who was executed by the British authorities in November 1920 for his part in a Republican ambush:

On All Saints' Day 1920 Kevin Barry was hanged in Mountjoy Jail, by the English because he was a soldier of the Irish Republic. On All Saints' Day 1922 Mountjoy Jail is filled with Kevin Barry's comrades and successors, soldiers of the same Irish Republic, who are being tortured because they are true to the same oath and faithful to the same allegiance. But their jailers and torturers are not English. They bear names such as Cosgrave and O'Keeffe, and they consist of men born in Ireland, who once honoured, or pretended to honour, Kevin Barry and serve the Republic for which he died.[58]

In January 1923 O'Malley was charged in connection with the Ailesbury Road episode: with 'taking part in an attack on the National Forces', 'aiding or abetting an attack on the National Forces', 'using force against the National Forces', 'having possession without proper authority of a rifle', and 'having possession without proper authority of a revolver'.[59] By this stage he had begun his recovery but was still in a very serious condition. He had suffered multiple wounds during the Ailesbury Road battle, and the Free State authorities were anxious to avoid any replication of the British authorities' execution of leading Easter rebel James Connolly in 1916. Connolly had been so badly wounded during the Easter Rising that he was unable to stand either for his trial or for his execution, and had to be tied to a chair to be shot. Revulsion at such treatment was widespread and the Free Staters were keen that O'Malley should not provide the occasion for similar outrage. In O'Malley's own words: 'The Free State wanted to execute me but I was too weak to be court-martialled.'[60] He was indeed seriously ill: surgeons informed him that he would never be able to walk properly again. But by May 1923 he was up for several hours each day. His mother, no militant Republican, was none the less deeply concerned about his condition. She wrote, in May 1923, to the Minister for External Affairs Desmond FitzGerald, expressing anxiety about her son's treatment and condition. FitzGerald replied with encouraging news of O'Malley's recovery and increasing health. But the pain of Marion's 'heart break' is clear from this correspondence. She felt that the Revolution had ripped her son from her: 'those wretched, awful Irish affairs have separated us for years'.[61]

O'Malley was gradually to recuperate during his 1922–4 imprisonment by the Free State authorities. The medical officer initially looking after his fragile health in Mountjoy Prison was Matthew Harris O'Connor. Grandson of the eminent nineteenth-century Irish nationalist Matthew Harris (1825–90), Matt O'Connor was a graduate of Cecilia Street Medical School—indeed, he had been a medical student with O'Malley. He became a Director of Pathology in the Free State Army and a Professor of Pathology in the Royal College of Surgeons. O'Connor had examined O'Malley immediately upon his arrival in Mountjoy in December 1922: he reported that eight of his nine wounds had 'healed completely', but added that there were six bullet fragments still lodged inside him and that the prisoner 'complains of weakness and is easily fatigued'.[62] In a different way, O'Malley was also helped through his recuperation by Molly Childers, with whom he corresponded copiously during these years. The American Mary (Molly) Alden Osgood (1874–1964: the daughter of Margaret and Hamilton Osgood, a socially prominent Boston family) had, in 1904, married Erskine Childers (1870–1922), the London-born author and convert to Irish Republicanism who had been executed by the Free State authorities in November 1922. Like her husband, Molly had adopted the cause of the anti-Treatyite Republicans. Seriously disabled from the waist down since childhood, Molly was strong-willed, determined, and impressively tenacious. Intelligent, sensitive, bookish, Romantic, and staunchly pro-Republican in the Civil War, Molly supported the Republican prisoners and it is in this context that her friendship with O'Malley flourished. O'Malley certainly developed an important friendship with her. A great admirer of O'Malley, she supported and, to a degree, mothered him during his recuperation: her letters, parcels, books, food, and her intimate, supportive friendship helped sustain him during this difficult period.

In May 1923 IRA Chief of Staff Frank Aiken gave the order for Republicans to cease fire and to dump arms. The Civil War was over, the anti-Treatyites defeated. But the conflict over the Treaty was far from concluded, and for O'Malley and the other Republicans who remained in prison the struggle was very much ongoing. Three months after the ceasefire order there came an important test of Republican strength. On 27 August 1923 there was held the first General Election under the recently adopted Constitution of the Irish Free State. The June 1922 election had clearly signalled popular endorsement of the Treaty. Even the Republican Seán O'Faoláin was to admit as much: of 128 seats the anti-Treaty candidates won 36 — 'If majority decisions count for anything that was final.'[63] In the 1923 election Republican candidates won 44 of the 153 seats but had no intention of taking them up. Abstention from this Dáil reflected the Republican view that the Free State body, like the Westminster Parliament before it, was an illegitimate usurper of power in Ireland. In loyalty to their ideal of an absolutely free, Republican parliament the prisoners and their comrades outside the jails looked for validation of their defiance. The pro-Treaty Cumann na nGaedheal Party had won 63 seats; but

O'Malley's friend and fellow anti-Treatyite, the leading Republican Peadar O'Donnell, was in no doubt about the Republicans' August 1923 achievement:

the result startled us. The official Treaty party only defeated the official Republican party by a narrow majority. The stubborn resistance of the mass of national opinion was no myth. We went half wild with delight in the prisons. They were whacked; we hadn't lost. After all the killings, jailings, and terrorism the mass of national opinion was still resisting the Treaty; the road back was going to be shorter than we had dared hope.[64]

Though in his own view 'totally unfit for the position',[65] O'Malley was elected as Teachta Dála (TD, member of the Dáil or Parliament) for Dublin North. Eighteen candidates had competed for the eight Dublin North seats, the Proportional Representation electoral system requiring that each successful candidate obtain a quota of 6,147 votes. O'Malley's first preference total was 4,602 (out of a total of 55,320 valid votes), thus making him the most popular of the four Republican candidates for the constituency. But it was not until the fourteenth count that he was elected, transfers from other candidates having raised his total to 5,410. Although this was not the required quota it was sufficient to ensure O'Malley's election as the eighth most popular candidate in this (the final) count. Not that he greeted his election with any great enthusiasm: 'I hated to be a TD.'[66] This rather anti-political theme in O'Malley's soldierly thinking recurs again and again; as to the immediate result O'Malley, like his fellow Republican TD Peadar O'Donnell, recorded the development as both surprising and encouraging.

A more painful political contest was soon to follow. Twelve thousand Republicans were held in prison after the anti-Treaty ceasefire, a reflection of the government's concern at the possibility of a resumption of the conflict. On 13 October 1923 Republican prisoners began a hunger strike which was aimed at securing their unconditional release from prison. O'Malley had opposed the plan but, typically, he participated in the campaign once it was decided upon, and he did so with striking resolution. Soon after the beginning of the strike O'Malley was moved, with some other prisoners, from Mountjoy Prison to Kilmainham Jail. This period of Dublin imprisonment was a testing one: badly injured even prior to the hunger strike, O'Malley faced a momentous challenge in enduring his forty-one-day fast. Among others, his mother was concerned. Signing herself Marion K. O'Malley, she wrote to her son's frequent correspondent Molly Childers on 28 October saying that she did not think Ernie equal to the hunger strike: 'I am greatly afraid he cannot live'.[67] O'Malley himself displayed a tough attitude: on the thirty-fourth day of the strike he wrote that 'It's rather hard to kill me after all. I am in good form, but my body is pretty weak and the doctors tell me all kinds of stupid things at times, but I tell them they have to reckon with the spirit and not the body.'[68]

On the evening of 22 November the decision was taken to call off the strike. It had collapsed, O'Malley later observed, 'without any definite promise of release. We had been defeated again . . . I expect many of us spent the same miserable hours in our cells as I did, after the decision had been arrived at.'[69] At the time, however, O'Malley's sense of being 'beaten and disgraced' was complemented by a more defiant assertion: 'I am not beaten in my heart as yet'.[70] Believing that the Free Staters 'understand our psychology as little as the English did',[71] O'Malley held that the Republicans would ultimately prove victorious, but that the achievement of the sought-after Republic would take a very long time.

It is possible that O'Malley's response was more robust than that of many of his comrades. It appears that the rather confused collapse of the strike resulted in considerable demoralization among the prisoners. Indeed, the strike strategy itself was a rather peculiar one: with thousands of prisoners simultaneously abstaining from food there was a high risk of some breaking the fast and therefore undermining the protest. The mood among the prisoners during this 1922–4 period as a whole was plainly not monochrome, reminiscences and contemporary accounts of the experience varying greatly in tone. The irrepressibly optimistic Peadar O'Donnell—a great admirer of the humorous novelist P. G. Wodehouse—offered a version of Civil War incarceration not entirely dissimilar to Wodehouse's version of British public school: japery, jollity, naive optimism, and boyish good humour pervading the wings, the sport, the educational classes.[72] Certainly, O'Malley's account—of books, classes, intellectual conversations, chess, wine, and dinner—bears a resemblance to university life (though the grimmer aspects of the experience should not be forgotten), and Frank O'Connor referred to Civil War imprisonment as 'the nearest thing I could have found to life on a college campus'.[73] The intimacy and shared purpose of these Republican prisoners gave the period an emotional charge, powerful at the time and affecting also in later memory.

Understandably, O'Malley himself swung greatly in his own state of mind. On occasions his physical condition combined with his sense of

political frustration to produce considerable melancholia. His comrade Frank Gallagher's prison diary records O'Malley's mood as 'low'
on 22 October 1923.[74] Yet O'Malley also exhibited an impressive mental and physical toughness and, like his Republican colleagues, he
held the struggle within the prisons to be a crucial part of the wider
political battle against the Free State. In January 1923 he had written
from Mountjoy Prison Hospital to the IRA Chief of Staff that 'The
men inside have certainly carried on their own little war'.[75] O'Malley
was eventually released from the Curragh Camp on 17 July 1924, one
of the last prisoners to be let out by the Free State authorities, and
returned to live with his parents at St Kevin's, 7 Iona Drive, in north
Dublin.

III

1924–1928
*The country fell into a state of apathy, after the Treaty with England, the Civil
War, and the rout of the Republicans.*

(Liam O'Flaherty)[76]

His reception at home was rather cool, his parents never having
endorsed his (or his brothers') Revolutionary Republicanism. O'Malley himself recorded that he had become severely isolated from his
family, from whom he had indeed been distant ever since his 1918
departure and his immersion in the Republican Revolution. Echoes
of solitude and separation are to be heard throughout his life. The
Republican movement was itself in a very weakened state at this time
(despite the IRA Chief of Staff's suggestion in August that 'On the
whole I think the Army is in a healthy state'),[77] and the Free State was
hardly the most hospitable of environments for the defeated anti-
Treatyites. Peadar O'Donnell later recalled 'a meeting of the wreckage
of the IRA, to reorganize the IRA' which was held after the release of
Republican prisoners. O'Malley had attended this gathering and had,
according to O'Donnell, asserted 'that the job of the IRA now was for
us to restore the morale that had been endangered by all the confusion
over the Treaty and so on'.[78] Certainly, the question of raising morale
was a vital one; Seán O'Faoláin referred to the early years of the Irish
Free State in terms of 'the disillusionment, the weariness of soul with
all patriotic emotion that . . . seem to be part of the inevitable after-
math of every nationalist upheaval'.[79] It is also true that Republican

leaders such as Aiken and de Valera had stressed at the close of the Civil War that it was important to keep the army together. Yet O'Donnell's recollections of the 1924 IRA meeting might bear more traces of his own views than of O'Malley's. The latter certainly held that there was considerable apathy in the mid-1920s Free State in relation to the national question, and was keen that this should be replaced by a sharper enthusiasm. But, unlike O'Donnell, O'Malley did not define his post-Revolutionary decade by immersion in IRA activity. He remained firmly Republican in his convictions and was held in high esteem by other Republicans; in 1924 he was nominated for the positions of Vice-President and Hon. Treasurer of Sinn Féin.[80] But the mid-1920s effectively mark a watershed in his career, with his moving away from full-time Republican activism and towards other objectives. Some of these—his writing projects, for example—were to have a strong Republican flavour and could (perhaps) be seen as the continuation of war by other means. But his post-1924 emphasis was increasingly that of the post-Revolutionary intellectual.

The IRA was still very much in existence. It was not, however, able to generate much momentum and, as the 1920s unfolded, it became increasingly marginal within the life of the Irish Free State. In 1926 Eamon de Valera led many of the anti-Treatyites towards constitutional politics with the founding of Fianna Fáil. This political party was to enter the Free State Dáil in 1927, to eclipse the more hardline Sinn Féin, and eventually to assume government of the state in 1932. As more and more from the anti-Treatyite constituency gave support to Fianna Fáil and to constitutional politics, so the IRA's rejectionist, violent approach came largely to be overshadowed. In Republican eyes the 1921 Treaty had many deficiencies; it none the less provided the basis for building a state to which the vast majority of twenty-six county nationalists could give allegiance. O'Malley in 1924 was far from enamoured with the Free State. But nor was he enthusiastic about the possibilities inherent in an IRA approach which looked incoherent and futile. It is crucial also to note that O'Malley himself was in very poor physical shape at this time ('There wasn't much left of me by the time the [hunger] strike was over')[81] and this effectively decided his immediate plans. With £5 from his father, £52 from the IRA,[82] and £100 advanced him by the White Cross, O'Malley set out for a recuperative visit to continental Europe in the hope that the rest and the climate would aid his physical and emotional recovery.

Setting out in 1925 he went via London and Paris to Spain and stayed with Irish contacts, Myles O'Moore of County Wexford and Margaret Barry of County Cork. Spending part of 1925 in Barcelona, he began to regain his health. Bullet wounds, the legacy of his interrogation by the British in the Anglo-Irish War, and the effects of the hunger strike had all combined to impair his physical condition. With characteristic self-drive and toughness, however, he set out to challenge and restore his body through mountain climbing in the Pyrénées ('I learned to walk again in the Pyrénées')[83] and by means of extensive walking through southern France, northern Spain, and Italy during 1925. As ever, he left a written record of his adventures: 'I had to climb on a razor edge crest . . . and at times it was difficult as one had to descend a little to avoid advancing on the sharp stones of the crest, which could very easily tear one's hands and legs. . . . As evening advanced . . . I was left by myself to read my tattered Shakespeare and study my maps.'[84] Equally typically, he was absorbed in studying those arts which would occupy and sustain him during his post-Revolutionary life: sculpture, church architecture, and the contents of museums and galleries. Solitude, self-reliance, mountains, landscape, churches, literature, art, and thoughtful autobiography: all themes which recur significantly during the various phases of his life.

In 1925 he stayed at the Irish College in Rome and also with some Irish friends in Florence where he particularly relished the treasures of the Uffizi Museum, with its outstanding collection of works by Italian masters. Until his return to Ireland in the latter part of 1926 O'Malley travelled further—in Italy and France—including a visit to his old IRA colleague Sean MacBride in Paris in August 1926. MacBride recalled O'Malley as having been restless and slightly disoriented at this time, as a result of his having been shattered by his Irish Revolutionary experiences. O'Malley himself felt that this recovery period was taking good effect. In April 1926 he wrote from the Pyrénées to his old Republican comrade Johnny Raleigh that 'My health has improved now and I feel in good form'.[85] The same message reached the IRA who, the following month, sent O'Malley a further £20 to help his finances until he should return.[86] The mid-1920s, therefore, were spent in recuperation, part of it in European sojourn; and while O'Malley kept in contact during this time with Republican friends such as Raleigh, the period epitomizes the transition from intense Republican involvement to the rather different, post-Revolutionary existence which was to follow.

In the second half of 1926 O'Malley returned to Ireland, £200 in debt, and went back to living at home with his parents in Dublin. His brothers' careers had progressed: Cecil had qualified in medicine and Kevin had almost completed his own medical studies. In October 1926 O'Malley himself returned to professional training, embarking for a second time as a UCD medical student at the Cecilia Street Medical School in Dublin. Other Revolutionaries, like C. S. Andrews and former IRA Chief of Staff Andy Cooney, were also students at the University. But it was not easy to adjust to this new situation. In November 1926 O'Malley wrote to Johnny Raleigh, 'I'm a second medical now trying to settle down but it's extremely difficult.'[87] Raleigh was a close and lasting friend; in April 1927 O'Malley was best man at his marriage to Bea Mooney in Limerick, and mutual loyalty bound the two men together. But old Republican links were now increasingly complemented by O'Malley's absorption in intellectual and artistic affairs. In 1928 he was a leading figure in the founding of UCD's Dramatic Club. Denis Coffey, President of UCD, was opposed to the foundation of a dramatic society in the University because he thought that the students would only waste their time at such activities instead of studying their academic subjects. But interested students (including O'Malley and the President's son, Donough Coffey) started a Dramatic Club within the already established Literary and Historical Society, the latter giving them some financial assistance. This Dramatic Club proved itself by successfully producing a play and so Coffey relented, allowing the UCD Dramatic Society to be established. His son Donough was elected first Director of this Society. O'Malley had therefore played a role in this artistic venture. Indeed, one of his fellow medical students at this time, N. J. McGahon, recalls O'Malley as having had far more interest in drama than in medicine.[88] Certainly, the dramatic interests were to be more crucial than any medical enthusiasm in determining the nature of O'Malley's subsequent career.

IV

1928–1935

The Irish in America or the Americans, even those friendly to Ireland, knew nothing about the reality of Irish life. I mixed mostly with Americans.

(Ernie O'Malley)[89]

The medical studies themselves were not progressing well. Shortly after his return from mainland Europe O'Malley had confessed to a

sense that he had 'just been drifting',[90] and something of this spirit
continued during the 1926–8 period. He felt out of place in the university, again failed his second-year medical exam, and found his life at
home irritatingly constricting. Ripe for the opportunity to travel again,
O'Malley's chance came in 1928. In the summer Frank Aiken, another
old comrade from the Republican Revolution and now a key figure in
Eamon de Valera's Fianna Fáil Party, approached O'Malley with a
suggestion which was to help alter the direction of his life. It was proposed that O'Malley should accompany Aiken on a fund-raising tour
of the United States on behalf of the newspaper, the *Irish Press*, which
de Valera was in the process of establishing. Fianna Fáil had been set
up in 1926 in order to organize anti-Treatyites into a practical, political
force which would be able to gain power and move forward in a direction more attractive to Republicans than that in which the then Free
State government—of the pro-Treaty Cumann na nGaedheal Party—
was leading. The key figure was the hugely symbolic Eamon de
Valera: survivor of the 1916 Rising; President during the post-1917 Revolutionary years of Sinn Féin, the Volunteers, and then of the Republican Dáil; elected President of the Irish Republic in 1921; the most
significant political opponent of the 1921 Treaty—de Valera was a
political giant in early twentieth-century Ireland. Having been
defeated in the Civil War of 1922–3, the anti-Treatyites had pursued a
policy of political rejectionism, abstaining from taking their seats in a
Free State Dáil (which they considered illegitimate). Shrewd, ambitious, pragmatic politician that he was, de Valera recognized the
potential here for long-term futility. Nor was he alone in this. When he
resigned as Sinn Féin President in 1926 he embarked on a new departure which was to take the bulk of anti-Treatyites with him. Establishing Fianna Fáil in May 1926, de Valera sought to draw both on the
tradition of militant nationalism which had energized the Revolutionary movement and on the reservoirs of power to be found in majority
democratic rule.[91] The new party, which quickly eclipsed the Sinn
Féin party from which it had split, built its appeal on a variety of foundations: the promise of constitutional progress towards ever greater
separation from Britain, the targeting of a range of social groups
through economic policies, the prospect of attaining genuine political
power in the state, and the appeal of figures—most conspicuously de
Valera himself—with Revolutionary prestige and charisma.

There was also the question of organization. Fianna Fáil offered
more effective local organization than their rivals, and the desire for a

newspaper also grew from this concern to maximize political mobilization behind the new nationalist project. As the Fianna Fáil leader himself wrote in May 1928: 'The newspaper is absolutely vital to the national cause. Without it all the efforts of the last ten years will be brought to nought.'[92] He expressed similar sentiments to O'Malley in November of the same year: 'The thing to keep in mind constantly is that without a newspaper it will be impossible to make any real national progress in our generation.'[93] By that stage O'Malley was himself actively involved in the *Irish Press* project, travelling to the United States in the company of Frank Aiken in pursuit of funds for the newspaper. He had arrived in New York in October 1928. With Aiken, he embarked on an exacting schedule of publicity and fund-raising among the American Irish community with the aim of raising sufficient American money by the middle of November. In some respects the task was one for which he was ill-suited. His sympathies were never wholly engaged by the political outlook of Fianna Fáil, a party whose pragmatic constitutionalism fell short of the purist Republican approach which characterized O'Malley's own favoured brand of politics. Moreover, public speaking formed a significant part of the USA tour and O'Malley was a poor public speaker; indeed, there is evidence that he found it difficult to make headway in the American *Irish Press* mission. But although the combination of political publicity and high-profile public attention did not particularly suit his inclinations, the trip had offered O'Malley an alternative to the less than ideal situation in which he had found himself in Ireland: as we have seen, living at home had been awkward and constricting while the medical studies were not progressing at all well. Again, the young Free State did not provide an especially agreeable atmosphere for Republicans. Many of those who had, like O'Malley, been on the losing side in the Civil War found themselves, again like O'Malley, travelling to the United States. For O'Malley himself, the visit to the States was to provide the opportunity for creating a second life.

While he was not entirely convinced by Fianna Fáil's politics, there can be no doubt that O'Malley was firmly convinced of the importance of establishing a newspaper of the kind envisaged by de Valera. In O'Malley's view there was

little need to stress the necessity for the paper: anyone who is at all familiar with the present day Irish press can see that it does not represent the country, that it does not interpret our national aspirations, that it has not a dignified independent outlook. . . . As a nation we are not a reading people, not a nation

of serious readers, hence newspapers influence our outlook more so than they
do that of most other countries.[94]

Frank Aiken made similar points:

The sacrifices of those who have struggled for the freedom of Ireland are as yet
without fruit, solely, in my opinion, because the daily papers in Ireland helped
the enemy. The fruit will be garnered only when we have a national daily press
that will sustain the courage of the people in a hard struggle and give a fair representation to the views of all who have ideas to express as to how best we can
shake off England's political and economic domination and secure the happiness and prosperity of our people. The proposed paper will do this.[95]

A Fianna Fáil paper, the *Irish Press* (the first issue of which appeared
on 5 September 1931, with O'Malley's friend Frank Gallagher as edi-
tor-in-chief) was presented by its founders as a national rather than a
party organ. De Valera—who had in early 1928 himself initiated a
fund drive for the paper in the USA—was the controlling editor, and
it was claimed that the newspaper would promote Irish culture,
industry, and interests—in particular against the threat of British
domination.

The American itinerary was demanding. The target was to raise
individual subscriptions for shares in sums of $100 and above, with a
view to raising an American quota of $500,000. In the latter part of
1928 O'Malley was in New York, Connecticut, Boston, Philadelphia,
Pittsburgh, Cleveland, Detroit, Chicago, Cincinnati, and Washington, DC. The early part of 1929 took him back to some of the same
places and also to Montana, Seattle, Oregon, Sacramento, and San
Francisco. In April 1929 O'Malley concluded his involvement in the
Irish Press mission, but decided to stay on in the United States which
provided him with opportunities to explore the new worlds of America
and of his post-Revolutionary imagination. From his earliest writings
during the Revolutionary era it is clear that the arts held O'Malley's
attention sustainedly and powerfully. Ironically, perhaps, art and literature held far more compelling appeal for him than did formal political argument or thought; the massive library which he was to build up
during his later life held comparatively little in the field of politics but
was impressively rich and diverse in literature and the arts. His time in
the United States offered such interests a chance to breathe freely.
Even while working for the *Irish Press* cause he had taken time to
indulge such interests: Friday 21 December 1928: 'Cincinnati, can-

vassed, visited Museum'; Friday 28 December 1928: 'New York, Metropolitan Museum'; Friday 1 March 1929: 'Chicago, visited Exhibition of Chicago painters'.[96] He admired distinctively impressive architecture, observing for example that New York's Woolworth Building had 'cathedral lines and a beautiful roof'.[97] New York, indeed, he came very much to like, appreciating the opportunities it offered for understanding modern artistic and intellectual movements. Away from the potentially stifling intimacy and memories of Ireland, he was in a position both to grow into the world of the humanities intellectual and also to produce fine work which addressed—from a helpful distance—the Irish Revolution to which he had so significantly contributed. He attempted to produce an alternative history of his country's epic Revolution, recording a Republican vision of these vital events and contesting the definition of Irishness as energetically in print as he had done in war. His writing was to be wide-ranging, including short stories and poetry as well as the more famous Revolutionary memoirs. And the material relating to Ireland fitted into a wider pattern: O'Malley was one of those distinguished writers who 'preserved received epic images of Ireland, conjured up in emigration'.[98]

In part, the quality and characteristics of his writing reflected the circles in which he mixed during his American sojourn. One of the distinctive aspects of O'Malley's post-Revolutionary life was his contact with artists and with other intellectuals. This was certainly true of his American experiences between 1928 and 1935. One example is his brief but striking acquaintance with the distinguished American photographer Edward Weston. It appears that O'Malley first (and vainly) tried to look Weston up in April 1929 in Carmel, California. Carmel was then a fertile ground for the nourishing of artists and in May 1929 the two men did manage to meet there. On 14 May the photographer had O'Malley to dinner, and the two men got on extremely well. On 25 May Weston took photographs of the Irishman which, perhaps more than any others, capture with precision O'Malley's intensity, concentrated reflectiveness, and piercing earnestness. O'Malley greatly admired Weston's photography. For his part, Weston was very impressed by O'Malley. Like many other artists and intellectuals, he was particularly taken with O'Malley as an intellectual who was also a man of action. After their dinner in May 1929, for example, Weston wrote in his diary that the Irishman's 'tales of his part in the rebellion—1916–1923—made me realize what a comparatively unexciting life I have had'.[99]

On 6 June 1929 Weston's diaries refer to O'Malley's departure. He travelled to Los Angeles and in July 1929 was staying in Pasadena, California. That summer, in Pasadena, he met the family of the Irish actor Peter Golden. Born in County Cork in 1877, Golden (a second cousin of Irish Revolutionary martyr Terence MacSwiney) had in 1901 emigrated to the United States where he involved himself in Irish nationalist activities as well as pursuing an acting career. Indeed, these two careers merged. An enthusiastic propagandist and organizer, Golden toured extensively in the United States performing poetry and oratory before large numbers of people in defence of the Irish Republican struggle. He died in Colorado in 1926, leaving a wife (Helen Merriam Golden) and three children (Terence (b. 1917), and twins Deirdre and Eithne (b. 1919)). Like O'Malley, Golden wrote much during his American exile; as with O'Malley, much of it was poetry and much of it had an Irish focus. Golden's *Impressions of Ireland* was based on a short visit to Ireland during 1922, and reflected his perceptions of the post-Treaty Irish political situation and his instinctive sympathy with the anti-Treatyite position.

Golden had met the American actress Helen Merriam while both were acting in Shakespeare's *Comedy of Errors*, and they had married in 1916. If Golden was an active propagandist for the Irish Republicans during the 1919–21 War of Independence period, then Helen, too, threw herself enthusiastically into supporting Irish nationalist causes. It was Helen and the three children whom O'Malley met in California in the late 1920s. Considerable shared interest existed between O'Malley and the Goldens—artistic, literary, theatrical, political—and the family were to become enormously important for O'Malley during the next few years. In September 1929 he visited Arizona's Grand Canyon with Helen and Terence Golden, the drive from Pasadena taking about a week. Moving on to Santa Fé, New Mexico, they discovered that an old friend of Helen's—the Irish writer Ella Young—was also then in New Mexico, staying slightly to the north in Taos. O'Malley and Golden visited Taos and, like numerous other intellectuals, artists, and bohemians of the period, quickly became addicted to the place. O'Malley was attracted by its beauty, but the culture of the setting was also appealing to him. If the travelling Golden family conjure images of Steinbeck, then the literary point of reference for Taos is more directly available in the form of the people whom O'Malley encountered there. Taos hosted an intriguing and distinctive artistic community, and its bohemian quality appealed to the Irish Revolutionary just as it had to Ella Young. The latter, who lived in California, had been staying with Mabel Dodge Luhan (who had discovered Taos in 1917 and had settled there, finding in it an antidote to the bourgeois respectability of her Buffalo, New York, background).

As with Carmel, this atmosphere suited O'Malley very well. In October 1929 he stayed on in Taos (in an Auto Camp cabin) and it was at this time and in this indulgent bohemia that he began to write his Revolutionary memoirs. Eventually published in two volumes—*On Another Man's Wound* (1936) covering 1916–21; *The Singing Flame* (1978) dealing with 1921–4—his initial approach was to write of the 1916–24 period as a whole. This reflected his political convictions: the Civil War of 1922–3 was in his view a continuation of the fight of Irish Republicans against British Imperialism, and so the Revolutionary period should be read as a continuous whole rather than as a War of Independence followed by a separate Civil War. In addition to drafting and meticulously redrafting these autobiographies, O'Malley also wrote many poems during this post-1929 New Mexican period. The poetic combined with the political, just as the absorption in New Mexico complemented the persistent Irish preoccupation. Indeed, the poetic infused the political: O'Malley's memoirs are distinctive in part because of their lyrical quality. And it was, in the end, work on Ireland which most energized him. He was later to argue that 'I really loved New Mexico deeply and I love it now, but I suppose Ireland—whatever way it is—is my destiny, less easy than the South West [of the USA] but here [in Ireland] are my roots, my people, and what I should write about'.[100] So, too, in the later 1920s and early 1930s O'Malley wrote, in the most artistic of exile settings, of Ireland and the Revolution. The setting helped to define the work. As we shall see, many of the striking qualities of O'Malley's books derive in part from the specific New Mexican context which produced them. In November 1929 Helen Golden and her daughter Eithne returned to Taos, where they stayed until February 1930; each evening O'Malley would come over to visit them and to read instalments of his unfolding memoirs. Drafts would be discussed and, in light of these comments, recrafted. The many-layered autobiographies reflect their having been many times refocused in this way.

Like O'Malley, Helen Golden had fallen in love with Taos and she therefore set about finding a house there. While she did so, and while she cleared up her affairs in Pasadena, O'Malley remained on in Taos. He was to stay there until the summer of 1930: writing, mixing with the

other bohemians in the locality, and immersing himself in this new set
of cultures. With the Goldens he visited—and was greatly impressed
by—Ácoma, an Indian pueblo 150 miles south-west of Taos. His other
friends in New Mexico included Mabel Dodge Luhan, Willard 'Spud'
Johnson (a journalist who had worked on the *New Yorker* and who ran
his own paper *Laughing Horse*), and Dorothy Brett (an English painter
of aristocratic background who, like Luhan, preferred New Mexican
bohemianism to the respectability of her upbringing). O'Malley also
became acquainted with the artist Georgia O'Keeffe, who lived in
Abiquiu, New Mexico.

   During the spring of 1930 O'Malley stayed (in its owner's absence)
in Spud Johnson's adobe house just outside Taos. He had a fever during April and May: this kept him housebound and he occupied himself by reading Johnson's large collection of books. Once recovered, he
worked with the Indians who were building Dorothy Brett's cabin
on the mountainside about a mile from the ranch in which D. H.
Lawrence had lived. Brett greatly liked O'Malley and this work helped
him out financially, enabling him to travel during late 1930 and much
of 1931: he spent time in Mexico and then (in the autumn of 1931) he
rented a little adobe house in the Spanish-speaking, blanket-weaving
village of Chimayó, New Mexico, about 50 miles to the south of Taos.
O'Malley's notebooks from this period reflect his preoccupations. In
August 1930 he spoke to a gathering of sixty or seventy people in Santa
Fé on the subject of Irish poetry, taking the subject through from the
ancient Gaelic period to the contemporary. In early 1931 in Mexico
City he was visiting museums and libraries; looking at frescoes, sculpture, and architecture; reading Chaucer; drinking a lot of tequila; and
feeling guilty about not finishing off his book ('the damned book on
which I am not able to do anything: I must write some of it tomorrow').[101] Absorbed in Mexico and preoccupied by Ireland, O'Malley
was troubled by a variety of issues. He was frustrated by his inability to
dig as deeply as he would have liked into Mexican culture, noting in
February 1931 that: 'Lack of the language keeps me from going any
deeper into the life, the life so vibrant and intense. I am on the surface,
a damned diletanti—or however it is spelt.'[102] Financial worries also
troubled him. He was not quite in the state described by his later
friend Samuel Beckett as the absolute impossibility of all purchase,
but he was certainly eking out a meagre enough subsistence, on the
basis of casual work such as that which had been provided by Dorothy
Brett. He was also suffering physically. In Mexico City in early 1931 he

noted that 'My back gives trouble these times: I suppose my ammunition [the bullets still lodged in his back] is moving about too much'.[103]

More positively, O'Malley met the talented American poet Hart Crane in Mexico and in the summer of 1931 lived briefly with him in Mixcoac, a suburb of Mexico City. The two men became fond friends: 'we drink a lot together—look at frescoes—and agree!' (Crane);[104] 'We became friends and remained friends to the end despite clashes from my sense of personal discipline and his lack of it' (O'Malley).[105] Literary, intellectual, and artistic, the two men shared much in outlook. The points about drink and discipline lend colour to our picture of O'Malley at this time ('Hart is a hard drinker: fifteen litres of beer the other day then I passed out')[106] and serve as a valuable antidote to the impression sometimes given of unadulterated asceticism and responsible austerity. As ever with O'Malley, the picture was more complex and varied. And as ever he made a powerful impression. Crane recorded in a 1931 letter to the writer Malcolm Cowley that O'Malley was 'the most quietly sincere and appreciative person, in many ways, whom I've ever met'.[107] The affection and respect were mutual, O'Malley observing of Crane: 'I liked him a great deal. He was generous, enthusiastic, and spoke the most amazing rhetoric, good rhetoric.'[108]

O'Malley returned to Taos in the autumn of 1931. From then until June 1932 he tutored the three Golden children, Terence, Deirdre, and Eithne. This arrangement was as pragmatic for O'Malley as it was agreeable to tutor and tutees: it paid for his board and food. Helen Golden had purchased an old adobe house and seven acres of land and horses in Talpa, at the mouth of the canyon of the Río Chiquito, about six or seven miles from Taos. The setting was idyllic (with alfalfa field and orchard) and the set-up rudimentary (no plumbing, no telephone, and no electricity). O'Malley lived in the 'mouse house', an adobe house (which smelt faintly of mice) next to the Goldens'. It was in this 'mouse house' that he taught the children. Along an entire wall of one of the house's two rooms he had a very large-scale military map of part of Munster: as ever, the Revolution stayed with him.

O'Malley's distinctive teaching style was typically uncompromising. Among other texts, he read the children Schopenhauer, and Samuel Butler's *Erewhon*. He made them read Shakespeare, taught them English grammar as well as literature, Spanish (he being but one step ahead of them in the textbook), history (for which he used D. H. Lawrence's *Movements in European History* as a text), and the history

of art. He was stern enough. For two months during the early part of
1932 Helen Golden was in hospital with pneumonia and O'Malley
took charge of the three children. He ran the household like a military
regime, as if the children were soldiers under his command. Daily
reports were required on the performance of their duties; time sheets
were filled out for each activity to ensure that their time had been well
used; each week one of the children was assigned the role of orderly.
Pragmatism, sternness, and the reversion to the familiar all combined
here with a certain measure of fun. Eithne remembers the teaching as
having been a major, and lastingly beneficial, influence on her life; if
O'Malley got on well with Helen Golden—they shared many interests
as well as fundamentally idealistic leanings—then it is also true that he
related well, if somewhat brusquely, to the children.

But he was keen to broaden his field of vision again and in 1932
returned to the vibrancy of New York City. Theodora Goddard, a
painter who had known O'Malley in New Mexico and who had herself
returned to New York, invited O'Malley to drive her car back for her to
New York. This he did in June 1932. In New York O'Malley was keen
to finish his manuscript, to get it published, and then to return home
to Ireland. He was also enthusiastic about developing contacts with
exciting intellectuals and artists. The American photographer Paul
Strand, whom O'Malley had known in New Mexico, put him in touch
with the Group Theatre and also with the Yaddo Corporation of
Saratoga Springs, New York. These two contacts were very fruitful.
Shortly after his arrival in New York in the summer of 1932 O'Malley
visited the Group Theatre for two days at Dover Furnace, New York.
Founded by theatrical enthusiasts Harold Clurman, Lee Strasberg,
and Cheryl Crawford—and involving such figures as the playwright
Clifford Odets—the Group, which first began to take shape in New
York in 1930, attempted to address the spiritual needs of its audience,
to dramatize harsh social realities, and to reflect (and reflect upon)
contemporary American life in a new form of theatre. Harold Clurman's emphasis upon spirituality and community rather than on materialism and individualism was one which O'Malley found appealing.
Of bourgeois background yet profoundly anti-bourgeois in spirit—
Clurman referred to Odets as 'a middle-class playwright . . . a poet of
the decaying middle class with revolutionary yearnings and convictions'[109]—the restless, dissatisfied intellectuals of the Group Theatre
offered idealism mingled with professionalism, and discipline mixed
with seriousness of purpose; each of these qualities appealed to and

was echoed in O'Malley. In contrast to the commercial cynicism of
Broadway theatre, the Group promoted an alternative, optimistic
vision of what the American future could hold. They projected ideas of
the death of the corrupt, old order and the birth of something new.
Against the background of the 1930s Depression, they veered notably
to the left, some of their number later running into difficulties with the
House Committee on Un-American Activities. But the Group's adherents were characterized and galvanized by a sense of urgent inquiry
into the condition of modern society (and by a desire, equally urgent,
to remedy its severe problems), rather than by dogmatic attachment to
left-wing ideology. Their work reflected tensions in the existing system
and looked to the creation of a new—though admittedly ill-defined—
social environment. Clurman in particular wanted the Group to represent a creative response to the problems of American life; more than
a theatre, it would be a movement.

As noted, O'Malley visited these ardent, idealistic bohemians at
their 1932 summer camp at Dover Furnace. O'Malley 'felt very much
at home' with them, and was impressed by their 'fine spirit' and 'great
comradeship'.[110] Representing the world of action as well as that of
intellectual fervour, O'Malley was one of the few outsiders whom the
Group welcomed. As on other occasions, his combination of intellectual force and Revolutionary experience impressed. Clurman, in
specific relation to O'Malley, observed that 'the closer to real life at its
realest' people were, the more they held the attention of the Group.
O'Malley, he added, was 'a symbol of the restless, adventurous, somewhat militant spirit that had descended upon us'.[111] Clifford Odets
also recalled O'Malley being a great success with the Group, remembering in particular that he had held them spellbound with stories of
the Irish Revolution. For his part, O'Malley shared many intellectual
currents with the Group (Clurman's enthusiasm for Lawrence, for
example, or Odets's interest in Schopenhauer) and they were among
the most exciting of his American contacts.

This 1930s collective endeavour failed to realize its ambitions,
though significant achievements were made. Their best plays, such as
Odets's *Awake and Sing!* and *Paradise Lost*, succeeded in evoking
tumult and dissatisfaction in striking ways, and their acting at times
succeeded in creating drama which engaged with the powerful insecurities and hopes then prevalent. It is not difficult to see their appeal
for O'Malley. In their belief in the political relevance of art, and in
their search for a new order which they only hazily defined, they

offered a familiar and entrancing atmosphere for the bespectacled, intellectual exile. The Group's shared vision of collective action expressed in the arts must ultimately be judged naive, but they did offer a dynamic response to the trauma of the decade and—given O'Malley's long-term commitment to the interweaving of politics and art—they were ideal comrades for him.

O'Malley's own reflections on America during the Depression are themselves intriguing. During July 1932, after his visit to the Group, he was unemployed in New York, trying to work on his book and simultaneously to look for more immediately remunerative work. In August 1932 he was to ruminate on this experience:

I had been used to the life east of Broadway and south of 14th Street. Men walking up: 'Have you a penny, buddy?' 'Can you give me 5 cents for a meal?' 'Spare a cigarette, mister?' Some faces tough and lined, others—but few— with pathetic gentleness, many shifty and cunning. It's hard to live there and not be affected by the terrible want. Street corner meetings every night, men talking in clichés. It's stupid. A shirted crowd mostly, waiting eagerly for a few honest, direct words; instead they get 'isms'.[112]

Having found himself in this rather depressing setting, O'Malley's introduction to the Yaddo Corporation came as a practical and intellectual blessing. Yaddo was run by George Foster Peabody and offered a haven for artists, writers, and composers, a place in which they could create and share their work. The mansion had been built as a summer home in the 1890s by Spencer Trask (a New York City financier) and his author wife Katrina. In 1900 the Trasks had formed the Corporation of Yaddo, a non-profit organization designed to maintain a residence and retreat for people pursuing creative and artistic work. After their deaths (Spencer died in 1909, Katrina in 1922), the several hundred acre Trask Estate in Saratoga Springs, New York—known as Yaddo—began (in June 1926) to receive its first guests. A home for artists, Yaddo was another of those sophisticated, intellectual settings in which O'Malley found a temporary home in these years. The Executive Director at Yaddo during 1926–70 was Elizabeth Ames. In 1932 Ames felt that O'Malley's work and his situation were 'rather special'[113] and she was therefore keen to invite him. O'Malley was very keen to have such an opportunity to write, and eagerly availed himself of this chance. He had already visited Yaddo for dinner in early July 1932 and, following Ames's invitation, was then resident there later in the year, from 16 August to 29 September. He was, he said, 'very well received' at Yaddo,[114] and the chance to work there concentratedly on his memoirs was a valuable one. The ascetic style of Yaddo suited O'Malley well enough. There was, indeed, something of a monastic quality to it. After breakfast at 8.15 the working day ran from 9 to 4, with an emphasis on silence in order that work be facilitated; life was kept extremely simple so that the maximum work could be achieved.

Yaddo has had a major influence on the careers of large numbers of artists, writers, and composers in modern America. Over two and a half thousand people have visited as artists, and residents there have included James Baldwin, Saul Bellow, Leonard Bernstein, Truman Capote, Aaron Copland, Carson McCullers, Flannery O'Connor, Sylvia Plath, and Alice Walker. The guest list during O'Malley's time included the composer Israel Citkovitz and the philosopher Sidney Hook. Such companions further enriched O'Malley's intellectual development, and Yaddo also enabled him to move ahead with his Revolutionary autobiography ('Here I am at Yaddo . . . I'm going to work like hell').[115] He was zealous to find a publisher, and again his Yaddo contacts were helpful. On 28 September 1932 George Leighton of *Harper's* magazine (New York) invited O'Malley to send him those sections of the manuscript dealing with his early life. This was on the recommendation of George Milburn (a guest at Yaddo during O'Malley's time there) who, on 19 October, wrote to O'Malley recommending that he indeed write to Leighton. Contact having been established, Leighton pursued O'Malley in November, hoping to find out more about the book and the possibilities for its publication. Nothing was to come of this, but Milburn was loyal in pursuing other options. On 17 April 1933 he wrote to Alfred Harcourt of the publishers Harcourt Brace regarding O'Malley's manuscript. Having considered the text, they rejected it in May 1933. Despite its later success, therefore, O'Malley's book was at this stage struggling to come to life.

Other, more personal developments were unfolding. In June 1933 Mariquita Villard—New York-born niece of Oswald Villard, editor and publisher of *The Nation* and *The New York Evening Post*—introduced O'Malley to Helen Huntington Hooker at a Hooker family Sunday luncheon in Greenwich, Connecticut. Mariquita was a friend of Helen and of her sister Adelaide, two of the four daughters of Elon and Blanche Hooker. Elon Hooker's family was of distinguished heritage but had not, in his childhood, been particularly wealthy. He himself had established considerable wealth, through his own successful Hooker Electrochemical Company. His wife Blanche was the daughter of a successful Detroit businessman. In this respectable, wealthy setting O'Malley provoked typically strong reactions (including some hostility from Elon). At the lunch he talked primarily to the two eldest Hooker daughters, Barbara and Adelaide; but it was the third child, the 28-year-old Helen, who was to change O'Malley's life. She was immediately attracted to the new visitor; later that afternoon she invited him to visit her sculpting studio where they talked and quickly became absorbed with one another. The relationship developed rapidly after this first meeting. O'Malley was at this time living on Charles Street in New York but had arranged shortly to go to Chicago to work as an Irish representative at the World's Fair. Keen to pursue Helen, he wrote to her in July 1933 from Chicago: 'Presently I am in the Irish Free State exhibit giving information with my tongue in my cheek. If you come to Chicago, and I wish you would, please look up that exhibit.'[116] The attraction mutual, Helen did indeed visit him at the Fair and the excitement of their relationship continued to flame.

O'Malley worked in Chicago from July to November and enjoyed the city well enough ('a good symphony orchestra and a really good collection of French paintings').[117] In New York again in December O'Malley re-established contact with Helen: 'Could you, please, when in town, and have time, meet me some place and time; I would like to see you again.'[118] He spent Christmas 1933 in Theodora Goddard's New York apartment and then in early 1934 stayed in the Bronx with the Citkovitz family (whose son Israel he had met at Yaddo in 1932). He had come to like the city, observing in January 1934 that 'New York's all right though. I like it. You're up against it so much and it's such a mad headache.'[119] At this time he knew people in the Alfred Stieglitz/Georgia O'Keeffe circle, of which his friend Paul Strand was a member. But social opportunities coexisted with financial difficulties. He commented of this 1934 period that: 'being so hard I organized New York so that I could be invited out to dinners about four nights a week, but that became too hectic as they were mostly society or semi-society functions and in the end I decided it was much better to be hungry.'[120] As ever, his intellectual work continued. He wrote numerous short stories, and in early 1934 worked for three months in the New York Public Library on Old and Middle Irish. In June 1934 he was focusing his powerful concentration on Donne and Shakespeare. But poverty was an equally persistent theme. In July 1934 O'Malley was a transient on Federal Relief in New York and, as such, was able to live in a house providing welfare-style accommodation. O'Malley's itinerant, American travelling life had often been difficult but, eventually, his resilience again became clear: 'This last year', he wrote to Paul Strand at the end of 1934, 'I went through several kinds of hell, and only last month was I able to realize that I was above defeat. That may sound presumptuous, but it's true. I touched bottom and found that at any rate.'[121]

In December 1934 he was still waiting to hear from Viking Press concerning the possible publication of his book. The delay in obtaining a publisher irritated him, but he had also been writing some short stories and had had some poetry accepted for publication. In January 1935 the American magazine *Poetry*[122] published O'Malley's poems 'Deirdre', and 'Mountjoy Hanged 1921'. In March 1936 his poem 'Indian' (relating to Zuni, in western New Mexico) appeared in the same magazine:

> From the mountain-side a ledge walked
> Into the hard grey light of noon
> As a cloud parts;
> With easy stride it took a beaten way
> Toward the cottonwood's splashed green:
> A greeting came without a greeting's word,
> An envoy of the peace of hills
> Passed softly on moccasin soles
> And vanished low on the arroyo's brim.
>
> The tawny earth was more of earth,
> Strong scents of greeny deerskin sage
> Made rich the low ground breeze.
> Bare rock slopes massed remote
> But near; mountain shades outstretched
> Angles, cool in welcome depths.
> A glow within our now more human clay—
> Radiance without, earth spell, hill gift.

While this reflected the entrancing hold which New Mexico had over O'Malley, 'Mountjoy Hanged 1921' had echoed his continuing Irish— and Irish Republican—interests:

> An ashen face from hempen rope
> Confronts the grey threat of a wall;
> Its memoried bone may swing above
> Loose rubbled death from time's onfall.

> The mind's antennaed waxen cast
> Beats courage from his shattered cry
> Drumming the echoing chord of hope
> On nerves that shook to see him die.
>
> Bone unto bone, his spirit cries
> Across slow ebbing of the years;
> Taut marrow of a man sheds dust
> To tread the meshes of our fears.

Poetry, penury, and Irish politics. As his poetry showed, O'Malley remained preoccupied with Ireland and by early 1935 he was more clearly able to see his way to returning there himself; in December 1934 he had been notified that he was to receive a pension for his Revolutionary activities and had, indeed, received an advance. This reflected the changing complexion of Irish Free State politics during the early 1930s. Following the general election of February 1932 Eamon de Valera's Fianna Fáil party had come to power. This marked an important turning point in Fianna Fáil's attempt to use the Free State's political structures as a means by which to undo the unacceptable features of the 1921 Anglo-Irish Treaty. The pro-Treaty Cumann na nGaedheal party had portrayed themselves as the party of responsibility, order, stability, peace, and law. During their years in government (1923–32), they did indeed lay the foundations for stable Irish democracy. Having accepted the necessity of playing by the Free State's rules, de Valera's party began the undoing of the Treaty shortly after coming to power: land annuity payments to Britain, the oath of allegiance to the British Crown, the office of Governor-General, the right of appeal to the Privy Council, British access to Irish naval facilities, and the 1922 Constitution were all undone during de Valera's constitutional crusade.

The new government in 1932 contained many of O'Malley's former IRA comrades. The losers in the 1922–3 Civil War were now in charge of the state against which they had then waged war. In the earliest years of Fianna Fáil rule there existed a deceptively cosy-looking relationship between the party and the contemporary IRA. Certainly, Fianna Fáil played on their Republican credentials. This was echoed in their attempts to look after current and former Republicans. Republican prisoners who had been jailed by the previous government were pardoned shortly after Fianna Fáil's accession to power. As well as this change in atmosphere, practical considerations were also altered—as

far as O'Malley was concerned—by the shift in political authority.
Frank Aiken suggested that satisfactory openings would be available to
him in Ireland, and in December 1930 Peadar O'Donnell had suggested to Frank Gallagher that O'Malley should be the literary editor
of the *Irish Press*. More crucially, the prospect of a military pension
made O'Malley's return from the USA feasible; as often, practicalities
helped determine his future. It was only when he knew that he would
get a pension that he felt he could go back to Ireland. On 4 February
1935 Frank Aiken wrote to O'Malley from the Department of Defence
in Dublin suggesting that a total pension of around £335 per annum
would be forthcoming on his return to Ireland and that 'If you were
here there would be no difficulty in getting the Military Service Pension fixed up within a week or two.'[123] The Department of Defence
had already informed O'Malley in 1934 that he was due a wound/
disability pension of £120 per annum for the 1932–6 period. (This
wound/disability pension was to continue into his later life as well.) In
July 1935 he was further notified that his basic annual pension, payable
as from 1 October 1934, would be £258.9.8. (In 1953 this figure was
increased to £336.0.7 per annum.) Thus the Revolutionary was provided with post-Revolutionary means of practical subsistence, and this
encouraged and hastened his return to Ireland. In the early spring of
1935 O'Malley, having outstayed his visa, smuggled himself back to
Ireland on a boat on which his brother Desmond was working. In May
1935 he therefore returned to live at home in Dublin, where his parents, and his siblings Paddy, Kathleen, Brendan, and Dessie still lived.

By the time of O'Malley's return to Ireland he and Helen were seriously considering marriage. They were very much in love. Indeed,
O'Malley—not usually effusive in his personal emotions—expressed
considerable tenderness, intensity, and emotional charge in his letters
to Helen from this period: 'I feel quite warm inside whenever I think of
you';[124] 'When I really feel anything most I miss you most';[125] 'it seems
impossible to live happily without you . . . please come as soon as you
can'.[126]

V

Today Frank Aiken called. He wanted me to stand for a constituency, then when I declined he wanted me to work in the general election, which I also declined.

(Ernie O'Malley)[127]

Without her father's knowledge, and despite his hostility towards O'Malley, Helen Hooker set out to visit Ireland in 1935. With her mother and her sister Adelaide she went, between 13 May and 2 June, on a Garden Club of America tour of Japan; then, with Adelaide, she travelled through Japan, China, Manchuria, Moscow, London, and (in August) to Dublin. In July Sarah Sheridan, who had worked for the Hookers for many years, arrived in Dublin at Helen's mother's instigation to assess the appropriateness of O'Malley's family. Armed with their social respectability and their medically oriented sons, the Malleys passed muster.

A more technical problem remained. Never having been baptized, Helen could not marry in Dublin. Ernie O'Malley and Helen Hooker therefore married on 27 September 1935 in a civil ceremony at the Marylebone Registry Office, London, with the marriage being solemnized in a Catholic religious ceremony at St James's Church, Spanish Place (a Catholic Church between Marylebone Road and Oxford Street).[128] He was 38 years old, she 30. Ernie's brother Kevin Malley was best man; also present were siblings Adelaide Hooker and Cecil Malley (who acted as witnesses) as well as Mrs Sheridan, and Ernie's sisters Marion and Kathleen and brother Brendan. After a small reception the couple had a brief honeymoon in London before returning to Dublin, where they first lived at 229 Upper Rathmines Road. The wedding made the news in New York, a reflection of Helen's social standing in society circles, with the *New York Times*, the *New York Herald Tribune*, and the *New York Sun* all carrying articles noting the event, the former two observing that Helen's younger sister Blanchette had married a Rockefeller (John D. Rockefeller III).

O'Malley's connections were not as socially elevated, but he did have a distinguished place in Ireland's Republican aristocracy and upon his return in 1935 he re-established contact with old comrades. Immediately after arriving in Ireland he had contacted Peadar O'Donnell and had—with O'Donnell, his wife Lile, and others—gone to Achill Island, County Mayo, for a week. But O'Malley rejected the available opportunities of diving into an Irish Republican political career. As already noted, many of his Revolutionary colleagues had become politicians. Similar options existed for O'Malley but he declined to pursue them. In a letter to his friend Johnny Raleigh, written from Dublin in June 1935, he recorded that he had recently 'met [Eamon] de Valera. At first he wanted me to run [as a parliamentary candidate] for South Dublin and so did most of his cabinet who were with him, but I put them off and acted, for me, very diplomatically.'[129]

If his social leanings were towards the undiplomatic, it is also true that O'Malley had never been particularly interested in conventional politics. His Revolution had emphatically been that of the Republican soldier, crusading behind the banner of nationalist certainty and relying on violence rather than political argument. This military record now offered him some compensations: on 11 July 1935 he was issued with his statement of Military Service for 1916–23 under the 1934 Military Service Pensions Act. This made considerable practical difference as O'Malley intended to return to student life. In 1936 he began, for a third time, to study medicine at UCD, registering once again for Second Medicine. One of O'Malley's fellow students from this period recalled him as having been 'a remote and awe-inspiring figure'.[130] It was the remoteness which struck another student contemporary, who remembers him as having been 'a rather aloof person who didn't fraternize much with the younger students'.[131] O'Malley rather gave the impression of not belonging to the class: he 'didn't really join in in any sort of student activities'; 'I'm sure he felt a bit of a square peg in a round hole'.[132] Aloof, preoccupied, quiet—certainly, this student episode was a difficult one for O'Malley. His age (he turned 39 in May 1936) made things awkward, and he seems to have found the studies themselves no more suited to his tastes than they had been during his previous attempts at the degree. During 1936–7 he studied medicine but did not sit for an examination. He threw himself into the work with resolution, writing to Johnny Raleigh in November 1936 that he was stuck into his studies, and observing the following month that 'I'm deep in physiology and feel sorry for myself'.[133] He was not greatly enjoying the work but was driving himself, spurred on partly by the fact that by this point three of his brothers (Cecil, Kevin, and Brendan) had completed their medical studies, while his sisters Marion and Kathleen were practising nurses. But he found it difficult to concentrate, to write, and especially to prepare for examinations. By the end of August 1937 Helen was clear that he would not be able to finish the degree.

She wrote to her father that 'I think he will not continue his medicine as it really is not possible for him to get screwed up to the exam. It is a matter of terrific pride with him but I am sure his nerves can't take it.'[134] O'Malley's battered nerves accentuated his difficulty in coping with post-Revolutionary life, and set some jarring notes against the overall diminuendo of his post-1924 existence.

For her part Helen favoured the idea that her husband should pursue literary affairs rather than continue being tortured by medical worries. By 1938 O'Malley himself was being frank about the subject, writing to Helen: 'I won't be sitting for my exam. I don't know enough about it.'[135] By this stage he had shifted more firmly in a literary direction. In the spring of 1936 O'Malley's book, *On Another Man's Wound*, was published by Rich and Cowan of London. The manuscript had been rejected by more than a dozen US publishers, but was accepted at once by Rich and Cowan. The 1935 contract for the book had guaranteed O'Malley a £40 advance (£20 on submission of manuscript, and £20 on publication), and royalties of 10% on sales (this percentage to rise as sales increased). On 14 December 1936 an agreement was reached between UK publisher Rich and Cowan and US publisher Houghton Mifflin (of Boston) about the work. Consequently, on 23 February 1937, it was published in the United States as *Army Without Banners*.

The autobiographical book was widely and enthusiastically reviewed in Ireland and elsewhere (the *New York Times* Book Review described it as 'a stirring and beautiful book'),[136] and it rapidly and rightly became recognized as a classic of Revolutionary literature. O'Malley's stylish, self-conscious, and imaginative record of the 1916–21 years established him as a significant figure within contemporary literary Ireland. Other literary developments were occurring. The *Dublin Magazine* published O'Malley's poems 'County Mayo' and 'Grannia to Diarmuid'. But it was the Revolutionary memoir which marked his literary arrival. On 7 August 1937 Lennox Robinson, the playwright and Honorary Secretary of the Irish Academy of Letters, invited O'Malley to become a member of the Academy. The Academy was to become virtually moribund after Yeats's death in 1939 and its importance should not be overvalued. But O'Malley's introduction to the body is of some interest. When Robinson wrote to O'Malley in August 1937 he informed him that his name had been proposed for membership of the Academy by Seán O'Faoláin and seconded by Frank O'Connor. In his autobiography *My Father's Son* O'Connor recalled that after a meeting of the Academy at which he and O'Faoláin had been trying to get O'Malley elected they had gone to the house of W. B. Yeats: 'Yeats greeted us with his Renaissance cardinal's chuckle and asked: "What do you two young rascals mean by trying to fill my Academy with gunmen?"'[137] O'Malley might well have enjoyed such an exchange. 'I don't mind being called a gunman,' he wrote to Desmond Ryan in 1936, 'we were, I suppose, though we didn't use that term ourselves.'[138]

While his admission to the Academy reflected O'Malley's literary arrival, there were also gloomier consequences following from the publication of *On Another Man's Wound*. In 1936 Joseph O'Doherty brought two actions claiming damages for alleged libel, one against O'Malley and his Irish printers and distributors (Dublin's Sign of the Three Candles Press), the other against O'Malley and the *Irish Press* (which had serialized the book). A barrister, Joseph O'Doherty had been born in Derry city but had strong family links with County Donegal. Involved from early on with the Irish Volunteers, O'Doherty had then become one of County Donegal's representatives in the first Dáil. Involved in the Anglo-Irish War, he subsequently took the Republican side in the Civil War, and was again elected a TD for Donegal in June 1922 and in August 1923. He later stood as a Fianna Fáil candidate in the elections of June 1927 (unsuccessfully) and 1933 (successfully).

O'Doherty claimed that a passage in O'Malley's book wrongly accused him of cowardly self-preservation during the War of Independence, by implying that he had refused to go on a Volunteer/IRA raid during the Anglo-Irish War. The passage in question referred to a raid for arms—a raid suggested by Michael Collins, then Adjutant General of the Volunteers—in Moville, County Donegal, on 1 October 1919. O'Doherty alleged that, although not named in the passage, it was clear that it was to him that O'Malley was referring when he described the refusal of a member of the Volunteer Executive to take part in the raid. O'Doherty claimed that the passage wrongly presented him as cowardly and dishonourable and that it therefore damaged his reputation. The issue came to trial in Dublin in 1937. O'Malley's defence was that the words in question did not refer, and were not understood to refer, to O'Doherty and that therefore there was no libel; moreover it was claimed that the facts as recorded in the book were true and had been expressed in good faith. 'I had to stand over what I had honestly remembered and had sincerely written. Also I knew that a series of libel actions could result.'[139]

Counsel for O'Doherty, J. M. FitzGerald KC, referred to O'Malley's book as a self-glorifying work and argued that it was extremely misleading in relation to the specific episode in question: rather than O'Doherty ducking out of the raid through cowardice, it had in fact been unanimously agreed without O'Doherty's intervention that, as a member of the Dáil, it would be improper for him to go on the raid. On 18 November 1937 Dublin's High Court decided against O'Malley: £250 in the action against O'Malley and the Sign of the Three Candles, £300 in the action against O'Malley and the *Irish Press*. This caused problems for O'Malley. When Helen told her father that the bailiffs had taken possession of the County Mayo house which she and Ernie were renting, Elon Hooker offered to pay. O'Malley in fact borrowed £400 in order to pay his share of the damages, and the matter was closed when in May 1938 the Eire High Court of Justice certified that O'Malley's £400 payment represented full satisfaction and settlement of O'Doherty's claims against him. O'Malley himself found the combination of the libel conflict and the medical studies depressing, observing in December 1937: 'The truth is that since I came back here with medicine around my neck for the first year making me miserable, and a libel action around my neck for another year I was more so.'[140] In particular, he was hurt by the failure of his old comrades to stand by him: 'I found it hard to obtain evidence. People who could verify facts and incidents in talk were reluctant to appear in court.'[141] Dispirited by this libel episode, and out of sorts with his degree, he decided to give up the medical studies.

These features of his life were typical in the disappointment which they brought. But other developments were more positive. He and Helen enjoyed exploring Ireland together. In the spring of 1936 they had spent several weeks in the south and west, visiting and photographing abbeys and ruins. Such activities reflected their intimacy built on shared artistic enthusiasm and absorption in Ireland. At Easter 1936 they went to Kerry with Johnny and Bea Raleigh. By this stage Helen was pregnant with their first child, and on 10 July 1936 Cahal Hooker O'Malley was born in Dublin. O'Malley received congratulations from, among others, one of his closest New York friends, Rebecca Citkovitz. He had informed her of Cahal's birth in a typically semi-legible epistle, and Citkovitz replied with charming irony:

So many words in your letter are a dark mystery to me, what with the shaking of the boat, what with your own naturally clear penmanship that they might be those long lost works of Sappho or Aeschylus or a Phoenician or Babylonian masterpiece, I just wouldn't know. I'm not certain whether you announce a son, a sin, an aeon, an exam, a job . . . a strange name follows which might be Consul, Consuelo, Cicero, Caesar, Caeculus, son of Vulcan, or the masculine of St. Cecilia. Anyway, whether it's a son or a sin, congratulations.[142]

In the autumn of 1936 the three O'Malleys visited Paris (where they bought paintings including works by Modigliani and Vlaminck) and then Corsica. In the summer of 1937 they again visited Paris; also in that year they travelled widely around Ireland, studying and photographing eighth- to twelfth-century Irish sculpture. Travel, friendships, family intimacy, and shared passion for the arts made this one of the warmer, more benign periods of O'Malley's life.

In the autumn of 1937 Elon Hooker provided a financial allowance for Helen which was of great practical assistance. Indeed the Hooker connection was to provide significant help in this respect and the pattern continued after Elon's death in 1938. Helen retained significant shares in her father's business and was given important financial boosts through the generosity of her mother. (Blanche's Christmas gift to the O'Malleys in 1940, for example, was over $10,000 worth of Hooker shares.) Money from Blanche's family had also been a help: D. M. Ferry, Junior had given Helen and Ernie $1,000 as their wedding present. O'Malley had also been given stock in the Hooker Electrochemical Company.

Armed with comparative comfort and keen to live in the rural west of Ireland, Ernie and Helen — in the autumn of 1937 — rented the Old Head Lodge, Killsallagh, Louisberg, in O'Malley's County Mayo. They used this as a base while searching for a house of their own on the Mayo coast. In 1938 they found it: Burrishoole Lodge, near Newport, County Mayo. This was an eight-bedroom stone house, set beautifully with a direct view of Croagh Patrick in the distance and of Burrishoole Abbey — a fifteenth-century Dominican Priory ruin — immediately across the water of a lagoon. Helen instinctively knew that this was *the* house, and in November 1938 they began to rent it. The house appealed on a number of levels. The stunningly lovely setting combined with the sense of a bucolic alternative to urban constriction; and O'Malley's patriotic attachment to rural Irish simplicity was complemented here by the long-standing connections the area possessed with O'Malley heritage. He was proud that the house had been built (in the early nineteenth century) on the site of O'Malley property. Helen was no less captivated with Burrishoole. Artistic and creative vision inspired her with possibilities for this Irish idyll and she soon began to improve the property, with work on the gardens and the construction of new buildings (including a studio) in the grounds. Such ambition, expensive as well as expansive, was to grow into a source of tension in the marriage. O'Malley's later comment reflected this: 'I tried to prevent her over-elaborate improvements but she was restless.'[143] Yet it is important to note the positive, enthusiastic quality of their early life together in Burrishoole, and later developments should not cloud this.

Coastal life (O'Malley possessed two boats — 'St Brendan' and 'The Blunderbuss' — which he used in the bay in all weathers) combined with continuing urban contacts. During 1938 O'Malley had spent part of May and June in London and part of July in Dublin, and his literary career was progressing in various ways. In 1938 *On Another Man's Wound* was translated into German and published (without O'Malley receiving royalties) as *Rebellen in Irland*. Further German editions were to appear during the Second World War in 1942 and 1943, and in each of the three editions between 4,000 and 6,000 copies were printed. The publisher was Alfred Metzner, a Berlin publishing company of which Dr Wolfgang Metzner was editor. The latter had taken a strong fancy to O'Malley's book: 'I was very interested in all sorts of struggles for liberation.'[144]

During most of 1939 O'Malley resided at Burrishoole. He was still working on a variety of writing projects, including the fine-tuning of the second part of his Revolutionary memoirs (taking the story from 1921 onwards). Visitors occasionally descended. In the summer Gerald Sykes, a leading figure from the American Group Theatre, visited Helen and Ernie at Burrishoole at the suggestion of Paul Strand. At this time O'Malley was engaged in taking photographs of Irish monuments, and he told Sykes that he had learned about photography from Strand during his time in New Mexico in the early 1930s. During the summer and autumn Helen's mother visited Ireland and stayed, for part of that time, at Burrishoole.

During the Second World War the O'Malleys spent much of their time farming in Mayo. Upon the commencement of hostilities in 1939 O'Malley had attempted to sign up for military duty in the Irish army, but had been rejected owing to his poor physical condition. Thus the soldier became a farmer: 'there was a war on. I felt that our farm should produce food.'[145] His notebooks concerning the farming are as obsessively meticulous as are his tireless scribblings on military and literary matters; in all such work he exhibited a relentless desire to put shape and order on things. Research, preparation, and cataloguing were all detailed in relation to a very wide range of activities ('*Calf at Birth:* dress navel and feet with dettol, 1 to 5 H_2O. Tie cord with string dipped in iodine. Rub down with straw; see that navel cord does not bleed too much. Sprinkle with salt and allow cow to lick').[146] Typically, great emphasis was placed on improvement—better drainage, better fertilizers, the most efficient organization of grazing—and O'Malley found some of the western farm workers frustrating in the extreme, eventually preferring not to employ local men.

Both O'Malley and Helen worked hard in the field. Indeed, Helen was dynamic, energetic, and visionary about the farming project and about Burrishoole more generally. She was keen to build up a model farm, and farm buildings continued to be built up until 1943. There had been problems with some of the neighbours, who had opposed Helen's intention to buy further land in the neighbouring peninsula. But during 1940 Helen proceeded with her building plans in Burrishoole (outhouses, a studio), although here friction developed with the more cautious instincts of her husband: 'I tried to keep her within reasonable limits of effort, but failed.'[147] Having initially rented Burrishoole, in September 1941 the O'Malleys actually purchased it. Burrishoole Lodge, together with about 40 acres of attached land, were bought in Helen's name. In 1942 she bought the adjoining lands (of over 30 acres). Thus by 1942 they had a 70-acre farm.

Literature and the arts continued to preoccupy them as well, however, and served as an antidote to their often frustrating farming existence. In December 1941 O'Malley wrote from Burrishoole that 'Helen and I have to go there [Dublin] every now and then to meet people who speak our own language. Here, nobody is interested in creative work . . . I have nobody to speak the language of books, literature, or criticism.'[148] In Dublin itself O'Malley could enjoy contact with figures such as the Belfast-born poet Louis MacNeice and the painter Jack Yeats. O'Malley and Yeats met frequently, corresponded warmly, and O'Malley bought a number of the painter's works. He was also to write tellingly on Yeats, and indeed during the late 1930s and the 1940s O'Malley spent much time attending, opening, and working to produce art exhibitions. Works from his own collection were sometimes used in these showings; he had, for example, two of his Jack Yeats paintings included in the London National Gallery's Yeats exhibition of 1942. Other artistic pursuits could rather better be pursued in Mayo. O'Malley was based there for most of 1940, and committed much of his energy to the collection of Irish folklore in the area around Clew Bay. He immersed himself in the late night sessions at which stories were told, and recorded large numbers of tales in his ever-detailed notebooks.

During this wartime period O'Malley was also a member of the Local Security Force and, in recognition of his previous military achievements, he was (in January 1942) awarded a 1916 Ribbon by the Department of Defence. There were also important family developments. On 8 August 1940 Ernie and Helen's second child, Etáin Huntington O'Malley, was born in Leinster Nursing Home, Fitzwilliam Street, Dublin. On 20 July 1942 Cormac Kevin Hooker O'Malley was born, also in Dublin (the father's profession being given on the birth certificate as that of 'author'). On 6 August Cormac was baptized at the Church of St Nicholas of Myra, Francis Street, Dublin. At the baptism a bowl was presented by the German minister to Ireland, Eduard Hempel, with whom Ernie and Helen were friendly.

Helen's own work as a sculptor was of enormous importance to her, as is reflected in the vast quantity and range of work which she was to produce over her lifetime. In 1942 she rented a flat at Fitzwilliam Place in Dublin; during much of 1942 Ernie and Helen were apart, she in Dublin and he in Burrishoole. An attempt was made to adjust this when in December 1943 Helen built a sculpture studio in Burrishoole. But by this stage, the marriage was struggling for life. Moreover, the wartime farming had, like many other aspects of rural Ireland, become frustrating for the O'Malleys. In February 1944 O'Malley broke his right leg while farming; the break took an age to heal and this accentuated his infuriation with the farm work. Between March and September 1944 he remained in Burrishoole, but from then until the end of the year he stayed in Dublin with Helen and the three children.

In the autumn of 1944 they—or, more particularly, Helen—bought a house at 15 Whitebeam Avenue, Clonskeagh, Dublin. In the autumn, too, Helen became submerged in work with the Players' Theatre. In November 1944 a number of young actors/actresses—Eithne Dunne, Gerard Healy, Harry Webster, and Liam Redmond—decided to leave Dublin's famous Abbey Theatre to found a new Company to be called the Players' Theatre. Lacking money but armed with experience, the new group aimed to promote the production of new Irish plays in an effort to revivify what they thought of as a moribund Irish theatre. The committee comprised Dunne, Healy, Webster, Redmond, and Helen O'Malley, whose keenness to move into the world of scenic design fired her interest in the new venture. O'Malley himself was unenthusiastic ('Her work was in sculpture I thought . . . I advised her to keep to sculpture and leave the theatre to theatre people')[149] and considerable tensions were to develop. The intrusion of the Players' group upon the O'Malleys' house, and the increasing intimacy between Helen and Redmond, caused great friction between Ernie and Helen. During the October–November 1944 period O'Malley committed himself to writing. He set himself a daily schedule of at least a morning's work on his various historical and artistic projects. Work, therefore, occupied them both; and by 1944 their intimacy with one another had greatly cooled.

VI

1945–1957

I went, 1955, to Paris with Cormac to get him accustomed to the Left Bank, the French way of life, painting, and the importance of French.

(Ernie O'Malley)[150]

The Second World War largely passed O'Malley by, with family concerns and his various avenues of work preoccupying him instead. Much of his time was focused during these years upon the arts. During the first half of 1945 he worked hard in helping to organize a Jack Yeats exhibition (the Jack B. Yeats National Loan Exhibition) which traced Yeats's development as an artist. It opened on 12 June 1945 at Dublin's National College of Art, to run during June and July. O'Malley had written an impressive introduction to the exhibition catalogue and had been a very active member of the organizing committee behind the venture. Yeats was tremendously appreciative of his efforts; in June 1945 he presented Ernie with a book of sketches inscribed: 'To Ernie O'Malley with many thanks for all the trouble about the Loan Exhibition of my painting'.[151]

The O'Malleys had also themselves become art collectors. Armed with money from Helen's family, and with acute artistic vision, they had been able to build an impressive collection of paintings. In March 1945, indeed, both had bought Yeats paintings at an exhibition at the Waddington Galleries, Ernie's choice being the beautiful, coastal 'Derrynane' (1927). This artistic enthusiasm they continued to share. Helen's theatrical involvement was more and more intense. On 12 February 1945 the Players' Theatre opened their first season with three plays presented at the Cork Opera House. Plays by Healy and

Redmond were performed, the Company remaining for a three-week season before proceeding on a short tour of the larger towns in the south of Ireland and then on to its first season in Dublin. On 6 March 1945 the Players' Theatre presented *The Black Stranger* by Gerry Healy at the Gate Theatre, Dublin. Helen, in the United States between June and December 1945, sought advice regarding Liam Redmond's work from her brother-in-law John P. Marquand—the successful American novelist who had married Helen's sister Adelaide in 1937. Marquand wrote in August 1945 that 'Mr Redmond has the makings of a first-rate playwright. My advice to him . . . is that he puts this play [*Rocks of Bawn*] aside and tries to write another and when writing it thinks of his characters, and gives them more of a chance to express themselves.'[152]

O'Malley's own writing was preoccupying and troubling him. For four months prior to Easter 1945 he was working steadily on the second volume of his Revolutionary memoirs. After that he appears never to have been able to write on the Irish Civil War, poor health and other writing commitments getting in the way. During Helen's visit to the United States Ernie looked after the three children and was based primarily at Burrishoole. In the autumn he was visited by Catherine 'Bobs' Walston whom he had met (then Catherine Crompton) in the States and whom he had again seen in Galway in 1941. Married to the future Labour peer Harry Walston, Catherine was the granddaughter of Sarah Sheridan, the Hookers' companion and confidante who had been sent over to Ireland to inspect the Malleys' credentials prior to Helen and Ernie's marriage. The Walstons had stayed in Burrishoole with the O'Malleys, and Catherine and Ernie were to become intimate friends. As with many of his friends, O'Malley shared with the Walstons a profound interest in the arts. They were well connected here. Sir John Rothenstein (Director of London's Tate Gallery) was a friend of theirs, and in December 1945 O'Malley brought Rothenstein to see Jack Yeats. O'Malley's plan was to set up an exhibition of Irish painters to show in Ireland and take to England, and for Rothenstein to set up an exhibition of English painters to show in England and take to Ireland. Other artistic projects were simultaneously consuming him. On 23 October 1945 he had opened Evie Hone's exhibition of paintings, stained glass, and drawings at Dublin's Dawson Gallery. And he was, during late-1945, buying more paintings than he could afford.

Christmas 1945 O'Malley spent with the children in Burrishoole, Helen returning from her USA visit immediately afterwards. Between

Mayo and Dublin, and between their various trips to England or the USA, Helen and Ernie were by this stage spending little time together. In mid-February 1946 Ernie travelled to London, staying at the Walstons' Piccadilly townhouse. He tried to arrange (or, rather, to have John Rothenstein arrange) art exhibitions in London, but Rothenstein was less enthusiastic. Even this first stage of O'Malley's scheme for reciprocal exhibitions failed, therefore, to materialize. During March and April O'Malley stayed with the Walstons at their large Cambridgeshire farm and during this time he mixed with a variety of artistic figures, including the distinguished English painter John Piper. Having returned to Ireland in the late spring, O'Malley then entertained Catherine Walston, Lady Barbara Rothschild, and Ludovic Kennedy in Burrishoole before returning with them to London to attend an opening at the Tate Gallery. Alternating between Burrishoole, Dublin, London, and Cambridge, O'Malley absorbed himself during these years in artistic interests. The work yielded much of value. In July 1946, for example, he published an insightful piece on the Irish painter Louis le Brocquy in the English review *Horizon*. Like le Brocquy, O'Malley found that much of his artistic world was focused inevitably on London. Having spent much of the summer in Burrishoole—some of it with Catherine Walston, who had rented a cottage on Achill Island—O'Malley returned to the English capital at the end of October. He was to remain there, staying at the Walstons' house, until the end of December 1946. Helen, too, was in London during that autumn, working on her theatre designs. But their respective work projects occupied them, by this stage, far more than did any mutual intimacy. The marriage had effectively ended.

The children, however, still had to be provided for. Intriguingly, in 1946 O'Malley entered the two boys for places at the English Benedictine public school, Ampleforth College, in Yorkshire. Cahal was scheduled to enter the school in the autumn term of 1950, and Cormac in the spring term of 1955 (Cormac: 'Though father fought bitterly against the British for patriotic reasons, he always approved of their educational system').[153] A distinguished school, offering a disciplined Catholic education as well as a widening of horizons, Ampleforth—a boarding school—would also solve the problem of where the boys would live. In late 1946 Helen stated that she wanted a divorce and that, as this was impossible to obtain in Ireland, she would be prepared to obtain it in the USA. She and Ernie therefore discussed the questions of custody and schooling for the three children. In October they had a series of meetings in London to try to settle these questions. Little had, however, been resolved by the time that Helen travelled to the States in November (where she was to stay until the end of March 1947). O'Malley was not keen on the idea of a divorce; but their emotional and, for most of the time in the late 1940s, their practical separation both underlined the fact that the marriage was moribund.

O'Malley's work was, by contrast, full of vigour. He published an article entitled 'Renaissance' in an edition of *La France Libre* (December 1946—January 1947) which focused on Ireland. He had also become involved with the Irish periodical *The Bell*. A valuable vehicle for literary, artistic, and social commentary, *The Bell* was founded by the writer Seán O'Faoláin in 1940. O'Faoláin edited the magazine until 1946; from that year until it ceased publication in 1954 *The Bell* was edited by O'Malley's old Republican comrade Peadar O'Donnell. Dissident intellectuals of Irish Republican pedigree, O'Faoláin and O'Donnell typified the spirit of the periodical. Offering wide-ranging reflection on (and often dissident criticism of) the society which the Irish Revolution had produced, *The Bell* had a very distinguished list of literary, artistic, and intellectual contributors, including not only O'Faoláin and O'Donnell themselves, but also figures such as Elizabeth Bowen, Hubert Butler, Edmund Curtis, Lynn Doyle, John Hewitt, Denis Johnston, Patrick Kavanagh, Donagh MacDonagh, Louis MacNeice, Flann O'Brien, Frank O'Connor, Liam O'Flaherty, Nano Reid, Lennox Robinson, Francis Stuart, and Jack B. Yeats. *The Bell* sought to survey and comment on Irish life, and indeed to cherish the best of it: '*The Bell* would particularly like to encourage articles on these—fine food, fine dress, fine furniture, fine drink, all the things that delight and satisfy the senses, all the lovely things that man makes as against the lovely things that are Nature's free gift to us and for which we deserve no credit.'[154] All of this suited O'Malley. As a dissident Republican intellectual who was committed to Irish independence, disaffected from aspects of the new Ireland, and keen on pursuing the artistic beauty and freedom which the new Ireland often rejected, it is not surprising that O'Malley should have become involved in *The Bell*. He had long enthused over the idea of some such venture. Indeed, in December 1923 he had commented to Peadar O'Donnell—at that time his fellow prisoner in Kilmainham Jail—that he was 'keen on a monthly paper' offering literary and art criticism, book reviews, short stories, and consideration of current affairs, history, economics, and geography.[155]

From May 1947 until April 1948 O'Malley was book editor for *The Bell*, and much of his time during this period was spent in pursuing contacts relating to this role — a role well suited to such an omnivorous bibliophile. Other projects were also occupying him. On 22 November 1946 Basil Taylor of the BBC's Third Programme Talks Department invited O'Malley to do a radio talk, either on art in the west of Ireland, or on American Indians. O'Malley accepted the offer, but refocused the subject. On 2 January 1947 he gave a Third Programme broadcast talk on 'The Traditions of Mexican Painting'. Introduced (misleadingly) as someone who had 'spent many years in Mexico', O'Malley reflected on Mexican painting within a context of his visual impressions of the place, arts, and people.

My first real experience of Mexico was in San Louis Potosi when I had come by road, or rather by a hypothetical road, across the northern desert. I was confused by facial types and at first, as is common enough, attracted by a superficial quality of romanticism in the colour and pattern of the land and its people. Faces were unlike the academic Greco-Roman European tradition. The mixture of Spanish and Indian had produced a race which varied between the two, but the basis was mainly Indian.

Here, then, was a folk tradition which was enriched in memory as I wandered through Mexico. It had strength, interest, and vitality. In colour, form, and design it was invariably aesthetically satisfying. This tradition of craftsmanship has affected the conscious artist and the popular hand worker in Mexico. At times, especially in the 19th and the early 20th century when taste was florid or banal, folk art kept its high purpose. In a time of resurgence, from 1910 to 1922, it was drawn on for inspiration by the conscious artist.[156]

In September 1947 O'Malley was again to appear on the BBC, this time as compère on the London Home Service for a pre-recorded edition of 'Country Magazine' from Eire. Having spent January and early February 1947 in London, O'Malley returned in the latter month to the Clonskeagh house in Dublin. Both Etáin and Cormac were sick, Helen was in the United States, and the children were in the charge of a nanny (Eileen Dineen) and a cook/housekeeper (Brigid O'Shea). In July 1947 Cormac and Etáin flew to the USA for a six-month stay, visiting aunts in Boston and New York and their grandmother in Greenwich, Connecticut. Later that month Cahal also travelled to the States. The visits were, in part at least, intended to allow the children to see their grandmother whose health was fading.

Helen also travelled to the USA, setting out on 16 October 1947 and remaining there for several months. Even before her departure, however, she and Ernie had scarcely been spending time together. Work preoccupied them. They had, it is true, overlapped for a week at Burrishoole immediately prior to Helen's departure in October. But before that Helen had been in London, working on theatre productions such as Paul Vincent Carroll's *The White Steed*. For his part, O'Malley spent most of 1947 in Burrishoole. His literary work absorbed most of his time. He was still working on various historical projects, had been elected Secretary of the Irish Academy of Letters (a post he held until 1949), and also had work relating to *The Bell*—the latter taking him to London in May and June 1947.

From early December 1947 until the spring of 1948 O'Malley was mainly based in Dublin, although he periodically visited Burrishoole. In May Helen returned from the USA and repeated that she wanted a divorce. O'Malley refused to consent, although their relationship was clearly under enormous tension. Their work projects pulled them in different directions. Helen's absorption in the Players' Theatre—in particular her increasing intimacy with Liam Redmond—offers a salient example. So, too, does O'Malley's concentrated devotion to his newest historical writing project: the interviewing of hundreds of Irish Revolutionary veterans concerning their exploits in the 1916–23 period. During 1948–54 O'Malley travelled widely throughout Ireland conducting interviews with over five hundred people. Distinct echoes can be heard here of his earlier itinerant life as a Revolutionary: solitary travels, in pursuit of those who had also been through the epic events of the Revolution. This episode can be read, at one level, as a poignant attempt to recapture the pivotal and most meaningful years of his life; there was a marked sadness to it—the physically damaged ex-Revolutionary, his private life in tatters, solitarily attempting to reassemble his purposeful Revolutionary youth. Characteristically, he worked with terrific zeal at the project; part of the work involved his taking extensive newspaper notes in Dublin's National Library to serve as a comparative source. The aim was to construct a military history of the Revolutionary period. Sometimes he would stay with friends (including some of his interviewees) and on other occasions he would sleep in his old Ford car. At the same time he acquired—and, again, transcribed in his numerous notebooks—a large number of Irish ballads and a large body of Irish folklore. Culture and politics were, as ever, intermingled.

On 30 May 1948 Cahal O'Malley was diagnosed as suffering from tuberculosis; in mid-June both he and Cormac were ordered to bed on account of the disease. When both boys were confirmed by x-ray as having the disease—the source was identified as having been the maid—they were confined to bed and for a year lived at home in Dublin (where they were taught a variety of academic subjects by their father). A nurse (Una Joyce) was hired to help with the boys who, after a year, made good recoveries. Etáin was sent, in August 1948 for over half a year, to live in County Dublin with O'Malley's friend, Mrs Sunny Clarke (in order to avoid TB). In September 1949 Cahal and Etáin were sent to Ring College, Dungarvan, County Waterford, a Gaelic-speaking school. Cormac remained in Burrishoole.

During April, May, and June 1949 Ernie and Helen lived together in Dublin. Apart from these months their lives in the late-1940s were effectively separate. In 1948 and in 1949 Thomas Gilchrist, Helen's American lawyer, came over to Dublin to see if some agreement between the two parties could be reached. No success was achieved on either occasion. Indeed, considerable bitterness had entered into the relationship by this stage. As is often the case, money and property provided battlegrounds. Helen and Ernie were not poor, by contemporary Irish standards. In 1948–9 Helen had an income, from her family, of approximately £2,500–£3,500 per annum. O'Malley's own finances were very variable. Around the time of his death in 1957 his bank balance was £2,005.14.8. During 1940–9 his highest balance was £1,436.10.1 (7 September 1948) and his lowest £78.8.8 overdrawn (28 January 1942). During 1950–7 his highest balance was £2,920.4.0 (16 May 1951) and his lowest £50.19.2 (1 September 1953). His problem was a periodical shortage of ready cash. On occasions this became quite pressing. In 1948 he had, as a precaution, corresponded with Sotheby and Co. of London about the possibility of their selling part of his library. On 15 December 1949 over four hundred of O'Malley's books were indeed auctioned, in his absence, at Sotheby's New Bond Street galleries. The works sold included a large collection of the works of W. B. Yeats as well as limited, signed editions of work by Liam O'Flaherty, Lady Gregory, and Padraic Colum. Other books sold on this occasion reflected O'Malley's wide-ranging intellectual tastes, including Patrick Kavanagh, Elizabeth Bowen, Seán O'Faoláin, D. H. Lawrence, John Donne, John Milton, John Bunyan, Miguel de Cervantes, Homer, and Shakespeare. From this Sotheby sale O'Malley made £486.5.0.

For her part, Helen's work included not only her theatrical interests, but also her continued commitment to sculpture. In 1950 she held her first one-person show of portraits in Dublin's St Stephen's Green Gallery. Her sculpture was not to be shown in the United States until 1953, when it was exhibited at the Taylor Museum in Colorado Springs. Helen's work included heads of many Irish figures including family (Ernie, Cormac, Etáin, and Ernie's mother Marion, with whom Helen had a strong relationship), writers (Liam O'Flaherty, Frank O'Connor, Peadar O'Donnell), actors/actresses (Liam Redmond, Siobhan McKenna), as well as figures from elsewhere (the writer John P. Marquand, Dr William Horsley Gantt—the Founder and Director of the Pavlovian Laboratory of Johns Hopkins University, Baltimore). Helen and Ernie shared a capacity for intense focus upon work and, while this had initially reinforced their intimacy, it gradually became another of those factors pushing the two partners away from one another. By 1950 the situation had reached its nadir. Helen was keen to leave O'Malley, but wanted custody of the children. O'Malley was resistant both to a divorce and to allowing the children out of his hands. In January 1949 Blanche Hooker, with her daughter Helen's backing, suggested to Ernie that the children come to the United States to convalesce from their illness in a more appropriate climate. O'Malley's brusquely cabled response—'Thank you for kind invitation but children remain in Ireland'[157]—was complemented by a fuller letter which more accurately reflected the essentially good relations which he and his mother-in-law enjoyed:

Thank you for your letter and for your kind invitation. The children, however, need one of their parents and that parent must stay with them, especially when they are ill, otherwise they have nobody to really trust. As far as I am concerned I will remain with them and that they know, consequently there is no necessity for their leaving; for what they need is rest, the cultivation of their imagination, and some little schoolwork: all of which they get here.[158]

If anything, perhaps, O'Malley had settled into the parenting side of domestic life rather better than Helen. Clearly, by 1949–50 the differences over how to bring up the children were compounding (and compounded by) the painful relations between wife and husband. Helen felt that Ernie's hard, unyielding approach to their upbringing had led to the children's illness. She argued that their post-TB recovery would be helped by their being removed to the drier and warmer climate available in the United States or in Switzerland. This O'Malley resolutely opposed.

Helen opted for a typically dramatic gesture, one which reinforces the view that O'Malley's post-Revolutionary life was as arresting and compelling as were his IRA exploits. On 28 March 1950 she took Cahal and Etáin from their school, Ring College, informing them that she was merely taking them out for the afternoon. Ernie had left instructions with the school's headmaster, An Fear Mor, that Helen was on no account to take the children away without his permission. The headmaster therefore went along to Dungarvan with Helen and the children; but he briefly left the hotel at which they were having tea and on his return found that Helen had briskly taken the children away. Helen, Cahal, and Etáin travelled via Belfast and Paris to New York. This kidnapping—and the word was used in relation to the event by Ernie, Helen, Cahal, Etáin, and Cormac—had, as we shall see, immense consequences for all involved. On 29 March An Fear Mor telegrammed O'Malley to inform him of the events of the previous day. O'Malley was at this point driving from Mayo (where Cormac was then staying) to Dublin. The police were alerted and were able to stop him at Mullingar, County Westmeath, and inform him of the incident. O'Malley exploded with rage, desperate and furious at Helen's gesture. The police searched for wife and children but by this stage they had left the country. On 3 April O'Malley was granted a conditional order of *habeas corpus* directing Helen to produce Cahal and Etáin, or to show cause for their removal, within ten days of the order.

In the United States Helen moved, later in 1950, to Colorado Springs and the two children went to school there. In Ireland, much of O'Malley's attention after the kidnapping of Cahal and Etáin was focused on the protection of Cormac. The boy, 8 years old in July 1950, stayed with his father and the pair shared their time between Dublin (where Cormac boarded at Mount Sackville Convent, Phoenix Park) and Burrishoole in the west. Their lives were isolated, the already remote setting of Burrishoole accentuated now by O'Malley's caution regarding those friends who might be suspected of sympathizing more with Helen than with himself in the separation. It is not that they had no visitors; during the summer of 1950, for example, John V. Kelleher (who was later to be Cormac's Professor of History at Harvard University) visited Burrishoole. But conditions there increasingly took on the appearance of vindicating Helen's concern about ill-health, and there is a cold, poignant, quiet, and haunted quality about this period. During O'Malley's time in Burrishoole his already far from robust health was not improved by the damp and cold conditions. After the break

with Helen there was not the money to improve the place or to maintain the staff necessary to run the farm. Eventually Ernie and Cormac
were to live in one room only, and without electricity or running water
the conditions were far from comfortable. Ernie's health was not good:
in February 1950 he wrote from Burrishoole to John Kelleher: 'I am in
bed as I have overdone it for my heart has been giving me trouble.'[159]

Legal hostilities with Helen continued. In the summer of 1950 she
applied for an injunction restraining O'Malley from being present in
Burrishoole, from removing livestock, furniture, and other possessions
from the property, and from interfering with the sale of such items.
The Dublin High Court refused to grant the order. Helen's claim was
that Burrishoole Lodge, together with all of the furniture and household goods contained in it, was her separate property. In June 1949 she
had instructed her solicitor (George Overend, a partner in the leading
Dublin firm A. and L. Goodbody) to put the house and lands at Burrishoole up for sale. The price, however, was high and no sale ensued.
Then in April 1950, after the kidnapping, Helen telephoned Overend
from the United States saying that he should press on with the immediate sale of Burrishoole, and also instructing him to organize for the
removal of all her furniture, household goods, and belongings from
the house. Overend set this in motion but O'Malley, later that month,
refused to allow the people sent to remove the various goods to do so.
He therefore prevented both the removal of the possessions claimed by
Helen and also the sale.

Having failed in her first legal assault (aimed at removing her furniture and gaining possession of Burrishoole), Helen then sued to evict
O'Malley from Burrishoole. The property had been taken in Helen's
name because, after the experience with the O'Doherty libel case,
they had not wanted O'Malley to own property in his own name lest
it thereby become vulnerable to further litigation. So although his
money (royalties from On Another Man's Wound) went towards the
buying of the house, the purchase was in Helen's name alone. In truth,
most of the money for the purchase had come from Hooker sources;
but the contest owed more to anger than to questions of historical
accuracy.

The solicitor representing O'Malley was Michael Noyk of Dublin;
Helen was again represented by Goodbody. In contrast to the style of
the latter leading firm, Noyk—who had represented Republicans in
the past—ran the O'Malley end of the struggle on a shoestring. The
Noyk/O'Malley case involved an attempt to establish from the letters

between Helen and Ernie that what O'Malley claimed to be the case—namely, that his money had gone towards paying for Burrishoole—was in fact true. In March 1951 O'Malley heard that it had been decided that the court application against him should be defeated with costs. After this setback Helen lost interest and O'Malley was therefore able to live at will in Burrishoole, which he did on and off.

There were, of course, more positive developments in his life. On 8 September 1950 the successful American film director John Ford had written to O'Malley saying that he was to make a film in County Mayo in 1951 and that he wanted O'Malley to be involved as his assistant on the project. During June and July 1951 Ford filmed *The Quiet Man*, with John Wayne, Maureen O'Hara, and Barry FitzGerald, the filming being based at Ashford Castle, near Cong, County Mayo. The film—released in 1952 and lastingly successful—was directed by Ford, produced by Merian C. Cooper, and based on a short story by the Irish writer Maurice Walsh, with a screenplay by Frank S. Nugent. In July 1950 Ford had visited Dublin and London on a preliminary trip in relation to *The Quiet Man*; in November 1950 he had prepared the ground at Ashford Castle. *The Quiet Man*, a romanticized celebration of pastoral Ireland, involved Ford shooting in Ireland for the first time. As a kind of local adviser, O'Malley was on set every day advising Ford about local culture and settings. He loved it, and enjoyed himself enormously in an atmosphere of great conviviality. He got on well with Wayne and O'Hara, and he liked the director in spite of certain temperamental problems ('I like Ford. He is difficult to work with and for at times, as he has a cyclonic temper').[160] Ford, in turn, was very keen on O'Malley. This is explicable enough. Of Catholic Irish-American background, with a profound interest in matters military, Ford was devoted to Ireland and held that it had suffered under suffocating alien influence: in all of this he and O'Malley would have nodded in agreement.[161] The Irish-American director had been impressed by O'Malley's IRA record and enjoyed the idea of having him as a friend and adviser on the set. Ford, in Maureen O'Hara's recollection, 'had a great deal of respect for Ernie. . . . He had such respect for Ernie. They would natter away like old buddies. . . . They liked each other. They were friends.'[162]

O'Malley's involvement in film was followed by his attempt to have reprinted the book which had represented another lyrical version of Ireland. On 8 September 1951 he wrote to Rich and Cowan asking that they consider reprinting *On Another Man's Wound*. The publishers

swiftly responded, however, that despite the work's excellence the state
of the market would not allow them to reprint it. A further setback
occurred two months later, with the initiation by Helen of divorce
proceedings. On 6 November 1951 she obtained an Interlocutory
Decree in Colorado, on her application for divorce from Ernie and for
custody of Cahal and Etáin. On 6 May 1952 the District Court, in the
County of El Paso, Colorado, decreed that Helen and Ernie were
divorced and that custody of Cahal and Étain should indeed be
awarded to Helen.

There were attempts to soothe relations. In the summer of 1952
Helen visited Ireland. She and Ernie met and talked for several days in
Dublin, he trying to persuade her to agree never to take Cormac.
Helen and Cormac spent time together—a considerable solace for the
former—but relations between Helen and Ernie remained taut and
painful. Helen's attitude towards Ernie in this period was more
changeable than were his feelings towards her. She remained uncertain about the end of the marriage, and tried without success to persuade her only recently divorced husband to remarry her. Indeed,
there is evidence that, from 1953 onwards, Helen experienced a feeling
of sorrow at having left Ernie and Ireland. She increasingly came to
idealize her time with O'Malley and indeed to romanticize Ireland
itself. The roots of this were hinted at in contemporary reflections on
her broader feelings with regard to Ireland: 'I have made my name as
an artist in Dublin. . . . My love of Dublin is very deep and will always
be. . . . My best years I gave to Ireland with all my heart and my soul
and [I] should be able to reap some of that richness now as I need a
quieter life.'[163]

While Helen wanted to reignite the relationship, O'Malley was hostile to the idea of their attempting again to live together. He certainly
did not want to remarry, writing in telling explanation to a friend in
July 1955 that Helen was 'an endless source of worry: no quietness,
improvident, and a doer of something or other'.[164] During that summer Helen visited Ireland, with Cahal and Etáin, and unsuccessfully
attempted to effect a reconciliation with Ernie. In a letter to Paul
Strand in August 1955, O'Malley recounted his ambivalent feelings:
'Helen wanted to remarry me, but I had had enough uncertainty and
the break up of a family. . . . Then I was upset as I thought I was not
doing my best to help the two children [Cahal and Etáin], but I could
see no way out of it. Worry I must avoid as much as I can and life with
Helen would mean endless worry and little touch with the two chil-

dren.'[165] Although he had been willing for Helen and Cormac to meet in the summer of 1952, he remained cautious about Helen's possible intentions towards the boy, and was very careful to limit access to him. In 1952 Cormac started at Willow Park School in Dublin, the preparatory school for Blackrock College, and on O'Malley's instructions could only be visited by either O'Malley himself or his friend and old Republican colleague Liam Manahan. In school holidays O'Malley arranged for Cormac to visit various reliably loyal people in different parts of Ireland. During the summer of 1952, for example, he stayed with the Kerrigans in County Donegal and the Duffys in County Roscommon. In the following summer, 1953, he stayed with O'Malley's brother Paddy in Greystones, County Wicklow, for a holiday. Understandably, Cormac's security and protection were paramount considerations for O'Malley after the 1950 kidnapping.

Other commitments also persisted, and key among them was his writing. In particular he remained concerned that a Republican record of the Irish Revolution be established. Early in 1953 he gave to Francis MacManus, General Features Officer at Radio Éireann, episodes of what were to become radio broadcasts on the Revolution. These were recorded by O'Malley in March and subsequently broadcast on the radio. The series of talks, entitled 'Raids and Rallies', dealt with episodes in the Anglo-Irish War involving IRA attacks on the forces of the Crown. After their broadcast, O'Malley was cheered by the response which the talks provoked from some of his old comrades ('The old lads seem to have been pleased for a number of them wrote to me').[166] By this stage his health had seriously, ominously deteriorated. On 12 March 1953 he had a heart attack, and was confined to St Bricin's Military Hospital in Dublin between March and May. The government in fact refused to give free treatment to the old IRA soldier, and his brother Kevin Malley and friend Johnny Raleigh between them paid O'Malley's bill. After the heart attack O'Malley's health remained poor. His capacity for travelling round pursuing his research projects was severely restricted and, together with his back injuries and the digestive problems caused by the 1923 hunger strike, he was often in considerable pain. His oft-noted irritability owed much to this. While recovering from the heart attack immediately after his departure from hospital, O'Malley stayed with his friends Christy and Annie Smith in Dublin. In the summer of 1953 he was able to return to Burrishoole. The place was in a very poor state: the gardens had become overgrown, damp ate into the ceilings, and (as noted earlier) the lack of comfort was not conducive to recuperation. But O'Malley adopted a familiarly resilient attitude. Writing to Paul Strand, one of his closest confidantes, in July 1953 he observed: 'Cormac is now eleven. We have a good time together and he learns from the sea and the countryside and sometimes from myself.'[167] During that summer O'Malley visited the Aran Islands (partly in order that Cormac should learn Irish) and then in August he and Cormac set out to visit the Walstons at Newton Hall, near Cambridge. They stayed with them there until January 1954, the hospitality, comfort, and agreeable, intimate company offering a welcome alternative to the eremitical existence at Burrishoole.

After a short period in Ireland early in 1954 O'Malley returned to the Walstons' Cambridgeshire home, basing himself there until the summer when he returned to Ireland and sold thirty acres of land, together with the cattle, in County Mayo. During the late summer he and Cormac spent two months at Burrishoole, before moving to 52 Mespil Flats in Dublin. The rented flat had four rooms, a kitchen, and a toilet. Two old Republican friends, Tony Woods and Johnny Raleigh, helped him to pack his books and paintings. The former were packed into the new flat, but some of the paintings were distributed elsewhere. Ernie's brother Kevin, a prominent heart specialist in Dublin, housed some of them; others went on loan to Limerick Art Gallery. The move was partly because of the inhospitable Burrishoole surroundings, and partly because O'Malley wanted to be nearer to Cormac's Willow Park schooling. But for the briefest of visits, Burrishoole itself remained uninhabited from their departure in 1954 until after O'Malley's death in 1957.

In many ways the crowdedly bookish Dublin flat suited his purposes very well. Cormac was easily able to come home from school every Saturday afternoon, and the location also facilitated O'Malley's access to the National Library. His research on the Revolution could therefore proceed. On days when he visited the library, he used to visit the Byrnes in their florist shop in nearby South Anne Street. A Republican family who had enthusiastically endorsed de Valera's Fianna Fáil, they used to have lunch brought over from Bewley's café in Grafton Street, and would share this with O'Malley on his frequent visits. O'Malley— consistently clad in old duffle coat, ragged jersey, tweed trousers, brown shoes, and brown glasses—was intensely compiling notebook after notebook of material from Irish newspapers of the 1916–23 period. In the autumn of 1954 Colonel Matt Feehan, editor of Dublin's

Sunday Press, heard that O'Malley was doing research on the 1916–23 troubles and asked him if he would write a series for the newspaper. O'Malley responded enthusiastically. Provided with a driver and a photographer, he was able again to travel in pursuit of his historical researches. Indeed, this 1954 initiative, which resulted in a series of articles in the *Sunday Press* between September 1955 and May 1956, gave O'Malley a new injection of energy. A version of the series — which also drew on the earlier Radio Éireann broadcasts — was to be published posthumously in 1982 as *Raids and Rallies* and, while the accounts are not perhaps as arresting or distinctive as his two-volume autobiography, they do none the less offer a valuable perspective on the Revolutionary rebels' activities.

In December 1954 O'Malley and Cormac travelled from Dublin to England where, once again, they stayed with the Walstons. Their — and particularly Catherine's — hospitality and friendship were important to O'Malley. But his relationship with England remained complex. In typically gruff manner he could be rather dismissive. 'England for me is an icy land, no interest in ideas or in talk and too frustrated with its own sense of authority from top to bottom';[168] 'This seems rude but I cannot talk to the English except aristocratic English or writers, taxi drivers, Cockneys, and some others. . . . There is an English stolidity which is very upsetting.'[169] But England had also provided him with much needed comfort and an intellectual-artistic base which he greatly appreciated during these later years. So, too, his visits to Paris allowed his interests to breathe more freely than they could in Ireland alone. On 26 March 1955 Samuel Beckett wrote from Paris in reply to O'Malley, who had announced to Beckett an impending two-week visit to the French capital with Cormac. Beckett, whom O'Malley had known for years through Irish connections, suggested that they meet on 12 April: 'Greatly looking forward to seeing you again, and Cormac.'[170] Though a sceptic concerning much that Irish nationalism prized, Beckett drew much of his writing from Irish experience, and his witty conversation and shared intellectual interests[171] also made him a welcome companion for O'Malley; Beckett was good company and an intellectually sympathetic drinking partner. In part, however, the French visit was planned with didactic fatherly purpose: 'I went, 1955, to Paris with Cormac to get him accustomed to the Left Bank, the French way of life, painting, and the importance of French.'[172] The French trip indeed reflected O'Malley's own Left Bank style — 'Much walking, smoking, fair enough drinking, and pictures'[173]—and he certainly cherished his times spent as an intellectual abroad: 'France, Spain, New Mexico, Mexico, Italy, are my second countries.'[174] Certainly this 1955 Parisian visit had offered rewards, and Parisian settings suited O'Malley's tastes. Back in Dublin in May 1955 he wrote to Jean McGrail (an American sculptress whom he had met in the Aran Islands in the summer of 1953) that 'Paris was cold enough. There were three warm days when it was delicious to sit with my back to Notre Dame in a sheltered place surrounded by trees in blossom.'[175]

In the west of Ireland during the summer of 1955, Ernie and Cormac spent the autumn in Dublin where O'Malley doggedly pursued his library research. By December, however, his health was very poor. The heart condition was bad, and his other injuries compounded the deteriorating situation. At the end of the year he was unable to work any further and recuperated during the Christmas period at Newton Hall, courtesy of the Walstons. During 1956 and 1957 he was in poor health and in considerable pain. Unable to commit himself to tasks too demanding, O'Malley none the less remained as active as possible. He helped to organize the groundwork for a Retrospective Exhibition of Irish artist Evie Hone's work, which was eventually to be held in Dublin in 1958. He visited Paul Strand in France in March 1956 with Cormac, and during April and May again acted as technical adviser to John Ford. The latter was working on *The Rising of the Moon*, filmed in the west of Ireland. The term 'technical director' was, on this occasion, rather too formal a term. Ford wanted O'Malley on the set more as a friend than an adviser; and again, the two men enjoyed each other's company.

On 1 May 1956 Cormac began school at Ampleforth College, as had been planned nine years earlier. He was to remain an Ampleforth boy until after Ernie's death the following year. In the summer of 1956 the two of them were again in the west of Ireland, enjoying a holiday in the Aran Islands, County Galway. That summer also brought Helen to Ireland, accompanied by her future husband Richard Roelofs. They met up with O'Malley in Dublin, and in August were married in Greenwich, Connecticut. The 1956 meeting was the last occasion on which Ernie and Helen met; by now, he had only a matter of months to live. In September 1956 his heart condition worsened and he was briefly hospitalized in Dublin. The Walstons hosted him from October until January, when he returned to the Mater Hospital in Dublin. The doctors acknowledged that nothing could be done to restore O'Malley's health and so, on 17 February 1957, he moved to stay with his sister Kathleen (Hogan) in Howth, County Dublin. Kathleen looked after him lovingly, and he appears to have had a comparatively serene last few weeks. On 17 March Cormac visited from England. On the morning of 25 March O'Malley died, aged 59. Heart failure was the cause of death.[176] On 27 March he was given a state funeral with full military honours. Among those attending at the Church of the Assumption, Howth, were the President Sean T. O'Kelly, the Taoiseach Eamon de Valera, and representatives of Government, Church, Judiciary, and Army. O'Malley was then buried in the Malley family plot in Glasnevin Cemetery, Dublin. The entire family—including Helen, Cahal, Etáin, and Cormac—attended the funeral.

The newspaper accounts upon his death demonstrated something of the standing which he had attained during his lifetime. The *Irish Press* referred to him as an 'outstanding figure of the War of Independence', 'one of the most colourful and courageous of the freedom fighters'.[177] The *Sunday Press* referred to him as 'a successful [Wolfe] Tone'—a description he would surely have enjoyed, given his immense admiration for the eighteenth-century United Irishman—and saluted many of his qualities: 'perfect soldierly bearing, fine intellectual qualities, quiet, but with an iron will, unemotional, but of a fierce unbending spirit, a countenance with all the strength and the fire of an old proud race untameable in servitude'.[178] The *Irish Times* referred to O'Malley as having been 'an almost legendary figure in the struggle for Irish independence'.[179] The *New York Times* described him as 'one of the most colourful fighters in the Irish war for independence'.[180] This reputation was to be posthumously enhanced, with the publication and republication of a series of O'Malley's writings. The first volume of his Revolutionary autobiography, *On Another Man's Wound*, was republished by Four Square Books of London in 1961, and then by Dublin's Anvil Books in 1979. It has remained in print ever since, as has the second volume, *The Singing Flame*, edited from an O'Malley manuscript by Frances-Mary Blake and published in 1978. In 1982 *Raids and Rallies* appeared (also edited by Blake). These books, as well as numerous other publications of O'Malley material (including a collection of his Civil War letters—*Prisoners*—in 1991), have presented his vision of his own experiences.

The opening chapter of this current book has introduced the man's Revolutionary and his later life in some detail in order that readers should have a foundation on which to build their understanding of the thematic analysis which follows. The place to begin the argument, both in terms of chronology and of historical significance, is with O'Malley the Revolutionary and it is to this that we now turn.

2

The Revolutionary

I

As a soldier, I had fought and killed the enemies of our nation.
(Ernie O'Malley)[1]

O'Malley's composer friend Israel Citkovitz recalled an occasion on which he was speaking, well after the 1916–23 Irish Revolution, to the Irish writer Denis Johnston. Citkovitz enquired after Ernie O'Malley, at which point Johnston 'looked scared and said, "Why, he's a killer!"'[2] This book is, amongst other things, about a Revolutionary gunman. The militant Irish Republican tradition within which O'Malley was influential is one which has been lastingly significant in modern Irish history and politics, and indeed in Anglo-Irish relations. Physical force, the approach central to the IRA's politics, must be understood if one is fully to appreciate Irish history.

O'Malley is particularly illuminating here. In the second volume of his autobiography he suggested of the Revolutionary period that 'I had given allegiance to a certain ideal of freedom as personified by the Irish Republic. It had not been realized except in the mind.'[3] What was this Republic of the mind? What was O'Malley's Revolutionary mentality in the 1916–23 era? According to O'Malley himself, there had been a certain vagueness of Republican ambition during the Revolution. Looking back from Mexico in early 1931 he observed of those who had fought in the Irish Revolution that 'their ideas of what freedom would realize were not definite'.[4] There was certainly considerable diversity among Republicans about what, for example, the phrase 'The Republic' actually meant. As one Civil War Republican and acquaintance of O'Malley, the novelist Francis Stuart, was later to put it there were 'practically as many visions of what the Republic entailed as there were people — and most of them completely unrealistic'.[5] But certain clear themes can be traced in O'Malley's own thinking, and can be related to the wider Irish Revolutionary experience of these years.

The first point to stress is O'Malley's commitment to soldiership itself: his politics were effectively military. As the quotation at the head of this chapter suggests, O'Malley saw himself during the Revolutionary period very much as a soldier. Politics were, to him, a matter of commitment and action. This is also how others tended to see him; his friend, Cumann na mBan Republican Sheila Humphreys, commented of O'Malley that 'he was a soldier, above all'.[6] The 1913–23 decade in Ireland witnessed a strikingly extensive militarism, and many within the IRA during the Revolution saw themselves primarily as soldiers. Charles Dalton referred to fellow IRA men Sean Treacy and Dan Breen as 'two of our greatest soldiers';[7] Breen referred to himself as 'a soldier first and foremost'.[8] And if IRA colleagues proudly bore their soldierly identity in public statements, then O'Malley himself, during the 1921 truce, described himself as 'anxiously looking forward to war'.[9] His interest in military matters was reflected in his extensive study of explosives, firearms, strategy, and the techniques of warfare; notebooks and lectures on such topics abound in his papers. O'Malley argued that, to be successful at guerrilla warfare, one needed 'dash and initiative';[10] he himself certainly exhibited considerable skill as an IRA leader. According to some, leadership and calmness in action characterized his Revolutionary contribution. As fellow Revolutionary (and later Republic of Ireland Taoiseach) Sean Lemass observed, 'I would say that was his main characteristic, the one that most people remember him for, this capacity to give leadership in action. He'd keep his head while all about him were losing theirs.'[11] The Rudyard Kipling reference here is, as we shall see, highly appropriate given O'Malley's complicated relationship with British influences. For the moment, let it merely be noted that O'Malley typified a soldierly politics which was prevalent in contemporary Republicanism. An t-Óglách, the journal of the Irish Volunteers — the

organization which was to become known as the IRA—presented the
Volunteers during the Revolution as 'a military body pure and simple',
and tellingly asserted that 'the successful maintenance of the Irish Volunteer is the one thing essential to the triumph of the cause of the Irish
Republic'. It was stressed that Volunteers 'should not allow their political activities to interfere with their military duties'.[12] Force was seen
as the only effective way of achieving national progress, and violence
was seen as having the intrinsic merit of proving the nation's worth.
O'Malley's colleague Liam Lynch (IRA Chief of Staff in the Civil
War) had argued in October 1917 that it was through armed resistance
that Ireland 'would achieve its nationhood'; he thought that 'the army
has to hew the way for politics to follow'.[13] Lynch's words clearly focus
the militant Republican argument. Violence was to undermine the
existing political order and to prepare the way for the creation of an
alternative governmental system more acceptable to the Revolutionaries. O'Malley was aware of the tension between this militant approach
and the more mainstream Irish nationalist tradition which preferred
constitutional methods to violent ones. Noting that many of the houses
in which he found himself during the Revolution had, facing each
other on the walls, pictures of Robert Emmet (United Irishman and
leader of the 1803 rebellion in Dublin) and Daniel O'Connell (leader
of early nineteenth-century Irish nationalism, and powerful parliamentarian), O'Malley wryly 'wondered what they would say to each
other if they could speak'.[14] In fact, O'Connell rejected revolutionism
and abhorred Emmet's rebellion.

A reflection by O'Malley's friend, the writer Seán O'Faoláin, illuminates O'Malley's soldiership, and specifically this complicated
relationship between the differing strains of Irish nationalist political
strategy in the modern period. In his fine biography of Daniel
O'Connell, O'Faoláin stated that

Republicanism is untraditional in Ireland in the sense that for the first one
hundred years or so of the modern Irish democracy—1800 to 1916, when the
Irish Republican Brotherhood stole Sinn Féin—the sole expressed and supported idea of the vast mass of the Irish people was for a hierarchical form of
society, based on the *status quo*; for the fullest freedom of action and opinion;
and for a native government of that order in peaceful union with Great Britain
under the symbol of the Crown.[15]

O'Malley found this book of O'Faoláin's 'sound enough: it keeps me
up late at night when I should be asleep',[16] and indeed he could live

with the idea that previous Irish generations—or even the current one—could be characterized as lacking in appropriate Republican commitment. For, according to O'Malley, one should lead the people rather than follow their expressed preferences. It is this notion of leading—or, if necessary, forcing—the people into the right position which emerges from O'Malley's contemporary evidence from the Revolution. Unlike his Republican colleague Peadar O'Donnell, who held that the people were fundamentally on his side anyway and needed only the merest of clarification prior to their becoming politically engaged,[17] O'Malley held that the people were considerably less reliable. During the truce period in 1921 he wrote that 'the IRA are popular and popularity is harder to face than contempt; the crowd cheering you today would cut your throat tomorrow, if they had the pluck'.[18]

Too strict a reliance upon electorally expressed preferences was, therefore, considered ill-judged. The people might vote against the prior rights of the Irish nation, against the proper direction of Irish history towards freedom. Militant Republicans, by contrast, could draw people along the right path, their vanguard actions preserving true Irish interests. If war was the continuation of policy by other means, then for many of its IRA practitioners the war was held to be superior to the political and had, for the moment at least, effectively taken its place. Republican soldiership thus carried with it an anti-political attitude, and O'Malley gave expression to this in typically piercing and memorable style: 'If [we had consulted the feelings of the people] we would never have fired a shot. If we gave them a good strong lead, they would follow.'[19] O'Malley was later to turn down the opportunity to become a politician in post-Revolutionary Ireland. He claimed to have shared 'the pseudo-military mind of the IRA and its fear of constitutional respectability',[20] and during the Revolution he certainly expressed considerable distaste for politics. He disliked the idea of being a member of the Dáil ('I will never be a TD—never';[21] 'I have made up my mind definitely not to function as a TD'),[22] admitted that at IRA Executive meetings and the like he had 'not the faintest ideas on policy or statesmanship',[23] and further observed that 'I'm afraid I have not one idea in my head as to policy. I know nothing of the application of freedom as I know nothing of the application of tyranny.'[24]

It is worth examining this anti-political trend in detail, so important has been its place in militant Republican tradition. Leading IRA man Liam Deasy exemplified the approach. Referring to the debate on the

1921 Treaty which had followed the end of the Anglo-Irish War, Deasy observed that 'Liam Lynch, Florrie O'Donoghue and I had received invitations to the debate and there, day after sad day, we had our first political experience which was unforgettable and most distressing'. The first political experience came after the war. Politics were held to be suspect:

From the first by-election in 1917 [Deasy wrote] we were never unduly influenced by election results. Our mission was to continue the Fenian policy, to rouse the country and to strive for its freedom. In our generation 'the voice of the people' as expressed by the Irish Parliamentary Party at Westminster was a spent force and the people were gradually but slowly coming to realize that nationhood would never be won by talk only. It had to be fought for, no matter what the cost.[25]

O'Malley himself had 'never liked the Parliamentary Party',[26] held that Irish Parliamentary Party leader John Redmond had in the First World War context 'offered Irish bodies in exchange for English promises',[27] and clearly demonstrated a neo-Fenian[28] impatience with politics. He and his IRA colleagues held that constitutional politics were impotent, and that the Home Rule project of John Redmond had only served to prove this. Parliamentary participation and British promises had failed to yield Irish self-government: 'The European war came and the promised Home Rule Bill was forgotten.'[29] The memoirs of O'Malley's Republican comrade C. S. Andrews illustrate the nature of Revolutionary Republican thinking: 'Redmond was the epitome of politicians in general and all politicians were regarded as low, dirty, and treacherous.'[30] A different approach was judged necessary.

Ireland here fitted into a broader pattern of European experience. The formative period for O'Malley's Revolutionary generation—the 1890s and the early years of the twentieth century—was characterized across much of Europe by disillusionment with the existing order, by the development of political Romanticism, and by the emergence of cults of youth and of violence. Revolutionary Ireland was distinctive and needs to be understood as such; but it was not out of step with wider European experience. Yet how did the IRA cult of youth and violence envisage force actually working in an Irish context? Comparatively small-scale military actions were intended to render Crown authority in Ireland ineffective. The 1919–21 IRA did indeed build up impressive momentum and the role of individuals like O'Malley was crucial to this process. There was great local variation, and much

depended upon the determined actions of a small number of committed individuals aiming to create the conditions for Revolution. In part
this echoed the military gesture of the 1916 rebels by whom O'Malley
had been so strongly influenced; 1916 was crucial to Republican thinking in part because it combined physical force gesture with the
attempted awakening of the sleeping nation. Symbolically, the Rising
was crucial to those who sought to rouse the dormant nation again during 1919–23. The events of Easter Week had been insufficiently dramatic to produce a national uprising, but they had powerfully changed
the direction of figures like O'Malley who were subsequently to build
a formidable Revolutionary movement. The latter was, however, a
movement which greatly differed from the 1916 enterprise. Its scope
was much broader, and its efforts to galvanize the Irish people into
Republican enthusiasm were more sustained and ambitious.

For O'Malley this process of Revolutionary galvanism was essentially threefold, involving inspiration, intimidation, and provocation.
First, inspiration. Revolutionary Republicans' conception of the
nation was a deeply Romantic one, dependent as it was upon the
notion of an innate national consciousness. Whether the metaphor
was one of awakening the sleeper or of restoring the dying to life, the
imagery repeatedly drew upon this powerful—though questionable—
idea of an inborn national sense. O'Malley epitomized the tendency
in typically quotable terms:

In general [he wrote of the Anglo-Irish War of 1919–21], the local IRA companies made or marred the morale of the people. If the officers were keen and
daring, if organization was good, if the flying columns had been established,
and if the people had become accustomed to seeing our men bearing arms
openly, the resistance was stiffened. When the fighting took place, the people
entered into the spirit of the fight even if they were not Republican, their emotions were stirred, and the little spark of nationality which is borne by everyone
who lives in Ireland was fanned and given expression to in one of many ways.[31]

O'Malley's Romanticism involved idealized visions of the peasantry
and this, along with many other aspects of his thinking, persisted
beyond the Revolution. In 1938 he advised a couple hoping to adopt an
Irish child 'to adopt peasant stock from Ireland as it has more good
blood in it than either middle or upper middle class'.[32] In such statements he sounded rather like his namesake Hugh O'Malley in Liam
O'Flaherty's novel *Thy Neighbour's Wife*: 'Peasants are the backbone
of a nation.'[33] But such arguments coexisted, as one might expect, with

a rather less enthusiastic attitude towards the actual peasants among whom he spent his Revolutionary (and, indeed, post-Revolutionary) years. In terms of Republican ideology, however, an essentially Romantic conception of the nation prevailed in O'Malley's mind.

Yet his notion of fanning the little spark of nationality involved a profoundly calculated form of inspiration. O'Malley was a hard-headed Romantic. He noted that minor IRA skirmishes were presented by Republicans as major battles, and he recorded the Republicans' shrewd recognition of the value of heroic gesture, magnified and distorted through publicity and propaganda:

Every one of our little fights or attacks was significant, they made panoramic pictures of the struggle in the people's eyes and lived on in their minds. Only in our country could the details of an individual fight expand to the generalizations of a pitched battle. What to me was a defeat, such as the destruction of an occupied post without the capture of its arms, would soon be sung of as a victory.[34]

Again, with reference to 1922, he wrote that 'Deep down [the people] could be stirred by something they would adjudge as heroic, however else it might appear to those taking part in it'.[35]

The people, therefore, could be inspired by the calculated gestures of Revolutionary violence. According to Republican orthodoxy, indeed, the people were overwhelmingly IRA sympathizers. Tom Maguire (Mayo) later informed O'Malley that 'I found the people very good. There was a fine response to the police boycott, and in moving around I found the people very good when I was on the run.'[36] But where the people did not sympathize, they could (as O'Malley observed) often be intimidated into acquiescence. O'Malley was frank about the degree to which many within the Irish nationalist community during the Revolutionary years were unconvinced about the IRA's violence. A 'good number', he observed of the Anglo-Irish War period, 'had their own reservations about the wisdom of the policy of armed resistance'.[37] Support for Sinn Féin did not necessarily imply support for IRA violence, and O'Malley's argument that acts of IRA violence had a stirring, inspiring quality which led people in their wake is perhaps less convincing than his steely description of the usefulness of intimidation:

At first [he wrote in 1923, of the Anglo-Irish War], police were inclined to get information but when people who talked loosely were located through the [IRA] intelligence system, or saw their friends suffer as a result of their looseness, things changed somewhat. For the enemy intelligence agents things were made so hot by the threatening and shooting of spies, and even more so by the clearing out of the local Royal Irish Constabulary garrison . . . people found it did not pay as 'England was far and protection a name', so people eventually learned to shut their eyes and close their mouths.[38]

The execution of alleged spies and informers by the IRA was common from the latter part of 1920 onwards. These killings, and the public depositing of the placarded bodies, suggested to the population a menacing combination of IRA intelligence and brutality. This was symbolic violence used to chilling effect, and it formed one of the main strands of Republican activity in the Revolutionary years. Pressure was exerted on a variety of targets,[39] and it could possess a distinctly menacing quality. In April 1920, for example, Edward Toole in County Tipperary received a letter concerning his wife Bridget, a barrack servant for the RIC at Rearcross. Signed by 'the Firing Party', this warned that 'Unless you withdraw the services of your wife from the local peelers within three days after receiving this notice you shall undergo the extreme penalty at the hands of the Irish Republican Army i.e. DEATH. . . . Please yourself now, but failing to carry out the order be prepared for death.' The letter carried a postscript alluding to an RIC Constable Finn whom the IRA had murdered nearby earlier in the month, with his eyes being blown away; Toole was warned: 'Remember Finn's eyes were missing, so mind yours.'[40] The following month a young woman, Bridget Keegan, who lived near Tuam, County Galway, was the victim of an attack by seven Republicans: having threatened to blow up her house unless admitted, they entered the house shortly after midnight on 1 May to punish her for fraternizing with British soldiers; armed, and with faces disguised by handkerchiefs, they took her out into the yard and—with shears and a singeing machine—one of the men cropped her hair; he turned to his colleagues and asked whether he should cut off her ears too, declared that he and his fellow attackers were 'out for Ireland free', and left the woman unconscious from shock and exposure (a condition in which she remained for some days).[41]

Intimidatory tactics were also used by the IRA in the 1922–3 Civil War. In August 1922 an IRA Operation Order stated that 'As almost the entire press is at present being used as a medium of enemy propaganda, you will see that the *Irish Independent, Freeman's Journal, Irish Times*, or any other hostile newspapers are prevented from being brought into your area for sale or circulation. Any which are brought in should be seized or destroyed.'[42] During the Civil War O'Malley was instructed by Liam Lynch to kill the editors of the *Irish Independent* and the *Irish Times* because of those papers' unsympathetic attitude towards the Republicans. He did not carry out the order, but he did write intimidatingly to the press during this period. In 1922, as Acting Assistant Chief of Staff of the IRA, O'Malley threatened the *Irish Times* in relation to its presentation of contemporary affairs.

A warning recently addressed to certain newspapers in Dublin has been ignored and no change has been observed in the tone of these journals since the warning was delivered. The Staff of this Command has [sic] now finally and carefully considered the whole question of the Dublin press and have [sic] decided that by allowing the present paper campaign to continue they would be committing a crime against the Republic.

The following alternatives are open to you: 1) Conduct your paper as a genuine free press, or 2) Hand over your journal to the Free State authorities to be conducted officially by them.

Failure to comply with either of the above alternatives will be regarded as a determination on your part to use the press as a military weapon against the Republic and will involve the same risks for you as are run by armed soldiers of the Free State Provisional Government.[43]

Inspiration and intimidation were complemented, in O'Malley's opinion, by arguably the most effective mechanism of IRA violence: the provocation of the state into actions of counter-productive harshness. As one recent commentator has observed, 'the IRA campaign [of the Anglo-Irish War] was not geared towards the achievement of a military victory in the conventional sense. The organization's strategy was rather to increase the level of guerrilla activity to such an extent that the political, military, and financial costs of the response would be judged too heavy by the British Government.'[44] Significant in raising the costs were the British reprisals (official and unofficial) which greeted the IRA campaign, and O'Malley fully recognized the value to the Republican cause of provoking the state's forces into precisely such a path. Writing of 1921 he argued in relation to the British authorities that 'Their campaign of terror was defeating itself',[45] and this view was shared by other Republicans. Leading County Clare IRA man Michael Brennan, in reference to 1921, commented that 'the British reprisals, instead of turning the people against us as the cause of their miseries, had thrown them strongly behind us'.[46] Indeed, by the spring of 1921 many people did tend to blame the British for the restrictions and inconveniences arising from the conflict. The British response to the IRA's campaign of violence was on occasions very brutal indeed. Moreover, it proved far from effective in dealing with the IRA, and in some ways actually worsened the situation for the authorities. In striking at guerrilla fighters there was a danger of affecting 'civilians' (O'Malley: 'The British . . . endeavoured to wage war on the people themselves, taking every one they did not personally know to be hostile')[47] and thereby causing or deepening disaffection from the state. This was particularly so because the British Government tended during the Anglo-Irish War to underestimate the scale of opposition in Ireland, and arguably because they failed to understand the enraptured Republicanism with which they had to contend.

O'Malley also recognized the tension between the various agencies of the Crown and held that this was heightened by the repressive violence employed in the fight against the Republicans. There was indeed a distinct lack of harmony between the various wings of the British forces, and on the question of reprisals O'Malley's view is supported by modern scholarship.[48] There is little doubt that British reprisals for IRA activity were crucial in delegitimizing Crown authority in Ireland. Within Ireland, as well as in Britain and abroad, many were disaffected from the reprisal measures adopted by sections of the British forces in Ireland during the Anglo-Irish War. The authorities drew a distinction between their own position — that of law — and the supposedly illegitimate position of their Republican opponents. When Crown forces acted beyond the scope of the law, or with undue harshness, this distinction became blurred. The rule of law was crucial to the British way; to subvert it and turn it, to some degree at least, against the British authorities was a powerful strategy. Admittedly, popular consent was never fully achieved for the IRA's actions — O'Malley himself is clear on that point — but it is also true that the 1919–21 period witnessed the effective undermining of British legitimacy across much of Ireland and ill-advised British harshness played its part in this process as the pursuit of revenge by both sides helped to intensify the conflict.

During the Anglo-Irish War, therefore, British strategies conspicuously failed to contain Irish Republican insurgency. To some degree the Republican guerrillas[49] succeeded in their objective: by the middle of 1920 in many areas of Ireland Republican authority was competing very effectively with that of the Crown and, while the 1921 deal with Britain fell far short of what many Republican activists had sought, it also underlined the degree to which British authority across much of Ireland had been subverted. From the perspective of physical force strategy, the key issue is this attempt to raise the costs of British counter-insurgency to an unacceptably high level. In this sense, perhaps, O'Malley could indeed be considered Clausewitzean ('If our opponent is to be made to comply with our will, we must place him in a situation which is more oppressive to him than the sacrifice which we demand'),[50] although O'Malley's lack of interest in policy rather set him apart from Clausewitz's emphasis on the political character of warfare. More generally, the IRA's strained relations with their own politicians cut across the great military theorist's insistence on the subordination of the military to the political leadership, and the Republican soldiers' rather dismissive and uncompromising attitude towards politics pushed them towards the position of replacing politics with war.

Yet political considerations undoubtedly provide the context for evaluating Republican soldiership in these years. First, there had to be a potential break between population and state for the Republican strategy to have any chance of success. British responses to IRA action could not have caused such major disaffection from the authorities had the Irish population been welded more firmly and uniformly to the state in terms of loyalty, and in terms of popular conviction about the legitimacy of the existing regime. This ties in with a second important point: namely, that Republicans had not only to undermine the existing order, but had also to provide an acceptable alternative. And here there had to be foundations to build on in the construction of arrangements which could command the allegiance of the wider population. The foundations of a Catholic, Gaelic, anti-British movement striving for a measure of political independence provided the base upon which to ground Republican rebellion during 1919–21. But these same considerations undermined the campaign of those Republicans—like Ernie O'Malley—who fought on for complete independence during the 1922–3 Civil War. During this latter conflict anti-Treatyites were unable to build the same level of disaffection from the state in part because the Irish authorities—Catholic, Gaelic, and clearly nationalist—could count on majority loyalty and on a widespread popular conviction of the state's legitimacy to a far greater degree than the British had been able to do during 1919–21. And the profound differences among the Republicans, which had been comparatively hidden during the 1919–21 period, were painfully opened up by the 1921 Treaty.

In O'Malley's view, therefore, IRA violence was a catalyst which acted in three specific ways: inspiration, intimidation, and provocation. Moreover, O'Malley saw physical force activity as liberating in itself as well as offering the means towards the achievement of liberation. Violence, he felt, could liberate Irish slave-mindedness;[51] and of 1918 he observed: 'I made the men manoeuvre in demesne land to rid them of their inherent respect for the owners. Even yet their fathers touched their hats to the gentry and to the sergeant of the police.'[52] Pride, collective identity, and a liberation from deference were all part of the IRA campaign. Its strategic logic did, it is true, possess a certain circularity. Officially, IRA violence was carried out in the name of the people. Yet the relationship of the IRA to the people was, in fact, far more complicated. To the extent that popular support existed, Republicans like O'Malley acted with sanction; to the extent that people did not support violence, Republicans acted specifically in order to stimulate them into giving their backing. Either way, Republicans acted. And this was a defining characteristic of the Revolutionary mentality; it was as much about creating the conditions for Revolution as about responding to them.

Much has been made in recent years of the élitist quality of the Revolutionary IRA's approach to politics. In part, this is merely an instance of the wider phenomenon of vanguard revolutionary movements, what O'Malley's friend Liam O'Flaherty referred to as 'that arrogant contemptuousness which seems to be characteristic of all revolutionaries'.[53] Certainly, the Revolutionary IRA did have a complicated relationship with democracy. Indeed, the anti-political attitude identified above carried with it distinct traces of the anti-democratic. O'Malley's style of thought has recently been characterized by one leading scholarly authority as 'fundamentally anti-democratic and also profoundly arrogant';[54] there is undoubtedly much in this charge. In place of the notion that legitimacy was determined by popular expression of opinion, the Republicans offered an alternative legitimism. Theoretically vesting authority in the people, in practice they demonstrated a marked reluctance to allow the people to decide the issue if the people took an unwelcome stance. The 1921 Treaty provided the clearest instance of this tendency, with clear popular majorities in favour of the agreement being brushed aside by the anti-Treatyites. O'Malley could certainly be contemptuous when the people failed to live up to his exacting Revolutionary demands. On occasions he openly dismissed the people's reliability and similar views persisted within Republicanism well into the post-Revolutionary period. O'Malley's Republican comrade Sean MacBride, for example, observed in 1934 at an IRA Convention: 'I have very little faith in the mass of the constitutionalist Republicans nor in the opinion of the mass of the people.'[55] This approach was that of a self-selecting élite knowing what was best for the people in whose name they ostensibly acted. And during the 1916–23 period Ernie O'Malley's aim was to jolt, to spur, to direct the people through forceful example; and the example of force could not, in his view, be allowed to wait for democratic sanction. What O'Malley sought was to achieve, through force, a par-ticular—in his view, a rightful—political arrangement and in doing so to bring about that popular endorsement which had been absent before the force was actually employed. This constituted a kind of democracy after the event, and this view lies at the heart of O'Malley's Revolutionary activism. The people who had not encouraged you to act would be won over by your unsanctioned actions. That being the case, you could then enjoy their subsequent legitimation of your prior activities.

Some fascinating material emerges from O'Malley's typically inci-sive reflections on these political questions. His honest acknowledge-ment of realities provides the key. He was prepared, for example, to concede that the 1918 general election—the bedrock of so much Irish Republican argument about the democratic foundation of Revolution-ary Republicanism—was on closer inspection a far more ambiguous episode, with the Irish Parliamentary Party and the Unionists winning large numbers of votes: 'That aspect of the election was forgotten, I expect, when the total number of seats won by the different parties were examined.'[56] Indeed, while the December 1918 election had seen Sinn Féin win 73 seats (compared with the IPP's 6, and the 26 won by Unionists), the party had only secured 48 per cent of the popular vote, and 59 per cent of the seats in contested constituencies. More people voted against than voted for Sinn Féin. Plainly, this does not erase the fact that Sinn Féin received an impressive endorsement in the 1918 general election, and O'Malley himself was not unduly troubled by levels of popular scepticism regarding militant Republican activity. He was confident that politics could be moved in a favourable direction by the Republican campaign of violence.

The attractions of O'Malley's approach to politics will be assessed later in this chapter, when we examine the reasons for his becoming and remaining an Irish Republican. First, however, it is important to place things in context by evaluating the anti-political cast of mind evident among O'Malley's Revolutionary generation. Excited disagreement can still be generated by consideration of, for example, the differing political approaches of the constitutional John Redmond and the 1916 rebel Patrick Pearse.[57] Similarly, views on the post-1916 Revolutionaries are widely divergent. Militant Republicanism in the Irish Revolution was founded on the premiss that constitutional nationalism was an ineffective form of politics.[58] An evaluation of the post-1919 IRA requires some assessment of the validity or otherwise of this central premiss, and consideration of John Redmond is therefore vital. Some recent scholars have argued persuasively that—contrary to Republican orthodoxy—Redmond and his Irish Parliamentary Party did indeed possess a plausible political strategy.[59] While many Revolutionaries held that physical force was necessary to the maintenance of the nation (O'Malley's friend and Republican comrade Maire Comerford, for example, argued that 'Pearse and Connolly, and the men who rose with them [in 1916], were convinced that a protest in arms was the only possible measure within their power to take, if the complete destruction of the Irish nation was to be averted'),[60] other people have rallied to the defence of liberal democracy and of that constitutional form of politics which Pearseanism rejected.

According to this latter view, neo-Fenian distaste for politics offered an appeal for some but also carried with it rather damaging consequences. Certainly, there were profound limitations to the IRA's anti-political approach: O'Malley himself

freely admitted that he possessed no administrative or governmental training, no plan of how he and other Republicans might use the independent Irish state to achieve their goals. He declared that he could never become a TD, again because of their lack of 'spirituality'. But it must be confessed that, while indeed Ireland's TDs do not strike even the most impartial observer as a spiritual bunch, they are the stuff of which democratic politics are made. Revolvers and Eng. Lit. were no preparation for creating a stable Ireland.[61]

Indeed, the anti-political instinct came close to scuppering the creation of that stable Ireland in the early 1920s. Anti-Treaty Republicans recognized political legitimacy as embodied in the pre-Treaty Republican parliaments, but when the Dáil voted aganst their Republic and, more significantly, when a popular pro-Treaty majority became clear, Republicans effectively rejected the right of the parliament or of the people to confer political legitimacy. The electorate clearly gave the

1921 settlement significant majorities in the elections of 1922–23, but this did not convince Republicans that the Treaty deserved to be accepted. The problem for those who retained their absolute commitment to the Republic was the gap which lay between, on the one hand, the rhetorical claims made by Republicans about Irish independence and, on the other, the practical fact that total independence for the whole of Ireland had never come close to being achieved in reality. The tragic Civil War of 1922–23 can be seen as the conflict between absolute claims and the inevitability of some form of pragmatic compromise.

But for many anti-Treatyite Republicans the Civil War represented a battle between principle and expediency. The quasi-religious—indeed, actually religious—interpretation of Irish nationalism which these people shared made compromise more unappealing still. How could one renege on a spiritual commitment, an absolute truth, a matter of sincere faith? It is also important to remember that, even within nationalist Ireland, the devoted Republican zealotry of the IRA represented only one strand of a wider spectrum of opinion. One cannot assume that those voters who had shifted from the Irish Parliamentary Party to Sinn Féin had necessarily left their old habits of thought and belief behind when they did so. 'The Republic' could mean a wide variety of things to a wide variety of people, and the number of people who—like Ernie O'Malley—espoused a purist Republican approach was always but a part of the broader nationalist community.

Moreover, condemned though the IPP was by militant Republicans, it was the parliamentary model which offered the basis for state-building when a section of the Sinn Féin Revolutionaries decided that the time had come to get on with practical government. When Ireland did achieve its partial independence in 1922, questions of electoral mandate and parliamentary practice became profoundly pressing. Not only do states have to consider the paramount importance of public order—and this state was born in the midst of Civil War—but those Revolutionaries who were now in government had responsibly to face the reconstruction of sustainable politics. Kevin O'Higgins, one of the most talented of the Free State leaders, had as a Sinn Féiner been contemptuous of John Redmond's constitutionalism. But O'Higgins the 1920s statesman had to face the task of rebuilding democracy in Ireland, and constitutionalism had more to offer here than had Revolutionary rejectionism. O'Higgins was himself to fall victim to the vengefulness of post-Revolutionary gunmen, being murdered by Republicans in 1927. By then, however, the Free State had moved considerably in the direction of peaceful democracy and O'Higgins had made a powerful contribution to this process. This achievement was highly significant: we should not underestimate the challenge which Civil War Republicans like Ernie O'Malley posed to the young Free State, and recent scholarship has suggested that the emergence of democracy out of the Irish Civil War was indeed a close-run affair.[62] To Free Staters such as O'Higgins the Civil War was a fight in defence of democracy itself. For his part, Ernie O'Malley—O'Higgins's opponent in the Civil War—also held that he was fighting for democracy. In O'Malley's view the Irish people had not been given a free choice on the Treaty: the British threat of war, should the Treaty not be accepted, undermined the argument that democracy was on the side of the Treatyites. In O'Malley's opinion Irish freedom, properly understood, involved complete independence and separation from Britain. This was a historical right, trumping the opinions of the contemporary Irish people and overruling the coerced acceptance of the 1921 agreement.

In later years, writing about the latter part of the Civil War struggle, O'Malley was to acknowledge a certain problem in the rigidity of IRA idealism: 'I saw a certain hardness in our idealism. It made us aloof from ordinary living, as if we were above it. There was insistence on principle, which often stood coldly out where immediate feeling was needed.'[63] Certainly, most anti-Treatyites of the 1922–23 period came within a few years to endorse an amended form of the Irish Free State, using its constitutional structures as the means for progress. The exacting intransigence of the 1922–23 Republican stance was replaced by a more flexible parliamentarian approach as, during the late 1920s, Eamon de Valera and Fianna Fáil came to the view that representative democracy offered the best hope of moving Irish nationalism forward. Indeed, de Valera came to espouse a strong allegiance to majority rule as the basis for order, and it was in pursuit of this goal that he enlisted O'Malley's help with the *Irish Press* in the late 1920s. Evolution rather than revolution came to be seen as the way forward for those who had opposed the 1921 Treaty.

But in the Civil War itself O'Malley typified the uncompromising militancy of IRA idealism. In this he was consistent with the stance he had adopted during the earlier Anglo-Irish War. It was a question of absolutes: Britain wrongly controlled Ireland, and force—rather than constitutional or electoral politics—would right this wrong. For O'Malley this was as true in 1922 as it had been in 1918. Defeat was preferable to compromise, and perhaps the attractions and the weaknesses of the physical force tradition are simultaneously evident here. O'Malley's IRA colleague Dan Breen could justify his Revolutionary violence on the satisfyingly simple grounds of 'the Irish people's desire for liberty, complete and untrammelled';[64] but any serious scrutiny of Irish popular opinion would have demonstrated that such simplistic interpretations failed to do justice to the actual complexity of political sympathies in contemporary Ireland.

II

[O]ne feels that one is always fighting for God and Ireland, for the spread of our spirituality such as it is, to counteract the agnosticism and materialism of our own and other countries.

(Ernie O'Malley)[65]

There were those within the Republican fold who exhibited a scepticism about the centrality of physical force within Irish Republican culture (O'Malley's friend, Peadar O'Donnell, suggested that Patrick Pearse had 'always elevated physical violence and self-sacrifice to a most impossible height'),[66] but there is no doubting either the importance of the physical force tradition during these years or O'Malley's profound commitment to it. In other vital ways, too, O'Malley reflected wider trends in Revolutionary Irish thinking during the 1916–23 era. As with other revolutions, the question of defining the national community was crucial; and as with other revolutionaries the Irish Republicans sought an upheaval which would lead to a recasting of society in line with their own ideology. The Irish Republican definition of the national community rested on a series of interconnected foundations: religious, cultural, historical, and political.

O'Malley and his comrades were, in the overwhelming majority of cases, Catholic Revolutionaries and this was very much a Catholic Revolution. The Catholic Church had played a vital role in influencing the intellectual formation of the Revolutionary generation. O'Malley's faith tended to be a private matter for much of his life, a personal affair not paraded or discussed. But it played a major role in defining his Revolutionary outlook. Of his childhood he observed: 'I had the accepted Catholic views of normality, in religion, morals, and behaviour; atheists were perverse, they sinned against the light. There was a pitying commiseration for them and for people of other religions.'[67] Educated by the Christian Brothers he, like the majority of his IRA colleagues, assumed a Catholic norm. Just as the Easter 1916 leaders (including the socialist James Connolly) were a profoundly Catholic group of rebels so, too, the 1919–23 Revolutionaries were deeply imbued with Catholic thinking. Talking of his University experience after the 1916 rebellion, O'Malley observed that 'The university was Catholic though not in title. . . . We were isolated from our countrymen who held other religious beliefs.'[68] Indeed, it is the very assumption that the Republican movement was, of course, Catholic which is striking from the sources. Michael Brennan, in his memoirs of the war in Clare, recalled of the IRA flying column that 'Attendance at Mass was of course dangerous, but I doubt if we ever missed Mass on a Sunday from the time the column was formed'.[69] During his imprisonment in the subsequent Civil War, O'Malley commented of his friend David Robinson, one of the few non-Catholics among the incarcerated Republicans: 'I feel of course that David's outlook on life is not ours.'[70] After the Republican hunger strike had begun in October 1923, it was suggested at the Sinn Féin Ard Fheis (Convention) that to support the strikers the Rosary should be publicly recited in every town and village in Ireland for six days, and seven times on the seventh day.

Indeed, both sides in the Civil War were deeply Catholic and this is historically explicable. The Penal Laws which, at least in theory, operated during the eighteenth century in Ireland were distinctive in the contemporary European context in being directed against the majority of the population, and had had the effect of tying Catholic laity and Catholic clergy more closely together. At the end of the century the United Irishmen—including O'Malley's hero, Theobald Wolfe Tone—attempted to transcend sectarian divisions but, as scholars of all hues testify, they manifestly failed to achieve this goal. During the nineteenth century Irish nationalism had come to be identified in practice with Catholic Ireland; for all his rhetorical flourishes, Daniel O'Connell was the leader of political Catholicism in Ireland, and the non-sectarian intentions of Young Irelander Thomas Davis in mid-century failed to prevail against the more powerful confessional politics which have so shaped modern Ireland. Thus, by the time that O'Malley's generation of Revolutionaries were born and had their outlook moulded, there was a close identification of political grievance, Catholic identity, and Irish nationalism. It was, in Irish Republican opinion, the Catholic people of Ireland who had suffered historical wrongs. Their land, their language, their economic development, and their independence had all been trampled upon by Britain and by Britain's (Protestant) representatives in Ireland. The Revolutionaries' definition of Irish history and of Irishness itself was profoundly linked to Catholic experience. Catholicism was a binding and defining force for Irish Republicans.

The sincerity of contemporary religious conviction should not be overlooked. Religious language and belief were important to large numbers of the Revolutionaries and O'Malley was no exception here. He became more deeply religious during the difficult period in prison during the Civil War—'I had learned to pray while in jail'[71]—but as we have seen his faith pre-dated this, and his Catholic faith and practice continued to be an important part of his life after the Revolution. In the mid-1920s he was still going to Mass during his European sojourn; the same was true in New York in 1928, in California in 1929, in New Mexico in 1930, in Mexico City in 1931, and in Ireland after his return from America (including the 1951 episode during which he was involved with John Wayne, Maureen O'Hara, John Ford, and others in the filming of *The Quiet Man*). The Catholic upbringing of his children was important to him, and while attendance at Mass became at times sporadic Catholicism remained an important part of his life.

The relationship between the Revolutionaries and their Church during the Revolution deserves serious consideration. While Irish Catholics have proved strikingly loyal to their Church in the modern period, they have also demonstrated a capacity for direct disobedience on certain key areas of Church teaching.[72] One example is the case of the Republicans during the 1922–23 Civil War. The Church explicitly condemned armed opposition to the Free State (even to the extent of excommunicating those who disobeyed this injunction) and the episode is instructive. O'Malley suffered from the excommunication: 'It has been terrible to have been so long deprived of the Sacraments. I get Holy Communion several times each week now.'[73] On 17 October 1923 he had been among a group of imprisoned Republican TDs who wrote to the Archbishop of Dublin to protest about the behaviour of prison chaplain Father Fennelly. The latter had refused to hear the confession of a dangerously ill hunger striker in Mountjoy Prison, and the TDs expressed concern that such an attitude could lead to hundreds of Republican hunger strikers being allowed to be 'in danger of death without the consolation of the sacraments'.[74] Spiritual consolation remained profoundly important to the Revolutionaries. Of course, one could remain a good Catholic while contravening specific political teaching by the Church. In reference to Republicans in prison during the latter part of 1923, O'Malley himself observed that 'Some men had become violently anti-clerical, but many thought the whole greater than the part, and that a Church should be judged by its spirit rather than by its ministers'.[75] The Revolutionaries were, there-fore, influenced by Catholic teaching and the overwhelming majority shared a specifically Catholic reading of Irish history and politics. But they were also capable of rejecting important aspects of Church teach-ing, and the influence of the Church was not one of mechanically applied pressure necessarily producing the desired effect.

Educational influence was important to the process, as will be demonstrated later in this chapter. It is also significant that the Revo-lutionaries tended to interweave their religion with their Republican-ism. God was held to sanction their activities, and religious notions of the efficacy of sacrifice and suffering were enlisted in Republican ser-vice. Indeed, these qualities were held to be ennobling in themselves as well as effective in producing other results. O'Malley wrote in November 1923 that 'The country has not had, as yet, sufficient volun-tary sacrifice and suffering and not until suffering fructuates will she get back her real soul'.[76] During the 1923 hunger strike, the IRA's Chief of Staff, Frank Aiken, wrote to the strikers and referred to their action as one which would educate their fellow men 'in the rights and duties of Christian citizenship'; the strike was interpreted as possessing moral and Christian dimensions:

You are now so removed from the world and all the lies and half-truths which confuse us in our everyday lives; your voluntary sufferings have so raised you above the mists that ordinarily obstruct our view that you are in a position to get a true perspective of what is worthwhile in life and how men should con-duct themselves: the passions they should suppress, the actions they should not do, the words they should not speak, the passions they should stimulate, the work and words they should do and speak. You have, in short, the opportunity of acquiring that self-knowledge which is the foundation of moral education; and of clearly seeing the objective on the map of life, and the roads to be taken by Christian Irishmen to reach that objective.[77]

Aiken picked up and developed similar themes a few days later in another epistle to the hunger strikers: 'we know that if one Volunteer . . . succeeds in setting the example to his fellow citizens by voluntarily suffering long drawn out tortures of the flesh and mind, and offering his life and sufferings to God for the Republic of Ireland, that the might and wiles of our enemies will be powerless to subdue the spirit that such a heroic sacrifice will awaken in her citizens'.[78] Indeed, according to Aiken, Republican suffering would purchase from God justice for the Irish nation. This is a vital point. Without understanding the religious conviction shared by these Catholic Revolutionaries, the nature of their commitment will elude us; in particular, the sacrificial element within Republican thinking was pervasive,[79] and was accentuated by the painful Civil War. As Dorothy Macardle, author of the classic Republican text *The Irish Republic*,[80] observed in her account of the 1922–23 conflict: 'Because there has been treachery in Ireland her destiny cannot be fulfilled without sacrifice greater than that shame — without the prodigal heroism, the extravagant sacrifice of the brave.'[81] Indeed, the sacrificial approach was sometimes presented as essential to the attainment of freedom; to put it in terms of which Eamon de Valera was fond, it was by a readiness to make sacrifices that nations were freed.

Just as Patrick Pearse had equated the patriot and the patriotic Irish people with Christ so, too, those Republicans who followed in the years after 1916 welded together notions of sacrifice, suffering, religion, and nationality. They also — and again Pearse is a relevant point of reference — celebrated the spiritual and the anti-material quality of Irish Republicanism, and here Ireland was held to provide a light by which other nations might be able better to see. Thus spiritual, anti-material, national, and Christian ambitions were interwoven: in O'Malley's words, from December 1923, 'one feels that one is always fighting for God and Ireland, for the spread of our spirituality such as it is, to counteract the agnosticism and materialism of our own and other countries'.[82] The leading figures from the Revolutionary period even acquired something of a sacred quality in the eyes of the enthusiasts. Charles Dalton, an IRA Volunteer and Intelligence Officer during the Anglo-Irish War, recalled in relation to the 1916 rebels that, 'Whenever I could get a photograph of one of the dead leaders I treasured it with a kind of sacred interest'.[83] And Romantic conceptions of Ireland contrasted its supposed spirituality with the materialism held to be characteristic of England. Ireland was, in the eyes of the Revolutionaries, to play a role in rescuing people from materialism. The Pearsean Terence MacSwiney, the Republican Lord Mayor of Cork who died on hunger strike in 1920, argued that 'We shall rouse the world from a wicked dream of material greed'.[84]

For O'Malley spirituality was a crucial source of strength; in his view the spiritual expression of nationhood was the key concept to consider, and it was because they represented the system which had stifled this expression that he held the RIC, the British Army, and the Free State Army deserving of the violence which the IRA had inflicted upon them. O'Malley focused much attention on Patrick Pearse and the echoes are indeed deafening. Near the end of his life Pearse had claimed of those who had led Ireland for the past twenty-five years that 'They have conceived of nationality as a material thing, whereas it is a spiritual thing . . . the nation to them is not all holy, a thing inviolate and inviolable, a thing that a man dare not sell or dishonour on pain of eternal perdition'. According to Pearse these people had seen nationality as a thing to be negotiated about rather than as something so sacred that negotiation was inappropriate. 'Freedom, being a spiritual necessity, transcends all corporeal necessities, and when freedom is being considered interests should not be spoken of.'[85] O'Malley read widely in Pearse, and the 1916 leader's spiritual approach greatly influenced and moulded O'Malley's Republicanism. O'Malley's stress on spirituality was not only a central aspect of his Revolutionary thinking, but also outlived his IRA career: writing to his Republican friend Sheila Humphreys in 1928, for example, he asserted that 'The spiritualistic interpretation of nationality is the only thing that matters'.[86]

Other echoes of Pearsean thought can be heard in O'Malley's philosophy. Suggestions such as Pearse's that 'Independence one must understand to include spiritual and intellectual independence as well as political independence'[87] chime harmoniously with O'Malley's views. Indeed, the two men shared much in their respective outlooks: an emphasis on the soul of the nation, on anti-modernism, on English crimes against Ireland, on the bankruptcy of parliamentary Irish nationalism, on the vital importance of inspiration in fostering and furthering the national cause. We have seen that for O'Malley religious imagery provided a way of describing and apprehending Republican experience: so, too, Pearse likened national freedom to a divine religion. The exalted, heroically inflexible Republicanism of the 1916 Pearse and of the 1919–23 O'Malley are inextricably bound together and share the attractions (and the drawbacks) of this enraptured style of politics.

Religion, therefore, provided one foundation of early twentieth-century O'Malleyite Republicanism. Interlocked with this was the second foundation stone: the Republican view of culture. Like other leading Republicans such as Michael Collins, O'Malley espoused the revival of Irish Gaelic civilization. Throughout his political writings he talks of race, racial qualities, racial similarities and differences; and throughout his writings he sympathizes with the ideal of cherishing and restoring a supposedly authentic Gaelic Irish culture. A cultural authenticist, O'Malley's approach echoed that of the nineteenth-century Irish nationalist Thomas Davis with his celebration of and absorption in the riches of Irish culture: literature, language, history, folklore, painting, sculpture, music, architecture. But O'Malley's generation celebrated an Irish culture perceived in part through the eyes of late nineteenth-century Gaelic revivalists. From the 1880s the efforts of cultural enthusiasts to create or recreate Irish language and pastimes flowered into organizations such as the Gaelic Athletic Association (1884) and the Gaelic League (1893). O'Malley's own relationship to Gaelic zealotry was complex and telling. But he undoubtedly shared the Revolutionary conviction that the revitalization of Ireland's authentic past was important if one was to preserve the life of the nation. The anti-material, anti-modern, and anti-urban were interwoven here: Gaelic renewal celebrated rural (especially small farm) culture against the intrusions of the urban and the foreign. During the period between the mid-nineteenth-century Irish famine and the early-twentieth-century establishment of the Irish Free State, the peasant proprietor came to dominate Irish rural society. These tenant farmers were transformed during the late nineteenth and early twentieth centuries into a landowning class with enormous influence on the development of Irish nationalist ideology. The myth of arcadian purity certainly held sway over many Irish Republicans and, in part, O'Malley shared this view: as with Gaelicism, so also with its rural setting O'Malley had a complex relationship. But there can be no doubt that cultural authenticism was an important foundation stone of Irish Republican thought.

The imposition of cultural order as defined by the enthusiast typically forms part of a revolutionary project, and the 1916–23 era in Ireland was no exception. Moreover, much of the fuel for this fire came from reserves of Anglophobia; as with nationalists elsewhere, Republicanism in Ireland has drawn much strength from definitions of what it is not, and of that to which it is opposed. Again, it is a complex picture; as we shall see, Anglocentrism also continued to influence Revolutionary mentality. But there was within Republican ideology a profound and pervasive Anglophobic resentment and Gaelic culture was defined as different from, and superior to, British culture. O'Malley recognized the importance of Irish language to the Revolutionaries ('Most of the officers and men in the recent [1916] Rising had had some knowledge of, or had been students of, Irish')[88] and in support of his political aspiration he offered a telling—and, for the historian, invaluable—account of the cultural basis upon which his political separatism rested. O'Malley stressed the distinctiveness, indeed the discreteness, of Irish culture. He suggested that British civilization was fundamentally alien to Ireland: 'We had fought a civilization which did not suit us. We had striven to give complete expression to the genius of the race.'[89] Of the 1919–21 war he claimed that 'the people saw the clash between two mentalities, two trends in direction, and two philosophies of life; between exploiters and exploited'.[90] Thus, the system against which he had fought was one which had retarded truly Irish development, and which 'had dammed back strength, vigour, and imagination needed in solving our problems in our own way. The spirit of the race was warped until it could express its type of genius.'[91] The Republican Revolution had, however, witnessed the eclipse of this Anglicized Ireland by a discrete, distinct Irishness: 'The enemy's Anglicization and snobbery, almost synonymous terms, had given way before a national zeal and the development of national consciousness.'[92] British civilization did not suit Ireland; the genius of the Irish race needed to be given room for its own, distinctive development; there was a clash between two mentalities or philosophies; the spirit of the Irish race needed to be set free, and the Revolution provided the means for doing so. This cultural interpretation—provided in O'Malley's subsequent writings on the Revolution, and evident in varying forms among the Republicans more generally[93]—provided a useful foundation stone upon which to build a justification for the uncompromising Republican political argument. If Irish culture was, as O'Malley suggested, discrete and distinctive, then the separatist struggle might appear to be entirely appropriate.

O'Malley's view that Irish traditions had been broken by British occupation—and that a renewal of authentic Irish culture was therefore required—drew on a particular reading of Irish history, and history was the third foundation stone of Republican ideology. The historic Irish nation was considered ancient, indivisible, and inclusive of all on the island; politically, culturally, and socially one unit, it had been so determined by history. Ireland had for centuries been, properly considered, one country possessing distinctive qualities of nationhood. O'Malley's close comrade Frank Gallagher, for example, held that even by the twelfth century Ireland had 'for centuries' been one in language, law, and culture.[94] English rule in Ireland was unjust and historical injustices validated present Republican actions. A sense of historically rooted grievance provided much momentum for Irish Republican advance. Moreover, history was perceived to be on the side of the Republicans, moving in their direction; historical developments suggested a directionality and a purpose in Irish experience. Just as Ireland was held to have a spiritual role to play in the world, so she had a historically determined and teleologically perceived right to independence. This sense of history was sustained more by emotional enthusiasm and attachment than by rigorous historical inquiry. The latter was too complicated a foundation on which to build national movements; for one thing, a detailed consideration of Irish history revealed that it carried within it as much potential for dividing people as for uniting them. But there is no question that history was seen as providing support for the Revolutionary stance. In O'Malley's case this is clear: 'There was a mental concept of the national struggle drawn from resistance to accumulative British aggression and from successive defeats over centuries.'[95] The Revolutionaries were a militant vanguard upholding the nation's highest aspirations, and these aspirations had been maintained during centuries of occupation. Looking back from the post-Second World War period, O'Malley argued that for a long time before the Irish Revolution Ireland had been a mental concept which, because the country was held by an outside power as part of an empire, 'could only exist as an independent country in the minds of those Irish who refused to surrender or to submit. For centuries there had been a condition of muffled war in which the people lived their own life apart from that of the conquerors whose right to rule was never accepted.'[96]

More boldly, Michael Collins was to argue that 'For 700 years the united effort has been to get the English out of Ireland'.[97] Both O'Malley's and Collins's arguments present historical simplifications. There was no united, seven-hundred-year effort at driving the English out of Ireland; and the people identified by O'Malley as opposing English involvement in Ireland represented but one strand of a much more complicated Irish response to Englishness and Britishness. Equally clearly, however, there was a tradition of hostility to Britain; and the argument from history was important to Republicans, offering the basis for an alternative concept of political legitimacy. To rival the established British authorities, Irish Republicans based their own claims to legitimacy on the premiss that, historically, British authority had no legitimacy whatsoever in Ireland. This view of history ignored the often positive relationship between Britishness and Irishness in the modern period. It also betrayed other weaknesses. That simply because early twentieth-century Republicanism sought the establishment of a fully separate, independent Ireland cannot be used as the basis for assuming that earlier Irish history necessarily pointed in that direction (or that the earlier Irish people would have wanted it to do so). It would, for example, be a historical absurdity to impute to the majority of nineteenth-century Irish people the kind of militant Republican sympathies espoused by Ernie O'Malley. Yet the very simplicity of the Republican view of history gave it considerable political charge. This charge was increased by the fact that those, like O'Malley, who held to this particular view of Irish history were prepared to act upon, to change, to drive history as well as to read and interpret it.

The mobilizing certainties of the Republican view of history—a story of British invasion and oppression, of cultural and political injustice—were tied in with the fourth foundation stone of Republican ideology: namely, a distinctive view of politics. As with contemporary nationalists elsewhere, early twentieth-century Irish Republicans held to a theory of self-determination. In the words of IRA Chief of Staff Frank Aiken, from November 1923, 'The great majority of the Irish citizens believe as a fundamental principle that the Republic of Ireland is a single sovereign nation whose citizens are entitled to frame their own destiny.'[98] According to this view, the people of Ireland had the right and the inclination to determine Ireland as a single and independent political unit. The inclination was held to have been demonstrated in the December 1918 general election—of which, for example, Dan Breen argued: 'It was the greatest manifestation of self-determination recorded in history. On the principles proclaimed by Britain and her allies, our claim to complete independence was unanswerable.'[99] As we have seen, the election was actually rather more complicated, and such arguments were less important to O'Malley than his stress upon the organic and spiritual unity of Ireland and its proper freedom and distinctiveness. An independent state would be a reflection of the freedom which true Irishness involved.

This separatist Republican approach to politics rested, therefore, on the assumption that Ireland was by right independent, and implied that the IRA's attacks on Crown forces were a matter of defending Ireland against a foreign intruder. Whether or not the (for example) RIC constable under attack was Irish, and whatever the circumstances of the attack, the constable was judged by Republicans to have represented the ultimate aggressor. English law in Ireland was held by Republicans to be illegitimate, a mechanism of oppression rather than the means of securing or maintaining justice. The 1916 rebels had proclaimed Ireland as a sovereign independent Republic. The 1919–21 Republicans stood by and defended that approach. To Ernie O'Malley the Republic of 1916–21, defended during the 1922–23 Civil War, represented legitimate political authority in Ireland. Other government, whether British or Free State, was a usurpation. Rather than the IRA being lawless criminals and gangsters, as their opponents sometimes suggested, they were in their own eyes defenders of the historically legitimate independent Ireland. O'Malley certainly held that the Free State government of the early 1920s had no rightful authority and that it represented a betrayal of the Irish Republic. In August 1922, during the early stages of the Civil War, he set out his Republican vision clearly enough when he argued that there existed a 'true line of tradition, in accord with the historic aspirations of this ancient nation for the absolute independence of Ireland'. As noted, such a view simplified the more complicated historical wishes of the actual Irish people: like Romantic nationalists elsewhere, O'Malley imputed to earlier generations an outlook which could only have been held in his own, later period. But this Romantic argument gained force from the apparent historical sanction which it offered. The Civil War Republicans were, according to O'Malley, in line with historic tradition: 'We are following in our present course the traditional, historic, and ascertained will of the Irish nation for absolute independence.'[100]

Assuming Ireland's right to complete sovereign independence, purist Republicans held that principle must not be trumped by the demands of expediency. The 1921 Treaty was rejected because it compromised the integrity of the Republic to which Republicans had given allegiance, the Republic which symbolized Ireland. An IRA Proclamation issued on 28 October 1922, with O'Malley as one of its signatories, declared that those responsible for entering into the 1921 Treaty had 'yielded to English threats of war', 'violated their pledges and their oaths', and acceded to an agreement which was 'subversive of the independence of the nation and destructive of its territorial integrity'. Independence from England, loyalty to the separatist Republic, the defence of the unity of Ireland—these were all part of

O'Malley's Republican vision. The October 1922 Proclamation was equally telling when it concentrated on the issue of legitimacy: the legitimate Republican Dáil had been replaced, and rightful authority in Ireland usurped, by a Free State government dependent on English force for its survival. For, according to this Republican outlook, it was merely the threat of renewed war by the English which had led to popular endorsement of the Treaty; the pro-Treaty authorities were aware, 'as everyone in Ireland is aware, that the people desire the continuance of the Republic and that given a free choice they would vote for it in an overwhelming majority'.[101] This Republican view held that the IRA were custodians of an ancient right to Irish freedom. Guarding that freedom was held to be essential, while the popular adoption of the Treaty was interpreted as a reaction only to temporary and unjust pressures — an expression of popular will which could not be allowed to interfere with the inherited right to absolute Irish freedom.

This aspect of Republican thinking is an important one and has proved persistently influential. It involves the opposition of two notions of the people. The views of the actual voters can be ignored if they contradict the views which the Republican élite hold to be essential to true Irishness. The historical Irish community is defined by a notion of freedom which is independent from the views of the people themselves: it is a political abstraction. It should not surprise us, therefore, that symbols were so vital to the Irish Revolutionaries. This is true from the 1916 Rising ('Few risings, one may think, have been conducted in any country with such a sense of the value of symbol')[102] to the symbolic emphasis evident in the Dáil debate on the 1921 Treaty, and into and beyond the Civil War. Symbols of freedom were of paramount importance to the Republicans; such symbols should not, in their view, be jettisoned or compromised by mere majority decision.

Indeed, those who rejected the designatedly authentic Irish identity were invalidated in Republican thinking. Those who disputed the Republican view were effectively defined as unIrish, and the binary quality of absolutist Republican politics could be brutal indeed. O'Malley identified those in Ireland who were loyal to the British authorities as being 'enemies of the Irish', while the IRA considered a person's anti-separatism to indicate that they were 'actively anti-Irish'.[103] This equation of separatism with Irishness represented an exclusive definition of the nation, and sought to deny the complexity of allegiances which Irish people displayed. Its ultimate endpoint was memorably expressed in O'Malley's chilling suggestion that 'The people of this country would have to give allegiance to it or if they wanted to support the Empire they would have to clear out and support the Empire elsewhere'.[104] Those Irish people outside the Republican community faced a grim situation according to this formula, and it was typical of O'Malley to record so frank a statement of Republican thinking. Indeed, the quotation brings us to one of the most crucial questions regarding Republican politics during the Revolution, namely the question of Ireland's (and particularly Ulster's) unionists. According to Irish Republican thinking the Irish nation was coextensive with the Irish island. All inhabitants were part of the nation and owed allegiance to it. The counter-argument is that the Republican assumption of historic Irish unity is fallacious, and that the partition which emerged in the 1920s properly reflected deep divisions: 'Nationalists are in the habit of referring to the "artificial partition" of the island. In principle, there is nothing artificial about the partition: it is a result of history, traditions, and demography. When Catholics decided to secede from the United Kingdom, Protestants seceded from the secession.'[105]

Such arguments bring us to the heart of the political problem which faced Republicans in the Irish Revolution concerning Ulster. Was the partition which emerged out of the 1921 Anglo-Irish Treaty a mutilation of the natural, national territory of Ireland, a British crime which caused lasting division in Irish politics? Or was the partitioning of Ireland in the 1920s a reflection, rather than a cause, of the profound cultural, religious, political, economic, and historical divisions in Ireland? There is no doubt where O'Malley's own sympathies lay. While he wrote and spoke little on the north of Ireland, his view was clearly anti-partitionist and he blamed England for fomenting Irish divisions. The unionists were seen as a minority of the Irish people, and the island of Ireland was taken to be the proper unit for democratic decision-making. Therefore, according to this Republican reading, it was an artificial majority which was created in Northern Ireland in the 1920s. O'Malley's views here tended to accord with those of his friends. Frank Gallagher—a fellow Republican prisoner during the Civil War period, and a leading propagandist for Irish Republicanism—held, like O'Malley, to the view that Irish unity was the natural order: 'The story has been told of how Ireland came to be dismembered against all common sense and against the interests of both parts of Ireland and of Britain. The idea was from the beginning not Irish, but British.'[106] Gallagher and O'Malley were on the Republican side in the Civil War, but their Free State opponents shared many of their views regarding the north-east of the island. It is not that the Irish nationalist tradition produced no dissenting voices. Moreover, the evidence was fully available, during the Revolutionary period and during the post-Revolutionary years in which O'Malley wrote his famous memoirs, on which to base a more detailed reading of (for example) Ulster unionist determination and reasoning. O'Malley's literary associate Seán O'Faoláin reflected some of these possibilities. 'No northerner', O'Faoláin wrote in his 1939 biography of Eamon de Valera, 'can possibly like such features of southern life, as at present constituted, as its pervasive clerical control; its censorship; its Gaelic revival; its isolationist economic policy.' O'Faoláin heard echoes between sectarian experiences north and south of the Irish border: 'the Protestant in the south has as little chance of getting his fair share of public appointments as the Catholic in the north. . . . Religion in the south is just as solidly organized as in the north, and is no less narrow-minded.'[107] The truth was that the themes providing Republican cohesion, identity, and purpose—Catholicism, Gaelicism, anti-Britishness, a particular reading of Irish history, separatism—divided as much as they united. Those Irish people whose views of religion, culture, history, politics, and Anglo-Irish relations did not accord with the Republican philosophy were excluded from the Republican definition of Irishness. The key aspects of Republican thinking which sustained Revolutionary momentum simultaneously cemented Irish divisions.

Unionists and Republicans in these Revolutionary years both displayed sectarian approaches, and some points should be noted here about this feature of contemporary Irish politics. It was certainly not the case that Protestants were unwelcome in Republican circles: quite the reverse. Colleagues of O'Malley such as Robert Barton and Erskine Childers prove this point effectively enough. But it would be short-sighted to ignore the profoundly sectarian quality of Irish politics in this period, and this was evident in Republican thinking in two senses. First, Republican ideology in practice defined Irishness in ways which effectively excluded most Irish Protestants. As noted, there was no objection to Protestants who adopted the cause of Irish Republicanism. But the fact was that Irish Protestant experience was interwoven with unionist politics every bit as much as Catholic Irish experience was tied in with nationalism. It was disingenuous to say that one rejected unionist politics but welcomed Protestants, given

that Irish Protestant religious communities were overwhelmingly oriented towards unionist politics, and for reasons every bit as explicable
as those which oriented most Irish Catholics towards nationalist sympathies. The few Irish Protestants who embraced Republicanism were
dissidents from their community, and it would be misleading to hold
them up as paradigmatic figures. Fundamentally, Irish Republicans
did not recognize the legitimacy of Irish unionism: they did not
acknowledge that historical experience had, not surprisingly, led the
bulk of Irish Protestants to identify with anti-Republican politics, just
as Catholic historical experience had produced so profound an attachment to nationalist politics.

That sectarian definitions were implicit within Republican ideology was acknowledged even by committed Republicans, such as
O'Malley's Civil War prison comrade George Gilmore (himself of
Protestant background). Of Eamon de Valera (the most influential
twentieth-century Irish Republican), for example, Gilmore observed:
'If I had to divide the people I knew into goodies and baddies, I'd put
de Valera among the goodies, but it would be with very great reservations because he had that very sectarian attitude.'[108] The point can be
well illustrated also by consideration of Anglo-Irish War IRA Chief of
Staff Richard Mulcahy who, like O'Malley, had been a medical student in Dublin and who also shared O'Malley's profoundly Catholic
world-view. In her detailed biography Maryann Valiulis states that
'Unquestionably, the most pervasive element in shaping Mulcahy's
values and beliefs was Catholicism'. Moreover, it is instructive to
reflect upon Valiulis's assertion that Mulcahy's 'vision was of a free,
united, Christian, Irish-speaking Ireland—virtuous and prosperous'.[109] This is a fair summary of profoundly held beliefs, and beliefs
which deserve respect from historians. Yet when this outlook is recon-
sidered from the perspective of, for example, Ulster unionists then the
picture looks quite different. If Ireland was to be 'united' then presum-
ably—and Irish Republicans did presume this—all the people of the
island were deemed to be part of the national unit. But then what of
Ireland being 'free'? What attraction could there be for unionists in
being 'free' from the state (the United Kingdom) of which they keenly
wished to remain a part? 'Christian'? In practice this implied Catholicism as far as the Revolutionaries were concerned; so what of Ireland's
Protestants? 'Irish-speaking'? Once again, there was a divisive as well as
a unifying quality to this emblem of national identity. 'Prosperous'? An
authoritative economic history has recently demonstrated that, for

example, 'average incomes in Ireland almost trebled between 1845 and 1914', that 'a whole series of proxies for living standards—wages, consumption, literacy, life-span, height, birth weight—argue for betterment between the Famine and the First World War', and that the notion that Irish industries declined as a consequence of the union with Britain at the start of the nineteenth century is in fact mistaken.[110] Thus prosperity was actually increasing in the period prior to Irish independence from Britain. Moreover, Irish experience under the union did not justify the Republican belief that industry had been stifled as a consequence of that union and (as post-independence performance was to demonstrate) there was equally little ground for the conviction that once independence had been achieved economic success would follow.

None of this is to demean the Republican vision of people such as Mulcahy or O'Malley. Their views were sincerely held and historically explicable. But it is vital to acknowledge the blind spot from which Irish Republicans suffered with regard to Irish Protestants: modern Protestant experience in Ireland had involved the development of political, religious, cultural, and economic allegiances which meant that the Republican separatist vision simply held no appeal for them. There was also a second, and more stark, strain of sectarianism within Republican politics in these years. Just as the Revolutionary period witnessed ugly incidents of sectarian violence directed by Protestants against Catholics so, too, the reverse was also the case. Sectarianism was widespread throughout the Ireland of the Revolutionary years, Catholic Ireland as well as Protestant.[111]

Such episodes of sectarian conflict heightened division within Ireland, and the Protestant-Catholic political relationship was certainly worsened by the violence of 1916–23. From a Republican perspective such as O'Malley's, the partition of the island in 1921–22 was disastrous. The nation was severed, and northern nationalists found themselves in a state within which they understandably felt marginalized. But Republicans had tended to ignore the division between unionist and nationalist, and found that they could neither coerce nor persuade Ulster's anti-nationalists into a united Ireland. Typically, O'Malley was in later years to observe with clarity the gap between Republican rhetoric and practical achievement. After the Second World War he observed that 'The partition question can always be raised by political parties for vote catching at elections, but being a question difficult of solution no practical move has really been taken to solve the difficulty.'[112] A 'question difficult of solution' it most certainly was, but Republican opposition to the partition of the island tied in with another key aspect of O'Malleyite politics: opposition to colonialism. O'Malley was hostile to the colonial system of which British rule in Ireland was an example. Revolutionary Republicanism was, therefore, part of a wider anti-colonialism and it is in this context that one should understand, for example, O'Malley's later comments on 'the evils of the colonial system' in nineteenth-century Mexico.[113]

O'Malley the Revolutionary stressed the importance of action, and of thought evolving within the framework of action. He was no political philosopher and, as we have seen, tended to dismiss his own conceptualization of politics. But political thought is not only to be found in the considered works of political philosophers, and this chapter has so far attempted to reconstruct O'Malley's Revolutionary ideology. For, while O'Malley sometimes seemed to downplay the importance of political principle (writing, for example, of the Treaty split that 'Personalities rather than principles seemed to have swayed many'),[114] it is undeniable that there was a powerful alternative ideology evident within the 1916–23 Irish Revolutionary movement. For adherents of the physical force tradition, politics during the Revolution was effectively a military matter; violence was to undermine the existing, illegitimate order and to facilitate a recasting of society in line with the Revolutionaries' own philosophy. Constitutional politics was held to be effete or impotent, and militant action was preferred to the reliance upon prior democratic mandate. Physical force activity would stimulate popular sanction, and simultaneously silence those not supportive of the Republican project. But it was also held to be liberating in itself and necessary to the maintenance of true Irish national traditions and aspirations. These, in turn, were founded upon a Romantic conception of the nation and were as uncompromising as they were sincere. The Revolutionary philosophy rested on religious, cultural, historical, and political foundations. There was a close identification between Catholicism, Irish Republicanism, and national identity; notions of sacrifice, suffering, and spirituality were interwoven with the expression both of religious and of national faith; and Catholic faith underpinned and intensified Revolutionary Republican commitment. An authenticist celebration of Gaelic (especially rural) revitalization added force to the definition of Irishness, and was tied in with a marked Anglophobia. Historical injustice was deemed to justify Republican resistance, and history was held to legitimize an alternative to British rule in Ireland. History demonstrated the essential unity and distinctiveness of Ireland and validated the Republican project (whatever the complexities of contemporary Irish allegiances). Republican politics involved an adherence to the theory of self-determination, and a belief that this justified independence from Britain; an absolutely independent Irish state would reflect the quality of true Irish freedom.

These elements of Republican thinking were interlinked with one another, and they both provided cohesion and stimulated division in Revolutionary Ireland. The definition of true Irishness as involving Catholic, Gaelic, anti-British, and separatist leanings gave considerable force and momentum to the Republican movement, defining the project in a powerful way. But it also excluded that significant body of Irish people whom Republicans claimed as part of the nation and yet whose views of religion, culture, history, and politics were excluded from the Republican definition of true Irishness. The lament that Irishness has on occasions been presented as 'a matter of aggressively displayed credentials'[115] was strikingly appropriate during these Revolutionary years.

III

The lack of organized social intercourse made the young discontented, especially in the towns. The wise domination of age, to some hard and harsh in the soul as the cancer of foreign rule, made volunteering an adventure and a relief.

(Ernie O'Malley)[116]

Having traced the contours of O'Malleyite Revolutionary thinking, we now turn to the question of explaining why he came to espouse this Revolutionary philosophy and, more broadly, why the Irish Revolution occurred. If one accepts the argument that Britishness was built on the strongly connected foundations of Protestantism, profits, and war[117] then it is not difficult to establish an explanatory framework within which to understand the development of early twentieth-century Irish Republicanism. Protestantism, profits, empire, and war all played a vital part in the forging of Ulster unionist commitment to Britishness. Conversely, negative reactions to particular experiences of religion, economics, and war were also crucial in leading some Irish people to reject British identity, and in generating the growth of militant Republicanism in Ireland. In broad terms, the perceived marginality of

Catholic Ireland within the United Kingdom—in terms of religion, economics, and war—provided the soil from which the new Irish Republicanism of the early twentieth century could grow.

As we have seen, O'Malley's own testimony bears repeated witness to the Catholic identity of his Revolutionary ardour and to the interlocking religious, redemptive, anti-materialistic, spiritual, nationalistic elements within his thinking. Catholic identity in Ireland provided the bedrock on which Irish Republicanism was based. O'Malley's associate C. S. Andrews (who was, like O'Malley, 'the end product of a Christian Brothers' education')[118] tellingly recalled in his own memoirs that 'We Catholics varied socially among ourselves but we all had the common bond, whatever our economic condition, of being second-class citizens.'[119] This perception, that Irish Catholics were not fully integrated into the state, is of the utmost importance for understanding the growth of modern Irish Republicanism; Catholic grievance and Catholic revanchism were mutually supportive and powerful themes in this period. In terms of economics, most of Catholic Ireland had failed to experience that dramatic industrial success which occurred in Ulster during the nineteenth century and which played a crucial part in welding north-eastern unionists to the British connection. The success of the north-east, and the nineteenth-century non-industrialization of most of Ireland, have been well treated in the academic literature.[120] The important point for this discussion is to recognize that while economics alone cannot explain partition, the economic success of Ulster did play a significant part in convincing unionists that their interests lay with—rather than apart from—Britain.[121] As to war, scholars have ably explained why there was considerable disaffection from the British war effort within Catholic Ireland.[122] Each, therefore, of these three foundations for the construction of Britishness—religion, economics, and war—left Ireland divided between those whose experience predisposed them towards the union and those whose experience led them to feel marginalized within the United Kingdom. Catholic Ireland did not fit neatly into a marginalized straitjacket—Catholic Irish responses to Britishness were profoundly complicated—but it remains true that religiously, economically, and in terms of warfare Catholic Ireland during and immediately after the First World War provided fertile ground in which separatist Republicanism could flourish.

Within this broad context the central question for Ernie O'Malley's biographer is: why did he do what he did during the Revolutionary years? A detailed answer to this question will in turn illuminate our reading of the broader Irish Revolution in which he played such an influential part. Explanations in terms of ostensible purpose ('I fight for my country in order to free my country') have to be treated with great respect; with that in view, the earlier parts of this chapter have outlined what O'Malley believed and what he aimed to achieve through his Revolutionary activity. No explanation of such a figure can be complete if one disregards such beliefs and expressed motivations. But intellectually satisfying explanations can only be arrived at if one also examines individual and social causes which have not necessarily any part in the publicly declared ideological programme of the Revolutionaries. The interaction of these two types of explanation is the key: it is not a case of people's actions being motivated only by a desire to achieve their publicly stated objectives, nor of their motivation being understood only in terms of social and individual causes obscured by the public programmes. Ernie O'Malley did act in pursuit of profoundly serious national objectives; but he and his comrades simultaneously acted—as he himself recognized—in response to a range of social and individual circumstances which public rhetoric often ignored. O'Malley's Revolution can only be properly understood if one explores in detail these social and individual circumstances. Here they will be examined under two broad headings. First, we will explore the reasons that soldiership appealed to O'Malley, in terms of professionalism and social background, the allure of adventure, and the assertive rebelliousness of youth. Second, O'Malley's complicated relationship to Britishness will be discussed: Britishness as providing an intellectual and imaginative framework, and an important source of ideas and influences; the tension between his Anglophobia and his Anglocentric absorption in much British culture; and the consequent appeal of a distinctively, explicitly non-British cultural nationalism.

Soldiership appealed to Ernie O'Malley prior to his becoming a Republican (during the early stages of the First World War he had been attracted by the notion of joining the British Army), so the idea that he became a soldier solely to free Ireland simply does not accord with the sources, including his own eloquent testimony. The attractions of soldiership for O'Malley were complex but can effectively be explained after close inspection of the available sources. For its part, Republican soldiership offered the reward of an attractive simplicity and certainty. O'Malley spoke approvingly of the 'awe-inspiring certitude, simple and direct' which one of his Republican comrades possessed,[123] and this identifies a crucial theme. The physical force Revolutionaries displayed considerable determination, resourcefulness, and resilience and were, in many cases, very able guerrilla fighters; part of their strength came from their exultation in a comparatively simple, sincerely held outlook. As we have seen, the IRA tradition rather scorned the blurred compromises of constitutional politics, preferring instead the purity of commitment to absolute ideals. This undoubtedly had its attractions, offering a rewardingly uncluttered view of purpose and historical certainty. The very grandness of the ambition derived from its simplicity: the ideal of an absolutely free, thoroughly revitalized, harmoniously purposeful Irish people was as attractive as it was politically implausible. But concentration on soldiership rather than on political detail allowed an avoidance of the complexities which would necessitate the compromise of unsullied ideals. Patrick Pearse is again of relevance here. His most accomplished biographer has referred to 'the essential simplicity of Pearse's mind',[124] and clearly there were psychological rewards to be found in following the Pearsean path. The latter-day Pearse himself had signalled this ('We have the strength and the peace of mind of those who never compromise')[125] and exhibited both the sincerity of commitment and the inflexibility of approach symptomatic of purist, militant Republicanism.

For O'Malley, soldiership also appealed in other specific ways. The concept of professionalism is important here. O'Malley approached his soldiership as a form of alternative professionalism and here we can find important evidence to help explain his rebellious career. A wealth of material testifies to the professionalism of his IRA career during the Anglo-Irish and Civil Wars. As with some other leading Republicans such as Richard Mulcahy,[126] Ernie O'Malley experienced his most successful professional period as a Revolutionary soldier. Salaried; committed to discipline, efficiency, and to the meticulous regularization of his forces; preoccupied with questions of duty, order, leadership, and rank—the picture which emerges is one of an almost obsessively professional IRA officer. In May 1920 An t-Óglách (the official IRA newspaper) stressed the vital importance of bringing the IRA's discipline and efficiency 'up to the highest pitch'.[127] The burden for achieving this, the paper continued, lay with the army's officers and it is here that the professionalism of people like O'Malley was historically important. One Anglo-Irish War veteran recalled O'Malley as 'a very strict disciplinarian. He didn't believe in any kind of social conversation or anything like that. He wanted to get down to business straightaway.'[128] Again, James J. Comerford, in his account of the IRA in Kilkenny, recalled that O'Malley 'looked for efficiency as well as discipline and training in the ranks of all IRA units. . . . When and while doing IRA work, O'Malley was a strict disciplinarian, a no-nonsense man, a fighting soldier of the IRA.'[129] He was meticulously keen on reports being written—on arms, on organization, on intelligence, on parades, on everything—and on procedural niceties being observed.[130] He was appalled when discipline was breached. In December 1919 he lamented the fact that IRA men were 'not disciplined enough, especially they do not suffer enough hardship. . . . Officers or men have not the faintest or at most only a very faint idea of military work, in general. They know very little of the organization and systematic training necessary to turn out an efficient soldier.'[131] When in early 1923 fellow IRA leader Liam Deasy pledged that he accepted and would aid in the immediate, unconditional surrender of Republican arms and men as required by the Free State authorities—and appealed to other Republicans to do the same—it was the 'rank indiscipline' of the act which appalled O'Malley.[132] He was strikingly strict. Madge Clifford (secretary to O'Malley during the June–November 1922 period) recalled of him as an IRA leader that 'He was very very strict on men in demanding work. He was friendly but demanding. He wanted the work done.'[133]

Some scholars have argued persuasively that the mismatch between levels of education on the one hand and employment opportunities on the other helps us to understand the emergence of the 1916–23 Irish Revolutionaries.[134] According to such arguments, lower middle class Catholics played a significant part in forging and driving forward the Revolution and these people's rising expectations, their desire for status, and their sense of status resentment under existing circumstances were key themes in early twentieth-century Irish politics. Living standards were indeed rising in Ireland in the period between the mid-nineteenth-century famine and the start of the 1914–18 war, and it is surely right that our attention be drawn to the issue of rising expectations. This is of relevance to Ernie O'Malley: indeed, social background and career questions are vital to any explanation of O'Malley's Revolutionary career. O'Malley fits the young, male, Catholic, non-northern, middle class, educated, socially mobile profile common among members of the Irish Republican élite of these years.[135] But in O'Malley's case the argument needs to be somewhat refocused. In particular, the important point is that the professional career offered by IRA officership matched O'Malley's particular social background, expectations, and aspirations. Of lower middle class background—his father was a solicitor's (and then a Congested Districts Board) clerk[136]—O'Malley was inculcated with the expectation of upward mobility and (more importantly) of professional performance. Law, medicine, and the army were the three respectable options;[137] O'Malley rejected the first, unsuccessfully attempted the second (as we have seen, he had twice failed his second-year medical examination at university prior to leaving home to become a Revolutionary), and resolutely pursued the third. It is important to avoid simplistic social determinism when examining such questions; certainly, in the Irish case, nomothetic arguments which crudely utilize class as the key explanatory mechanism for the Revolutionary period remain thoroughly implausible.[138] But the particular relevance of specific social circumstances is vital to any proper understanding of the individuals who effected the Irish Revolution. In O'Malley's case lower middle class expectation (even ambition) played a crucial part in the formation of the Revolutionary.

But the attractions of soldiership were compounded, for O'Malley as for others, by the quality of adventure. The excitement of IRA activities breathes through contemporary and subsequent accounts of the Irish Revolution and the question of adventure merits consideration in our explanation of O'Malley's Revolutionary involvement. In April 1923 O'Malley recalled having had 'some grand exciting times' during the Anglo-Irish War.[139] There was indeed considerable drama during these years; the mood of adventure pervaded the experiences of O'Malley and his closer associates, among whom one frequently found that adventure set one apart from the banal and the quotidian. Molly Childers described her involvement in the 1914 Howth gun-running in the following exalted terms: 'That great adventure made my spirit eternally young because it tore away finally and for good the last bonds that attached me to humdrum safety and shelter.'[140] Having broken from ordinariness, some of the Revolutionaries were later to find it difficult ever to reconcile themselves again to the everyday.

In O'Malley's own case it is worth considering his enthusiasm for that most dashing of Irish Republican heroes Theobald Wolfe Tone, with whose rebellious soldiership O'Malley certainly identified. Tone was an important influence on O'Malley in the crucial, crucible period immediately after the 1916 rebellion and the appeal was in part the swashbuckling, soldierly quality which the eighteenth-century patriot's memoirs suggested. O'Malley coupled Tone and Pearse as Republican exemplars and after Pearse's Easter Rising it was to Tone that O'Malley turned: 'Delving amongst a heap of books which were in my study I found a first edition of Wolfe Tone's *Autobiography* in two volumes and this I read.'[141] Seán O'Faoláin was later to identify Tone as the prototype on whom would-be revolutionaries in Ireland modelled themselves, and in O'Malley's case this ties in with the appeal of adventure and also of a particular kind of bravado frequently in evidence during his Revolutionary career. Faced with the prospect of imminent execution early in 1923, he closed off a letter to a comrade with apparent insouciance: 'Another bit of lead won't do me any harm.'[142] For adventure overlapped with other appealing qualities: reckless gesture carried with it certain rewards in this period—we can see this clearly in O'Malley's own career—and the attractions of soldiership were accentuated by the prospect of prestige. O'Malley's comrade C. S. Andrews reflected usefully on this in relaton to his own experience as a Republican soldier: 'in the popular estimate of any nation, volunteer soldiers who have seen active service enjoy greater esteem than any other section of the community. I had fought in the Black and Tan War and in the Civil War. By the standards of most wars the amount of fighting I did was trivial but nonetheless it was enough to earn me the chrism of combat.'[143]

Prestige, significance, pride, heroism, dignity, purpose, self-esteem, power, and adventure could all be woven together in the Republican garment, and such themes could outlive the Revolution itself. Just as Dan Breen was to revel in the glamour of his 'outlaw' IRA status,[144] so also many post-Revolutionary political careers in independent Ireland were, in part at least, founded upon the lasting cachet derived from such careers of Republican adventure. O'Malley was characteristically revealing in his reading of this feature of the Revolution. As he observed of the Anglo-Irish War: 'The lack of organized social inter-course made the young discontented, especially in the towns. The wise domination of age, to some hard and harsh in the soul as the can-cer of foreign rule, made volunteering an adventure and a relief.'[145] Reflections such as this illuminate one of O'Malley's distinctive quali-ties as a Revolutionary. Most such enthusiasts explain their own and their comrades' actions in terms of ostensible purpose; O'Malley's piercing observations about the Revolution in Ireland are intriguing because he is unusually prepared to mine a richer vein of causation.

IRA volunteering was, he argued, about freeing Ireland from Britain; but it was also about freeing volunteers from their parents and from the social stagnation of their lives. Clearly, neither kind of explanation is adequate without the other. It is in the interaction between the stated political project and the social, intellectual, economic, imaginative, and other forces at work on the Revolutionary, that satisfying explanations are to be reached. It is in O'Malley's preparedness to discuss both lines of approach, and in his ability to provide candid and evocative depictions of relevant material, that much of his attraction lies.

If adventure, relief, and independence were offered by IRA activity, then it is also important to follow through the point about the generational tensions to which such themes related. The formative period for the 1919–23 Republican élite was the 1890–1914 period; young men in early twentieth-century Ireland tended to be in a position of subordination to key authority figures (fathers, priests, employers) and one crucial aspect of the Revolutionary years was inter-generational tension. O'Malley was certainly clear that the Republican fight was of and for a younger generation, and he offers considerable evidence about the motivating power which generational tensions had in producing the Revolutionaries. In his own case home life was 'wearisome', his parents annoyingly 'strict'; to adopt the Republicanism of which they and their circle so disapproved, and to break so dramatically from the family, established his independence in a very striking way and enabled him to find his feet with a distinctive swagger. Moreover, O'Malley observed the way in which the growth of military activity connected more generally with emancipation from parental authority: 'men who were gradually being led by minor activities began to become more confident and more independent of their people's control. Eventually one's people had not the slightest say in matters nor did they attempt it.'[146] His observations (in relation to the IRA of 1920) that 'we saw things through the eyes of youth',[147] and that 'By degrees the stern parental discipline was broken, and youth learned a certain independence',[148] help to concentrate attention on the dynamics of Republican enthusiasm. Comradeship, group identity, and the power of the militant public band reinforced the attractiveness of IRA involvement here. Republican activity provided a means of escape from stifling parental authority and social stagnation. Inter-generational conflict helped to stimulate Revolutionary activism, and O'Malley's telling reflections during these years testify to a politics of Romantic youth.

Adventure is also central to O'Malley's complicated relationship with Britishness. The importance of British influences and frameworks in influencing and producing militant Irish Republicanism has often been inadequately appreciated by scholars and observers (overemphasis on the Gaelicist framework has partly contributed to this process), and full consideration of his relation to Britishness is vital to an understanding of Ernie O'Malley's Revolutionary activities. O'Malley would gruffly and understandably have scoffed at the idea that he was British. But it is undeniable that British ideas, frameworks, and influences were a vital part of his life and help to explain why he developed as he did towards a particular kind of Irish Republicanism. Scholars studying modern Ireland have in different ways begun a thorough exploration of the Britishness of much Irish experience,[149] and this need not indicate alignment which any particular school of history. For example, writers of varied inclination are all agreed on the importance of understanding the British influences operating upon the eighteenth-century United Irishmen.[150] So, too, with Ernie O'Malley—an early twentieth-century Republican who celebrated the United Irish legacy—it is crucial to appreciate the nature of the British framework which so significantly contributed to his ideas and actions during the Irish Revolution.

The place to begin is with the First World War or, more specifically, with O'Malley's British-filtered experience of it. Just as the IRA of 1919–21 adopted an organizational structure which followed the lines of the British Army so, too, O'Malley's individual military experience carried with it many British echoes. When the 1914–18 war began O'Malley had intended, like his older brother, to join the British Army.[151] After he had been converted to an alternative patriotism in an alternative army the British military resonances remained. He retained friendly contacts with his brother and with other British soldiers ('Frank and I were bound by affection. We had always stood by each other. My beliefs did not make any difference to him nor did they to his fellow-officers. It was easier to talk to men who had fought').[152] O'Malley read official British military books (praising the material contained therein) and enjoyed his military discussions with his British army brother, a theme echoed later by his friendship with figures such as Robert Barton and David Robinson (Irish Republicans who had both been officers in the British forces). Of the articles published in the *Irish Volunteer* dealing with guerrilla warfare, he singled out for praise those which expounded material in official British Army textbooks. He sought out military texts unavailable in Ireland but obtainable in London, and within his extensive military library he held British Army publications on topics including musketry, artillery, and bayonet fighting, and acquired texts such as a 1917 edition of the HMSO *Field Service Pocket Book*, which contained sections on the system of command in the field, the general organization and functions of the military Staff, discipline, courts martial, and so forth.

On occasions observers have found it difficult to recognize some of these aspects of O'Malley's experience. Modern-day Sinn Féiner Gerry Adams, referring to O'Malley's book *On Another Man's Wound*, has suggested that the title phrase was intended to relate to the usurping of power by non-Republicans in independent Ireland on the backs of those (like O'Malley) who had fought during the preceding war.[153] In fact, O'Malley used the phrase in his book to refer critically to the way in which Irish Republicans 'dismissed the agony, blood, and misery of the trenches as we dismiss another's sorrow'.[154] Moreover, O'Malley continued to respond sympathetically after the Revolution to those Irish people whose patriotism had been expressed by wartime involvement in the British forces. Again, in a recent book dealing with inter-war Irish Republicanism, Conor Foley has O'Malley organizing attacks on Armistice Day marchers in 1920s Dublin.[155] O'Malley's actual attitude was, in fact, far more interesting: 'I "did" Grafton Street', he wrote in November 1926, 'looking at the Poppy wearers and feeling sympathy for them for many had relatives killed I am sure.'[156] O'Malley's complex response to the First World War—becoming a Republican separatist while retaining close affinities with British Army culture—forms an intriguing part of Ireland's wider experience of that conflict. If 1914 did indeed inaugurate 'the age of massacre',[157] then Irish experience tragically fits this wider pattern. Not only did large numbers of Irish people, nationalist as well as unionist, fight and die for Britain in the First World War, but Ireland's own age of massacre was to unfold during, after, and partly because of this wider conflict.

In his literary as in his military culture the Revolutionary O'Malley was inevitably British-influenced. He was among the most bookish of gunmen, the 'love for books' which he described himself as possessing in 1923[158] continuing into his post-IRA life: 'I am eternally tempted by books and reading.'[159] Many of his fellow Irish Republicans were themselves inclined to bookishness, and a significant number also shared his heavily British literary interests. Like other Republicans of the period O'Malley exhibited a self-improving attitude—restless, self-driving, relentless — and this is evident in his letters from prison in the 1920s. He established numerous projects and programmes of study and, tellingly, these often involved British sources. 'I have mapped out a course in English literature,' he wrote in July 1923, 'and am endeavouring to follow it.'[160] Some months earlier he had written from prison that 'I have a decent library now and have ample time to browse deep in Chaucer, Shakespeare, Dante, and Milton so it's not a bad old world'.[161] He loved Shakespeare (reading the sonnets in the Four Courts during June 1922), Stevenson, Austen, Buchan, Scott, Dickens, Shelley, Keats, Browning, Blake, Chaucer, Milton, Lamb, Hazlitt, Johnson, Bennett, Galsworthy. Writing in 1923, he listed the material which he had read and in doing so cited roughly four times as many British authors as he did Irish ones. Moreover, the authors over whom he most enthused were British.[162]

Nor was he unique in this. O'Malley the Revolutionary had, for example, read and been influenced by Thomas Carlyle and here he definitely fitted into a broader pattern, Carlyle having been claimed as the 'unrecognized founding-father of Irish national rhetoric'.[163] Moreover, notable Republicans such as Peadar O'Donnell and Frank Ryan, no less than Seán O'Faoláin, testified to the influential attachment which they had to British literary culture. O'Donnell wrote of his prison excitement over Defoe, Shelley, Dickens, Stevenson, and Wodehouse, and (with characteristic impishness) of his enthusiasm for Shakespeare:

I don't remember on what day of the week I finally escaped from prison but it was on a Wednesday that I saw a copy of Shakespeare in the officers' lavatory when I was outside having a bath; I stole it! Well, listen here, there's no punishment I could ever receive for that theft that would exceed the joy its capture gave me. I'm telling you, Shakespeare was a great man, and I would suggest to the British ruling class that the least they can do when they jail folk like me is to present each of us with a copy of his works. It is true that in this case I rescued Shakespeare from a few of my countrymen but that must not be used as an argument to resist my plea, for it is only that section of my countrymen who can be hired to serve the Empire who would use Shakespeare in a lavatory.[164]

Visiting Ireland in 1922 the actor and poet Peter Golden, with whose family O'Malley was later to become intimate, recalled overhearing 'a group of young Republican soldiers discussing the relative merits of Shelley and Keats',[165] and this leads us to a vital point regarding O'Malley and regarding the Irish Revolutionaries more generally. For while O'Malley was considered by many to be 'a romantic figure',[166] it is also important to recognize the role played in his career by Romanticism itself. Frank O'Connor's identification of the relationship between Shelleyan Romanticism and Irish nationalism is striking here.[167] O'Connor specifically pointed towards the celebration of death, to which might be added: the exaltation of passion over reason and of emotion over critical intellect; the glorification of emotion and of heightened sensitivity; an exciting emotional intensity; the celebration of imagination and of beauty; youthful idealism and the dreaming of great unfulfilled projects; a pervasive sense of yearning; a sentimentality; and even a poignant recognition that the actual could not be moulded to fit the ideal. O'Malley's profound love for Shelley, Keats, Wordsworth, Blake, Coleridge, Byron, Goethe, Hugo—reflecting his strikingly, though not exclusively, British intellectual framework—is clearly pertinent to this argument. So, too, are statements such as those of O'Malley's comrade C. S. Andrews that during the Revolutionary years his reactions 'were based mainly on emotionalism and enthusiasm. I rarely thought; I felt.'[168] This is echoed in other sources,[169] and in the Romantic conception of the nation which Irish Republicans tended to hold. Irish Republican nationalism was powerful in part precisely because it did rely on sentiment: these Revolutionaries were less inclined towards the scientific and the economic than towards the imaginative, the Romantic, and the literary. And such an approach had a definite appeal. Liam O'Flaherty commented in connection with one of his fictional characters that 'Faith has a great advantage over reason as a criterion of life's phenomena, in that it grants the believer precious moments of otherwise unattainable happiness';[170] this reflection could stand for the experience of many contemporary Irish Revolutionaries.

If O'Malley was deeply read in English Romantic literature, and steeped in Romantic ideas and influences, then he also fitted in with a contemporary poetic patriotism which, again, brings us to his complicated relation to Britishness. Modern observers have noted the resemblances between Irish poet-patriot Patrick Pearse and British poet-patriot Rupert Brooke. It is more interesting still that Ernie O'Malley himself recognized such connections and, typically, was immersed in the work of both poets.[171] Other poetic figures also capture this British–Irish interweaving. An example is Francis Ledwidge, an Irish poet whose work O'Malley enjoyed. Born in County Meath in 1887 and dying in the British forces in 1917, Ledwidge was 'at one and the same time a British soldier, an Irish nationalist, and a sympathizer with the Easter Rising in Dublin'.[172] What are we to make of such interconnections? Plainly it would be absurd to concentrate exclusively on the echoes between Irish and British experience; as we will see, O'Malley's roots went deep into uniquely Irish, distinctively anti-British sources as well, and these are vital to any explanation of his Revolutionary career. But it is crucially important to stress that British and Irish history—even when concerning a Republican separatist such as O'Malley—is not a matter of exclusiveness. Rather, it must be understood in such a way that one is appreciative of the interweaving between the two, and of their connectedness as well as their separateness.

These themes have been highlighted in relation to O'Malley's military and literary culture, and can be usefully illuminated by consideration of one of O'Malley's favourite authors during the Revolutionary period: John Buchan. There are paradoxical connections between O'Malley (the Catholic, Irish, Republican anti-Imperialist) and Buchan (the Presbyterian, Scottish, Tory Imperialist).[173] O'Malley made many approving references to Buchan's work, and his library contained many of Buchan's books. O'Malley read and enjoyed Greenmantle—Buchan's 1916 adventure—while a Republican prisoner in Mountjoy Prison. The novel, which was the second in Buchan's Richard Hannay series, had been written in part to entertain the British troops during the First World War; there is a pungent irony in its having entertained this particular soldier of the Irish Republican Army. Yet it remains true not only that the First World War and post-First World War culture depicted in Buchan's Hannay novels resembles that portrayed in O'Malley's writings on the Irish Revolution, but also that these O'Malley–Buchan resonances are not surprising given that the two men actually shared many intellectual and cultural influences. The O'Malley–Buchan connection is illustrative both of the themes running through the Irish Revolution, and also of the intellectual framework which informed O'Malley's thinking. In each case the causes behind his Revolutionary experiences become clearer.

First, there are many themes shared between the fictional memoirs of Buchan's hero and O'Malley's autobiographical accounts. The romance of adventure is evident in both, as are the essentially apolitical attitude of the hero-narrator and the celebration of serious, professional soldiership. Both sets of dramatic exploits involve an overwhelmingly male culture, and in both worlds courage is glorified and action and adventure are enthusiastically celebrated in a youthful, boyish spirit as a preferable alternative to suburban routine and dullness. The countryside against which these adventures are set is represented in terms which enhance the patriotic quality of the narratives. For both authors, visions of landscape are made to serve distinctly patriotic purposes. Indeed, both O'Malley and Hannay are zealous map enthusiasts, and with O'Malley there existed a direct connection between knowledge of land, intimacy with country, and Republican commitment. His passion for geography grew out of his Davisite desire to know the country intimately from every possible point of view: historical, literary, artistic, musical, architectural, and geographical. O'Malley often used distinctly Hannayesque language ('The [Free] Staters are awful rotters to fire on girls')[174] and other striking similarities exist. Hannay's adventures feature the appearance and recurrent reappearance of intimate, loyal, male comrades who form a self-selecting band of saviours (Sandy Arbuthnot, Peter Pienaar, John Blenkiron); so too do O'Malley's (Seamus Robinson, Sean Treacy, Frank Gallagher). Again, the culture of spies and repeated disguise pervades both sets of adventures, as does the celebration of young comrades' selfless sacrifice for the national cause.

In reading *Greenmantle*, therefore, O'Malley escaped into a culture and a world which were deeply and favourably familiar to him. And this brings us to our second point: close examination of the two authors' influences and mutual connections helps to contextualize these undoubted resonances between the heroic characters—one fictional, one autobiographical—whose adventures they relate. As so often with O'Malley the paradoxical can, after sustained reflection, be seen to be entirely logical. The notion that 'Irish' and 'British' should be understood as categories which are essentially discrete from one another is one which obscures at least as much as it clarifies. Certainly, in the case of these two authors there exist many mutual resemblances; despite their differing political sympathies both men drank substantially from the same well of ideas and influences. Buchan and O'Malley were romantic, storytelling patriots who provided valuable sources for the historian of the early twentieth century. Furthermore, immensely talented though they were, each man produced historical writing which later readers will judge to have suffered from a certain over-romantic inclination. It has been noted, in reference to Buchan's history of the 1914–18 conflict, that 'his view of war was too celebratory and romanticized to be entirely accepted in the long term'.[175] For all their unquestionable strengths, the same would have to be argued in relation to O'Malley's accounts of the 1916–23 Irish wars, *On Another Man's Wound, The Singing Flame*, and *Raids and Rallies*. And if Hannay's romantic adventures resembled those contained in O'Malley's writings, then the roots of this similarity can in part be traced to the fact that Buchan and O'Malley shared similar tastes in reading. Both men immersed themselves enthusiastically in Stevensonian romantic adventures. Buchan's biographer, Janet Adam Smith, observes that Buchan's 'view of what constituted a "romance"' came largely from Robert Louis Stevenson, and establishes the strong influence which Stevenson had on Buchan.[176] O'Malley, too, derived much of his sense of the 'romantical' and of 'adventure' from Stevenson, whom he loved and frequently praised.[177] Indeed, O'Malley and Buchan possessed shared tastes in much of their mutually wide reading. Both men enjoyed Scott, Dickens, Thackeray, and Arnold. Each adored Shakespeare: 'I like Shakespeare best' (O'Malley); 'the greatest of all poets' (Buchan).[178] Both relished the writings of literary scholar Arthur Quiller-Couch. O'Malley was steeped in and liked the work of Shakespearean scholar Andrew Cecil Bradley—again, the celebration of imagination is a conspicuous theme[179]—while Buchan for his part had been taught by Bradley at Glasgow University. O'Malley read deeply in the art historian and critic Walter Pater, expressing his 'love' for him in 1923;[180] Buchan chose Brasenose at Oxford in part because it was Pater's college.

Other similarities complement these bookish connections. Both O'Malley and Buchan wrote patriotic accounts of conflict which assumed that their respective nations fought in defence of a righteous cause and that they unquestionably held the moral high ground. Both celebrated the clean, chivalrous fight. Again, both men were imbued with the sense that patriotic sacrifice would produce a fruitful harvest. Each man stressed the cross-class quality of patriotic commitment, and each suggested the possibility that some new social pattern might emerge from military struggle. Speaking of his Volunteer Company, O'Malley asserted: 'We . . . were mixed: professions, unskilled labour, students, government clerks, skilled labour, business men, and out-of-works. . . . There were no class distinctions. One judged a man by his previous training, courage, efficiency, and ability; results by zeal and willingness to learn.'[181] Again, with reference this time to Republican prisoners in 1924, O'Malley remarked: 'It was hard to distinguish, as one walked around the camp, the professions or occupations of the men. . . . We were prisoners, it did not matter about one's position or education, here all ranked equally. . . . There was a recasting, a new shaping of values.'[182] In turn, Buchan stressed the cross-class composition of the First World War British Army; and he suggested that 'If we can carry that great brotherhood of the trenches into the years of peace, and make a better and a juster England, where class hatred will abate because class selfishness has gone, then, by the grace of God, this war may yet rank as one of the happiest events in our history.'[183]

These echoes can be further amplified. A list, for example, of English historian G. M. Trevelyan's favoured authors—Macaulay, Carlyle, Meredith, Shakespeare, Scott, Milton, Shelley, Keats—mirrored O'Malley's tastes; Trevelyan (like O'Malley) admired John Buchan and (like Buchan) was enjoyed by O'Malley; Trevelyan, like Buchan and O'Malley, had been strongly influenced by Bradley.[184] Again, Erskine Childers provides a useful point of reference. This English-born writer who embraced Irish Republicanism was admired both by Buchan and by O'Malley. Much has been made of the supposed riddle of Childers's career—his shift from British loyalty to Irish Republicanism—but, like O'Malley, Childers appears perplexing only if one assumes the most rigid of divisions between Irishness and Britishness. Just as the flavour of boyish, spy-ridden, patriotic adventure in his novel *The Riddle of the Sands*[185] resembles O'Malley's Revolutionary world, so, too, the territory he inhabited of complex interaction between Britishness and Irishness also likened him to O'Malley, another Irish Republican profoundly influenced by a complex relation to Britishness.

These echoes between O'Malley, Childers, and Buchan are profoundly revealing. My suggestion is not that reading John Buchan's novels caused O'Malley to become a Revolutionary (although Buchan's influence can, perhaps, be detected in the way in which O'Malley later wrote up his own Revolutionary adventures), nor is it the point of my argument to claim that there is anything automatically peculiar about an Irish Republican drawing intellectual or imaginative sustenance from the riches of British culture. My point is rather that we should appreciate the precise nature of the intellectual and other influences at work on the Irish Revolutionaries, and that such appreciation is necessarily incomplete unless O'Malley's British influences and frameworks are recognized. The shared cultures evident in O'Malley and Buchan are illustrative of key aspects of the Irishman's Revolution, and also of the world of influences which moulded that Revolution.

In explaining O'Malley's Republicanism, however, one has to delve more deeply into the complications of his relationship with Britishness. British influences, sources, and frameworks were vital to him; he was, in many ways, both Anglocentric and Anglophile. But the explanation of his Revolutionary commitment lies in the tension between these leanings on the one hand and, on the other, his Anglophobia and his position within a culture which was marginal to Britishness. Repulsion as well as attraction, hostility as well as intimacy, characterized O'Malley's relation to Britain. For alongside his enthusiastic immersion in so much British culture must be set, for example, his suggestion in 1923 that as a youngster he had possessed 'the inborn hate of things English, which I expect all Irishmen inherit'.[186] As noted earlier, O'Malley belonged to a Catholic Ireland which was economically and religiously distinctive within the UK, and there is no doubt that Britain was to him both intimate and alien. As is often the case, the simultaneous existence of apparently contradictory truths offers the key to historical explanation. In significant ways he was marginal to Britishness and, indeed, was markedly Anglophobic. Yet he was simultaneously too British to be able to assume a comfortably distinct, alternative self-definition. It is not surprising, therefore, that O'Malley sought so energetically for distinctively non-British and anti-British expression: his Anglocentrism sharpened rather than blurred the zeal with which this quest was undertaken. Militant Irish Republicanism — Catholic, Gaelic, Anglophobic, and devoted to economic autarky — offered a multiply satisfying identity which bestowed prestige, self-esteem, and dignity, and which stressed Irish independence and distinctive authenticity.

The means as well as the separatist ends of O'Malley's Revolutionary politics involved a rejection of Britishness. So, too, did his attitude to Gaelicism, and indeed his response to cultural nationalism merits serious consideration. As we have seen, the articulation of a cultural nationalist thesis formed a significant part of his Republican argument and O'Malley without question adopted an emblematic Gaelic identity. Just as Jacky Whelan became Seán O'Faoláin so, too, Ernest Malley became Earnán Ó Máille, and while he had not come to Republicanism through the Gaelic League he did join the Gaelic League after his Republican conversion. Moreover, he repeatedly noted the important role which Gaelic enthusiasm had played during the Revolution. He stated that most of his post-1916 colleagues in the Volunteers had joined the Gaelic League, and asserted that Gaelic

Leaguers 'stressed the incentive of the language towards propagandist nationality; few had disinterested literary values'.[187] It is significant that in O'Malley's later notebooks—in which he compiled research on the Revolutionary period—particular attention was paid to such passages as that from Batt O'Connor which argued that 'The Gaelic League and the Gaelic Athletic Association were the two chief sources from which the Irish Republican Brotherhood recruited its members'.[188]

In O'Malley's own case the significance of the Gaelic identity lay in the energy and ambivalence evident in its invention. For O'Malley recorded publicly that his Irish was 'poor',[189] and privately that he lacked 'Gaelic tradition and outlook'.[190] To his son's recollection that 'I can never recall hearing father talk Irish'[191] should be added O'Malley's own typically layered remark in December 1923 that 'I know very little Irish; I should be ashamed, but really I'm not'.[192] The only partially convincing Gaelic reinvention of himself should not, however, cause it to be treated lightly. The consciousness that some apology was required for one's lack of Gaelic credentials in itself testifies to the importance of this feature of the Revolutionary experience, and scholars have documented the precise nature of that importance.[193] In O'Malley's case, it was the tension between marginalized Anglophobia and Anglophile Anglocentrism which rendered his Gaelic reinvention both urgent and problematic. O'Malley's Gaelic self was implausible and imperative for precisely the same reasons.

That the Gaelicist approach was a valuable and appealing part of the Revolutionaries' programme is not, however, in doubt. As O'Malley's writings testify, the pursuit of dignified distinctiveness played a very major role in motivating the Revolutionaries. Subservience ('Long domination had worn down a large percentage of the race to subservience or aping snobbery')[194] was to be replaced by a more defiant stance. During the Revolutionaries' youth there had developed a sturdy linguistic revivalism in which the Gaelic League played a central role, and this culture offered considerable social, psychological, and political rewards. The Gaelic cultural inheritance was a powerful resource, a large reservoir on which to draw, and was employed to strengthen the claim to political independence. Republicans were keen to use Gaelic cultural enthusiasms to further their own political purposes, and many in cultural organizations were equally keen that Gaelicizing passions should be harnessed in precisely this way. Certainly, the Irish language was celebrated by separatists as a symbol of national distinctiveness and O'Malley was attracted by the idea that a less Anglocentric culture should flourish in the new Ireland. In 1928 he argued that 'For a century the official interpreter of foreign news to us in Ireland has been England. We see the world through her eyes and is it any wonder that she is able to impose something of her mentality? Even some amongst us of the Republican faith have been influenced, have learned to take the hostile point of view for granted and have lost some independence of thought.'[195] There was some irony in such reflections—O'Malley sympathized with such a view in part because he himself shared something of that very Anglocentric culture which he here decried. Indeed, his pursuit of cultural purism grew directly out of the fact that he was (like so many Irish and British people) hybrid, drawing on heterogeneous sources.

Important in giving definition to the distinctively, proudly Gaelic Revolutionary view were certain of Ireland's Christian Brothers' Schools. It has often been remarked that the revival of Irish cultural nationalism during the late nineteenth and early twentieth centuries was tied up in some way with the CBS, and this deserves serious consideration. For while it is difficult to be precise about the direct influence which O'Malley's O'Connell School experiences had upon the emergence of his Republicanism, some important points can be established as a way of providing a context for understanding his political development. The first point is that the CBS provided secondary education for urban, Catholic boys from the lower middle classes, and this section of late nineteenth- and early twentieth-century Irish society produced a highly significant number of the 1916–23 Revolutionaries. Of particular relevance to O'Malley's case is the question of upward social mobility. As noted, O'Malley's family background instilled in him a sense of professional expectation, and certainly the ethos of the CBS was such as to reinforce the belief that comparatively less well-off boys should better themselves educationally and socially.

Second, it should be noted that the CBS had offered during the nineteenth century a distinctive approach to history and culture. Irish history was taught by the Brothers as a major subject; and a significant theme in their version of Irish history was that of Irish struggle and resistance in the face of English intrusion and invasion. In addition they tended to stress the sufferings which the Irish had experienced at the hands of the English, and to emphasize the glories and riches of the Gaelic civilization which English involvement in Ireland had eroded. For O'Malley's generation of Republican Revolutionaries the ideological resonances of this teaching are fairly clear and it is arguable that the Christian Brothers' influence helped to undermine British rule in Ireland. But a third point should be mentioned. That the CBS represented an important influence on the early twentieth-century Republicans is not in dispute; but it would be wrong to jump too eagerly for a straightforward causal relationship here. Barry Coldrey's excellent study of the Christian Brothers[196] shrewdly avoids too mechanical or simplistic a model for CBS influence, suggesting instead that the impact of the Brothers' schools involved the intensification and reinforcement of Catholic nationalist values rather than their creation. Certainly, in O'Malley's case, there is evidence that while the Brothers helped to develop an interest in history and even a sense of national grievance, they were not responsible for inculcating a sense of Revolutionary necessity in their pupil. An intriguing passage from an early draft of *On Another Man's Wound* records that 'At school with the Christian Brothers . . . we learned Irish history, a story of oppression'. But O'Malley continues by recalling that according to the Brothers' version

[Patrick] Sarsfield and [Henry] Grattan seemed to be more important than [Theobald] Wolfe Tone and [James] Fintan Lalor. Daniel O'Connell was a greater deliverer than Hugh O'Neill or Red Hugh O'Donnell or Owen Roe [O'Neill]. [John] Redmond seemed to carry on the tradition of Charles Stewart Parnell. The Fenians were referred to as a gallant effort; boys were pleased to think that their forefathers had been out in '67, '48, or '98 [the Irish rebellions of 1867, 1848, and 1798], but it was a vanished past: one did not think of it in such terms now.[197]

Ireland, therefore, was presented as having had a distinct history and one which included a tale of oppression by England; but the parliamentary tradition of Grattan, O'Connell, Parnell, and Redmond was preferable in modern times to the more militant efforts of those such as Wolfe Tone or the Fenians. None the less, the introduction of nationalist argument created a framework within which Republican conviction could be placed. O'Malley recalled, for example, that he had been selected at school to participate in a debate, speaking on the side which defended the view that the First World War 'was not Ireland's war'; in preparing his case he came across arguments and material which he had not previously encountered.[198] Such episodes formed part of his developing political outlook, and lay behind his ostensibly sudden conversion in 1916.

Moreover, the Brothers did help to bolster a pride and confidence in Catholic Irishness, and Dublin's O'Connell School, which the young Ernie O'Malley attended, was ably placed to do this as one of the most successful of the CBS. The strong nationalist environment of his school contributed to the development of O'Malley's Republicanism; if the 1916 rebellion excited from him a Republican response, then it was a response which was grounded, in part at least, on a familiarity with a positive case for nationalist readings of Irish history and culture. A disproportionate number of those participating in the Easter Rising had been educated by the Christian Brothers and indeed the socialization process at work in the CBS helped to foster the ideas and orientation of many of the 1916–23 Revolutionaries. Ernie O'Malley's conversion to Republicanism, dramatic though it appeared, should be seen within this wider context.

A further note should perhaps be sounded. Mechanical explanations of the Irish Revolution sometimes flounder on their failure to listen sensitively to the particularities of individual experience. This would be true of any attempt to suggest that the CBS in any straightforward way caused the Irish Revolution. For while a significant number of O'Connell School pupils—past and present—participated in the Easter Rising, for example, it is also true that others educated at the school responded to that patriotic First World War era by fighting in the British Army. A similar point should be remembered in relation to O'Malley's Medical School experience at UCD. The atmosphere at the School in O'Malley's time was far from anti-nationalist. Very much the Catholic university, the UCD setting can be seen, particularly after 1916, as a consolidating influence upon O'Malley's emerging Irish Republicanism. Cecilia Street medical students took part in the 1916 Rising, and prominent figures in the Irish Revolution such as Kevin Barry and Richard Mulcahy had, like O'Malley, been students in the UCD Medical Faculty. Yet it is also true that numerous graduates and students of the Medical School fought for Britain during the First World War; there, as elsewhere in Ireland, there was evidence of the political divisions sharpened by the 1914–18 conflict. Being a student at Cecilia Street or a pupil at the O'Connell School did not necessarily push one into the IRA. Indeed, no single cause or influence can satisfactorily be held to explain (or come close to explaining) why people joined the IRA during the Revolution. Broad brush strokes can suggest important themes, and the significance of particular educational influences is certainly one example. But while wide patterns of influence can and should be pointed out, they must be approached with a sensitivity to the uniqueness of each individual's experience. It is in the specifics of individual experience that we will find the most intellectually satisfying explanations of the Irish Revolution.

Against the background of religious and economic marginality within the UK during the First World War, O'Malley's individual development towards and then within Irish Republicanism can be carefully traced and explained. No monocausal explanation will suffice. But when all of the particular features of his Revolution are pieced together then a clear picture emerges. Republican soldiership appealed to him for its essentially apolitical simplicity, for its un-doubted glamour, and as a means of fulfilling professional expecta-tions; social background was important here, especially in the light of his difficulties with university medicine; so, too, was the appeal of sol-dierly adventure and excitement, which offered an escape from quo-tidian dullness and stagnation; the assertive rebelliousness of youth was important, the IRA simultaneously offering a means of fighting against both British Imperialism and also the dullness and restrictions of subservient home life. Much of the framework for this soldiership was, ironically, provided by British influences and sources (military, literary, and imaginative). Much of O'Malley's Romantic Revolution-ary perspective was drawn from British roots. Just as post-1922 indepen-dent Ireland owed much of its shape to British influence, framework, and example,[199] so, too, the anti-British Revolutionaries who fought to achieve that independence themselves drew deeply on British sources. In O'Malley's case, crucially, the tension between a marginal Anglo-phobia and an Anglophile Anglocentrism rendered cultural and polit-ical Irish separatism attractive, and this attractiveness was intensified and reinforced by CBS schooling. The riches of distinctively Irish culture provided reserves from which he could draw considerable sustenance.

None of these factors singly would have produced the Revolution-ary; between them, however, they did precisely that. Two further points should be stressed. First, this explanation is not intended to offer a model which accounts for the 1916–23 Irish Revolution as a whole. Rather, it explains Ernie O'Malley's Revolution and is specifically sensitive to his particular experiences. And the explanation offered here must be approached with an eye to cumulative historical devel-opment against these complex, personal experiences: O'Malley's day-by-day choices involved responses to particular combinations of circumstance and thus led incrementally towards his Republicanism. The decision to leave home and become fully immersed in IRA activity came at a difficult point in his medical studies and against the background of a sharply problematic relationship with his parents. Similarly, the earlier impact of the 1916 Rising reflected, for example, regionally and personally specific connections. This can helpfully be illustrated by consideration of O'Malley's references to John MacBride, whose native town was Westport, County Mayo, in the west of Ireland. Having fought for the Boers against the British, MacBride—a leading Irish Republican Brotherhood (IRB) man—was eventually to be executed in May 1916 for his part in the Easter Rising. O'Malley had known MacBride slightly in Dublin—his parents had known the MacBrides in the west—and this personal connection heightened the young student's angry response to the post-Rising executions: 'I had felt resentment at the death of the others; now a strange rage replaced it. I had known MacBride.'[200] Of the latter, O'Malley recalled:

I might speak of his kindness to us as children, how when visitors came he talked and laughed with us and we learned to drop 'our best company manners' and feel at ease. He told us stories of the Boer War, promised me an unminted gold coin, which had belonged to the Boer mint which had to be hurriedly evacuated at the approach of the British. . . . He spoke of the horrors of the British internment camps where the women and children died like flies.[201]

As with physical force Republicans of a later period, it is important not to ignore such personal stimulants to rebellious response. Certainly MacBride's Anglophobic influence over the impressionable O'Malley was, if anything, increased by his execution. O'Malley had been impressed by MacBride's soldierly Boer War stories, and there is no doubt about the political direction of his influence, a public statement from the IRB man in 1914 neatly capturing his views: 'No man can claim authority to barter away the immutable rights of nationhood: for Irishmen have fought, suffered, and died in defence of these rights. And . . . Irishmen will always be found to snatch up the torch from the slumbering fire, to hold it aloft as a guiding light, and to hand it on, blazing afresh, to the succeeding generation.'[202] Individual decisions must, ultimately, be judged against consideration of precisely such personal, unique connections. Second, however, it is equally true that many of the themes covered in this chapter do reflect important wider trends, and help illuminate the broader political movement of these years. O'Malley struck people as unique, and so he was. But in much of his conditioning and in many of his attitudes he might stand as an emblem of his whole Revolutionary generation.

3

The Intellectual

I

You have to be very self-supporting to live in the Irish countryside, I mean intellectually self-supporting.

(Ernie O'Malley)[1]

The establishment of the Irish Free State in 1922 was followed by an attempt to consolidate a distinct Irish identity in political, economic, and cultural terms. Sinn Féin ideology was given a practical testing ground in the new opportunities available to the young Free State. The ideology of the early twentieth-century Revolutionaries celebrated the peasantry as an anti-modern alternative to the supposed evils of industrialized society; arcadianism was crucial to the national self-image, the peasants and the land helping to define true Irishness. Ernie O'Malley, too, celebrated an idealized peasantry and shared a positive vision of rustic Irish culture. In the post-Second World War years he observed: 'I had decided rightly or wrongly that the children should be brought up in the country. In Burrishoole [County Mayo] they had sea and land. As the children grew up they would have the reality of land and a tradition of folk belief and of folk imagination which they could later discard: but it would be imbibed not from books but from people.'[2]

Much of O'Malley's post-Revolutionary experience, indeed, testifies to his attachment to rural Ireland. In the mid-1940s he wrote lovingly of his native County Mayo in a passage reminiscent of *On Another Man's Wound*:

The most interesting part of the county is the sea edge and its background, which can best be seen either from a boat or on a height. . . . The bareness and austerity of the hills withdraws them from human contact, yet small white-washed houses contact remoteness and emphasize the struggle with land. People eager for the relaxation of good talk can rise suddenly out of bog depth or come down from hill height. Curve and outline satisfy the mind while changing colour makes them close to the heart.[3]

In letters from the mid-1950s he was to underline such sentiments: 'my heart is in Clew Bay';[4] 'A city is strange enough to me, as you are unrelated to earth, sky, or sea.'[5]

But (as is often the case with revolutionaries' attachment to the arcadian) there was also a tension between the ideal and the lived experience. This was sharpened by his sustained involvement in the practical business of living in the west of Ireland for much of his post-Revolutionary life. A letter to his New Mexican pupil and friend Eithne Golden, written in 1940, aptly characterizes something of O'Malley's complicated response to rural Ireland. He wrote of Ireland that 'This is a hard, cruel, and bitter country, but its faults are balanced by its virtues of humanity, kindliness, and faith. . . . You had best see it on the ground and in the country, when you have clay in your boots and salt water on your hands: in the city you might see it intellectually but around too many drawing-room fires.' But later in the same letter he also observed that 'You have to be very self-supporting to live in the Irish countryside, I mean intellectually self-supporting. There is no art, no library worth a small curse, no one who writes or paints near to you: very few people who read.'[6]

This last point was echoed again and again in O'Malley's thinking. In a post-Second World War manuscript he observed that 'Intellectual life in Ireland is difficult for many reasons, chiefly because the audience is limited.'[7] As a sophisticated writer and reader (few other farmers in his Mayo neighbourhood, for example, were likely to be reading Isaiah Berlin), O'Malley found rural life on occasions deadening and limiting. The inertia caused him considerable frustration, and although Dublin offered an antidote even this did not necessarily suffice. O'Malley wrote to his wife Helen early in 1937: 'It's a pity

Dublin is so slack about music as I would like to hear Brahms' symphonies again, some of his quartets and piano music, and also Beethoven's.'[8] This is why London offered such repeated attractions for him (as for other Irish Republican intellectuals), and there were echoes here of his friend Brendan Behan's comment that 'I really could not see why two small islands off the coast of Europe . . . required four capitals. One is enough, and we should live off the better one, which is in England.'[9]

O'Malley was caught between celebration of, and frustration with, a patriotically frugal and introspective Ireland. He testified to the problems of intellectual life in post-Revolutionary Ireland, but was also a conspicuous example of its great achievements and potential. As during the Revolution so, too, O'Malley the post-IRA intellectual was both energized and restricted by a nationalist framework, and was both exhilarated and frustrated by the idyllic yet often torpid west. Scholars have noted the post-Revolutionary swing in Ireland away from Revolutionary romanticism towards disenchanted realism.[10] In O'Malley's case, however, it was less a case of moving from one to the other than of experiencing the two simultaneously during the post-1922 era. O'Malley the intellectual in the new Ireland was both dissatisfied realist and persistent romantic. The land and the peasants had, like the Revolution itself, significantly disappointed him; but he retained his faith none the less. Indeed, he greatly lamented the decay of the rural west which he identified near the end of his life: 'The remoteness from a sense of time and from the passage of time is the most extraordinary thing about Aran. It is sad to see a people wither away when the fish leave them, or when they depend too much upon government subsidies. Most of the young people leave the islands.'[11]

None of this should cause us to ignore the strength of O'Malley's love for rural Ireland. But it does complicate the picture of the man and thereby brings him into more identifiable and helpful focus. Moreover, O'Malley's experience here was part of a broader set of tensions in post-Revolutionary Ireland. The ideals of the Revolutionary ideologues and enthusiasts were powerful in providing a sense of purpose and identity in the new Ireland; cultural nationalism helped to define the character of the post-1922 Irish state. But it is also true that Revolutionary ideals sat awkwardly with some key Irish realities. Orthodox definition and popular experience did not necessarily match one another neatly, and this is the setting for understanding O'Malley's intellectual development. Many intellectuals found the post-Revolutionary context wearying and constricting. Samuel Beckett's brilliant heresy, the 1938 novel *Murphy*, caustically refers to the 'civilized world and Irish Free State', lampoons Free State censorship, celebrates leaving Ireland, and hilariously detonates cultural nationalist orthodoxy.[12] O'Malley and Beckett were friends, and O'Malley's reflections on the author are telling. In a letter from 1956 O'Malley observed that there were 'Very few sculptors in Ireland, very few painters, very few anything, indeed. Yet Sam Beckett is Irish and he is regarded as of being important in France as he writes in French. He is an aloof man whom I like a good deal, interested in painting and in music, but not much of a talker save, I expect, in Paris.'[13] Significantly, Beckett had (like many other talented Irish intellectuals) left Ireland. Such exile both reflected and reinforced Irish intellectual isolation; and O'Malley's own life in rural Ireland itself reflected isolation. Looking back on the early stages of the Second World War he observed that 'We were considerably isolated in Burrishoole—a trip to France and to Corsica, frequent journeys to study sculpture, but no organized society'.[14] In December 1948 he wrote from Burrishoole to Frank Gallagher: 'Here, a strange timeless world. I don't read papers. I have no wireless. Each week I go out to Mass at 8 a.m. in a trap. That is as much as I see of the outside world, which I expect is yet there.'[15]

This was a particular version of cultural isolation, and one which mirrored O'Malley's simultaneous enthusiasms for the rustic and for the urban. But his attitudes also relate to the wider question of Irish isolationism, and to the cultural conflicts which surrounded it. Just as he had misgivings about certain aspects of the Gaelicization project (in a post-Second World War piece he referred to the independent Irish state's 'insistence on compulsory Irish in schools and for government appointments' and added: 'Whatever the sincerity of motives involved, the results were inclined to travesty the intention'),[16] so, too, he opposed certain other ways in which cultural orthodoxy was implemented in the new Ireland. Crucial here was censorship. O'Malley's Revolution had been characterized by his belief in the pursuit of freedom: imaginative and artistic, as well as political. The authorities in the Irish Free State/Éire adopted a more restrictive attitude towards independence of thought, and the new Ireland became characterized by a stifling cultural censorship. The 1923 Censorship of Films Act enabled an official film censor to protect people from what were judged to be obscene, indecent, blasphemous, or immoral works. The 1929 Censorship of Publications Act—reflecting attitudes which had

roots in the attempts of pre-independence Catholic enthusiasts to censor the immoral[17] — gave a Censorship Board the power to ban publications which were considered obscene or indecent. The legislation
was aimed in part at popular magazines and newspapers which were
held to be unsavoury, but it had a severe impact on serious intellectual
life. Over the ensuing decades many books were proscribed, a large
number of them by important Irish writers. O'Malley's friend, the
American scholar John V. Kelleher, was later to observe (in 1945) that
'Every Irish author of any standing is represented on the list of banned
books' and that 'Since the Act went into effect, about 1500 books have
been proscribed, including just about every Irish novel worth reading'.[18] This cultural protectionism was intended to guard the distinctive, the local, the truly Irish. But protecting the morals and culture of
the nation in this way undoubtedly led to a closed rather than open
attitude to cultural and literary influences, and contributed to Irish
cultural impoverishment and isolation.

    Such a stance ran contrary to O'Malley's own intellectual and cul-
tural life, and it would be possible to characterize him as a dissident in
a culture where intellectual closure rather than intellectual emancipation was the norm. He was politically unorthodox— the views which
he held regarding the Civil War, and which were posthumously to be
published in *The Singing Flame*, cut at the root of the Free State's
official ideology and represented a thoroughly dissident account of its
origins and emergence—and this had cultural implications too. After
the Revolution O'Malley kept in touch with ex-Revolutionaries who
had become politicians, but gravitated more and more towards those
of the Revolutionary generation whose sympathies lay in intellectual,
artistic, and cultural enthusiasm. His vision of a new Ireland had
involved a cultural emancipation, and his intellectual friends in independent Ireland were closer to this ambition than were most of his
political ex-comrades. Towards the end of his life, in 1955, O'Malley
wrote: 'Unfortunately Irish Catholic priests are so art-hostile, due to
the destruction of artistic instinct in Ireland for four hundred to five
hundred years; yet it could have been recentred, the aesthetic instinct,
if any of the successive cabinets were interested, any one member, I
mean.'[19] This was a point to which he alluded elsewhere, the absence
from Irish high political life of figures interested in 'art, literature, or
the things of the mind which lead to planning for time'.[20] Cultural
revolutionaries rarely get the revolution they desire, and O'Malley was
unquestionably disappointed by some of the developments which

occurred after 1922. Here we are back to the Romantic yearning for unachieved change, and again it is important to recognize that what gave Irish cultural nationalism much of its cohesion and meaning also carried with it less appealing aspects. The conservative climate in the early years of independent Ireland—an atmosphere in which Catholic guardians sought to protect people from evils as varied as communism, dance-halls, jazz, and extramarital sex—was a climate which many of the population welcomed. Hostility to the closed nature of the cultural protectionist project must be accompanied by recognition of this fact.

Indeed, O'Malley the post-Revolutionary intellectual represented that strand of Republican thinking which was dissident within the Ireland which the Republican Revolution had produced. A significant point of reference here is The Bell, which opposed the implementation of crude censorship (Peadar O'Donnell in 1947 referring to the censors as 'a board of censors of really formidable backwardness')[21] and which championed a more enlightened approach to cultural life in Ireland. In 1950 O'Donnell, as editor of The Bell, was stressing the social value of the journal: 'A magazine which associates serious writers and their public for mutual challenge and stimulation becomes a social influence of considerable usefulness, especially in Ireland where our writers merely draw the material for their work from Irish life but find their public abroad.'[22]

The Bell featured work by many important and talented writers. Much of the magazine's driving force came from people with Republican backgrounds who had become dissatisfied with key features of the Ireland that the Revolution had produced. The Bell was a significant vehicle for expressing such dissatisfaction, and O'Malley fitted into this project of offering constructive and subversive interventions in Irish cultural life. A Christian, Republican intellectual, but one with independent and sceptical perspectives, O'Malley was well suited to O'Faoláin and O'Donnell's journal. O'Faoláin thought there was a deep-rooted strain of anti-intellectualism in the Irish mind;[23] de Valera's Ireland was certainly characterized by a continuation of the cultural censorship prevalent during the pre-1932 years, and some aspects of the Fianna Fáil approach clearly jarred with O'Malley's understanding of Irish Republicanism. He broadly sympathized with the celebration of a rural, Gaelic, and Catholic Irish identity, and to that extent the Ireland of de Valera's 1937 Constitution suited him well enough. But O'Malley's relation to de Valera's Ireland was complicated by his dissidence from the cultural isolationism which it encouraged.

He was not straightforwardly dissident from the mainstream nationalist culture of these years, nor entirely orthodox within it. Like his
friend and colleague at *The Bell* Peadar O'Donnell, he was capable
both of celebrating western arcadianism and of recognizing certain
problems with western realities. O'Donnell himself was deeply sceptical about de Valera's Ireland, referring in *The Bell* in 1945 to the
Fianna Fáil leader's 'St Patrick's Purgatory outlook' and suggesting
that 'a little less frugality would be a blessing'.[24] The following year
O'Donnell wrote (again in *The Bell*) that 'de Valera has been a failure
as head of the Fianna Fáil government. Under him Irish youth have
been forced into exile on a scale that threatens our survival as a people.
He has no sense of people in his body, and looks out over our industrial
problems with the frugal standards of a peasant, or a monk.'[25] By the
mid-1940s, indeed, O'Donnell had reached the view that Ireland's
problem lay in there being too many people on the land and too few in
employment in the towns. He maintained throughout his life a class-
based view of Ireland's problems and of what he held to be the appropriate solutions. While O'Malley did not share O'Donnell's socialist
critique of independent Ireland, he did exhibit a hard-headed appreciation of some of the difficulties implicit within the new state's nationalist orthodoxy. This, indeed, was one of the qualities of pure Republican
thinking in the post-Revolutionary years: the cultural dissidence of
those who had conceived of a fuller emancipation than that achieved
in Free State/Éire practice. From O'Malley's perspective the key
enemy was intellectual and cultural insularity, and much of his private
and public intellectual work was aimed at countering such a tendency.

The Bell represented one branch of the Republican family, proxim-
ity with old comrades being an important feature of O'Malley's post-
Revolutionary life. But—as during the conflict with the British
itself—there were some tensions and problems also in this later period
among the comrades. O'Malley tried to build up a book review section
in *The Bell*, but reviewers were hard to find and English publishers
were not always enthusiastic about sending books to the journal.
Moreover, there were problems with Peadar O'Donnell. According to
O'Malley, O'Donnell was 'a bad judge of literature' and was far from
reliable as editor: 'Not since October [1947]', he wrote in March 1948
'have I received the galleys of reviews. Even then the editor did not
take my selection of reviews, but made a choice of his own.'[26]
But close contact with talented Irish intellectuals was a vital part of
O'Malley's post-IRA life. As with Peadar O'Donnell, so also with Liam

O'Flaherty O'Malley had an intriguing friendship. All three men were born in the west of Ireland in the 1890s (O'Donnell 1893, O'Flaherty 1896, O'Malley 1897), all three were involved in the Revolution and had taken the Republican side in the Civil War, and all three contributed significantly to Irish letters in subsequent years. The melancholy, gloomy mood of much of O'Flaherty's work—the fog-bound, rainy, bleak, heavy, depressing world of The Informer (1925), Mr Gilhooley (1926), or The Assassin (1928), for example—is starkly different from that brighter atmosphere which pervades O'Donnell's writings. O'Donnell's comparatively cheery treatment of the Irish Civil War in The Knife (1930) can, for instance, be contrasted with the much darker tone used by O'Flaherty in 'The Mountain Tavern' (1929). O'Malley greatly admired 'The Mountain Tavern', and his own account of the Civil War (in The Singing Flame, for example) was nearer to O'Flaherty's melancholy reading than to the merry mood of O'Donnell's Civil War autobiography, The Gates Flew Open (1932).

O'Malley read widely in O'Flaherty's work. He liked the historical novel Famine (1937),[27] just as O'Flaherty liked On Another Man's Wound (especially its 'cold military approach').[28] Both men had been wounded in war, O'Flaherty while fighting in the First World War British Army in 1917 and O'Malley several times as an IRA man during the Irish Revolution. In O'Flaherty's case, and almost certainly in O'Malley's, this encouraged a subsequent tendency towards the melancholic. There were many differences between the two in the way they handled their intellectual life; O'Flaherty's tendency to throw himself into causes but as quickly retreat from that world of action into a private world of imagination, for example, greatly differed from O'Malley's more sustainedly engaged approach. But they did both form part of a dissident, ex-Revolutionary body of intellectual opinion. Much of O'Flaherty's work was banned in Ireland and he, like O'Malley, was instinctively opposed to the closing out of expression (O'Flaherty wrote to Jonathan Cape in the late 1930s that 'I have always been opposed to action for libel and as I believe in freedom of the press for myself, so do I believe that others should enjoy it in equal measure').[29] And both O'Flaherty and O'Malley held, even during these early years of the new state, that the imagined freedom for which the Revolutionaries had fought was somehow mocked by the practical realities of the new Ireland.

Liam O'Flaherty is a helpful guide also to other important aspects of O'Malley's intellectual life. O'Flaherty's Dostoyevskian quality, for example, points us towards O'Malley's interest in the great Russian writer. O'Malley read Dostoyevsky extensively ('his fundamental understanding of people is the best I know')[30] and was exhilarated by him. In prison in 1921 he 'read *The Brothers Karamazov* . . . I began *Crime and Punishment*. I was so excited that I could not sleep well. The mental excitement of Dostoyevsky came over to me, it put my mind in a whirl of delight and warmth and overstimulation. I re-read the books. They changed the cell.'[31] This feverish intellectual energy was a persistent characteristic of O'Malley's. Indeed, there was something in him of the Raskolnikovian intellectual: tortured, troubled, tormented, restless. His own writing was of immense urgency and importance to him, and could cause him considerable anxiety (references such as that in his notebook for 26 January 1931 — 'I'm not getting any writing done'[32] — populate his private writings). Moreover, there was in O'Malley's mind a clear connection between troubled mental excitement and his own commitment to Republican nationalism. In a fascinating manuscript draft of *On Another Man's Wound* he linked his parents' lack of nationalism or patriotism to their having had 'no unrest of mind'.[33] Dissatisfaction with what existed here combined with precisely that Dostoyevskian exhilaration which pervaded O'Malley's intellectual life.

Artists and intellectuals — including Samuel Beckett, Edward Weston, Paul Strand, the Group Theatre, Louis MacNeice, and Hart Crane — were frequently, repeatedly impressed by O'Malley. In part it was his considerable intellectual flexibility and power which attracted such people to him. Partly, also, it was his combination of letters with dramatic action. O'Malley's friendship with the Belfast-born poet Louis MacNeice is instructive here. It was O'Malley the post-Revolutionary intellectual whom MacNeice came to know; yet O'Malley the man of action could not be separated from O'Malley the writer. As MacNeice's biographer has observed, 'MacNeice hated the violence he [O'Malley] represented, but could not help admiring the man of action, raconteur, and author of a brilliant memoir, *On Another Man's Wound*'.[34] This echoes MacNeice's poetry ('We envy men of action')[35] and it also resembles the responses of other intellectuals and artists towards O'Malley.

More extended consideration is, perhaps, due to O'Malley's friendship with the brilliant American modernist poet, Hart Crane. Born in Garrettsville, Ohio, in 1899, Crane was to write some of the most powerful of modern American verse. His books *White Buildings* (1926) and

The Bridge (1930) demonstrated his importance, a significance recognized by—among others—T. S. Eliot.[36] Crane was the recipient of a Guggenheim Foundation Fellowship in 1931, to pursue creative work in Mexico. He went to Mexico City and it was during this period that he and O'Malley spent time together. Tragically, Crane was shortly to die (committing suicide in April 1932) but the two men's brief encounter is of great interest in relation to O'Malley the intellectual. O'Malley read Crane's work, took extensive notes on it, transcribed Crane's poems into his collection of notebooks, and thought the American's work highly significant. The two men (both roving bohemians at this stage) obviously enjoyed each other's company, but also shared intellectual and artistic tastes and aims. Both were absorbed at this time in Marlowe, Shakespeare, Donne, Jonson, Blake, Wordsworth, Melville, Whitman, Baudelaire, Dostoyevsky, Pound, and Eliot. Both men celebrated the vigour and spirituality of Mexican painting and had shared interests in traditions of European art.

Their huge reading—both were omnivorous—and artistic range therefore helped to bring them together. So, too, did their spiritual ambition for literature. One of Crane's aims in his masterpiece *The Bridge* was to produce an epic which would use episodes from American history to encourage the growth of the spiritual consciousness in the individual. The poem drew richly on mythology, history, and literature, employing a distinctive view of the past to support a faith in the spiritual possibilities of a less materialistic American future. Crane lamented that the USA had, in his view, become enslaved to materialism. But he demonstrated an optimistic faith in future possibilities. *The Bridge* was an exhortation to idealism, using New York's Brooklyn Bridge as a symbol of spiritual faith and deploying the past as inspiration for future hope.[37]

O'Malley noted in Crane this search for spiritual values, observed his use of the past for this purpose, and welcomed the tremendous vigour of his poetry. He also identified Crane's great faith, observing of the poet that 'He believed in America, in its creative ability'.[38] Resemblances shout out here between the two men's intellectual projects. The idealist viewing his country's past in ways which promoted a spiritualistic, anti-materialistic view of its possible future; the repudiation of materialism by means of presenting examples of idealism in one's nation's history; the pursuit of cultural rebirth through arts, literature, and imagination; the search via one's writing for nobility, beauty, and for the higher spirit—all of these are evident in Crane's eclectic national epic, but are also evident in the Irish writings on which O'Malley was engaged at this time. Moreover, broader points emerge on closer inspection of the two writers' relationship. Crane was interested in the epiphanic moment for the artist and in what that could reveal. In 1927 he argued that 'One should be somewhat satisfied if one's work comes to approximate a true record of such moments of "illumination" as are occasionally possible. A sharpening of reality accessible to the poet, to no such degree possible through other mediums.'[39] This raised important questions concerning the relationship between poetry and science. Crane's view, as expressed in 1930, was that 'That "truth" which science pursues is radically different from the metaphorical, extra-logical "truth" of the poet'.[40] He saw poetry as the intuitive pursuit of absolute beauty (again, there were definite echoes here of O'Malley) and held that the poet was inspired and could see things which were denied in ordinary experience. He therefore disputed the view that poetry was practised and indulged in by dreamers, that it merely entertained or supported the psychological well-being of poets or readers but could not contribute to our knowledge of objective reality.

Among the others whom O'Malley met in these years of bohemian sojourn was the American poet Robinson Jeffers (1887–1962). He had met Jeffers and his wife Una in the thriving artists' colony at Carmel, prior to visiting Taos, and they had also then spent time together in New Mexico. O'Malley read and took notes on Jeffers's work, and their shared literary enthusiasms (Shakespeare, Milton, Wordsworth, Yeats, Homer) were compounded by shared interest in Ireland. Una Jeffers had been enthusiastic to explore Irish culture and this prompted the Jeffers to visit Ireland for an extended period in late 1929. They greatly enjoyed their wide-ranging Irish travels ('we've been in every county of Ireland except one [Wexford]'; 'Ireland pleased us most and England least'), though some of the poet's observations were sharply pointed enough ('The people are Irish Catholics here [Knocknacarry, County Antrim] . . . therefore as primitive and kindly and dirty as anywhere in the west').[41] Politically, there were significant differences between the two men. Jeffers's views were complex. He had many left-wing and liberal friends, though his own politics were those of a sceptical conservative, with little belief in the human capacity for the amelioration of society. O'Malley, too, mixed with people exhibiting a wide variety of political sympathies. But his own politics were some distance from Jeffers's aristocratic version of élitism; in 1937 Jeffers described his politics as: 'Ideally, aristocratic and republican: freedom for the responsible elements of society and contentment for the less respons-ible'.[42] O'Malley also forged a close friendship with the American photographer Paul Strand. Again, New Mexico provided the fertile territory for friendship to flourish, but subsequent letters and contacts testified to a continuing intimacy and mutual understanding. The photographer thought very highly of O'Malley ('I know you are a man of vision and inner strength'),[43] so much so that he suggested they work together on a book, taking a village or group of Irish villages, with Strand taking the photographs and O'Malley writing the text.

Sadly, this project did not materialize. But it is illustrative of the interconnectedness between O'Malley's American and his Irish intel-lectual concerns and contacts. Jeffers, Strand, and Crane—who had known (and read W. B. Yeats with) Padraic Colum—evinced an inter-est in Irishness, and O'Malley's intellectual life was persistently focused on Ireland and on Irish connections and concerns. Back in Ireland after his 1928–35 travels, he participated in a number of Irish intellec-tual bodies such as the Irish Academy of Letters, and the Bibliographi-cal Society of Ireland. Both of these are revealing. As Seán O'Faoláin told O'Malley in relation to the Academy, there was a major problem that so few Irish writers lived in Dublin. O'Malley recognized this, and was fully aware of the difficulties facing intellectuals in independent Ireland. Certainly, the role of the Academy itself should not be over-stated. Peadar O'Donnell's view, that from the start 'an air of make-believe'[44] had surrounded the body, establishes the key here. But the Academy did reflect some of O'Malley's concerns and something of his standing. Aiming to promote creative literature in Ireland, the body was intended to afford recognition to the country's writers in an atmosphere which was in many respects less than favourable. It opposed the restric-tive censorship prevalent in the state. Moreover, it had associated with it some of the most powerful names in modern Irish letters. Established by William Butler Yeats and George Bernard Shaw, it had held its first meeting in 1932; present at that meeting were some of the key literary figures in Irish life during this period, including Yeats, Frank O'Connor, George Russell (AE), and Lennox Robinson.

O'Malley's membership of the Bibliographical Society of Ireland is significant: he was a committed bibliophile, with an impressively wide intellectual range. His unquenchable desire for book-buying resulted in a massive personal library, a collection through which he worked his way omnivorously; hundreds of notebooks testify to his wide-ranging literary and intellectual hunger. If he was fastidious and particular about the precise editions of the books which he sought and bought, then he was equally detailed in his attention to their contents. And this obsessive note-taking was a long-standing habit; his Revolutionary comrade Sean Lemass recalled of the O'Malley of 1922 that 'he wrote down . . . meticulously, everything that happened . . . he had this notebook . . . in which he was always writing'.[45]

In contrast to the myth of the boisterous, boozy, Behanesque Irish writer, therefore, we have in O'Malley a sensitive, troubled, earnest, almost neurotically perfectionistic intellectual. His massive intellectual range and his hunger for ideas are equally impressive. Linked into a significant culture of post-Revolutionary intellectuals, O'Malley reflected the tensions prevalent in independent Ireland: enthusiastic attachment to Republican nationalist belief coexisted with dissidence and dissatisfaction. His Republicanism had involved a vision of cultural and intellectual freedom, and he sought to further this through his reading and writing, through his interconnected Irish and non-Irish intellectual preoccupations. In particular, his research and writing on the Irish Revolution saw him attempt to further those ideals for which he had fought during 1916–23.

II

Writing has helped me to work certain prejudices out of my system, to clarify experience.

(Ernie O'Malley)[46]

O'Malley's standing as an Irish Revolutionary is defined as much by his writing as by his military career; 'O'Malley's books are regarded as the most literary record of the events of the Revolutionary period'.[47] He felt compelled to write, observing in 1934 that 'I yet have the feeling of not justifying my existence when I don't write something; maybe I'll get rid of that, but it seems to me an ethical code and perhaps my only one.'[48] That he considered his writing to have enabled him to work through 'certain prejudices' is intriguing. O'Malley's writings on the Irish Revolution offer both an imaginative, intelligent statement of the Republican case and also considerable evidence that O'Malley himself had matured into a decidedly post-Revolutionary state of mind. It was not that he jettisoned his Republican convictions; these remained with him throughout his life. But during the 1920s there was a definite shift on O'Malley's part from Revolutionary soldiership to intellectual preoccupation. The two careers are clearly interwoven. As noted in the previous chapter, intellectual forces played a very significant part in forming O'Malley the Revolutionary soldier; and an argument could definitely be made that O'Malley's books have had a variety of subversive influences. But with the mid-1920s we see a post-Revolutionary nationalist keen to express his Republican sympathies through the pen rather than the gun.

This, indeed, provides the key to appreciating O'Malley's important writings on the Revolution. He began a first draft of On Another Man's Wound with the question, 'How does one reconstruct a spiritual state of mind?'[49] This captures the central purpose of O'Malley's autobiographical masterpiece: the reconstruction of a decidedly spiritual mentality, of a Revolutionary state of mind which he wanted to depict for the purposes of personal as well as political record. The record he produced was an outstanding legacy to leave behind him. O'Malley's memoirs, in particular On Another Man's Wound and The Singing Flame, stand out from the majority of Irish Revolutionary autobiographies: sophisticated, layered, subtle, stylized, crafted, ambitious, and intellectually powerful, these works contrast starkly with the more naive writings of some of O'Malley's Revolutionary comrades (such as Dan Breen, Tom Barry, or Liam Deasy). Imagination—so important a part of O'Malley's political formation—was crucial also to the distinctiveness of his writings on the Revolution. If one considers O'Malley's work from the perspective of I. A. Richards's 'four kinds of meaning' (sense, feeling, tone, and intention)[50]—and given O'Malley's interest in Richards this is, perhaps, not entirely inappropriate—then something of his writing's quality becomes clear. In terms of drawing attention to a state of affairs, of expressing authorial feeling, of choosing appropriate literary colours, and of intending a powerful effect, O'Malley's books resonate with striking authority. In particular, the tone chosen by O'Malley is often strikingly, self-consciously evocative. In describing the lurid, night-fire panorama at Hollyford Barracks in County Tipperary (which O'Malley and his IRA colleagues were attacking in May 1920), he recalled:

For a few moments, while we watched the roof, there was a quiet interval, then flames sprang violently to life again, yellow-red in licking spray. . . . I was about to die, I believed, and yet with no conscious effort on my own part my mind seemed to be busily noting the little inconsequential details that were taking place around me. . . . When I looked down, the small village was splintered with orange light which climbed up the sides of the houses and showed up the darkened hills which seemed to move as flames wavered. Light was reflected off windows while shadows edged the spattered illumination. It was a Caravaggio canvas, that scene which I firmly thought would be my last.[51]

This distinctively imaginative picture is further illuminated by consideration of O'Malley's fuller view of Caravaggio, in whom he took a sustained and committed interest. O'Malley observed that 'Caravaggio emphasized literal observation and emphatic description'; he also argued that in Caravaggio one finds 'violent, unusual effects of light' and 'the expression of melodramatic emotion', and he argued of Caravaggio that 'He had imagination and genuine talent, but he aimed at producing a vivid shock of surprised agreement in the spectator'.[52] O'Malley crafted his work painstakingly through years of diligent attention and chose allusions with considerable care; his Caravaggio imagery in describing the 1920 IRA attack on Hollyford Barracks is characteristically revealing both in its arresting evocation of a particular episode, and also in what it reflects of O'Malley's sophisticated literary intention.

Responses to O'Malley's On Another Man's Wound—the only one of his books to be published during his lifetime—chimed with its distinctive quality. The Irish Press reviewer found it 'difficult to speak about [On Another Man's Wound] otherwise than in superlatives', and held that O'Malley's was the best book yet written on the Anglo-Irish War.[53] American reviews were also highly eulogistic. The New York Herald Tribune described Army Without Banners (the title of the American edition) as 'a superbly written narrative of high personal and national adventure'.[54] The Boston Sunday Globe reviewer suggested that O'Malley's book was written 'with clarity of conviction' yet 'without rancour and with a serenity of restraint which lifts it far above any volume of the kind I know of'.[55] The praise is still forthcoming. In the Irish Times early in 1996 the distinguished writer John McGahern described On Another Man's Wound as 'the one classic work to have emerged directly from the violence that led to independence and the foundation of the state', adding that the book deserves 'a permanent and honoured place in our literature'.[56] Scholars have likewise been drawn to the book (and to O'Malley's other published writings) for their insights into the period and for their articulate expression of Irish Republican thinking.

Some of these responses help focus our attention not only on the literary qualities of the book, but also on O'Malley's place within the

1. Ernie O'Malley, 1929

2. Ernie O'Malley, 1933

3. Helen Hooker, 1930

5. Ernie O'Malley, John Wayne, and Cormac O'Malley, 1951, during the filming of *The Quiet Man*

4. O'Malley family, Dublin 1946. Cahal, Etáin, Helen, Ernie, Cormac (left to right)

6. Ernie O'Malley, 1954

7. Ernie O'Malley, Cormac O'Malley, with horse (Sheila) and dog (Rommel), 1951

wider Irish intellectual context. For example, the novelist Francis
Stuart has written positively of O'Malley's work,[57] and Stuart's
endorsement is intriguing. He met O'Malley during the Civil War and
also during the 1930s, was impressed by his integrity, and thought him
a true Revolutionary. Stuart's own reflections on the 1930s grouped
himself with Samuel Beckett and Louis MacNeice as Protestants who
'didn't take any note of society' and who in fact left Ireland: 'We were
dismissed, almost totally, in favour of writers like [Frank] O'Connor,
[Daniel] Corkery, Seán O'Faoláin, who were thought to represent the
new Irish spirit.' In contrast to his own triumvirate, Stuart maintains,
these writers 'flattered society by commenting on it'.[58] Stuart celebrated the notion of dissidence, of taking the outsider's unacceptable
position, and here there are useful indications regarding O'Malley's
intellectual positioning. He did not fit neatly into either of Stuart's
1930s triumvirates. Instead, he shared features with both: as we have
seen, O'Malley can be connected with O'Connor and O'Faoláin as
with Beckett and MacNeice. The key feature, and it is one to which
Stuart points, is the combination of idealism with sceptical distance.
Even his detractors would acknowledge O'Malley's idealism; his
capacity for scepticism, for ambivalence, and for heterodox opinion
are likewise indisputable. Indeed, it is these latter characteristics
which make his writings so frequently compelling. A committed Irish
Republican, he simultaneously expressed doubts about some of the
faith's foundations. An Irish separatist fighting to free Ireland from
British rule, he simultaneously recognized that more politically neu-
tral forces (such as generational conflict) were vitally important in producing the Revolution.

These reflections are present in O'Malley's Revolutionary mus-
ings,[59] but they reach their most polished expression in his later writings. The key here is established in a letter from O'Malley to Sheila
Humphreys in 1928, shortly before the period when he wrote his Revolutionary memoirs: 'I have the bad and disagreeable habit of writing
the truth as I see it, and not as other people (including yourself) realize
it, in which we are a race of spiritualized idealists with a world idea of
freedom, having nothing to learn for we have made no mistakes.'[60]
The truth as he saw it contained much Republican orthodoxy, but also
much else. He was sceptical about the exaggerated presentation of
IRA activities, and was particularly wary of some of the myths which
grew up around himself. Writing of the period of his internment in
1924, he observed: 'I was told stories of myself, what I had said or done

in different places. I could not recognize myself for the legend. . . .
People saw us as a myth, which bore little relation to ourselves.'[61] It
was not that O'Malley rejected such myths entirely: he recognized
their political value, and his writings themselves clearly helped to
establish his own cultic status in Republican tradition. But he expressed a certain resentment at the constriction which such expectations imposed on him. The layered nature of his carefully crafted
autobiographies provided scope for reflecting this ambivalence.
Indeed, the setting for his writing is crucial. In 1935, shortly before his
return to Ireland, O'Malley observed that 'Here in America I have
been cut away from my own country where I found I was developing
into a symbol.' America had helped O'Malley 'to find something of
myself'.[62] His memoirs were written some years after the Revolutionary upheavals which they describe, and the distinctive American context within which they were substantially constructed goes far in
explaining their particular qualities. During the 1928–35 years in
America O'Malley worked on the 1916–24 period as a whole; although
the 1936 book (*On Another Man's Wound*) concluded its story in 1921,
the posthumously published material dealing with the post-1921 period
was also significantly developed during these American years.

The most significant episodes for this writing occurred during
O'Malley's times in New Mexico, Mexico, New York, Yaddo (Saratoga
Springs), and Boston. Emigration offered great rewards and opportunities: new contacts, people, and settings provided the atmosphere in
which O'Malley's writing could flourish more imaginatively and freely
than in early Free State Ireland. *On Another Man's Wound* is, among
other things, emigrant literature; and the lyrical quality of its Ireland
owes much to the accentuation of attachment which prolonged
absence fostered in O'Malley. He missed and adored Ireland (upon his
return there in 1935 he rhapsodically celebrated its rural beauty: 'The
country is amazingly beautiful I think, but I don't know if I confuse my
aesthetics with my actual love of every square inch of it').[63] But
thoughts of Ireland also sharpened for him the advantages of the
United States; his responses were ambivalent. Writing from Chicago
in 1933, for example, he reflected that 'America seems such a good
country when I think of Ireland and Ireland such a pleasant place
when I think of America that it is hard to resolve my doubts'.[64]

O'Malley could be contemptuous about certain forms of sentimentality, and he approached his emigrant period with a typically vigorous
sense of its opportunities rather than with mawkishly expressed

regrets.[65] Certainly the 1928–35 sojourn was productive in terms of creativity. O'Malley approached his writing with an impressive seriousness, and found and refined his distinctive style during these years, with his accounts of America echoing his writings on Ireland. See, for example, his growing interest in landscape evident in his depiction of Arizona's Grand Canyon from September 1929: 'White granite base to red cliffs a blue like that of the sea in the distance, which later turned out to be cloud shadows on a mountain length running at and to the west; the white grey base rounded and moulded continues to follow the mountains in spirals.'[66] O'Malley was entranced also by the landscape and setting of New Mexico: its romantic quality, beauty, wildness, peace, and unspoilt character. Writing of the South-West he observed that 'one is always conscious of space'.[67] Eithne Golden later recalled how much he 'loved New Mexico',[68] while Mabel Dodge Luhan (whom O'Malley came to know in New Mexico, and who had earlier brought D. H. Lawrence to Taos) observed that 'Taos had something wonderful in it, like the dawn of the world. Lawrence always called it pristine. . . . Everyone is surprised at that first view of Taos Valley—it is so beautiful.'[69]

Part of the attraction for O'Malley lay in his sympathy with the Indians. Antonio (Tony) Mirabal was a Taos Indian with whom O'Malley was to identify particularly closely. O'Malley considered Mirabal a close friend during his time in Taos, and was drawn to him in part because Mirabal was militant in defence of the Indians' interests. Luhan herself (1879–1962) had discovered Taos in 1917 and settled there. She was from a well-to-do family in Buffalo, New York, and had lived, prior to Taos, in Europe and in New York City. Rejecting what she saw as the emotionally stunted, routinized world of bourgeois Buffalo, she had reacted against its rich, dull safety and had travelled. Her pursuit of spiritual satisfaction and her emotional intensity both suited her to the artistic commune culture which characterized the Taos world: anti-materialist, anti-bourgeois, bohemian, authenticist, and hostile to mainstream America. A leading figure in contemporary New Mexican bohemia, Luhan epitomized its self-consciousness and its reactive celebration of the primitive.

New Mexico during this period was a major centre for the arts in the United States. In particular, Santa Fé and Taos had become focal points of some significance. Alice Corbin Henderson had arrived in New Mexico in 1916 and had been one of the first writers to settle in Santa Fé; Mary Austin—a celebrant of Pueblo Indian culture—had arrived in 1918 and had founded the Santa Fé writers' colony. Similarly, Taos had become an artistic centre. Bert G. Phillips and Ernest L. Blumenschein—both of whom had studied painting in Paris—together arrived in Taos in 1898 and founded there the Taos Art Colony. In 1915 the Taos painters formed the Taos Society of Artists, which was to survive until 1927. Painter Georgia O'Keeffe and photographer Paul Strand had arrived in New Mexico shortly after the First World War. Mabel Dodge Luhan was herself behind the establishment of an impressive writers' colony in Taos, and the often colourful people in this aesthetic colony just over fifty miles north-east of Santa Fé provided O'Malley with his setting for much of the 1929–32 period. Taos held a certain glamour: its intellectuals, artists, and bohemians coincided in a refuge from industrial America and from urban materialist conceptions of progress, in an atmosphere of spiritual rebellion, and in a sophisticated intimacy.[70] Among the Taos Luhan circle in which O'Malley mixed were Theodora Goddard (a New York painter who left the city to go to Taos in 1929); Dorothy Stewart (1898–1954, another painter from New York); Miriam Hapgood de Witt (1906–90, author of a valuable memoir on Taos,[71] in which she remembered O'Malley as a romantic character); Dorothy Brett;[72] Robinson and Una Jeffers (who were close to Luhan and often visited Taos); 'Spud' Johnson (poet, critic, and publisher of an irreverent magazine, *Laughing Horse*);[73] and the Irish writer Ella Young. It was to meet Young that O'Malley had first visited Taos. Having met up they discussed a whole variety of topics at length, and Young advised O'Malley about the writing of his memoirs. Indeed, when the Goldens initially returned to California in late 1929, O'Malley stayed on in Taos partly with a view to Ella Young helping him write his book. Young's possible influence is intriguing and may offer one part of the explanation for the distinctive style of *On Another Man's Wound*. An Irish poet and mystic, Young had gone to the United States in 1925 and was to lecture for years on Celtic Mythology and Gaelic Literature at the University of California at Berkeley. Imaginative, flowery, and with theosophical leanings, Young believed in the fairy people of Irish legend and also in nature spirits, held that trees and plants had conscious personalities with which she could communicate, and was convinced that animals had psychic powers which humans did not possess.

Brought up on Malory and Tennyson; enthralled by *The Iliad*; possessed of a great regard for Patrick Pearse; acquainted with Pearse, Thomas MacDonagh, W. B. Yeats, Maud Gonne, Padraic Colum, and AE—Young's framework was one which, to some degree, suited O'Malley well. Like him, she had been in Dublin during the 1916 rebellion (which she described as 'a poet's Rising')[74] and, again like O'Malley, her political sympathies were to go to the Republicans in the 1922–23 Civil War. She celebrated the 'magic'[75] of the west of Ireland, loved and gathered Irish folklore, and favoured a lyrical approach to the romantic beauty of Ireland.

Thus her advice to O'Malley (such as the suggestion that 'I think that a big book like your book on Ireland takes *time*. One must stop now and then and do something else to let the work of the book mature in one's mind')[76] should be seen within their shared world-view and similar leanings. Young, for example, offers in her own auto-biography lyrical depictions of rural Ireland, and likens New Mexico to Ireland: 'This stone-pure mountain-guarded land [New Mexico] is one after my own heart: it reminds me of the stony reaches of Western Ireland—of Connemara where the white horses of faeryland thrust untameable heads from wine-dark shadow-encompassed mountain tarns. I shall love this country';[77] O'Malley, in discussion with Young in Taos, 'compared the Aran Islanders to the Indians',[78] and his own writings offer a strikingly lyrical presentation of rural Ireland: 'I looked forward to Spring: broken land, brown, umber, upturned, earth smells awakened by the rain. The wild daffodil quivering on pliant stem, purple-frittered wild iris, the delicate cream of the primrose backed by its crimpled leaf and the rich golden glory of the sedate crocus.'[79] So the poet's encouragement and help reinforced O'Malley's leanings towards a particular kind of imaginative celebration. Sheer distance from Ireland heightened his lyrical appreciation; but so, too, did some of the key influences upon him in his exile.

On O'Malley's arrival in Taos, Young was staying with Mabel Luhan. Luhan hosted large numbers of visiting artists and intellectuals (including Georgia O'Keeffe and Ansel Adams) in her book-packed house. Many of the people in the Luhan circle were, like Luhan herself, absorbed in writing their memoirs. O'Malley, Brett, Luhan, Young, Hapgood de Witt, and others were all autobiographers. This culture also played a part in the formation and definition of O'Malley's memoirs. He and his friends during these years read material out to each other, discussed each other's work frequently and at length, and shared many ideas and responses; in this setting O'Malley wrote and rewrote, drafting and recrafting his work meticulously. His pains-taking, perfectionistic approach is reflected in the quality of the prose achieved,[80] and also in some of his other reflections (such as his concern that authors should not dash work off hurriedly, nicely captured by his statement after the publication of Peadar O'Donnell's fourth novel in five years, *The Knife* (1930), that 'I hope that Peadar will not turn into a mass production merchant').[81]

O'Malley's reflections on Ireland were also affected by his response to the indigenous people. He greatly liked the Taos Indians and their communal, respectful attitude to land. But, fascinated though he was, he found them not the easiest to know: in Taos in September 1930 he noted that 'Their customs are difficult to know as an Indian hates to be asked questions'.[82] He also warmed to the Mexican Indians during his visit to Mexico itself. In late 1930 the painter Dorothy Stewart decided to spend the winter in Mexico and suggested the idea to Theodora Goddard and to Ernie O'Malley, both of whom responded positively. They drove down to Mexico City—the bumpy drive on rough roads causing O'Malley some pain on account of the bullets in his back—and upon arrival in Mexico O'Malley separated from the painters. Though they kept in touch, O'Malley preferred to explore in a more solitary fashion.

O'Malley's thoughts in and on Mexico are illuminating. As noted, he liked the Indians. In Mexico in early 1931 he wrote in his notebook of the Indians there: 'perhaps I'm prejudiced in favour of their race'.[83] Indeed, O'Malley read the Mexicans in ways which echoed and coloured his representation of his own country. Initially attracted by a romanticism in the Mexican land and its people, O'Malley came to stress the 'strength' and 'vitality' of Mexican folk tradition and the way in which this folk tradition was drawn upon during a period of national resurgence. All of this resembled his view of authentic Irish culture, as did his remarks about the 'battle for indigenous expression' in the Mexican arts, or concerning the way in which Mexican artists 'inspired by revolutionary zeal' sought to make the history and struggles of their country live in public.[84] In March 1931 O'Malley talked of the inhabitants of pre-colonial Mexico having had their bodies and souls broken by the Spanish conquest, and argued that the Spanish conquest 'smashed their [the pre-colonial inhabitants'] legitimate pride [and] retarded the development along their own lines. . . . This smashing of a nation's soul to me is the worst feature of Imperial rule.'[85] Here we have distinct echoes of his observations regarding Ireland, both those written before and after his exile. Consider, for example, his stress in November 1923 upon the importance of Ireland regaining her

'real soul';[86] and compare his observation in *The Singing Flame* that
the rule of the British Empire in Ireland had 'stifled the spiritual
expression of nationhood', 'retarded our development', and 'dammed
back strength, vigour, and imagination needed in solving our problems in our own way'.[87] Mexican reflections both echoed and reinforced his view of Ireland. O'Malley celebrated energy, vitality,
forcefulness, vigour, and directness in the Mexican setting just as he
did in the Irish (and, indeed, elsewhere: see his reference to 'the vigorous, direct touch of Albrecht Dürer',[88] one of his favourite artists).

Writing in 1947, O'Malley suggested that Mexico was of interest to
Ireland, having long been subject to foreign domination, and that the
country 'has made and is now making an important contribution to art
history'. Comparisons were significant: just as the Mexican Indians'
culture had been destroyed by colonialism, with the Indians not appreciating the contribution of their race to world history, so similarly,
O'Malley argued, the Irish of the eighteenth century had been 'isolated
from and unaware of their achievements in the past. They had with-
drawn from the conscious life of their conquerors as if they were living
in another dimension.'[89] The links here between imagination and political freedom are important. O'Malley conceived of freedom as involving both formal political and lasting cultural emancipation. National
freedom and individual, intellectual freedom were interlinked. In this
sense the writing of politics by means of imaginative autobiography was
appropriate, with the personal and political being intricately interwoven. O'Malley's disciplined, carefully layered autobiographies repeatedly bear this out. His use, for example, of personally resonant literary
reference to amplify a political point is telling. Herman Melville's 1851
masterpiece *Moby-Dick* is put to such use: O'Malley loved the book,
read and re-read it often, took extensive notes on it, read it to his children, and discussed it with friends. Much in the book appealed to him:
the sea, Melville's recognition that one's own experiences are far more
effectively communicated to the reader if backed up with research on
the subject more generally, and his obsessively meticulous taxonomic
detail. Melville's unresting and brilliantly allusive book is drawn into
O'Malley's account of the Irish Revolution; in prison in 1924 he
lamented the low quality of reading material which absorbed his fellow
Republican inmates and tried to remedy the situation:

When one gave them a decent book they invariably read it and asked for
another by the same author, or another on the same subject. I gave them my

books. *Moby-Dick* was a favourite. I had copies of it sent in to me for the men. I had re-read it many times, now I knew some of it by heart. Was not the white whale the whale of empire which devoured us, or was it the idea of freedom, which would make *brus* of us until we could improve the harpoon of a social system that would bring it alongside.[90]

The literary and the political, the personally exciting and the nationally significant, were interwoven in O'Malley's intellectual world. Books, and the life he absorbed through them, made sense of his personal and political history. Now he would write his own book, with the same objectives.

O'Malley's carefully composed and subtle autobiographies represent an important record of the Irish Revolution, and plainly exist in a different category from mere annals or reportage. Written and rewritten over a lengthy period, crafted some years after the events themselves, and substantially drafted some distance from Ireland and from Irish sources, these memoirs present both treasures and problems for the historian. It has been suggested that O'Malley is 'a more reliable guide to mentality than to reality',[91] and this identifies a crucial point. Thus, O'Malley's record of the flavour, drama, and passion of the Revolution is important, as are his powerful exposition of the Republican argument and his evocation of Republican sentiment. This should not blind us to those places in the works where misrepresentation occurs. Arguably, indeed, it is precisely the books' engaged quality which makes them so useful in evoking the Republican mentality; straightforward, accurate reportage would not have conveyed the essence of the Republican crusade.

Thus, for an obvious example, the passages of direct speech from O'Malley's Revolutionary conversations should not be—and were not intended to be—taken as verbatim accounts of historical episodes. Rather, they communicate views, character, and sentiment in ways which their author thought significant. Other unreliable details are, perhaps, more interesting to the professional historian. In his account of the 1916–21 struggle, for example, O'Malley cited Sinn Féin's 1917 declaration of intent with regard to the achievement of an Irish Republic: 'Sinn Féin aims at securing the recognition of an independent Irish Republic.'[92] He omitted to quote that part of the Sinn Féin statement which reflected the tension within the movement as to whether or not a fully separatist, Republican stand should have been taken. The actual, more equivocal, 1917 statement had read: 'Sinn Féin aims at securing the international recognition of Ireland as an independent

Irish Republic. Having achieved that status, the Irish people may, by referendum, freely choose their own form of government.'[93] Similar cases occur in the treatment of the Civil War. In his account of the August 1923 General Election O'Malley refers to his own election for Dublin North and suggests that, ironically, the transfer of 'the second preference votes of the Free State Minister for Defence, Dick Mulcahy, had given me my quota'. O'Malley's point here was that the division over the Treaty was characterized by a fundamental senselessness: 'How could one arrive at the point of view which gave him [the Free Stater, Mulcahy] first preference and myself second?'[94] In fact, this is precisely what did not happen in the election: of the 15,858 Mulcahy second preference votes reallocated to other candidates, O'Malley received only 47 (he was eventually elected without reaching the quota).[95]

The value of O'Malley's books lies less in the precise accuracy of their detailed historical record (which is questionable) than in their reconstruction of a Republican enthusiasm, of a particular Revolutionary mentality. He sought to present an account of the Revolution from a committed Republican perspective and created one of the most evocative and striking versions of that Republican case. He was not a historian, a point on which he is clear in the introduction to *On Another Man's Wound*: 'This is not a history. Dates I considered unimportant. Our people seized imaginatively on certain events, exalted them through their own folk quality of expression in song and story.'[96] This quotation usefully sets the tone of the book, for imagination and exaltation colour the work distinctively. But O'Malley the post-Revolutionary author did research deeply into history. As ever, it is important to trace the development of his approach at its different stages. His early enthusiasm for history at school—'I liked history and read outside my course'[97]—should not be confused with the later development of this interest when, for example, he became a subscriber in the 1930s to the newly established *Irish Historical Studies*. This (the joint journal of the Irish Historical Society and the Ulster Society for Irish Historical Studies) was a serious historical journal the first number of which appeared in 1938. O'Malley, indeed, began subscribing in 1938, and was a subscriber also in the 1940s and 1950s. The journal's editors, the historians R. Dudley Edwards and T. W. Moody, set out something of their purpose for this important intellectual initiative in the 'Preface' to the first number of *IHS*. Influenced by English example, and in particular that of the Institute of Historical

Research in London, Edwards and Moody were setting out to produce a journal which would fill what they thought of as a professional void:

in Ireland there is no counterpart to the Historical Association and the Institute of Historical Research in England, nor of the journals of these bodies, *History*, and the *Bulletin of the Institute of Historical Research*, respectively. Nor is there any periodical of the type of the *English Historical Review*, the *Revue Historique*, or the *American Historical Review* . . . the Irish historian is severely handicapped by the absence of any journal exclusively devoted to the scientific study of Irish history.

Moody and Edwards hoped that the journal would be 'of service to the specialist, the teacher, and the general reader who has an intelligent interest in the subject'.[98]

The journal certainly offered much to O'Malley, who felt it important that a continuous tradition of Irish scholarship be firmly established. Many of the topics covered in *IHS* related closely to his historical interests. Volume One (1938–9), for example, contained pieces dealing with Anglo-Irish local government in the late fifteenth and early sixteenth centuries, with Hugh O'Neill, with the plantation of Ulster, and with the eighteenth-century United Irishmen; Volume Two (1940–1) included work dealing with Poynings' Law, and with the United Irishmen. Thus, O'Malley's serious historical interests were nurtured by this new development in Irish intellectual life. He delved deeply into historical reading. This did not focus exclusively on Ireland — he read work by many authors, including R. H. Tawney, J. E. Neale, A. F. Pollard, and the pages of the *English Historical Review* — but his interest, not surprisingly, did concentrate most sustainedly upon Ireland. He read the work of Edmund Curtis, and the journal of the Cork Historical and Archaeological Society; he worked extensively on Ireland under the Tudors, taking lengthy notes in particular on Hugh O'Neill and on the late-sixteenth-century Spanish Armada; he became absorbed by T. W. Moody's influential and erudite book, *The Londonderry Plantation 1609–1641* (published in 1939); he was interested in the mid-seventeenth-century Cromwellian settlement; and he held that the early modern European context was vital for understanding the development of Irish history and that, in particular, the then prevalence of religious persecution established the proper context for understanding the emergence of Irish divisions.

O'Malley, therefore, displayed an impressive intellectual range in his historical reading, drawing on the newly professionalized work which covered a broad canvas. The tremendously extensive, obsessively detailed notes which he took year by year provided him with a sturdy foundation, and with material on which to base more published writings than in fact emerged. He tended towards perfectionism. Having written in New Mexico and New York the first draft of what was to become *The Singing Flame*, he felt it unfinished; by the early 1950s he also had drafts of the *Raids and Rallies* material and of his biographical study of County Longford IRA leader Sean Connolly. Pressures and distractions slowed down the process of finishing and publishing more books. As he himself put it, towards the end of his life, 'Family, becoming a farmer, and other things—having a wife mostly—threw me off my real work.'[99] Unfinished and unpublished though much of his writing remained, the work does add significantly to our view of the man. The 50,000 words written on Sean Connolly (1890–1921) reflect O'Malley's keenness that biographies be written of the Revolutionaries and the political figures of the period. He wrote the study with a view to reaching those from a generation which accepted what freedom there was in Ireland without knowledge—from books or from memory—of the struggles in the past which had won that freedom. The Connolly book was intended to be the right kind of record, of which O'Malley thought there were far too few: 'As a race we have not kept records, nor have we written in anything but the sparsest way about movements or organizations which have influenced the past seventy years.'[100] When historical episodes were indeed scrutinized, it was by no means an encouraging story which emerged, but O'Malley remained keen that the exploration should be pursued and that honest, tough lessons should be learned as a consequence. In an untitled manuscript draft from the post-Second World War period, for instance, he detailed his views on the Irish Civil War, which had

split the comradeship of united effort, weakened the nation by bitterness and harsh memory, and made people doubt intention and motive. . . . One immediate result of this strife was a new understanding and an unromantic realization of ourselves as a people. At one time it had been easy to blame the British for our faults and easy to interpret them in terms of conditions forced on us by historical necessity; now, some learned to analyse cause and effect, to blame themselves and to face the evil necessity of power.[101]

III

Oh beauty, beauty, now you hold
Me captive in your thrall.
Spread but your wings and take your flight,
I follow at your call.

(Ernie O'Malley)[102]

Ernie O'Malley read and wrote vast amounts of poetry. As ever, his invaluable notebooks bear witness to the focus of his concentration. Whitman, Dickinson, Yeats, Frost, Pound, Eliot, Cummings, Crane, and Auden occupied much of his attention during his North American sojourn. He was fascinated by the development of poetic styles as evident in such writers. So, too, he took extensive notes on Shakespeare's sonnets—his literary companions from the Civil War days—and he also retained his long-held interest in the poetry of Patrick Pearse, whose verse his own early poetic scribblings had resembled. But it was only during the late 1920s that O'Malley began to write large numbers of poems. The O'Malley poems published in the mid-1930s by *Poetry* (the American magazine of verse edited by Harriet Monroe) reflect his approach rather well: impressions of New Mexico and re-creations of Ireland vied with one another. As we have seen, O'Malley's Irish reflections during his American period helped define and produce his important prose works; his poetry from these years is characterized by some similar colours. His poem 'Connemara', for example, distinctly resembles lyrical episodes from his autobiographical prose:

Bleak hungry land,
Strewn rock, blue mountain bulk.
Grey with mists of despair,
Sea lashed by storming waves,
Wind beaten, wind moulded.
Bare the pattern of life
Woven by your elements.
Nature's moods in your eyes,
In your proud heart old song.
Lost grace in your courtesy.
Strength of word in Gaelic speech.
Grey, bleak, hungry land
Haunting us, calling us back.[103]

The same terms ('bare', 'haunting', 'grey', 'hungry') are all deployed in relation to the same part of western Ireland in *On Another Man's*

Wound.[104] But O'Malley's poetry sometimes also displays his sympathies through a rather lighter expression:

'Dislikes'

I do not like a well-trimmed lawn
As billiard table for a fawn.
Nor an undoggy, mannered pug
That blends so gently with a rug.
I do not like a womaned man
Starched til he is pale and wan.[105]

O'Malley's poetry is not sustainedly serious in the way that, for example, that of his friend Hart Crane assuredly was. But much can none the less be learned from it. O'Malley's poetry pointed towards his increasingly artistic and intellectual preoccupations during the inter-war years. 'Peace' (1935):

A table to work at in the centre of a room
Ink and a pen, paper and a chair
Light from a window and four walls
That is content after long wandering
That is peace within four walls.[106]

His poems demonstrated the extent to which he had become entranced with New Mexico. See, for example, his celebration of the New Mexican 'Sunset':

Bright beauty comes to bless the hills
before the calm of night;
pain is remembered with a song
and anguish with delight.[107]

In particular he celebrated the peace of New Mexico in his poetry, and extolled the many qualities of the Indians there: 'New Mexico':

Who has seen the Indian smile
Inwardly, with pleasing face,
Has sensed the glory of this land
Guarding well its strength of grace.[108]

Simultaneously, the poems show that he remained very much absorbed in Ireland, and his poetry helpfully amplifies this point. This had been true of his earlier poetry — 'To Ireland' (1926):

Fair Lady, I offer up to you
This little sheaf of words: 'tis true

> That you may find them worthless, dull
> Then know, please, that my heart's too full
> To write of you e'en though I think
> So much, and hover on the brink
> Of words.[109]

But it was true also of his later work, in an exile period during much of which he felt distinct pulls towards returning to Ireland.

O'Malley's poems frequently reflect his lighter side (often hidden in much of his other writing) and indicate his many preferences (repeatedly celebrating mountains, trees, animals, birds, and in particular the natural setting of the west of Ireland). They also reflect his essential Romanticism. 'Beauty's Pilgrim' has him exclaim,

> Oh beauty, beauty, now you hold
> Me captive in your thrall.
> Spread but your wings and take your flight,
> I follow at your call.[110]

'Ecstasy' is a frequently recurrent word throughout O'Malley's poems, and with the ecstatic immersion in beauty we reach a point of central importance. In *The Singing Flame* he made an explicit link between the pursuit of beauty and his political commitment: 'If I could find an acceptance of the two lives, that of the struggle, and that of one's own development in the feeling of beauty and all its shades which I could not express—that would be an ideal.'[111] These two Romanticisms—the aesthetic and the political—would fulfil his ideal if he were able simultaneously to combine them within himself. O'Malley's intellectual life, and in particular the nature of his writing, makes full sense only if one appreciates this point.

If connections exist between the two struggles for emancipation, then there are also other echoes between the separatist and the aesthete evident in his poetry. An honest simplicity of approach:

> Oh love be kind
> As you are good
> And you will find
> Me all you should[112]

coexists on occasions with a striking, adolescent naivety:

> You smiled at me
> And my heart beat
> Exceedingly

You spoke to me
And it was like
To ecstasy

You touched my hand
And I was straight
In Fairyland.[113]

But—and again the echoes from his political writings are clear—there
is also a profound self-consciousness in some of O'Malley's poetry.
Consider this Jekyll-looking-at-Hyde, Stevensonian poem from 1928:

I looked into the glass that night
Before I went to bed
And there my soul scowled out at me
As if it had been wed
To hate and sin and misery.
Twas shrivelled, bent and old.
With shifty glance it eyéd me
As if it had been sold.
And when I took away my eyes
And looked back at the glass
It still glared out with malice grim
Nor did the vision pass.[114]

Again, O'Malley's poem 'Doubt' refers tellingly to 'The certainty I
lack' and also to doubt's being 'as hard as hunger' to endure.[115] And his
variety of mood and attitude is suggested in an O'Malley poem from
February 1928:

Like to a stringéd harp
Through which a changing wind
Blows gusts, now soft, now sharp
Veering from harsh to kind
Is the kingdom of my mind.[116]

Just as his lasting scholarly interest in poetry reflected his pursuit of
erudition, therefore, so his attempts at his own poetry vigorously
demonstrated many important features of his imaginative, intellectual,
and emotional life.

IV

I . . . made for the National Gallery [London] tripping over English people feeding pigeons in Trafalgar Square. That's their emotional outlet. Bomb frontier towns in north west India and compensate by being soppy to pigeons in Trafalgar Square. The Gallery was a joy so I remained there as long as I could.

(Ernie O'Malley)[117]

As the above quotation demonstrates, O'Malley's increasing immersion during the 1930s in the world of the arts was not accompanied by the removal of his sharp convictions concerning British political iniquity. But his post-Revolutionary framework was essentially artistic, intellectual, and—as ever—wide-ranging in its influences. Much of his concern, indeed, lay with the avoidance of parochialism and of Irish isolation. In the mid-1940s he contributed an essay entitled 'Renaissance' to an edition of *La France Libre*, the Irish section of which also featured contributions by writers such as Patrick Kavanagh and Frank O'Connor. O'Malley's own piece reflected his ongoing convictions about the Irish Revolution ('En 1916 apparut un mouvement de résistance qui mobilisa peu à peu les ressources de la nation, et qui fut, dans l'Europe contemporaine, le premier mouvement de résistance efficace' [In 1916 there appeared a resistance movement which, gradually, mobilized the nation's resources, and was the first effective resistance movement in contemporary Europe])[118] and this essay is also instructive regarding O'Malley's view of contemporary Irish circumstances:

L'Irlande est essentiellement éloignée des affaires mondiales. Jusqu'au traité de 1922, une partie de son énergie fut dirigée, sans régularité d'ailleurs, vers la conquête de la liberté politique. Depuis un siècle et demi au moins, l'Irlande était coupée de tout contact avec le continent; et sa population, privée d'échanges intellectuels ou artistiques tangibles et féconds, n'était capable ni d'avoir elle-même ni de provoquer chez les autres peuples un genre de réactions qui pût faciliter la compréhension. Elle avait d'instinct du respect et de l'affection pour certains pays, notamment pour la France, l'Espagne, l'Italie et les peuples opprimés, mais ces sentiments correspondaient à une «compréhension du cœur» qui n'avait rien à voir avec l'avenir politique ou intellectuel des pays étrangers. [Ireland is, essentially, remote from world affairs. Up till the Treaty of 1922 [*sic*] part of her energy was directed, albeit intermittently, towards the achievement of political freedom. For at least a century and a half Ireland had been cut off from all contact with the continent; and her population, deprived of meaningful and fruitful intellectual or artistic exchanges, were not capable either of producing in themselves or of inducing in other peoples the kind of reactions that might have made understanding easier. She had instinctive respect and affection for certain countries, notably France, Spain, Italy, and oppressed peoples, but these sentiments corresponded to an 'understanding of the heart' which had nothing to do with the business of understanding foreign countries' political or intellectual future.][119]

This picks up themes which O'Malley addressed elsewhere about Irish isolation and it also reflects the connections between his views of the Revolution and his wider social and cultural considerations regarding Ireland's place in the world. For while O'Malley's most important body of written work focused on his earlier Revolutionary enthusiasms, his writing was much broader than this. Other artistic, intellectual, and social interests lengthily preoccupied him, and important continuities and links bind together his Revolutionary and his artistic work. This is clear, for example, in relation to painting. O'Malley was committed to a serious appreciation of painting, as of the wider arts. Ever the patriot, he was also keen on the preservation and celebration of the arts in, of, and for Ireland. He was a member in 1945 of the Friends of the National Collections of Ireland, a society whose purpose was to secure artistic works and historic objects for Irish national or public collections. But he also possessed a discerning eye, and became an effective and committed art critic.

Moreover, O'Malley's approach to painting reflected his wider enthusiasms: 'when a tradition loses life, vitality, and spiritual feeling artists break away from the tradition of their fathers and grandfathers and are vitalized by their own fresh vision and by inspiration from a neglected aspect of the past'; 'Art is a thing of the spirit'.[120] Vitality, vigour, and spirit were crucial to his political vision of the nation as to his artistic approach. And O'Malley had displayed a thirst for aesthetic knowledge and nourishment during his Revolutionary career: a letter to the artist Estella Solomons, written from prison in November 1923 shortly after the end of his forty-one-day hunger strike, captures something of his early artistic preferences and obsessions, not to mention his rather demanding approach to correspondents:

I am very interested in art, especially in the older Italian, Spanish, and Dutch schools. Above all I love Albrecht Dürer's etchings and woodcuts. I know nothing of modern art, just a little of modern etching. . . . Could you please send me a well illustrated book on Dürer? If you have not one could you, please, get me one? Also I would like any old art periodicals or books which you could spare and do not want.[121]

Keen to celebrate the locally distinctive while avoiding the parochial, O'Malley sought to balance rusticity with sophistication. In 1939 in Burrishoole, County Mayo, he reflected: 'I dream of pictures down here and read of them: seeing them is another matter.'[122] The paintings on which his imagination fed were drawn from an impressively wide range of artists. He studied and was absorbed by Fra Angelico, Botticelli, Louis le Brocquy, Caravaggio, Cézanne, Chagall, Degas, Donatello, Dürer, Evie Hone, Gauguin, Giotto, van Gogh, Goya, Greco, Mainie Jellett, Kandinsky, Klee, Leonardo, Maillol, Mantegna, Matisse, Norah McGuinness, Michelangelo, Modigliani, O'Keeffe, Picasso, Pissarro, Nano Reid, Rembrandt, Renoir, Rouault, Rubens, Velazquez, Vlaminck, Zurbarán.

O'Malley spent much time visiting galleries, and was particularly taken with novel developments. In late 1942, for example, he was impressed by the exhibition, 'In Theatre Street', at Dublin's Contemporary Picture Galleries (an exhibition of theatre design). He also wrote fluently and with considerable talent about a wide range of artistic subjects. Typically meticulous attention was, for instance, evident in a manuscript piece on a Goya *Portrait*: a verbal depiction of the painting was followed by O'Malley's more imaginative responses, in particular his celebration of Goya's importance in restoring vitality to Spanish painting and in evincing another of O'Malley's favourite qualities, vigour. Indeed, one can sense O'Malley's identification with the spirit of the painter as he observes that Goya 'ended eighteenth century painting and by himself began the new century. He is individual, the new type of artist who fights for his own ideas and who says what he thinks . . . his sense of colour is new, fresh, and vigorous.'[123] But of particular interest, perhaps, is O'Malley's work on Irish painting and its context. A fascinating piece from January 1947 dealt with contemporary Irish attitudes towards painting, and broadened out into a reflective consideration of the context and condition of intellectual life in Ireland. Remote and otherworldly, undisciplined, emotional, and friendly, Ireland was, according to O'Malley, 'seldom indifferent for one must take sides not only on political issues but even on the worth of a play or on the obvious superiority of your native county'. Censorship—'an insult to intelligence'—prevented Irish readers from experiencing the work of their own writers, and there were problems too with the atmosphere in which Irish painters found themselves: not many people, he argued, were interested in art and there were few commercial galleries. But significant artists there were, and O'Malley was very much in the vanguard as one of their most enthusiastic and thoughtful supporters. Jack Yeats and Nano Reid were of weight, and Dublin-born Evie Hone was 'possibly the most important artist in [stained glass] in western Europe'.[124]

Hone's death in 1955 greatly upset O'Malley: 'Today in London I heard sad news. Evie Hone is dead. She was the best glass worker in western Europe.'[125] Having been trained in London and influenced by a subsequent period in Paris, Hone had imbibed the influences of Braque, Matisse, Picasso, and Chagall. She impressed O'Malley as precisely the kind of distinctive, non-parochial talent Ireland should be producing. O'Malley bought work by Hone, including 'May Morning', 'The Crucifixion', and 'Still Life', and indeed he and Helen together built up an impressive collection of paintings. O'Malley owned many works by modern Irish artists, including Mainie Jellett's 'Study for Clew Bay', a Norah McGuinness 'Landscape', and numerous works by Jack B. Yeats, including: 'Dinner in a Room in Sligo', 'Death for Only One', 'Paper Bags for Hats', 'Reverie: On a Train from Sligo' (this last bought from Dublin's Dawson Gallery for £300, and paid for in three instalments during 1945–7). Hone (1894–1955), Jellett (1897–1944), McGuinness (1903–80), and Yeats (1871–1957) between them occupied much of O'Malley's artistic attention. Yeats in particular was important to him. London-born son of the portrait painter John Butler Yeats (1839–1922) and brother of the poet William Butler Yeats (1865–1939), Jack was trained in London but concentrated much of his work on Irish subjects. O'Malley greatly enjoyed the freshness, subtlety, and vitality of his work, and was understandably impressed by the painter's inventiveness with magnificent colours and by his powerful imagination. He celebrated the way Yeats responded to the physical surroundings of the west of Ireland, and also the way he interpreted the life there: like O'Malley, Yeats drew much of the inspiration for his work from Ireland. O'Malley liked Yeats the man (whom he thought 'wise, human, kind'),[126] and took detailed notes on his paintings. The two men appreciated one another. Yeats sold some of his work directly to O'Malley (the 1937 oil, 'Death for Only One', being sold by the artist, for example, in 1939), and they were for a time in frequent contact (O'Malley: 'Once I went to see him when I was in Dublin almost once each week. I am very fond of Jack').[127] Their conversations would range from paintings to literature (in the late 1930s they decided that 'There is no poetic content in [George Bernard Shaw's] words . . . and yet he has dramatic content')[128] and this Yeatsian connection further underlines O'Malley's involvement in the small but important world of post-Revolutionary Irish modernism.

Indeed, his absorption in Yeats pre-dates the painter's achievement of wider popular recognition in the 1940s, and here O'Malley deserves credit for his acuity of vision. He justifiably considered Yeats 'the most important painter this country has yet produced',[129] and observed of him that 'To Irish landscape Yeats has brought a fresh vision and a creative palette. . . . His development . . . is primarily that of a colourist, who surprises, enchants, and disturbs, with his economy of means, sureness of touch, and that sense of inevitability which makes his paint induce one to study and study again a canvas, which to a casual observer, may seem a fortuitous improvization.'[130] There is something in the argument that, during the early twentieth century, Irish Republicanism drew sustenance from an isolationist, Sinn Féinish approach whereas artistic modernism in Ireland concentrated its focus on wider, international connections. But O'Malley's international perspective and Jack Yeats's sympathetic, detailed observance of the parochially Irish both testify to a more complicated situation. Certainly, O'Malley the post-Revolutionary Republican shared with Irish modernists the view that the most effective way of raising standards was by means of exposure to, rather than avoidance of, wider influences. And Yeats the internationally influenced modernist devoted much attention to portraying in vividly evocative, sensitive ways the distinctively local Ireland which the Republicans helped to create.

O'Malley had close involvement with other important Irish artists, including the highly original Louis le Brocquy (b. 1916), who was also a friend of Jack Yeats, and who met O'Malley through his mother, Sybil le Brocquy. O'Malley influenced the Dublin-born painter (le Brocquy: 'He taught me much, in Burrishoole, in Dublin, in the Forties, through his gentle but passionate ideas on art, on life')[131] and, indeed, le Brocquy later recalled that he had been 'devoted' to O'Malley 'during the war years in Ireland'.[132] The two men became good friends; they met mostly in Dublin and sometimes in Burrishoole, O'Malley helping le Brocquy to discover the west. O'Malley greatly respected the painter's work, and devoted to it a 1946 piece in the English review *Horizon*. In this he sensitively traced le Brocquy's influences and development, and stressed the importance to Irish art of wider influences (appropriately enough, perhaps, as this is something echoed throughout le Brocquy's career in terms of international influences and settings):

As nineteenth century and contemporary work is very poorly represented in Irish galleries, students have had to depend on visits to Europe for analysis, understanding, and stimulation. The need for the steady influence of good examples of creative work, which can meet prejudice or change it to acceptance or understanding, was most felt during the [Second World] War. Indeed, until generosity enriches this deeply felt want, people and painters here will remain isolated from first-class minds expressing contemporary ideas in terms of paint.[133]

Le Brocquy combined a profound sense of Irish identity with an openness to international settings, influences, and perspectives. This suited O'Malley's own sympathies, and le Brocquy's work features in the collection which the O'Malleys between them built up. So, too, does the work of many other Irish artists: Hone, Jellett, McGuinness, and Yeats have been referred to, but mention should also be made of Paul Henry (1876–1958), Cecil Salkeld (1904–68), Nano Reid (1905–81), Patrick Hennessy (1915–80), Gerard Dillon (1916–71), and Anne Yeats (b. 1919). O'Malley was keen on the establishment of a national painting tradition in Ireland ('In paint also a tradition of seeing and of understanding has yet to be established'),[134] but the O'Malleys' collection also included artists drawn from wider settings: John Piper and Henry Moore; Georges Rouault and Aristide Maillol; Amedeo Modigliani; and the American photographer Paul Strand. The English painter and designer John Piper, and the English sculptor Henry Moore, were of interest to Ernie O'Malley and, indeed, reflected his concern that Irish attention be paid to wider frameworks as well as to domestic work. Writing in *The Bell* in 1947 he concentrated attention on a Dublin exhibition of contemporary English drawings, paintings, and sculptures; this included pieces by Moore and Piper themselves ('Henry Moore and John Piper have a good showing of sound work') and was important as 'the first comprehensive showing in Dublin of contemporary English work'.[135]

The inclusion of Strand's work in the O'Malleys' collection is also significant. Photography played an important part in the lives of Ernie and Helen: they worked together on photographing a wide range of Irish subjects, while O'Malley's friendships and interests stretched to

Strand, Edward Weston, Alfred Stieglitz, and Georgia O'Keeffe. With Strand, O'Malley was especially close. He admired the man's work ('He is a fine photographer')[136] and the two coincided in California, New Mexico, and on O'Malley's visits to Paris. Their letters indicate considerable affection and respect, reflected in the aforementioned plan to collaborate on a book.

Painting and photography were complemented in O'Malley's artistic world by a profound interest in sculpture. From 1937 onwards O'Malley made considerable effort to study Irish sculpture from the twelfth to the seventeenth centuries. He was especially interested in medieval Irish religious sculpture and architecture. He visited and photographed large numbers of monasteries, read up on them, and exhibited here once again a Thomas Davis-like enthusiasm for knowing and understanding all things Irish. Sculpture was something shared with Helen—herself an accomplished sculptress[137]—and for Ernie it was profoundly important: 'Sculpture is a definite and important heritage which should be a source of true pride to our imagination and to our eyes, and a challenge to creative inspiration.'[138] It should also, in O'Malley's view, be great fun: 'the proper way to see sculpture is with sun and plenty of whiskey'.[139] This was not just a matter of Irish settings. In Mexico in 1931 O'Malley was preoccupied studying local sculpture, and his lasting interest in architecture should, perhaps, be seen in connection with this. Again, his travel reflections are telling. He took intrigued note of New York's architecture on his arrival there in October 1928: 'The skyscrapers did not seem so gigantic, perhaps because the smaller buildings were ten to twenty stories high. Some skyscrapers looking like houses of cards built up at random—bare, raw looking—others were rectangular, but had some ornamentation; few were beautiful.'[140] He did consider many of the buildings in the southern part of Manhattan to be beautifully proportioned, and after a few days in the city concluded that 'It is only from on high that one can appreciate New York'.[141] He was particularly struck by the Woolworth Building, New York's tallest until 1930 and surely one of its most beautiful. Decisive, often dramatic, essentially aesthetic judgements characterize him here as in so much of his life.

V

'[A]n imaginative story: the best of its kind I have ever read.'[142]
(Ernie O'Malley, on Kafka's *The Castle*)

As noted in relation to Jack B. Yeats, O'Malley's relationship with artistic modernism was significant in terms of his intellectual development and setting. With literature, O'Malley moved from the typically anti-modern Revolutionary view of the 1916–23 period, to an enthusiastic embracing of modernism during his post-Revolutionary life. There is nothing necessarily anti-Republican about this at all. O'Malley took methodical, systematic, copious, hugely detailed notes on James Joyce, but the recent attempts to challenge the idea of a revisionist Joyce[143] render that less surprising, perhaps, than some would initially assume. Similarly, we have seen with Hart Crane that there was a notable overlap in terms of influences, literary ambitions, and outlook. A case could also be made to suggest that O'Malley's keenness on D. H. Lawrence fitted neatly with his consistently held political views: Anne Fernihough's recent depiction of Lawrence's anti-Imperialistic aesthetics might provide scholarly grounds for such an argument.[144]

As reflected in Fernihough's argument, Lawrence cannot neatly be fitted into either a straightforward left-wing or right-wing ideological framework. Ernie O'Malley (deeply read in Lawrence, and even jokingly accused by some of his New Mexican friends of trying to emulate Lawrence with his red beard) is equally difficult to fit into either ideological pigeon-hole. This is an important point, for O'Malley's Irish Republicanism was tied in with his wider views of intellectual life and of international politics. And in the post-Revolutionary era vital intellectual and political battles could not easily be evaded. O'Malley's friend Louis MacNeice is again of relevance here. Despite their friendship, there were important differences between the two men. They shared some similar interests, but their intellectual and political approaches were divergent in significant ways. MacNeice the Protestant northerner was profoundly sceptical about what he saw as the Romantic assumptions crucial to Irish nationalism. Disaffection, distance, and unavoidable attachment to Ireland are there in both men, but in distinctively different ways. O'Malley reflected critically on aspects of the Irish Revolution, but very much as a Republican who was disillusioned with Republicans' failure rather than with their political project itself. Not surprisingly, given his origins, MacNeice's scepticism is written in a quite different key:

> The bombs in the turnip sack, the sniper from the roof,
> Griffith, Connolly, Collins, where have they brought us?
> Ourselves alone! Let the round tower stand aloof
> In a world of bursting mortar!
> Let the school-children fumble their sums
> In a half-dead language;
> Let the censor be busy on the books; pull down the Georgian slums;
> Let the games be played in Gaelic.[145]

This poem ('Autumn Journal', written in 1938) brings us to another telling difference between the two men: their divergent approaches to the Second World War. In the west of Ireland in 1942 MacNeice stayed in a hotel in County Mayo in which the German Minister to Ireland (Eduard Hempel) was also staying. Hempel (who was not a member of the Nazi party, but who was prepared to explain the National Socialists' policy towards Jews 'primarily' in terms of the Jews' own behaviour after the First World War)[146] was a friend of O'Malley, and the latter offered MacNeice a letter of introduction — which the poet gruffly refused. Unlike MacNeice's, O'Malley's attitude towards Hempel, and indeed towards the Second World War itself, was fundamentally ambivalent.[147] O'Malley followed reports of the war (not least through the British newspapers) but the conflict was essentially remote from him, especially when he was in Burrishoole.[148] Indeed, he deliberately stood some way back from partisan involvement in this world conflict. In response to the objection that one of his friends during this period was a Fascist, he observed: 'As if that made any difference. I can't carry round my wars with me all the time. Goodness knows I have enough hangover from fighting against an Empire to quarrel with ideologies. . . . People are more important to me now, anyhow.'[149] Personal friendship overruled ideological objections.

O'Malley was fundamentally sympathetic to the Irish government's policy of neutrality during the Second World War. For most of the state's inhabitants, neutrality made good sense for both pragmatic and symbolic reasons. In O'Malley's view, neutrality was 'more than anything else an expression of nationality and a determination to pursue that attitude of mind in spite of adjacent and distant pressure'. He recognized that Ireland was '(in essence) remote from world affairs' and that this remoteness was increased during the war: 'As the war developed Ireland became more indrawn and isolated.'[150] This isolation was partly justified for O'Malley by a conception that the British and German protagonists were roughly deserving of equal sympathy (or the lack of it). In July 1940 he answered his son Cahal's question 'Are the Germans bad?' with the verdict: 'No worse than the English at times.'[151] On occasions his Second World War sympathies seem to have leaned towards the German side. In November 1941, for example, he recorded that he thought it 'a realistic view' to argue that 'the Germans dominate Europe and the sooner they can get along with the new order and put it to work the better'.[152]

O'Malley was not a Fascist; on 5 November 1936 in Dawson Street, Dublin, he had, for example, chaired a meeting of Irish Republicans in sympathy with the anti-Franco forces in Spain. This was a dissident gesture in contemporary Ireland, where sympathy for Franco was widespread, and the meeting had prompted a severe response from the *Irish Independent*. The paper claimed to have 'taken its stand with the Pope and with the Irish Hierarchy'; in contrast, the newspaper asserted, the Dawson Street group had 'insulted the name of decent Irish Republicanism by their vile suggestion that Irish Republicans have any sympathy with the murderers of priests and the destroyers of churches. The dead who died for Irish freedom would turn in their graves at the suggestion that Irish Republicanism is to be compared with Spanish anti-God communism.'[153] During the 1939–45 world war there were significant sections of Irish society which actively favoured the Nazis.[154] O'Malley was not part of that group. But his ambivalent attitude during the war is instructive, emerging in part from a reluctance to back the British, from a sense of weariness with ideological battles, and from a belief that Irish neutrality made sense both symbolically and practically.

Moreover, O'Malley's intellectual life cannot accurately be assessed without reference to wider ideological themes in contemporary Europe. The key point to stress is that left and right during the early twentieth century frequently drank from the same well of ideas and O'Malley, like many other intellectuals of the period, defies neat categorization. He could seem clearly anti-Fascist, as in the following comment on W. B. Yeats: 'as a human being he tended to become an Irishman founded in the eighteenth century, close to the Anglo-Irish who held their lands—their lands confiscated from our people—and their prejudice. As I reread his remarks I see how retrograde from the point of essential freedom he was. Lady Gregory might have helped him, but Yeats went his own Fascist way.'[155] But, as noted, he could also at times show sympathy for the Second World War Germans, and the early 1920s Republican world which he had inhabited indisputably echoed many themes of continental Fascism: the emphasis on sacrifice, the cult of youth, the celebration of militarism, the anti-democratic slant, the desire for the rebirth of ancient culture. Key to O'Malley's thinking was a persistent anti-bourgeois sympathy (common among the right as among the left in the early twentieth century), a conviction that the materialistic, soulless, egotistical, commercial modern individual should be opposed with a spiritually richer alternative. This sense was evident in his Revolutionary enthusiasm and was also relevant to his contacts in New Mexico (with the Taos circle), in Mexico (with Hart Crane), and with the Group Theatre.

The anti-bourgeois opposition to commercialism echoes one of the most influential of artist intellectuals, Richard Wagner. O'Malley listened to, read, and took notes on Wagner (part of his enduring enthusiasm for what some would still be brave enough to describe as serious music). He was also interested in Bach, Beethoven, Berlioz, Bizet, Brahms, Bruckner, Chopin, Debussy, Donizetti, Dvorak, Franck, Haydn, Handel, Liszt, Mozart, Mendelssohn, Prokoviev, Puccini, Rachmaninov, Ravel, Rimsky-Korsakof, Rossini, Scarlatti, Schubert, Schumann, Scriabin, Shostakovich, Sibelius, Richard Strauss, Stravinsky, Tchaikovsky, Vaughan Williams, Verdi, Walton, and Weber. Typically, he embarked upon an extensive range of relevant reading and scholarship and, as ever, took lengthy notes on such work. These bore testimony to his unrelenting discipline: he meticulously worked through, for example, the works of Beethoven, cataloguing those he needed most urgently to listen to in depth. He ordered them by type (symphony, piano sonata, string quartet, trio) and then subdivided each of these groups listing in order those which he prioritized from each type of work. And, as suggested above, the musical interests related to wider themes and Wagner is perhaps the most telling illustration. The great nineteenth-century German composer reminds us, for example, about the possible complexities of Romantic revolutionary thought. The Wagnerian conception of revolution involved purging the German nation of Jewishness, and his revolutionism has been seen to point both to left and right: both anti-Jewishness and socialism were important to his revolutionary thinking. So, too, Irish Republican Revolutionism held complexities: within the Irish Revolution the racial and the Revolutionary were tightly interwoven.[156]

This consideration of the wider social and cultural implications of listening to music is in line with the approach advocated by, among others, Professor Edward Said;[157] and Said's work highlights other crucial aspects of O'Malley the intellectual. In his 1993 Reith Lectures, broadcast on the BBC, Professor Said argued against the professionalization of intellectual life, preferring instead what he described as intellectual 'amateurism, literally, an activity that is fuelled by care and affection rather than by profit, and selfish, narrow specialization'.[158] Rather than seeing intellectual life as something involving certified expertise, rigid specialization, a bias towards the powerful, and a paid role within the structures which sustain the powerful, Said argued instead for the engaged, amateur intellectual: one whose range is broad, who transcends narrow specialism and sees the larger picture, who seeks to advance freedom and knowledge, and who speaks for the weak and unrepresented rather than for the powerful. In some ways, O'Malley might be seen as a precursor of Professor Said's idealized intellectual. He was a talented intellectual working outside the established structures. In contrast, for example, with Louis MacNeice — who had obtained a First in Mods and in Greats at Oxford University, and who had become a university lecturer — O'Malley's intellectual life was comparatively unblessed by formal, institutional recognition. He had never completed his university degree, and he operated outside rather than within society's formal structures for intellectuals (experiencing the Chomskian advantages and drawbacks of such a position).[159] Moreover, O'Malley avoided narrowness of specialization. His research included European and wider history, painting, music, sculpture, literature, and politics; and he attempted to draw together the various themes which he encountered in each of these fields. Espousing the cause of freedom and greatly venerating knowledge, repeatedly adopting the role of the dissident rather than adhering to comfortable orthodoxy, and even using the BBC to denounce the evils of colonialism, O'Malley fits Professor Said's description rather neatly.

But Said's work also points us to more complicated questions which are vital to our understanding of O'Malley's intellectual setting. Many scholars have sought to place Irish experience within the explanatory framework of colonialism. This has yielded much intriguing work, and when presented by intellectuals such as Said it has often been illuminating. But the serious student of O'Malley's Republican and post-Revolutionary experience must register doubts about the inclusiveness and explanatory power of this approach. Let us consider the matter a little more closely. Said has, for example, defined Imperialism and colonialism as involving the metropolitan subjection and settlement of 'distant' territories, and yet seeks to depict the British–Irish relationship according to such a paradigm. He talks misleadingly of 'Europe's special ways of representing' Ireland, thereby implying that Ireland has somehow existed outside Europe (a notion which looks distinctly implausible to those familiar with Irish history). Moreover, Said rather simplistically concentrates on 'resistance' to Imperialism and colonialism as the defining response of the 'native' culture. Even if one were to accept the inclusion of Ireland within this Imperial or colonial framework, the concentration on resistance rather than integration is only possible if one ignores the experience of vast numbers of Irish people in the modern period, people whose experience has been far less determined by 'resistance' than Professor Said's account would suggest.[160] Irish people's experience has been more complicated than simply to have involved, or been defined by, resistance to British influence or power. Many Irish people embraced as much as they resisted. Moreover, even in the case of Ernie O'Malley—than whom there could be no more active resister—the response to Britishness was very ambiguous. To suggest that resistance should somehow serve as a definition of authentic Irishness is to rely on casual assumption rather than on a rigorous examination of the evidence.

This point can be expanded to include discussion of wider themes in which O'Malley was deeply interested. Said argues, for example, that 'Irish people can never be English any more than Cambodians or Algerians can be French', and also that 'India, North Africa, the Caribbean, Central and South America, many parts of Africa, China and Japan, the Pacific archipelago, Malaysia, Australia, New Zealand, North America, and of course Ireland belong in a group together'.[161] These assertions are distinctly misleading. The division into the exclusive categories of 'Irish' and 'English' misses the point that, for many Irish people in the modern period (and not just Ulster unionists), it is Britishness rather than Englishness which is important; for these Irish people there was nothing mutually exclusive about the categories of Irishness and Britishness.[162] Moreover, it is far from clear that the regions in Said's lengthy list actually do belong together as he suggests. Certainly, there are strong economic arguments to compel an alternative view, and it might be suggested that colonial and post-colonial frameworks actually fit Ireland rather poorly.[163]

Indeed, the colonization-resistance-decolonization model does appear rather crude when applied to Ireland and, tellingly, its exponents often appear ignorant of recent historiographical argument. The post-colonial model can be rather a constricting one and, certainly, the post-colonial framework ill-fits Ireland in key respects. Scholars such as David Lloyd have employed a post-colonial approach to Ireland with some ingenuity, but have on occasions simplified the political in order to retain their strict theoretical model. Thus, for example, Professor Lloyd's undefended assertion that there was something *artificial* about the creation of Northern Ireland[164] implies that there was something more *natural* about a non-partitioned Ireland. People may feel this to be true. But it surely requires demonstration rather than mere assumption, particularly given the significant body of recent scholarly literature which confounds such a traditional outlook. The irony is that the profoundly anti-colonial Ernie O'Malley was so tireless and devoted in exploring the scholarly literature of his own day—the newly established *Irish Historical Studies*, for example—that he more than anyone would have been dissatisfied with casual, orthodox assumption. His restless pursuit of the most persuasive intellectual argument was one of his greatest and most enduring strengths.

The Companion

I

I have ever been singularly fortunate in my good friends for they have proved to be true and straight, but always something has happened to them so that now I am often afraid to make friendships.

(Ernie O'Malley)[1]

This book represents an attempt to interweave the various strands of Ernie O'Malley's life—the political, the military, the intellectual, the personal—in the belief that unless one sees the full picture then none of its sections or constituent parts can properly be understood. The current chapter examines O'Malley the companion—friend, colleague, husband, father—and endeavours to unveil something of his layered, complex personality.

O'Malley devoted much of his later life to recreating the exalted days of Revolutionary companionship; paradoxically, he had made few close friends during the Irish Revolution itself. Indeed, he was hard to please in terms of friendships throughout life, his description of childhood—'few real chums but what I had were staunch'[2]—being appropriate also to much of his later experience. His son's recollection of O'Malley's enthusiasms—emphasizing 'wine, books, and friends'[3]—is underlined by comments such as that made to O'Malley's brother

Kevin by Rebecca Citkovitz in 1949: 'He is very loyal to old friends.'[4]
Citkovitz, a devoted American friend from his emigrant years, wrote
extensively to O'Malley after his return to Ireland. Her lengthy letters
showed affection, respect, and loyalty, and just as O'Malley could
inspire such strong reactions so, too, he retained a loyal sense of attachment in turn to his intimates. This is evident in the continuation of old
Republican connections—Johnny Raleigh, Sheila Humphreys, Frank
Gallagher—and in the desire to record in writing the Republican
commitment and quality of those with whom he had fought: *On
Another Man's Wound* can, in part, be seen as a gesture of loyalty to
old friends and comrades, as well as an imaginative re-creation of the
irrecoverable past. But loyalty to individuals could also cut across the
political divisions of Irish life. O'Malley remained on good terms with
some who had taken the opposite side in the Civil War (a not uncom-
mon experience in post-1923 Ireland). Among his post-Revolutionary
friends, for example, he included Dr Matt O'Connor. As we saw in
Chapter 1, O'Connor had been the Senior Medical Officer in Mountjoy, and had been in charge of O'Malley when he was badly injured
during the Civil War. He had exaggerated the poorness of the Republican's medical condition in order that the Free State authorities
should not execute him; after the Civil War the two men remained
good friends for many years.

As this indicates, O'Malley's friendships were on occasions sharpened by the extremity of harsh circumstances. Loyalty was prized in
part because, like so many during the First World War and its after-
math, people had been lost and intimacies shattered.[5] Moreover, just
as the Revolution severed friendships, so also much of O'Malley's post-
Revolutionary experience was to reinforce his emphasis on the importance of loyalty. The Revolution had, in his view, been betrayed; this
was compounded by the libel case in the 1930s, by the painful death of
his marriage during the 1940s and early 1950s, and by his consequent
separation from two of his children. If these events sharpened his
appreciation of loyalty, they also reinforced his tendencies towards
solitude and isolation. Eithne Golden later recalled of O'Malley that
'He was a loner . . . he wasn't a very sociable person.'[6] His Revolutionary wanderings were, of their nature, largely solitary—in reference to
1918–23 he recalled 'having to depend on myself always for five
years'[7]—and his later emigrant sojourn echoed this again. He wrote,
for example, to Frank Gallagher in 1930 from Santa Fé, New Mexico:
'I miss the talks we used to have, here where I have nobody to talk to.'[8]

But there is no doubt that the persistence of this theme throughout his life reflects a measure of personal preference. O'Malley himself put it partly down to impatience ('I am impatient by nature and I can put up with a great deal of solitude at times').[9] It also indicated the emotional wariness characteristic of the highly sensitive. O'Malley had good friends and many of them attested to his agreeable qualities as a companion. But he was not instinctively gregarious, was not particularly keen on being the focus of attention socially, and tended towards the shy and the private. Most of all, he was guarded about emotions and preferred not to be questioned about the personal. Reticent, reserved, hostile to prying attention, he could seem cold as well as self-reliant, aloof as well as sensitive. This should not obscure from us his capacity for intense passion—his daughter's description of him as 'having the capacity to be passionate but cold'[10] nicely captures something of the combination—but the preference for privacy and space was undeniably an important aspect of the man's personality. He had, as his daughter again recalled, 'a deep need of solitude and silence'.[11] The recollections of Jean McGrail are instructive here. McGrail first met O'Malley during the mid-1950s in the Aran Islands, which she used to visit each summer. A New York sculptor, she found in O'Malley a man of shared artistic interests and the two became friends. O'Malley, she recalls, was a contemplative, private man who would never talk about personal or family matters. Self-reliant, direct, strict with himself, clear about his own likes and dislikes, the O'Malley of McGrail's recollections[12] is recognizable from the many other sources which depict the man's personality.

Some of this went back to the austere, distant quality of O'Malley's family upbringing—'There was very little love in the family. I can honestly say that I never loved my parents, but I respected them.'[13] This was reinforced as his experiences developed after he left home in 1918. Itinerant soldiership, the loss of comrades, the split over the 1921 Treaty, solitary travel in Europe, displaced medical student life in the 1920s, wandering through intellectual bohemia in the United States— all of this cumulatively encouraged solitude, self-reliance, and toughness. O'Malley could be hard, stern, and flinty in his attitudes towards self and others. Tough-mindedness incorporated a certain stoicism: O'Malley commented (in relation to 1918) that 'My body was hardy enough. I had an Erewonian [sic] contempt for disease'[14]—a reference to Samuel Butler's satirical *Erewhon*, which depicts a place in which illness was considered criminal, immoral, and worthy of punishment. Indeed, though O'Malley had an eye for quality and luxury which bordered at times on the sybaritic, he could also exhibit a measure of asceticism and austerity. During the Revolution he was keen to guard resources frugally, to account for them in detail, and to be spartan rather than flabby in terms of one's own needs. Sobriety and restraint were prized by some — though, to his distress, not by all — of his comrades. IRA Chief of Staff Frank Aiken, for example, urged Republicans in 1923 that 'we must respect ourselves and make sure to keep ourselves — and every organization with which we are associated — clean and temperate'.[15] In O'Malley's case this related also to discipline, and he was as severe on himself as on his men.

Disciplined and tough-minded, O'Malley tended to be direct and to say precisely what he thought of people regardless of their sensitivities. Not unduly polite, he was contemptuous of the demands of petty propriety; Eithne Golden recalled that 'He never bothered being on his best behaviour for anybody's benefit. . . . He would have *scorned* to be on his best behaviour.'[16] Uncompromising in private as in political life, O'Malley provoked strong reactions, negative as well as positive. This owed something to his demanding expectations, which could deepen both friendships and divisions. In 1933 O'Malley visited Joseph Campbell (1879–1944), the Belfast-born poet and Irish Republican who spent the late 1920s and the 1930s in New York. The two men shared many similar tastes and influences in their reading, were both committed Republicans (Campbell had been an active member of Sinn Féin during the Irish Revolution and had been anti-Treaty during the Civil War), were both obsessed by Ireland during their American exile, and also shared similar hobbies (including mountain walking). Fruitful ground, one might have thought, for an amiable meeting. In fact, O'Malley's demanding attitude led him to dismiss Campbell for being insufficiently lean and hungry: 'I went to see Joe Campbell once. It was a shock. Fat, gross, and cushioned, living I thought on an Irish background; sentimental in retrospective and untrue to what might have been himself . . . he has fallen between the armchairs.'[17]

Demanding as he was, he was inevitably disappointed. He was scornful of those ex-Revolutionaries who became 'soft, content to remind themselves of their former integrity and idealism as they made use of them for political or economic purposes'.[18] He, by contrast, would stay pure, in a manner denied to those who embraced the despised trades of politics and compromise. O'Malley's mother, Mar-

ion Malley, was an extremely purposeful, driven, and driving character, and her children evidently inherited something of these qualities.
Ernie certainly did so, characterized as he was by a self-punishing
relentlessness. He made few concessions, for himself or for others, and
was as exacting as he was self-driving. As a result, O'Malley was capable of sustained, concentrated work. As a Revolutionary and as a writer,
he set himself demanding schedules and pursued them with a striking
intensity. Zeal and commitment threaded through O'Malley's life,
personal as well as political, and helped produce great achievements
as well as sharp pain. In all of his projects O'Malley displayed a nervous intensity—again, the comparison with Dostoyevsky's Raskolnikov
suggests itself—and his restless energy combined with a meticulous,
determined earnestness. Single-mindedness blurred, on occasions,
into obsessiveness. O'Malley's vast collection of detailed notebooks,
catalogues, and lists testifies to this, as do remarks such as that of
Eamon de Valera in 1928 (in relation to O'Malley's *Irish Press* mission): 'Many thanks for your report of 5 November. You need not go
into such detail in future.'[19] The constant record-keeping and the tireless compilation of notes reflect the insecurity of a dynamic but self-
taught intellectual driven on by doubt and by a hunger for greater
certainty and knowledge. It is also important to note that, as with many
people who had experienced the European conflicts of the 1914–18
period and after, O'Malley's nerves were more taut than would otherwise have been the case. The memory of violence was compounded by
a legacy of constant physical pain, and O'Malley's often-noted irritability must be understood partially in these terms. Again, the wider
post-First World War context is important here. O'Malley's experience
reflected the ways in which war impacted upon an equivocally respon-
sive Ireland: the different soldierly routes chosen by Ernie and his
brother Frank indicate this, as do O'Malley's comparatively empa-
thetic reflections concerning those Irish people who fought in a war
from which he maintained a certain distance.[20] The central legacy of
the war related to its awful human cost, and here O'Malley again
echoed the wider experience of the period. Ulick O'Connor (who, like
his father Dr Matt O'Connor, knew O'Malley) likened the nerve-
damaging effects of O'Malley's Revolutionary experiences to the
effects of First World War horror upon those who had been in the
trenches; O'Malley's 'nervous system had been shattered by the events
that he'd been involved in'.[21]

O'Malley's intensity annoyed some, but it also made him colourful, dramatic, searching. His nervous intelligence and vigorous alertness combined to produce strong likes and dislikes, and made him a distinctive companion. His determined pursuit of goals and his resoluteness of purpose made him a committed colleague, friend, or opponent. Stubborn in attachment to principle, he could be as difficult as he was compelling; the very qualities that made him engaging could also make him profoundly difficult to live with. Awkward at times, he could—and did—fall out badly with people. Robert Herbert provides an illustrative example. Herbert—Librarian and Director at the Limerick Public Library, Art Gallery, and Museum—had helped O'Malley by housing some of his paintings in Limerick from the late 1940s. In February 1956 O'Malley wrote to Herbert complaining about the condition of some of these pictures upon their return to him: works by Yeats, Hone, Modigliani, and Vlaminck now had, he suggested, damaged frames and damp stains. It was an ill-tempered letter and provoked a reply of similar flavour. Herbert responded with surprise at the tone and the content of O'Malley's epistle, defended his treatment of the paintings, and commented that 'When I find you listing as faults "frame slightly apart in all the corners" and "the frames of all the pictures on which you inserted labels need to be cleaned in this spot", I cannot help suggesting that you use a hammer in the first instance and a sponge in the latter.'[22] O'Malley could be brusque, temperamental, intolerant, arrogant, blunt, and gruff. Used to being obeyed as a leading IRA officer, he carried his authoritarian expectations into his post-Revolutionary personal dealings. He could certainly be contemptuously dismissive of people, groups as well as individuals. Consider, for example, his 1940 observation that Americans were 'too much impressed by momentary trends, in art as in business'.[23] Proud, by his own admission, O'Malley could also be arrogant in his judgements. As with the tireless notetaking and cataloguing, however, such decisive dismissals might owe as much to underconfidence as to its opposite.

Clearly, O'Malley possessed a wide variety of emotional and temperamental colours. It would be misleading to concentrate exclusively on his more serious side: his lighter touches were also vital to his personality. Although not naturally gregarious, O'Malley could—in certain comfortable company—enjoy considerable conviviality. The writer and broadcaster Ludovic Kennedy, who met O'Malley on a visit to Ireland in the late 1940s, found him 'excellent and amusing company',[24] and he was not alone. In August 1951, for example, after the effective conclusion of his legal battle with Helen, O'Malley gave a dinner in Burrishoole in honour of his solicitor Michael Noyk. The dinner was a feast: elaborate, with expensive wines and many locally derived dishes. 'Liver-kidney Rosgiblin' referred to the Rosgiblin land which O'Malley had purchased and on which he kept cattle; 'Mackerel grilled Carrowkeel' echoed Carrowkeel, land which Helen had purchased; Chateau Mouton Rothschild 1929 underlined the fact that O'Malley was capable of departing from asceticism in style.[25] Indeed, close inspection of the evidence reveals a side of O'Malley here which is often missing from existing accounts. He enjoyed drinking sessions with John Wayne during the filming of *The Quiet Man* in 1951, just as he had earlier enjoyed tequila, Chianti, and Mescal in Mexico in 1931 (echoing D. H. Lawrence: 'mescal . . . to get brutally drunk on').[26] In the early 1930s, indeed, he had observed that 'It's hard to live in a country where you cannot have wine for meals'.[27] He noticed women as well as wine: in Albuquerque, New Mexico, in December 1930 he observed that 'The girls exude sex with a wiggle of the[ir] bottoms, a tiggle of their hips, a smell of scent and an alarming make up.'[28] In Mexico the following month he wrote in his notebook that he liked 'the unabashed way they look at a girl here: yesterday in the park there was a girl with rolled stockings and her overcoat was tightly pulled up where she leant on her beau's arms; all the coach drivers stopped, put their heads out of the windows, all the male passers by turned their heads—nothing surreptitious about it.'[29] His asceticism was not unbending, and his earnestness could give way to a sense of humour and fun. Peadar O'Donnell challenged the view of O'Malley as one who was too severe: 'He had a very live and quite a mischievous sense of humour . . . the picture of him as a severe person without any sense of fun would be completely wrong'.[30] He was a serious man, and could be very severe; but, not surprisingly, there was at times and with certain people a lighter, gayer side. His daughter ably captures something of the mixture in recalling that 'he had great capacity to laugh . . . but he was a lone eagle ultimately'; 'to talk personally didn't interest him'.[31]

If, like his favoured author Herman Melville, he loved a good laugh (Melville: 'a good laugh is a mighty good thing, and rather too scarce a good thing; the more's the pity';[32] O'Malley: 'A sense of humour is too often lacking in creative work'),[33] then this points to a softer side of his personality, the side remembered in particular by those who knew him in his later years. Maureen O'Hara's recollection of the O'Malley of 1951, for instance, is typical here: 'a charming, soft old teddy bear . . . a lovely man to be around, a lovely man to talk to'.[34] If this cuts across the usual picture of the man, then it adds one more layer to the personality as we have so far unveiled it: loyal, solitary, self-reliant; sensitive, emotionally wary, private, shy, reticent; austere, tough-minded, stoical, disciplined; intransigent, demanding, capable of arrogance, relentlessly self-driven, intense, earnest, and determined; dynamic, restless; by turns intolerant, dismissive, and convivial; charismatic, fascinating, compelling, and difficult.

II

All that is important is to tell you that I love you very much and that I know we must be married before the autumn.

(Ernie O'Malley to Helen Hooker)[35]

This is, in part, a love story. When Ernie O'Malley met Helen Hooker in June 1933 in Connecticut a new and crucial phase of his life began. Helen Huntington Hooker (1905–93) had been born in Greenwich, Connecticut, was schooled there and then for five years in Miss Chapin's prestigious private school in New York City, from which she graduated in 1923. Talented in a number of directions, Helen in 1923 won the American National Junior Tennis Championship. This success reflected parental enthusiasms and family tensions. Her father, Elon Huntington Hooker (1869–1938)—who had himself been college champion at tennis in his undergraduate days at the University of Rochester—was ambitious for his four daughters. Helen's enthusiasm for an artistic career was not shared by her parents, but having achieved the tennis victory she argued (with typical vehemence) that she had fulfilled a parental ambition and that she should now be allowed to follow her own chosen paths. These involved, primarily, sculpture and, secondarily, travel, dance, and a general commitment to the arts. On sculpture she worked in New York with Mahonri Young, Edmund Amateus, and William Zorach, and in Paris with Émile Bourdelle. She also studied wood carving and had considerable ability as a painter. Widely travelled, she had a breadth of artistic experience based in part on these experiences: Leningrad, Moscow, Oberammergau, and Athens all played their part in influencing her artistic outlook. There was no formal training. But there was much exposure to diverse artistic talents and situations, which built up her own distinctive talent and vision.

Sculpture was in part a rebellion against family culture. Helen was extremely proud of her family, but tension undoubtedly existed. Elon Hooker and Blanche Hooker had four daughters—Barbara (b. 1901), Adelaide (b. 1903), Helen (b. 1905), Blanchette (b. 1909)—and both parents played a significant part in O'Malley's story. Elon's philosophy, though profoundly different from O'Malley's, was an equally demanding one. Hooker once wrote that 'The product of a life is the quality of accomplishment multiplied by its quantity'; in a speech in 1935 he declared that 'Individual achievement, self-reliance, and thrift are the foundations of progress and security'.[36] Hooker's family was of distinguished lineage: Elon was a direct descendant of Thomas Hooker,[37] and six governors of Connecticut and Massachusetts were in his line of ancestry. During his own childhood, however, the family was not blessed with great wealth. Born in Rochester, New York, Elon went as an undergraduate to the University of Rochester, graduating from there in 1891; in the autumn of 1892 he began to study engineering at Cornell University, New York, graduating in civil engineering in 1894 and having a Ph.D. conferred upon him in 1896. While attached to Cornell he studied in Zurich and Paris. He became a civil engineer, and in 1899 was appointed Deputy Superintendent of Public Works for the state of New York by the then Governor Theodore Roosevelt. Energetic, ambitious, talented, driven, Elon in the early years of the century founded the Hooker Electrochemical Company whose innovative electrolytic process produced chlorine, caustic soda, and hydrogen, and whose Niagara Falls plant went into operation in January 1906. During the First World War Hooker Electrochemical expanded its operations and by 1918 the company was producing bleach, caustic soda, and fifteen new chemicals with a chlorine base. A flourishing, innovative businessman, Elon Hooker survived the early 1930s Depression better than many, the chemical industry not suffering as drastically as did some others. In 1920 Hooker ran unsuccessfully for the Republican nomination for Governor of New York. This, then, was an able, determined businessman, with interests in science and politics, with a breadth of experience, and with a distinct set of convictions about respectability, the duties of business in relation to politics and society, the importance of achievement and of education, and the value of self-reliance and individual initiative. Hostile to radicalism (whether from left or right), Hooker believed in a capitalism characterized by social responsibility, and in the interweaving of democracy, progress, and business. During the 1930s he spoke in defence of democratic capitalism against the threats of Fascism and of communism and socialism.

In January 1901 Elon had married Blanche Ferry (1871–1956), the eldest daughter of Dexter Mason Ferry (1833–1907) of Detroit, Michigan, and of Addie Elizabeth [Miller] Ferry (1841–1905). Ferry himself was a successful businessman, a self-made entrepreneur who became a wealthy and leading citizen of Detroit with Republican Party connections. Born in Detroit herself, Blanche graduated from Vassar College, New York, in 1894, and so Helen Hooker had an educated, financially successful, respectable, conservative, socially prescribed background. Achievement and appropriate accomplishment, money and social propriety: these were the bedrock of her WASPish upbringing. By marrying an Irish Catholic ex-Revolutionary, a wandering, unemployed, and moneyless writer of unyielding and dissident opinions, Helen was rebelling as much against her family as O'Malley himself had rebelled against his own when endorsing Revolutionary Irish Republicanism. The conflict of cultures and personalities was evident at the first meeting between O'Malley and the Hookers in 1933. O'Malley recalled the Hookers as having been hostile to Ireland, the Irish, and Catholicism (Elon was Baptist; Blanche, Christian Scientist). Ernie and Elon instantly clashed. At that first luncheon they had quarrelled about the American Indians, O'Malley defending them against what he judged to be Hooker's insulting remarks. Hooker gave instructions after this episode that O'Malley should not be invited to the house again. The Irishman was judged to have been disrespectful, subversive of Elon's authority and of appropriate social behaviour. Later, the two men were to attempt a better relationship. Neither O'Malley nor his father-in-law were particularly prone to gushing effusions of private emotion. But after Ernie and Helen had married, Elon and O'Malley made an effort to establish cordial, sensitive, and respectful relations. Shortly after the wedding in 1935 O'Malley wrote to Elon Hooker noting that he understood how trying the episode must have been for him. O'Malley went on to outline how he and Helen were keen to settle down 'to a fixed programme of work in Dublin this winter'—a phrase guaranteed to please Hooker—and expressed the hope that Elon would stay with them in Dublin on his next visit to Europe.[38] Hooker replied in a similar spirit.

I have been interested in the plans for the new home in Dublin and your university work to complete preparation for the profession of medicine. . . . It has not been easy to write—your letter is appreciative of that—but my only interest is in Helen's long time happiness and the worth while success of those dear to her. Even so it is difficult to be reconciled to a life for her and her children so far away from home traditions, her friends, and what life had in store for her here. She is a wonderful girl—gifted and worthy of personal achievement. She has chosen—and I hope wisely—to trust her future to you. May God bless you both and make the hard places easier.[39]

In time, Elon even read O'Malley's book and appears to have enjoyed and appreciated it. But their initial contact was much more frosty.

Helen, however, was not someone to be put off by parental disapproval; it might even have sharpened her determination. The Hooker girls were spirited, able, goal-oriented; Helen was imperious, tenacious, energetic, and impatient. Treated by her father in a pushy way—he wanted his daughters to win—Helen responded in an equally assertive way: dynamic, determined, energetic, adventurous. In the late 1920s, years before she had met O'Malley, she had visited Russia with her close sister Adelaide in a typically boisterous endeavour. As the sisters' account of this trip recalled, 'Our reasons for being there at all were curiosity and cussedness. We didn't know much about Marx and Lenin, but from father's description they were bad enough to be interesting.'[40] In Russia Helen looked at churches and at icons, presaging the artistic interests which she and Ernie were to share. Indeed it is possible to trace much that explains the shared world which Helen and O'Malley were to inhabit. In a letter from the late 1940s Adelaide wrote to O'Malley that 'Helen has always required a world of swapping aesthetic ideas with people and would wither without this';[41] this judgement is close to the mark and sharply identifies one of the bonds tying Ernie and Helen closely together.

Like Ernie, Helen possessed a wide range of interwoven qualities and experiences: talented, artistic, widely travelled, very determined, driven, steely, and capable of sharp focus on a cherished project. As with Ernie, the list might be extended to include what are, perhaps, less flattering characteristics. She could be capricious, undisciplined, with a tendency to dart flittingly from one project to the next. A certain lack of confidence made her unwilling to subject achievement to open or formal assessment; she compensated for this by being intransigent and extremely self-focused. Having met in 1933, their relationship grew intimate during the remaining part of O'Malley's American period. O'Malley's striking looks and searching, intense blue eyes captured Helen's attention immediately. Helen—beautiful, sophisticated, with blue eyes as captivating as Ernie's—was equally glamorous. But more than physical attraction united them. Interests in literature, painting, sculpture—on their first meeting Helen had 'seemed to be interested in the fact that I knew about sculpture and painting'[42]—combined with a shared enthusiasm for drama and theatre. Travel had expanded the vision of both, and the two widely travelled artists—Helen's passport, issued in April 1935, described her occupation as that of 'Artist'—met on the territory of the arts.

For O'Malley, Helen also represented a certain freedom from the past. With no Irish or political connection, she was nothing to do with the disappointments of the Irish Revolution, and engaged with him in an area of his life—the artistic—which remained intact. Artistic, spirited, talented, and sexually alluring, she was to captivate O'Malley as much as he did her. For her own part, Helen referred in a letter to her mother (written some months after having first met O'Malley) to 'his Irish charm and courageous spirit'.[43] Part of the attraction for her was what she held to be O'Malley's untamed quality—'my wild Irishman'[44]—and this was interwoven in her view with his intellectual and literary ability. Moreover, and rather paradoxically, Helen rebelled against her family by her association with O'Malley, while simultaneously seeing in him something of her father. Both she and Ernie were to acknowledge this, and the authoritarian, educated, opinionated, goal-oriented, well-focused qualities of the two men underline it.

Ernie and Helen fell deeply in love. Helen's sister Adelaide reported her to have been 'happier than I have ever seen her'[45] on her wedding day. For his part, O'Malley wrote intimately to Helen in April 1935, shortly after he had left New York for Massachusetts, the letter reflecting a tension between his declamatory roughness and the more tender vulnerability which she brought out in him:

I did not think the sight of your peaked helmet disappearing could make a bus seem so desolate. . . . I'm afraid our last few months in New York have had too much an air of unreality and strain and yet I am only too glad for these months. The problem of reality in my country has yet to be faced. It is a bitter country and one without pity. That you have to realize but on the whole living there makes for a reality that I miss in America. I mention this because I don't want any romantic idea of the country to obscure its actuality. . . . All the rest of this letter is really unimportant. All that is important is to tell you that I love you very much and that I know we must be married before the autumn.[46]

O'Malley's relationship with Helen during these early stages produced his most effusive expressions of personal emotion. This did not come easily to him: in another spring 1935 letter to Helen he observed: 'I really find it hard to write to you, mainly I expect that I never before had to put on paper what I now feel, and written words seem very stilted and formal when it is a question of expressing very personal emotions and feelings.'[47] From a family background characterized more by formal respect than by expressed intimacy, O'Malley had moved straight into experiences of loss, defeat, displacement, and perceived betrayal; and then, self-imposed exile. All this reinforced his inclinations towards privacy and reticence. This new relationship allowed—at least, for a time—his softer emotions to breathe more freely. But his marriage, as so much else of his post-Revolutionary life, would be racked by irreconcilable tensions.

III

I have had some trouble with Helen for some years due to what might be called incompatibility.

(Ernie O'Malley)[48]

Ernie and Helen remained in love for some years after their marriage in September 1935. Touches of romantic sentiment are frequently evident during the early years of their Irish life, O'Malley, for example, writing from Dublin to Helen in London in 1937 that 'The house is very lonely without you'.[49] By the mid-1940s, however, the marriage had effectively broken down. A number of frequently interlocking themes help to explain this. The first concerns the Irish world which they idealistically entered together in 1935. The *Irish Times* appreciation of Helen Hooker upon her death in 1993 remarked on her having had 'an ardent love affair with Ireland'.[50] This is a justifiable observation, for Helen exhibited a genuine enthusiasm for Ireland. Writing to her father in 1936 about her adopted island she said that 'There are many really lovely people here and I like the informal way of life so much'.[51] But this was, unfortunately, only part of the story. Attuned to Connecticut and New York City, Helen missed the social sophistication of her Hooker world. This milieu had in some ways been constraining for her, and had placed her under pressures from which Ireland seemed to offer emancipation. But there were costs, too, in leaving America behind. In Burrishoole Helen missed the world of theatre and metropolitan sophistication. Dublin was, in the end, no substitute and Ireland became profoundly difficult as well as enthralling. Writing from Dublin to an American friend in July 1946 she sounded very much like Elon Hooker's daughter:

I see no Americans over here or girls like yourself, and it was reassuring to find that some of the things which make life difficult for me in Ireland are not really individual problems, but racial problems. The intensity of the American temperament and drive towards the goal, or ambition, is so different in us than in the Irish girl—both our methods of attaining it and the speed with which we approach it.[52]

More sharply, she had written to her mother at Christmas 1943 that 'I don't believe life in medieval Russia could be any harder than it is in Ireland in 1943. . . . I well understand why the average person of any ability leaves.'[53] Ernie had himself written to Helen from Burrishoole some months earlier that 'This is no civilized place for you to live in'.[54]

It is important here to register precisely the kind of world from which Helen's Ireland differed. One way of focusing this is to consider the work of Helen's brother-in-law, the American novelist of manners John P. Marquand (1893–1960). Adelaide Hooker married Marquand in April 1937. The latter, a Harvard-educated best-selling author, concentrated much of his attention on the depiction of a culture about which he felt most ambivalent: that of the (typically) Harvard-trained, successful business or law professional, the commuter from Connecticut to New York City, the wealthy character surrounded by bourgeois propriety and defined according to a precisely graded social stratification. Hard work, conservatism, responsibility, respectability, and achievement: Marquand's novels could be describing Elon Hooker's world.[55] O'Malley had many Marquand novels in his library but, although we have noted some echoes between O'Malley and Elon Hooker, the two men were essentially of different worlds. More importantly, despite Helen's at times difficult relationship with her family, the world which Marquand so closely studied was one which substantially defined her expectations. From this world County Mayo at times seemed painfully remote.

A further illustration of this can be found if one looks to another of Helen's sisters, Blanchette. The youngest of the Hooker girls, Blanchette married John D. Rockefeller III in November 1932. They were married in New York's Riverside Church at West 122nd Street, a huge building modelled on Chartres's thirteenth-century Gothic cathedral. Construction on the church had begun in 1927, the first service being held there in 1930. The building's twenty-floor tower—the

Laura Spelman Rockefeller Memorial Tower—rises 119 metres above
the street, and contains the seventy-four bell Laura Spelman Rockefeller Memorial Carillon, a gift from John D. Rockefeller, Jnr. in
memory of his mother. Helen's sister had, therefore, been married in a
vast neo-Gothic church which her father-in-law had been wealthy and
socially significant enough to fund and to define. The gap between
this world and that of Helen's adopted life in Ireland was great. So, too,
was the distance between Helen and Ernie over their respective
approaches to discipline. Both could be very focused on projects. But
sustained organization—so important a quality for Ernie—was not
Helen's preferred style. Etáin O'Malley recalls of her parents that 'he
felt that she was emotionally undisciplined—and she was';[56] for his
part, O'Malley himself claimed that Helen 'would not hold to any discipline for a length of time',[57] and thought her lacking in disciplined
concentration. He thought her irresponsible and, in particular, found
her attitude towards money problematic: 'She has no sense of money.
A great deal of trouble arose out of this habit of hers of not paying
debts. Nor did she keep a budget.'[58] In his view she was spendthrift,
and he thought her improvements to Burrishoole extravagant and
over-elaborate. Again and again he stressed the financial point, an
example being his exasperated letter to Helen in September 1943: 'The
telephone is to be used for emergencies only. It costs money and I
don't know with a double house where money is to come from . . . you
have got to live simply for the very good reason that there is no
money.'[59] There is considerable evidence to support the view that
Helen was less disciplined than her husband in terms of the latter's
preference for a cataloguing precision; she was certainly less cautious
than he with money. Whether or not these tendencies represent a flaw
in character is more questionable; that it represented an increasing
problem in their marriage is indisputable.

So, too, the physical aspect of the marriage caused some problems.
Physical attraction had been an important feature of their relationship
from the beginning, but there were differing attitudes and demands.
According to O'Malley, there developed 'friction about sleeping
together . . . Helen's idea was that if there was trouble it could always
be settled by sleeping [together]. If I had a row with Helen I would find
it hard to make love to her. It would have to wait until the right mood
came, in peace.'[60] Moreover, while sexuality and sensuality were crucial to Helen's relationships with men, O'Malley's physical injuries—
in particular the severe back pain from which he persistently

suffered—and his more general ill-health were inhibiting. More broadly, this related to the more affectionate and intimate aspect of their life together. Helen certainly felt that O'Malley isolated himself from her, and that he would not share the intimacy necessary for a full relationship. In a letter of 1946 she accused him of having been unwilling genuinely to share life with her: 'Perhaps you need to be alone the rest of your life but I have already had to spend much of my life with you alone and without companionship of heart or act.'[61]

These difficulties caused frustrations and mutual jealousies, some of which tied in with another key area of difficulty in the marriage, namely that of work. The children's recollections help to point the way here. Etáin has observed that 'My mother and father were both married to their goals',[62] and has also referred to them as having been 'two very undomestic people'.[63] The concentration on work priorities certainly contributed to the drawing apart of the O'Malleys, especially given the striking stubbornness of their determination: Cormac tellingly described Helen as 'a "no compromise" person. . . . There was this blind stubborn streak, this indomitable force, this utter belief ultimately in her own opinion, which could not be trained or transmuted.'[64] Something similar could be argued about Ernie and, when allied to both partners' familiarity with being obeyed, this proved a severe problem. Both independent-minded and both rather inflexible, the married combination was hard for either of them to sustain. Once again, the zeal which produced impressive achievements could also prove destructive.

Helen's work—particularly in theatre—grew to absorb her profoundly. She wrote to her mother in 1947 that 'The world of the theatre is so exciting and absorbing; that possibly is part of its charm, one has not time to think of oneself at all and therefore forgets one's personal worries'.[65] In her husband's view, she would have done better to concentrate on one field—sculpture—rather than (as he saw it) flitting between theatre and decorative arts as well. He especially took against the Players' Theatre project: 'She [Helen] wanted me to act on a board to read plays. The board as far as I remember consisted of actors . . . I had never liked actors. They were too extrovert, given to too much acting off stage. They had usually an exaggerated idea of their own importance.'[66] It was not that O'Malley was uninterested in theatre: his connections with America's Group Theatre and his student work at UCD both testify to that. But the Players' Theatre was, he felt, an unhelpful distraction for Helen and one which intruded on their life.

This became more difficult as Helen and the Theatre's Liam Redmond (1910–91) — a UCD graduate, actor, and playwright, then in his
mid-thirties — became more closely involved with one another. Helen
kept a large photograph of Redmond in her bedroom during the early
period of the Theatre in the mid-1940s, and the Players came on many
evenings to 15 Whitebeam Avenue to use the O'Malleys' home as a
base. Ernie protested about the use of the home in this way but Helen
remained insistent. By 1946 O'Malley was unwilling to meet the Players socially in his house. Not surprisingly, perhaps, a sharp-edged jealousy developed. Helen had undoubtedly become very close to
Redmond in the course of their involvement in the Theatre. By 1948
the tension with O'Malley was painful. In July of that year Ernie wrote
to his sister Marion [Sweetie] that 'Helen has involved herself too
much with Liam Redmond' and that 'It would be a relief if Helen
would go away for a while, for as long as Redmond is two doors away
[the Redmonds also lived in Whitebeam Avenue] she is a cause of
trouble'.[67] But while O'Malley felt that Helen's work had taken her in
unwelcome directions, he also recognized rightly that the problems
were not all on one side: Helen 'had always told people that I was
"difficult". That was true, I was.'[68] Inflexible about many aspects of his
life, he was rigid about his work schedule and was preoccupied with
his research and his writing during much of the 1940s. In December
1946 Blanche Hooker — Helen's mother, and somebody who was sensitive to both Ernie and Helen — wrote perceptively, fairly, and with
some wisdom to Ernie: 'Helen has very marvellous strong qualities and
equally strong weak ones. I should say the same of you and neither of
you is likely to change under the method you have been pursuing most
of the time since you have been married.'[69]
     Just as discipline exacerbated financial differences, therefore, work
was bound up with sexual jealousy. Not that the jealous anger was uni-
laterally directed. Sarah Sheridan — the woman who had been sent to
Ireland by Blanche Hooker in 1935 in order to vet the Malley family —
had a granddaughter (Catherine Crompton) with whom the
O'Malleys became friendly. Catherine ('Bobs') married wealthy Englishman Henry (Harry) Walston in 1935 in the USA, and settled in
England. The O'Malleys knew the Walstons and spent time with them
in both England and Ireland. But it was the friendship between
Catherine and Ernie which grew most important. O'Malley plainly
meant a considerable amount to Catherine Walston — 'You are very
dear to a lot of us, Ernie . . . your relationship with me is unique in my

life'[70] — and Helen grew profoundly jealous. Assuming that Catherine and Ernie's intimacy must be based on sexual involvement, Helen was, by the latter part of 1946, openly making such allegations. Such clashes reflected and deepened the conflict within the marriage, and the situation by the mid-1940s was irretrievably dire. Cormac's judgement that the split between his mother and father had the qualities of 'a real civil war'[71] nicely captures the flavour of the personal tragedy. At times, things became genuinely ugly, and it was the cumulative overlapping of various problems which produced this situation. A later recollection of O'Malley's illustrates the combined tensions over money, sexual jealousy, work, and friends:

In February [1945] she [Helen] began to ring up my friends for money. I protested. She would not stop. One day I went into her room, told her to stop. She refused. She said she would do as she liked. If I didn't like what she was doing I could leave the house. It was her house anyhow. She struck me as I tried to take the phone out of her hand. I smacked her on the bottom or on the face. Next day her face was blue in spots.[72]

After Helen returned from her 1945 visit to the United States, O'Malley recalled that she 'told me that I was neurotic, that I badly needed psychoanalysis. A psychiatrist in New York who listened to her stories about me said I was definitely a very bad case close to insanity. He looked at a photograph of me and said definitely I was the type and that was what he actually expected me to look like.'[73]

As outlined already, this attrition led to a dramatic separation, kidnapping, and divorce. (Newspaper attention to the O'Malleys' explosive relationship shows that the glamour of the much mythologized gunman still adhered, as well as underlining the fact that the couple represented something of a colourful distraction from the often depressingly monochrome Ireland of this period.) O'Malley objected to Helen's apparent incapacity to make decisions; she objected to his quick judgements on any situation. Ernie was impatient, with a bad temper, and was emotionally uncommunicative, private, solitary; Helen's fiery temper was combined with emotional effusiveness and flirtatious gregariousness. Incompatibility coexisted with powerful, possessive love, and the consequent frustration and constriction killed the relationship. The poignancy of this dying marriage is painfully reflected in the sources, Helen writing in 1948 to her mother, for example, about the sundered relationship with Ernie that 'Nothing can ever hurt me so much again'.[74]

Most tragic of all, perhaps, were some of the developments involving the three children. Ernie and Helen's approach to the three children both reflected and, on occasions, contributed to the ending of the marriage. There had been good times as a family, O'Malley reading or story-telling with the children by the fire, Cahal recalling that his father would 'weave wonderful stories' for them as children;[75] sailing in the bay ('Burrishoole has in ways been associated with our name since the tenth century and I was anxious to bring the children up related to land and sea until they grew up');[76] listening to music together; engaging in (typically serious) discussions and focusing on literature—*The Iliad, The Odyssey, Moby-Dick, Gulliver's Travels*[77]—but enjoying also much laughter. His children preserved a treasured legacy of imaginative stimulation: Etáin: 'he loved imagination'; 'I certainly spent my whole childhood inside books'; 'He read every day . . . to us'; 'My love of language started with father reading poetry and prose aloud to us'; 'Certainly the impact of wanting quality I get from both my parents.'[78]

The sharp break of 1950, with the kidnapping of Cahal and Etáin, ripped the family apart. Helen later felt guilty about the removal of the two elder children to the United States, and certainly the rupture caused problems for them. Etáin's observation that 'Kidnapping is a very serious criminal offence and should be. And . . . we all suffered very deep scars from that',[79] reflects something of the pain. Arguing that, effectively, she had both Ireland and her father stolen from her, she notes that 'I certainly have felt uprooted.'[80] Cahal and Etáin had comparatively little contact with their father after 1950 (Cahal: 'A real loss. And I wish it had been otherwise');[81] the omission of either child from Ernie's will—uncertain of how Cormac would be provided for, Ernie left everything to him—underlined the break which had occurred. In the summer of 1955, for example, Helen, Cahal, and Etáin visited O'Malley in Ireland, but his response to his two older children was self-protective and cold: 'My attitude was, let the children search me out if they wanted to establish a contact, for I realize on meeting them that I have one child, Cormac, whom I must bring up as an Irishman'.[82] There is a poignant cry preserved in a letter written by Etáin from Greenwich, Connecticut, in 1952 to her father in Ireland: 'You don't know how much I want to go fishing and sailing again, Oh Daddy Dear when will I see you?'[83]

5

The Legacies

This book has outlined Ernie O'Malley's Life, examined his career as a Revolutionary, considered him as an Intellectual, and reflected upon him as a Companion. But what of his Legacies? Four questions suggest themselves. First, did O'Malley leave behind him any significant intellectual, artistic argument? Second, what are we to make of his political legacy in Ireland? Third, has this case study exploring O'Malley's career anything important to tell us about our understanding of the wider phenomenon of nationalism? Fourth, what overall perspective can be reached in drawing the book's various themes together in conclusion? This chapter will focus attention on contemporary concerns (is O'Malley of importance to us today?) and broaden out the range of his significance (is he of more than merely local or sectional interest?); the answer to each of these questions is, I believe, undoubtedly positive.

I

First, then, did O'Malley leave any significant intellectual, artistic argument? It is clear that he left behind him an impressive body of writings on political history and on art, and also that he influenced and assisted people such as Louis le Brocquy and Jack Yeats. I would argue, however, that beyond these particular legacies lies the broader one of a vision or perspective which pervaded much of his intellectual life. It is this vision which most pressingly demands our attention. In his survey of *The Irish*, Seán O'Faoláin stated that his paramount question was to ask what each event he examined had contributed 'to the sum of world-civilization'.[1] This demanding standard of judgement is fitting also for O'Faoláin's friend Ernie O'Malley, who was sustainedly attached to the notion of wide cultural horizons. O'Malley's aim was to balance an appreciation of the distinctively local with a preparedness to evaluate according to international standards, and to use the outstanding—whether Samuel Beckett, James Joyce, Franz Kafka, or T. S. Eliot—as a measure for the achievement of perspective. This avoidance of insularity sat awkwardly with the authenticist celebration required of Sinn Féinish patriotism, but O'Malley strove to celebrate the locally distinctive while recognizing the quality of the internationally impressive. As with his view that the politically powerful should cherish that which sensitizes, so too there is much of value in this attempt to combine local and international perspectives.

In balancing the local with the international, O'Malley also attempted to balance a commitment to the democratic with a strong sense that hierarchies of (often élitist) discernment had to be preserved. Art echoed politics here: O'Malley typified that strand of Irish Republicanism which simultaneously acted in the name of the people while disavowing much that the people actually believed. In artistic and intellectual terms, O'Malley espoused the wide dissemination of ideas. But, like his friend Louis MacNeice, he was pulled by competing impulses concerning élites and culture. MacNeice's 'Autumn Journal' crisply captures their dilemma:

> habit makes me
> Think victory for one implies another's defeat,
> That freedom means the power to order, and that in order
> To preserve the values dear to the élite
> The élite must remain a few. It is so hard to imagine
> A world where the many would have their chance without
> A fall in the standard of intellectual living
> And nothing left that the highbrow cared about.
> Which fears must be suppressed. There is no reason for thinking
> That, if you give a chance to people to think or live,
> The arts of thought or life will suffer and become rougher
> And not return more than you could ever give.[2]

Suppress though he might, O'Malley had a distinctly Arnoldian strain to his thinking and this is a vital point. He quoted Matthew Arnold (the great nineteenth-century critic) during the Revolutionary period,[3] took extensive notes on his work, and was to acknowledge in March 1931 that 'I still think him [Arnold] the clearest-souled Englishman of his century'.[4] Arnoldian balance was not O'Malley's style, but Arnoldian intellectual snobbery undoubtedly was.[5] Hostile to the vulgar and the philistine, O'Malley's intellectual élitism involved him in displaying a certain disdain for lower culture. Aspects of the people's actual life had repelled him during the Revolution;[6] so, too, he scorned literature, ideas, and art which were, in his view, less than serious. Arnold's celebration of the countryside — 'The Scholar-Gypsy' was well known to O'Malley — and his enthusiasm for the English Romanticism of Coleridge, Byron, Shelley, and Keats are very clearly echoed in O'Malley. Similarly, the two men's shared hostility to intellectual and aesthetic narrowness underlines the likenesses between them.

O'Malley, therefore, sought to cherish the local while judging by wider standards; and he aimed to preserve serious ideas and culture while supporting the notion of democratic and widespread access to such riches. This point is of profound relevance to our own period. In the late twentieth century, for example, Matthew Arnold has become a focus for fierce debate about culture. Battle lines in such debate have often been drawn between, on the one hand, canonical conservatives (preserving and validating culture which is held to be serious, superior, and durable) and, on the other, more relativistic progressives (explicitly disavowing the notion of cultural canons, and preferring the relativistic assumptions implicit in the Cultural Studies discipline). Hostility to Arnold has, at times, seemed like a badge of politically correct cultural orthodoxy; his Victorian confidence in cultural pronouncement and evaluation have been seen by some as characterizing reaction and narrowness. O'Malley's early twentieth-century reflections fall between the death of Arnold (1888) and the birth of Cultural Studies, and in some ways he helpfully blurs the sometimes over-neat division line between them. For O'Malley was aware not only of a wide diversity of cultures — in Europe and America — but also of their simultaneously powerful attractions. 'Cultures' rather than 'culture' interested him. Yet he was, in much of his intellectual formation, a late Victorian. For the most part he studied and absorbed himself in what might still be termed 'high culture'. He firmly believed in rigorous standards and in the possibility of establishing hierarchies of, for example, literary quality. He sought to be sensitive to the competing riches of rival cultures, without shedding his capacity for judging that which he considered more serious, durable, and worthy of sustained scrutiny.

O'Malley at times resembles a kind of neo-Arnoldian, and again this is an important feature of his legacy to later generations. He would, for example, have been as horrified as Allan Bloom at the death of intellectual life within modern families, at the demise of a reading culture among the young, and at the apparent incapacity of many modern students 'to distinguish between the sublime and trash'.[7] And, like Bloom, he believed in the appreciation, conservation, and transmission of inherited cultural riches. Indeed, this formed a crucial part not only of his view of art, but of his political philosophy. O'Malley's ideal was to accept his two lives simultaneously: that of the political struggle and that of the development of a personal, profound sense of beauty.

II

Second, what are we to make of Ernie O'Malley's political legacy in Ireland? Is he of interest and significance only to those fascinated by, or supportive of, militant Republicanism? My argument is that O'Malley's career, beliefs, and outlook are illuminating for anyone with an interest in modern Irish politics. Indeed, the material in this book points to conclusions central to our understanding of modern Irish political life. For while the primary task of the historian is to reconstruct a world from the past, it is also true that such reconstruction can help to illuminate more contemporary events. As with other Irish Republicans, Ernie O'Malley's legacy has been claimed by various groups and individuals in defence of their own preferred forms of political activity or principle. Most of these claims rest on too narrow a purpose and on too shaky a historical understanding to be intellectually impressive.

But there are more important ways in which O'Malley's legacy carries a resonance for current politics. Eric Hobsbawm has recently suggested that the historian's major task 'is not to judge but to understand even what we can least comprehend'.[8] Viewed in this light, modern Ireland presents the historian with a profound challenge. There have existed in twentieth-century Ireland two starkly opposed views of the world in the form of unionism and nationalism. Difficult (if not impossible) to reconcile—with their differing approaches to culture, religion, history, politics, symbolism, and economics—their respective communities have often found it very difficult to comprehend one another. This makes it vital for scholars to understand the divided past as fully as possible. The case of Ernie O'Malley—one of the most robust and gifted of modern Irish Republican nationalists—might help Irish unionists towards understanding themes which often seem to defy comprehension (the Republican physical force tradition, its causes and dynamics). It might also prompt Irish nationalists to reflect on those aspects of their own tradition which explain and justify unionist opposition to nationalist ambitions. Irish politics cries out for a move beyond insistent, traditional simplicities: reconceptualizations are required on all sides, unionist as well as nationalist, in London as well as in Dublin.[9] Crucial to this flexibility is a fuller understanding of the various political traditions involved. While, for example, it would be unfounded simply to equate a fidelity to Pearsean Republicanism with the Irish national good, neither is it realistic to ignore so important a tradition in Ireland as militant Republicanism.

Within the latter tradition Ernie O'Malley raises striking questions. He helps us to understand both the characteristics and the causes of the physical force movement. Not only are the sources particularly rich in relation to O'Malley, but his dual role—as staunch Irish rebel, and as fiercely independent mind within the Republican camp— makes him doubly interesting to the historian. His dissident voice challenges aspects both of anti-Republican and of Republican orthodoxies. One feature of this which is worthy of particular consideration is the way in which tensions produced historical change. Throughout this book we have seen repeated evidence of the generative power of tensions within O'Malley's experience: tensions between marginalized Anglophobia and Anglocentric Anglophilia, between the rural and the urban, between the popular and the élitist, between the modern and the anti-modern, between the ascetic and the indulgent, between the parochially distinctive and the internationally distinguished. The competing pull of these forces frequently lay at the root of O'Malley's development.

Similar dynamics have underlain Irish political developments in the period after O'Malley's death, and it is also true that his particular experiences have been echoed by more general trends in Irish politics. For while O'Malley's experience was distinctive, it formed part of a

wider political trajectory and here we find evidence of some of the
most profound forces and tensions in modern Irish history. The relationship, for example, between liberal democracy and ethno-religious
national sentiment has been one of the most significant in twentieth-
century politics, and Irish experience in the decades after 1916 demonstrated the ways in which these forces could tussle and interweave.
Revolutionary reaction against Britain involved rejection not only of
British rule in Ireland, but also of the form of politics which accompanied it: the IRA philosophy was one which eschewed strict attachment
to democratic principle. Yet the goal of Irish Republicanism did rest
on rhetorical adherence to democratic notions, and once the Revolutionaries attained power they adopted a very British form of parliamentary politics. The ethno-religious national sentiment which could not
breathe within the UK temporarily destabilized Ireland. But the fact
that the destabilization did indeed prove temporary owed much to the
internalization within Ireland of that very political tradition of liberal
democracy against which so much IRA activity was directed.

Ernie O'Malley's compelling quality owes much to this very fact:
that tension determined many of the developments in his life. The
paradoxes in his experience involved his being characterized simultaneously by what might initially appear to be mutually exclusive qualities. This makes it easier for people to find in O'Malley a wide range of
differing legacies. In this, O'Malley echoed some other leading figures
in the Irish Republican pantheon, including one of his own heroes,
the eighteenth-century United Irishman Theobald Wolfe Tone.
O'Malley, like the historian W. E. H. Lecky before him, thought that
Tone stood out from among the commonplace of Irish conspiracy;
and Tone, like O'Malley, has been frequently enlisted as an Irish
Republican exemplar. O'Malley himself was attracted by Tone, whose
legacy was full of complications and ironies. Unsympathetic to romantic Gaelicism, anti-Papal, and lacking in understanding of the
Catholic peasantry, Tone was a paradoxical figure to gain celebrity as
the founder of a movement which in its modern guise has cherished
Gaelicism, Catholicism, and peasant culture. Committed to the healing of divisions between Ireland's various religious groups, Tone's
name has been repeatedly attached to militant separatist campaigns
whose result—whatever their intention—has been to deepen the division in Ireland between Catholic and Protestant. O'Malley left behind him equally paradoxical implications (illuminated by his own
reflections and writings) and these stand out as part of his legacy.

While etching himself into Irish Republican history through his memorable autobiographies, he also displayed considerable scepticism
about physical force notions of the heroic. The enduring romance of
Irish Republicanism, which still holds many in its grasp, is both sustained and subverted by O'Malley's accounts.

It would be quite wrong to underplay O'Malley's sincere and lasting
commitment to Irish Republican ideals. But it would also be misleading—and unworthy of his own questioning intelligence—to ignore the
scepticism he displayed about aspects of the physical force tradition,
and it is vital to note how his post-Revolutionary attitudes marked a shift
in emphasis. In the mid-1920s his active involvement in militant
Republicanism effectively ended. His writings represented a continuation of his struggle, and he was happy enough that his work should
influence the next generation. In 1945 he was asked if he would allow
certain passages from *On Another Man's Wound* to go into an anthology for schoolchildren and replied: 'Certainly, I give consent. It can't
do school children any great harm.'[10] As a young man O'Malley had
felt that thought should be turned into action (in this he resembled, for
example, Erskine Childers);[11] but while his later writings defended and
explained his youthful Republican violence, the post-Revolutionary
O'Malley believed that new approaches were now appropriate. The
Revolution had deepened Irish divisions between nationalist and
unionist, Protestant and Catholic, and also between nationalists
themselves: O'Malley certainly felt that the Civil War split was one
which required healing. In a post-Second World War piece regarding
wartime neutrality he welcomed the fact that 'Men who had fought
against each other in the bitter Civil War met again as comrades. . . .
The healing of the aching sores resulting from the Civil War were [*sic*]
for some the most important result of neutrality.'[12] Even more
significant, perhaps, was his 1948 observation that the new multi-party
coalition government 'may do some good. It should help to break down
the political hatred of the Civil War. . . . if a younger crowd get into politics a man may be judged on his merits in the year of 1947 and not
those of 1916 or 1922. That again would be a change for the better.'[13]
This marks a refreshing break from the notion that Revolutionary pedigree drawn from the mythic 1916–23 period should determine later
political worth. As with so many key Republican figures, therefore,
O'Malley's attitudes on close inspection defy easy classification. Any
picture which is to do justice to his views must be delicately painted
and must attend to intricate detail; ambiguous images should leap out

from the canvas when viewed from different angles, as with the Jack Yeats oils which O'Malley so much admired. Accordingly, efforts to enlist this complex man for current projects should be inspected very carefully indeed.

Efforts to claim O'Malley's political legacy have on occasions come from surprising quarters. In an important and intriguing speech in Coleraine (Northern Ireland) in December 1992 the UK Secretary of State for Northern Ireland, Sir Patrick Mayhew, used Ernie O'Malley as one of the pegs on which to hang the British government's reconciliatory message to contemporary Irish Republicans:

I recently learned how the letters of an IRA leader of the 1920s, Ernie O'Malley, warmly recognize the cultural riches of the very country against which he had just been fighting with such determination. The cultural achievements of each country draw on and enrich the other. There is therefore no place in anyone's thinking for cultural superiority, let alone hegemony. . . . In a mature and tolerant society there should be ample scope for the development of different cultural expression, which does not pose a threat to, or express itself in hostility towards, those of a different tradition, but which will enrich society as a whole through increasing enjoyment of its very diversity.[14]

This fascinating speech drew attention to key questions relevant to our understanding of Irish politics, and it cast Ernie O'Malley in an interesting light. O'Malley's experience does indeed demonstrate the profoundly enriching interaction of the cultures of Britain and Ireland. But the attempt to use him as a symbol of liberal potential undeniably has its limitations. He combined a richly Anglocentric personal culture with a deep political hostility to British rule in Ireland. Indeed, as this book has argued, it is precisely the interaction of O'Malley's Anglocentrism and his Anglophobia which helped generate his IRA violence in the first place. Moreover, as a young Revolutionary, O'Malley's outlook was one which achieved focus and momentum precisely through its lack of pluralistic tolerance.

But his post-Revolutionary reflections do contain within them the seeds of a different perspective,[15] and it is worth considering O'Malley in relation to that modern scholarship which has sought to reassess the political legacy which he epitomized. Many recent authorities—Roy Foster, Charles Townshend, Tom Garvin, and George Boyce among them—have drawn on O'Malley to illustrate modern Irish history. There has during the last generation been a scholarly interrogation of some of the assumptions traditionally central to Irish nationalist thinking. The Northern Ireland conflict has sharpened the focus of some in looking at the past—politics and history never being far apart in Ireland—and has certainly increased both the output of writings on Irish history and the sense of urgency associated with them. But the reappraisal of supposed nationalist verities pre-dates the eruption of that conflict in the late 1960s. Aspects of Sinn Féin ideology—economic protectionism, cultural closure, Catholic triumphalism, rustic celebration, irredentism regarding the north, Gaelicism, physical force—had been fraying at the edges within the Republic of Ireland before the Ulster crisis emerged in the late 1960s.

   In recent years, this reappraisal has moved on considerably. Thus, for example, the idea of Irish unification as a foreseeably feasible goal has been questioned by the work of economists who have demonstrated its economic impracticality. So, too, the investigations of political scientists have reflected the ways in which the development of the Republic of Ireland's popular and high political cultures have militated against the prioritizing of unification. Indeed, the notion that the people of the island of Ireland unproblematically form one single nation may have been irretrievably displaced. So, too, have the notions that Irish identity should be defined by a separatist stance in relation to Britain or that too narrow an Irish identity even be sought out. As Roy Foster has argued, there has been all too persistent an emphasis through much modern Irish history on constricting and exclusive definitions of what it is to be Irish; Foster's desire to see the emergence of 'a more relaxed and inclusive definition of Irishness, and a less constricted view of Irish history'[16] brings us to the heart of the scholarly reappraisal alluded to above, and links directly to questions concerning the political legacies of a Revolutionary such as Ernie O'Malley.

   This is why a study of O'Malley's life is resoundingly relevant: for many of the issues on which such debates have focused are significantly illuminated by the case of this Republican nationalist. An important historical figure in the crucible years of the new Ireland, O'Malley compelled attention then and still does. Charismatic, dynamic, and talented, he gave powerful expression to many ideas which have remained central to a wide range of Irish nationalists: the Catholic, Gaelic, and separatist definition of the nation; the physical force tradition; the spiritual emphasis at the heart of his brand of Irish Republicanism. The evidence he provides points to the fact that zealous attachment to such ideals brought damage as well as achievement, exclusion as well as cohesion. O'Malley's exciting but ultimately

unsatisfying life does not demonstrate that Irish experience is fully
encapsulated in a purely orthodox, Anglophobic separatism; as we
have seen, this failed to satisfy O'Malley himself. Rather, this story
points to the reasons underlying the emergence of a powerful Republicanism which changed the course of modern Irish politics. In doing so
it reinforces a theme repeatedly in evidence in the pages of this book:
that modern Irishness has persistently involved overlapping layers of
experience (even where these might initially seem to have contra-
dicted one another), and that definitions and explanations of modern
Ireland are only convincing if they register this fact. Inclusiveness
rather than exclusiveness provides the key to understanding and
explaining the history of O'Malley and his times. O'Malley was both
excited by rural Ireland and profoundly frustrated by it; both emanci-
pated by America and desperate to return from there to Ireland; he
both celebrated physical force heroics and doubted them; he was both
a supporter of Gaelicist ideals and aware of the damaging potential of
such orthodoxy in practice.

   All of this reinforces the need to avoid simplification. Just as with
other leading figures in Irish history, considerable sensitivity is
required. The tendency towards revising the less credible existing
orthodoxies must not involve the swinging of the pendulum towards
vilification: a balance is required, and one which treats people's ideas
and experiences seriously. Thus, in acknowledging the brutal and divisive features of 1916–23 Irish Republicanism, one should not lose sight
of the profound attachment to its principles which motivated many
such as O'Malley. Yet the complexity of the picture demonstrates that
Revolutionary certainties provide a shaky foundation on which to base
political philosophy. The IRA of the Irish Revolution sought to build a
united nation; and yet the violence left nationalist Ireland cut in two
for decades, and further deepened divisions between unionists and
nationalists. The Revolutionaries rested faith in defining notions of
Irishness which united many, but which simultaneously excluded
large numbers of Irish people. As Professor George Boyce has recently
observed, 'the terms "Irish" and "Ireland" were used formally and
informally by Catholics as a description of themselves. This forced
many northern Protestants to deny their Irishness.'[17] Plainly, these
reflections do not apply only to one side in the Irish conflict: exclusiveness and damaging violence have characterized unionists and also
the British authorities. This is a point worth stressing when people — of
every side — look to a simplified version of history to justify contempo-

rary brutalities in relation to Northern Ireland. Such validating certainties offer some comfort and are frequently used to sanction political violence; historians tend instead to offer complexities which
subvert both the comfort and the sanction.

Perhaps the central feature of O'Malley's Irish political legacy concerns the Revolutionary rejection of constitutional nationalism. Later
generations can assign a priority to certain episodes in the past which
may not, at the time, have been especially significant; other episodes
may be unfairly demoted. This is where O'Malley is particularly
instructive. The case of the Redmondite constitutional nationalists, for
example (no less than that of the defeated side in the Irish Civil War)
deserves to be evaluated on its own merits rather than through the lens
of those who rejected and defeated it. This is an important point, for in
evaluating the militant Republicanism of 1916–23 it is vital to consider
the constitutional politics which it effectively replaced during the Revolutionary years. Much modern scholarship points to the unrealistic
quality of militant Republican expectation, and also questions the
plausibility of the Republican axiom that constitutional politics will
fail to deliver and that force is therefore necessary. In fact, violence has
tended to remove from Irish conflict that very flexibility required if
progress is likely to be made. The Pearsean Republicanism enthusiastically endorsed by Ernie O'Malley (and central to his Revolutionary
politics) was founded on a rejection of constitutional nationalist politics as being impotent and irrelevant. Some scholars still seem
impressed by this logic.[18] But an alternative view suggests that it is, perhaps, less than compelling and that the Republicans' rejection of constitutional politics was unfortunate. O'Malley himself was clear that
Redmondism had failed, that its approach should be rejected, and that
successful politics had to be based on a more aggressive brand of Irish
nationalism. He referred scornfully to 'the Redmondites and their
system of corruption';[19] in contrast, recent detailed scholarship points
instead towards the Irish Party's fundamental honesty.[20] Again,
O'Malley's suggestion that 'Only by fighting had Ireland ever gained
its own self-respect or any practical advantage'[21] looks naive and simplistic when set against the respective historical records and legacies of
constitutional and physical force Irish nationalists. Moreover, John
Redmond's approach reflected an attempt to reject bigotry, and the
legacy of such efforts should be valued in the context of a Northern
Ireland conflict which has repeatedly been exacerbated by a celebration of narrowness and chauvinism. Militant Republicans' exclusive

definitions of authentic Irishness, no less than their intimidatory practices, arguably offer unhelpful legacies for modern Ulster.

The rejection of Redmondism was echoed later in the Republicans'
hostility towards the popularly endorsed 1921 Treaty, for again there
emerged the issue of one's attitude towards constitutional mandates.
Indeed, one's assessment of O'Malley's political career centrally
depends on this question concerning constitutional politics, and it is
one of undoubted significance in modern Ireland. The issue is raised
both in O'Malley's preference for Pearse over Redmond and also in his
rejection of the Treaty: should one respect popularly expressed political preferences and the compromises which they usually entail, or
should electoral endorsement be obscured by a preference for uncompromising, aggressive vanguardism? O'Malley was surely consistent in
his maintenance of the view that—in 1922 as in 1916 or 1919—strict
observance of popular Irish preferences would have led Irish Republicans to eschew the use of physical force. His argument was that, in
each case, a Revolutionary élite could lead the people through militant example rather than follow their prior preferences. If one accepts
this approach, then O'Malleyite Republicanism will hold some
appeal; if not, then constitutionally pursued compromise appears the
more promising and less divisive route to political progress. Ernie
O'Malley was an enraptured Romantic Revolutionary. His glamorous
reputation among Irish Republicans substantially derives from the
uncompromised perfection of his Republican dream; this uncompromising quality both defines his appeal and clarifies his political
impracticality.

III

The third question concerning the legacies of Ernie O'Malley is this:
has this study of an Irish Republican nationalist anything important to
tell us about our understanding of the wider phenomenon of nationalism? I would argue that O'Malley's concern about the ways in which
posterity would view him has been of enormous benefit to historians,
and not just to those interested in Ireland. Contemporaries such as
Todd Andrews and Frank Gallagher produced fascinating written
accounts of the Irish Revolution; the subtlety and complexity of
O'Malley's memoirs are, perhaps, even more striking. O'Malley not
only illuminates our reading of militant and other forms of Irish

nationalism, but may also help to clarify our understanding of nation-alism as a wider phenomenon. For example, the pattern of antipathy, respect, and emulation on the part of nationalists towards their oppo-nents is not confined to relations between Ireland and Britain. In an important book, Liah Greenfeld has argued that the historical devel-opment of nationalism can best be explained by means of the concepts of prestige and *ressentiment*, combined with the elements of inferior-ity and emulation which have characterized the relations between nationalists of different countries. Her argument is that, against the domestic background of shifting national élites and the redefinition of social hierarchies, questions of dignity and prestige have rendered various nationalisms appealing at key historical moments. Moreover, she asserts the importance of a series of complicated relationships between newly emerging forms of nationalism and their prior existing rivals. Nascent French nationalism, she argues, was defined and char-acterized by a sense of resentment and inferiority towards England and was further influenced by (and emulative of) English prior example. So, too, Russia's attitude towards the west and Germany's toward France and England evinced this explanatory mixture of resentment, inferiority, influence, and imitation. Nationalism having first sprouted in England, its subsequent development—according, at least, to Greenfeld—can be traced in terms of these complicated national rela-tionships.[22]

Greenfeld's argument echoes the detailed evidence for early twenti-eth-century Ireland too closely for it to be casually dismissed. Shifts in domestic élites, the redefinition of social hierarchies, the prestige-bestowing qualities of a new form of nationalism, considerable resent-ment towards England (coupled with a telling weight of influence and emulation,[23] and significant evidence of a sense of inferiority)—each of these components has a crucial part to play in helping us to under-stand the Irish Revolution. In O'Malley's case the 'inborn hate of things English' coexisted with a sizeable degree of British influence, and with glimpses of a sense of what he ironically called 'the superior-ity of the English';[24] and the Revolution was undoubtedly set against the background of shifting élites and hierarchies. Greenfeld's empha-sis on the relationship between nationalism and individual dignity— 'The concept of the nation presupposed a sense of respect toward the individual, an emphasis on the dignity of the human being'[25]—again relates to O'Malley's own career, interweaving questions of national and personal self-esteem and self-confidence. So, too, does her stress on the role played in the development of nationalism by dissatisfactions, tensions, and insecurities relating to identity.

Greenfeld's broad, sociological approach illustrates the possibilities inherent in general treatments of nationalism for enriching our understanding of Ireland. Many other examples from the massive literature on nationalism could be cited. Definitions of the nation and of nationalism are famously problematic.[26] But a working assumption such as that employed by scholars such as Eric Hobsbawm — 'any sufficiently large body of people whose members regard themselves as members of a "nation", will be treated as such'[27] — points us to some of the ways in which specific Irish experience can be illuminated by theorists of nationalism. For such a definition would plainly allow early twentieth-century Irish nationalists their nation. But it would also recognize that there existed a significant body of people — most notably those concentrated in the north-east of the island — who clearly did not form part of the Irish nation as defined by Irish nationalists. Again, Elie Kedourie's classic study of *Nationalism* offers useful scepticism about some of the pieties held dear by nationalist enthusiasts: 'Experience — bitter experience — has shown that contrary to the dreams of Mazzini and President Woodrow Wilson national self-determination is a principle of disorder, not of order, in international life.'[28] This relates back to the point drawn from Hobsbawm. For the very situations in which self-determination is most hailed as a necessary principle — instances of conflict over boundaries, and over the relation between state and nation — tend to be those in which the principle is of least help. As elsewhere, so also in Ireland disputes about the appropriate unit of self-determination are liable to remain fierce and unresolved. Should the unit of self-determination be the people of the island as a whole, as O'Malley and many other Irish nationalists would hold? Or should Ulster unionists be allowed to self-determine their own future within the state set up in the early 1920s to reflect their interests?

The influential work of Ernest Gellner, with his salutary warnings about the dangers inherent in accepting nationalist rhetoric on its own terms, again offers useful insights. Recognizing that essentialist definitions of the nation are less helpful than might be desired (such definitions being too frequently undermined by important exceptions), Gellner opted instead to stress the relationship of nationalism to modernity. Nationalism was presented as a function of modernization, a result of industrial social organization; it resulted from 'the erosion of the multiple petty binding local organizations and their replacement by mobile, anonymous, literate, identity-conferring cultures'.[29] 'The essence of nationalism in the West is that a High—literacy-linked—culture becomes the pervasive, membership-defining culture of the total society.'[30] Such an approach helpfully identified nationalism very much as a modern phenomenon arising from specific historical circumstances rather than one which was given, self-evident, and ancient. Again, Gellner powerfully stressed the vital role of education in relation to nationalism, education being necessary to the new mobile culture, and tension between local educated classes and the metropolitan centre helping to stimulate nationalist development.[31]

Work by scholars such as Greenfeld, Hobsbawm, Kedourie, and Gellner provides a valuable context for the understanding of national-ism, and much of it is clearly helpful in examining Irish nationalism, Republican or otherwise. But it might be suggested that a case study such as the present one—of a particular Irish Republican nationalist—prompts a measure of scepticism about such general, wide-angled treatments. It is here that our exploration of O'Malley's nationalism helps us to approach the wider nationalist phenomenon more mean-ingfully. Theorists of nationalism often except Ireland from their gen-eral patterns,[32] and this might perhaps reinforce our doubts about the applicability of too strict a general model to specific Irish experience. Arguably, it is dangerous to start with such theorizing. Scholars such as Gellner display a greater interest in the general 'why?' of nationalism as a world phenomenon, than in the distinctive qualities of, differ-ences between, or differing nuances within particular nationalisms.[33] His grand, causal narrative of nationalism has comparatively little to say in explaining why individual nationalists opted for particular brands of faith, why they split over specific issues, or why they dis-agreed over policy or over political emphasis. My argument is that more closely focused scholarly studies offer, ultimately, more satisfy-ing explanations of such human behaviour. With Ernie O'Malley it is clear that both his cumulative, month by month development, and also the particular combination of influences and circumstances press-ing upon him at any given moment along that path of historical devel-opment, were uniquely peculiar to him. Without recognizing and documenting this truth it is impossible to delineate, much less explain, his nationalism in any adequate way.

Thus while historical sociology looks at typologies and can provide very helpful definitions,[34] the qualifications to such an approach are acknowledged even by its advocates. Distinctiveness and difference

are as significant as is any putative general similarity among nationalists; indeed, it is questionable whether general accounts of nationalism
accurately depict anybody's specific experience except in rather
blurred images.[35] This book concentrates on a distinctive nationalist
intellectual in the hope that dialogue between its specificity and the
more general treatments of nationalism as a wider phenomenon might
yield a productive tension.

In a sense, the key point here concerns the individual. Studies of
individuals are a necessary complement to work focused on aggregates
or collectivities. In the case of the Revolutionary IRA the importance
of very varied local and individual initiatives in stimulating and
defining the conflict perhaps underlines the need for biographical
monographs.[36] In a compelling recent article Michael Hopkinson,
author of the most scholarly account of the Irish Civil War, has rightly
noted the tendency of scholars dealing with the 1910–23 period in Ireland to offer either biography, or accounts which strongly emphasize
the role of leading figures. Hopkinson suggests that such an approach
has had damaging implications for our longer-term historical understanding. According to this view personalized historiography has, for
example, obscured our vision of important institutions and Hopkinson
calls on historians of twentieth-century Ireland to write 'on themes not
dependent on the chronology of an individual's life or on a straightforward narrative of events'.[37]

Ernie O'Malley might perhaps have disagreed. In December 1948
he wrote to Frank Gallagher: 'I have been reading Frank O'Connor's
Michael Collins. It is a strange medley of information and misinforma-
tion. Collins had colour but leant less to fighting Ireland than O'Connor thinks, but then he wants to create a realistic legend or rather to
back up a legend. It is a pity that there have not been a few other
biographies written. One of Griffith is needed.'[38] O'Connor certainly
did stress Collins's fighting role ('It was quite plain, he did not give a
damn for any political organization which did not subserve the interests of the fighting men'); and although the author thanked O'Malley
among those who had helped him in writing the book, this particular
biography plainly failed to satisfy O'Malley's idea of appropriate biographical treatment. Yet both O'Malley and O'Connor believed that
their writing on the Revolutionary period was in some way addressed
to an audience which was ignorant of—even indifferent to—the struggles of that era. In different ways the modern context, to which
Michael Hopkinson's argument relates, is also one in which the Irish

Revolutionaries are frequently viewed from a position of ignorance and indifference. Frank O'Connor could write in 1937 that 'A new generation has grown up which is utterly indifferent to the great story that began in Easter 1916. It is even bored by it.'[39] This could be applied with even greater force to later generations.

This biography is not constructed as 'a straightforward narrative of events'; but it is written in the belief that, popular ignorance and apathy notwithstanding, biographical treatments of figures such as O'Malley retain an important place in Irish intellectual life. Hopkinson's own account of the Civil War, *Green Against Green*, depends very heavily upon O'Malley sources, much of the book's detail being drawn from O'Malley's individually distinctive writings or interviews. Moreover, Hopkinson himself acknowledges that local initiative during the Irish Revolution was vitally important in stimulating the changes which occurred during those years, and indeed in determining their varied pattern across Ireland. Small numbers of individuals did have a distinctively personal influence in driving things in particular directions. That these directions were not always those which had been sought in no way undermines the general point: Revolutionary zealots such as Ernie O'Malley changed the course of modern Irish history. To appreciate their thinking and their practice it is important to see the wider context, and this book represents an attempt to do precisely that. A purely chronological structure has been eschewed in order that wider themes and broader developments can be interwoven with O'Malley's individual life. But the idea that individual experience is uniquely distinctive and complex, and the conviction that significant individuals can make a marked difference to historical change, together demand that the peculiarities and intricacies of biographical detail be addressed. Irish Revolutionary Republicans—like members of nationalist movements everywhere—were of very varied beliefs, ambitions, backgrounds, qualities, and sympathies. Biographical studies are essential to ensure that these differences are not blurred or ignored, as they can be in more general treatments of nationalism.

IV

More personally, perhaps, what conclusions can be drawn about Ernie O'Malley? What overall perspective can be reached in drawing the book's various themes together? Ulick O'Connor recalled a telling

occasion on which he, at that time a student with an ability at conjur-
ing, had been asked by O'Malley to entertain his two sons, Cormac
and Cahal.

It was suggested that I go and entertain the two boys, who were ill . . . I remember that it was rather difficult for me to get there . . . and I remember going
along—I had quite a big case full of stuff—and I went up the stairs to the two
boys and I did a performance for them. I entertained them for an hour. And I
remember being very struck by the lack of grace, really, that Ernie had. He
admitted me into the house almost as a paid performer, showed me upstairs—
he was inside with a friend . . . —and then showed me out. And I could see that
there was a side to his character that was insensitive to what was going on in
other people's minds. . . . And I think it was due to the fact that his nervous system had been shattered by the events that he had been involved in. And that
therefore it was almost as if that sensory area had been cut. . . . Because I don't
think he was by nature an insensitive person.[40]

Insensitive, cold, graceless—and yet lovingly keen to provide enter-
tainment for his children; the O'Malley presented by such episodes, a
man damaged by youthful adventures, is a poignant and quiet figure.
Adjustment to post-Revolutionary life had proved difficult. Sadness
and a series of fractures and disappointments characterized much of
O'Malley's experience from the mid-1920s onwards. Family, friends,
and politics all let him down in various ways. Intimacy remained crucial to him, but it brought pain and loss more frequently than it did
comfort and calm.

O'Malley himself acknowledged that his obsessive idealism might
have been too rigid, and much of his displacement and isolation
surely resulted from this. Formidable resolution and courage—exhibited in episodes such as the 1923 hunger strike—displayed depths of
commitment which could create and destroy with equal force.
Hostile to the mundane, O'Malley was uncompromisingly extreme:
equally committed in his soldiering, his writing, and his personal
intimacies. Romanticism was his leitmotif. Indeed, given his interweaving of political, religious, and philosophic interests, his Revolutionary disappointment, his ill-health, and his marital unhappiness,
O'Malley might even be considered as something of a Coleridgean
figure. With his creative and destructive zeal, and with a private
life no less turbulent and dramatic than his Revolutionary career,
O'Malley's story is one of commitments and disappointments of
equal profundity. Loyalties and wounds both remained from the Revolution; but it was the latter which gradually gained ground on him.

Burned and hurt, the post-Revolutionary O'Malley appears very much as a post-First World War figure, with pain, loss, and poignancy repeatedly in evidence.

Yet there remained an undoubted glamour about him. His friendship with Catherine Walston epitomized this side of his life. Beautiful, wealthy, and self-consciously outrageous, Catherine inhabited a world which typified the less austere of O'Malley's many settings. Sexually adventurous (Walston's affair with Graham Greene was only one of a large number of extramarital liaisons), Catherine provoked jealous rage from Ernie's wife, and shared with him a lasting friendship. Contact with her—and he spent much time in his later life at the Walstons' elegant Cambridgeshire country house—was echoed by other glamorous associations: from John Wayne to Michael Collins, and from Maureen O'Hara to the Taos bohemians. O'Malley was both man of action and agonizing intellectual; in this he surely resembled another glamorous figure, the similarly mysterious and romantic T. E. Lawrence. Numerous people commented upon the physical similarity between the two men, and the connections go further: self-conscious intellectuals, both were brooding yet committed to action. O'Malley read Lawrence's *Revolt in the Desert*, and took notes from Robert Graves's *Lawrence and the Arabs*. He noted Lawrence's Irish connections, his undergraduate taste for French poetry, and his huge appetite for reading. He also copied out from Graves the following passage, which surely carried for O'Malley some echoes of his own life: 'he [Lawrence] is not even a single-minded romantic: he clearly despises his romanticism and fights it in himself so sternly that he only makes it more incurable.'[41]

O'Malley's mind was instinctively subversive, independent both of orthodoxy and of authority. A talented and widely praised writer, he displayed an honesty and consistency as he attempted to enrich his life with meaning through intellectual endeavour. Arguably, his writing provided a redemption in later life and saved him from post-Revolutionary oblivion. As a roving literary intellectual, O'Malley stood outside society and yet came to be esteemed for his imaginative reconstructions of it. His accomplishments are all the more impressive for his being essentially self-taught; and this culture of self-improvement stayed with him throughout. It was evident in his fastidious approach to his books: whether collecting, reading, annotating, or cataloguing them in his obsessive lists. And if the impulse to collect and list reflects a certain insecurity, then this surely lies at the heart of

his restless intellectual energy. Such energy stimulated him to impressive achievements. Crucial also to the value of his work were
his breadth of interests (history, painting, sculpture, music, literature)
and his range of contexts (Dublin, Mayo, New Mexico, New York,
Saratoga Springs, Paris). O'Malley's reflections on Ireland gained richness owing to this avoidance of narrowness. Similarly, his writing
strikes so powerfully in part because he combined the ability to depict
with the capacity for dramatic action. His re-creation of the Republican world of 1916–23 is doubly resounding because he was equally
significant as writer and as leading Revolutionary participant.

    The Revolutionaries had constructed an alternative politics; in his
later life O'Malley existed in the bohemian counterpart of this world,
avoiding mainstream experience whether political or intellectual.
More at home in the arts than in formal political life, he indulged his
imaginative preferences in defence of his passionate convictions: his
belief in the Irish Republican cause, his celebration of the imagination, vitality, and vigour of Irish life, and his robustly defiant hostility to
deference. All this seems clear enough. But it is important always to
recognize the ambiguous in O'Malley; this is in some ways the fundamental point about him and can be illuminated by brief consideration
of one of his friends. Christopher Ricks has brilliantly examined that
celebrant of oblivion Samuel Beckett and, in particular, the ways in
which Beckett treated death and life through language which was itself
simultaneously alive and dead. Cliché, for example: 'A cliché is a dead
piece of language, of which one cliché might be that it is dead but
won't lie down.'[42] Words of antithetical sense also served Beckett's
purpose here, cancelling themselves out by simultaneously implying
their own opposite: 'cleave', 'in charge of', 'quite'—and 'certain'. As
Ricks notes, the word 'certain' can indicate both precision and impre-
cision: 'Are you *certain*?'; 'There was a *certain* amount of sympathy for
the proposal.'

    This also offers a helpful way of understanding Ernie O'Malley.
O'Malley is compelling and exciting precisely because he contains
within himself leanings, sympathies, and experiences of what might
be termed antithetical sense: intellectually élitist and a committed
defender of popular culture; profoundly urban and absorbed in rural
values; enthusiastic for local tradition, attachment, and sentiment, and
yet keen to avoid the constraints of the parochial; Anglophobic and
Anglophile; both enthralled by and sceptical of the heroic strain in
militant Irish Republicanism; fiercely committed and persistently

ambivalent; simultaneously hating and loving exile. All this suggests
that there is room indeed for a Beckettian reading of O'Malley's *certain* ideal of freedom': 'I had given allegiance to a certain ideal of freedom as personified by the Irish Republic. It had not been realized
except in the mind.'[43] In the several spheres which he inhabited—
Revolution, writing, art criticism—his ability to occupy at once the
role of enthusiast and subversive raised echoes which still reverberate
today. Interpreting O'Malley is rewarding and difficult because of
such dual qualities. His collaboration with John Ford can, for example, be seen as a typically ambiguous gesture. There was considerable
strain between the image of rural Ireland presented in the idealized
Quiet Man and the frustrations and fractures of O'Malley's actual contemporary Irish experience. So also there exist many other strikingly
ambiguous images from his life, and these are instructive about wider
Irish experience. O'Malley does not provide any kind of norm for Irish
society, since it is precisely the complexity and uniqueness of his story
which helps us to make sense of it. But there are certainly family
resemblances linking O'Malley's experience to that of the broader
Irish community. These are frequently ambiguous, being characterized by the simultaneous existence of apparently contradictory realities. Emigration both as painful rupture and as positive opportunity;
the Irish relationship with Britishness being characterized by a profound hostility and by an enriching intimacy; simultaneous pride in,
and dissatisfaction with, the distinctive localisms of Irish culture;
attachment to, and scepticism about, physical force Irish Republican
orthodoxy—each of these tense relationships is evident in Ernie
O'Malley's experience and reflection. That they also form a major part
of modern Irish culture and politics renders him as important as he is
endlessly compelling.

Going through the country I often felt as would a traveller on a railway journey
as he looked at the passing life about him, dissociated from it. The people had
to live the round of the soil and solve its problems of economic and of living
relationships, which were more of living than my relation to the fighting effort
only; beneath the will necessary for the action and decision needed for command was my other less resolute and retiring self. The strain was there always,
but work kept it away. Always alert and steeling myself, wondering if peace
would ever come, yet pushing on officers and columns to make the fighting
more thorough, feeling what the unarmed people were going through, but
planning operations that would bring down on them more than equivalent
brutality.[44]

Notes

1 THE LIFE

1. O'Malley to Childers, 26 Nov.–1 Dec. 1923, in R. English and C. O'Malley (eds.), *Prisoners: The Civil War Letters of Ernie O'Malley* (Dublin: Poolbeg, 1991), 69–93.
2. O'Malley to Ames, Summer 1932, Archives of the Yaddo Corporation, Saratoga Springs, NY.
3. C. S. Andrews, *Dublin Made Me: An Autobiography* (Cork: Mercier, 1979), 256.
4. As in Oscar Wilde's play, there are certain complications surrounding the name Ernest. Unlike Wilde's play, however, a little clarification at the start might be helpful. Ernest Bernard Malley came later to add the O' to his name and became most commonly known as Ernie O'Malley. A number of variations, including Earnán O Máille and Earnán O'Malley, occur during his career. In this book he will be known, as he most commonly was during his lifetime, as Ernie O'Malley.
5. E. O'Malley, *On Another Man's Wound* (Dublin: Anvil, 1979; 1st edn. 1936), 19–22.
6. O'Malley to Childers, 26 Nov.–1 Dec. 1923, in English and O'Malley (eds.), *Prisoners*, 70.
7. O'Malley to Childers, 26 Nov.–1 Dec. 1923, ibid. 71.
8. D. Fitzpatrick, 'Militarism in Ireland 1900–1922', in T. Bartlett and K. Jeffery (eds.), *A Military History of Ireland* (Cambridge: Cambridge University Press, 1996), 394.
9. O'Malley to Childers, 26 Nov.–1 Dec. 1923, in English and O'Malley (eds.), *Prisoners*, 72–3.
10. D. G. Boyce, *Nationalism in Ireland* (London: Routledge, 1995; 1st edn. 1982), 313.
11. *Public Attitude and Opinion in Ireland as to the Recent Outbreak* (15 May 1916), Bonar Law Papers, HLRO BL 63/C/3.
12. For a variety of very differing opinions, see M. Ni Dhonnchadha and T. Dorgan (eds.), *Revising the Rising* (Derry: Field Day, 1991), and P. Bew, *Ideology and the Irish Question: Ulster Unionism and Irish Nationalism 1912–1916* (Oxford: Oxford University Press, 1994).
13. O'Malley to Childers, 26 Nov.–1 Dec. 1923, in English and O'Malley (eds.), *Prisoners*, 70.
14. O'Malley, *On Another Man's Wound*, 27.
15. Ibid. 32.
16. O'Malley to Childers, 26 Nov.–1 Dec. 1923, in English and O'Malley (eds.), *Prisoners*, 73.
17. O'Malley, *On Another Man's Wound*, 9.

18. Ibid. 38.
19. O'Malley diary (13 Oct. 1928), Cormac O'Malley Papers, PP.
20. O'Malley to Humphreys, 25 Dec. 1923, in English and O'Malley (eds.), *Prisoners*, 129.
21. O'Malley to Childers, 5–7 Dec. 1923, ibid. 110.
22. O'Malley, *On Another Man's Wound*, 62.
23. O'Malley to Childers, 26 Nov.–1 Dec. 1923, in English and O'Malley (eds.), *Prisoners*, 74.
24. O'Malley was registered for courses in the UCD Faculty of Medicine for the Academic Session 1915–16 (First Medicine) and for the Academic Sessions 1916–17, 1917–18, 1926–7, 1927–8, and 1936–7 (Second Medicine)—information courtesy of the UCD Office of the Registrar. He never completed his medical studies.
25. R. E. Childers, *The Riddle of the Sands* (Harmondsworth: Penguin, 1978; 1st edn. 1903), 27.
26. For a stimulating treatment of Griffith, see P. Maume, 'The Ancient Constitution: Arthur Griffith and his Intellectual Legacy to Sinn Féin', *Irish Political Studies*, 10 (1995).
27. O'Malley, *On Another Man's Wound*, 60–1.
28. Ibid. 73–4.
29. O'Malley, handwritten notes (n.d.), Cormac O'Malley Papers, PP.
30. Summary of Outrages against the Police, week ending 16 May 1920, PRO CO 904/148.
31. O'Malley, *On Another Man's Wound*, 150–5; cf. D. Breen, *My Fight for Irish Freedom* (Dublin: Anvil, 1989; 1st edn. 1924), 107–10.
32. O'Malley, *On Another Man's Wound*, 218, 221.
33. J. Maher, *The Flying Column: West Kilkenny 1916–1921* (Dublin: Geography Publications, 1987), ch. 8; see also J. J. Comerford, *My Kilkenny IRA Days 1916–1922* (Kilkenny: privately published, 1980; 1st edn. 1978), 280.
34. E. O'Malley, *Raids and Rallies* (Dublin: Anvil, 1982), 156.
35. ' "Do you think you are going to beat us?" said the Major; "you're going to answer questions, do you hear?" he shouted. . . . He hit me hard in a passion, smash after smash. I got up from the floor. My cheeks were cut, blood ran from my forehead into my eyes. My eyes were swollen, it was hard to keep up the lids. . . . The blood in my eyes made the room a distorted jumble of reds and blues. A hot, salty taste of warm blood flowed down my throat, and through my lips when I took breath' (O'Malley, *On Another Man's Wound*, 250).
36. Inspector General's Confidential Monthly Report for Jan. 1921, PRO CO 904/114.
37. O'Malley to FitzGerald, 25 Aug. 1921, FitzGerald Papers, ADUCD P80.
38. O'Malley interview with Gilmore, Ernie O'Malley Papers, ADUCD P17b/106.

39. Private Sessions of Second Dáil, 17 Dec. 1921.

40. E. O'Malley, *The Singing Flame* (Dublin: Anvil, 1978), 41.

41. For election details, see Michael Gallagher's invaluable *Irish Elections 1922–1944: Results and Analysis* (Limerick: PSAI Press, 1993).

42. Quoted in T. de Vere White, *Kevin O'Higgins* (Dublin: Anvil, 1986; 1st edn. 1948), 96.

43. O'Malley, *The Singing Flame*, 11.

44. O'Malley to Childers, 23 Nov. 1923, in English and O'Malley (eds.), *Prisoners*, 58.

45. M. Hopkinson, *Green Against Green: The Irish Civil War* (Dublin: Gill and Macmillan, 1988), 72.

46. O'Malley, *The Singing Flame*, 101, 120.

47. Ibid. 125.

48. O'Malley, Statement concerning ASU Dublin (26 Oct. 1949), Cormac O'Malley Papers, PP.

49. T. Garvin, *Nationalist Revolutionaries in Ireland 1858–1928* (Oxford: Oxford University Press, 1987), 142.

50. O'Malley, *The Singing Flame*, 172.

51. Ibid. 160.

52. S. Bean Ui Dhonnchadha (Sheila Humphreys) in U. MacEoin (ed.), *Survivors* (Dublin: Argenta, 1987; 1st edn. 1980), 346.

53. 'Batt was such a friend of our family's and of Republicans at the time, that we know perfectly well he didn't give it away' (Sheila Humphreys, interview with the author, Dublin, 26 Feb. 1987).

54. Brief for Counsel on behalf of Earnon O Maille (*sic*) (11 Jan. 1923), Cormac O'Malley Papers, PP.

55. O'Malley, *The Singing Flame*, 186–7.

56. *Irish Times*, 6 Nov. 1922.

57. *Poblacht na h-Eireann*, 7 Nov. 1922.

58. Ibid. 3 Nov. 1922.

59. Brief for Counsel on behalf of Earnon O Maille (*sic*) (11 Jan. 1923), Cormac O'Malley Papers, PP.

60. O'Malley, handwritten notes (n.d.), Cormac O'Malley Papers, PP. In January 1923 O'Malley expressed his concern 'that I may collapse at the trial through weakness, and the enemy may state I collapsed through funk' (O'Malley to Lynch, 10 Jan. 1923, Twomey Papers, ADUCD P69/7 (10)).

61. O'Malley to FitzGerald, 22 May 1923, Desmond FitzGerald Papers, ADUCD P80/313 (6). Marion signed this correspondence as 'O'Malley' rather than 'Malley'.

62. Senior Medical Officer's Reports, 27 Dec., 29 Dec. 1922, Files of the Dept. of the Taoiseach, NA S 1369/17.

63. S. O'Faoláin, *De Valera* (Harmondsworth: Penguin, 1939), 102.

64. P. O'Donnell, *The Gates Flew Open* (London: Jonathan Cape, 1932), 178–9.

NOTES 217

65. O'Malley to Childers, 12 Nov. 1923, in English and O'Malley (eds.), *Prisoners*, 47.
66. O'Malley, *The Singing Flame*, 238.
67. O'Malley to Childers, 28 Oct. 1923, Cormac O'Malley Papers, PP.
68. O'Malley to Plunkett, 15 Nov. 1923, in English and O'Malley (eds.), *Prisoners*, 50.
69. O'Malley, *The Singing Flame*, 262.
70. O'Malley to Childers, 23 Nov. 1923, in English and O'Malley (eds.), *Prisoners*, 58.
71. O'Malley to Lynch, 14 Jan. 1923, Twomey Papers, ADUCD P69/7 (2).
72. O'Donnell, *The Gates Flew Open*.
73. F. O'Connor, *An Only Child* (Belfast: Blackstaff, 1993; 1st edn. 1961), 259–60.
74. Gallagher diary, Gallagher Papers, NLI MS 18,356 [4].
75. O'Malley to Lynch, 10 Jan. 1923, Twomey Papers, ADUCD P69/7 (9).
76. L. O'Flaherty, *The Assassin* (Dublin: Wolfhound, 1988; 1st edn. 1928), 65.
77. Chief of Staff Report to Executive Meeting (10 Aug. 1924), Ernie O'Malley Papers, ADUCD P17a/12.
78. Cormac O'Malley interview with Peadar O'Donnell, Oct. 1970, Cormac O'Malley Papers, PP.
79. S. O'Faoláin, *Constance Markievicz* (London: Sphere, 1967; 1st edn. 1934), 10.
80. Ernie O'Malley Papers, ADUCD P17b/190.
81. O'Malley, Handwritten Notes (n.d.), Cormac O'Malley Papers, PP. During the Revolution O'Malley had sustained numerous injuries: to his wrist and ankle in 1918, his shoulder and hip in 1920, his feet and eyes in British custody in 1920–1, and his multiple bullet wounds inflicted during his capture in Nov. 1922.
82. Chief of Staff to Minister of Defence, 19 June 1925, Twomey Papers, ADUCD P69/6 (36).
83. O'Malley to Monroe, 10 Jan. 1935, Cormac O'Malley Papers, PP.
84. O'Malley, European diaries, Cormac O'Malley Papers, PP.
85. O'Malley to Raleigh, 15 Apr. 1926, Cormac O'Malley Papers, PP.
86. Chief of Staff to O'Malley, 31 May 1926, Twomey Papers, ADUCD P69/39 (13).
87. O'Malley to Raleigh, 21 Nov. 1926, Cormac O'Malley Papers, PP.
88. He also recalls O'Malley being 'a bit of a braggart' who 'boasted a lot of his exploits' (N. J. McGahon to the author, 11 July 1990).
89. O'Malley, Autobiographical Notes (c.1950), Cormac O'Malley Papers, PP.
90. O'Malley to Gallagher, 12 Nov. 1926, Cormac O'Malley Papers, PP.
91. 'Fianna Fáil was, from the beginning, totally electorally orientated. The party's ideals would be realized by winning a parliamentary majority; desired changes would be effected by the actions of a Fianna Fáil

government' (R. Dunphy, *The Making of Fianna Fáil Power in Ireland 1923–1948* (Oxford: Oxford University Press, 1995), 77).

92. De Valera to Walsh, 12 May 1928, Walsh Papers, Box 26, NYPL.
93. De Valera to O'Malley, 30 Nov. 1928, Cormac O'Malley Papers, PP.
94. O'Malley, handwritten notes (1928), Cormac O'Malley Papers, PP.
95. Aiken, *Irish Press* promotional letter (1928), Cormac O'Malley Papers, PP.
96. O'Malley diaries, Cormac O'Malley Papers, PP.
97. O'Malley diary (15 Oct. 1928), Cormac O'Malley Papers, PP.
98. R. F. Foster, *Paddy and Mr Punch: Connections in Irish and English History* (London: Allen Lane, 1993), 300.
99. Weston diary (14 May 1929), Centre for Creative Photography, University of Arizona, Tucson.
100. O'Malley to Golden, 10 July 1955, Sax Papers, PP.
101. O'Malley notebook (Jan. 1931), Cormac O'Malley Papers, PP.
102. O'Malley notebook (Feb. 1931), Cormac O'Malley Papers, PP.
103. O'Malley notebook (1931), Cormac O'Malley Papers, PP.
104. Crane to Cowley, 2 June 1931, in B. Weber (ed.), *The Letters of Hart Crane 1916–1932* (New York: Hermitage House, 1952), 371.
105. O'Malley to Monroe, 10 Jan. 1935, Cormac O'Malley Papers, PP.
106. O'Malley diary (1931), Cormac O'Malley Papers, PP.
107. Crane to Cowley, 2 June 1931, in Weber (ed.), *Letters of Hart Crane 1916–1932*, 371.
108. O'Malley to Monroe, 10 Jan. 1935, Cormac O'Malley Papers, PP.
109. Clurman, in C. Odets, *Six Plays of Clifford Odets* (New York: Random House, 1939), 424, 426.
110. O'Malley to Strand, 13 July 1932, Strand Papers, Centre for Creative Photography, University of Arizona, Tucson.
111. H. Clurman, *The Fervent Years: The Story of the Group Theatre and the Thirties* (New York: Hill and Wang, 1957; 1st edn. 1945), 86.
112. O'Malley to Strand, 19 Aug. 1932, Strand Papers, Centre for Creative Photography, University of Arizona, Tucson.
113. Ames to O'Malley, 9 Aug. 1932, Archives of the Yaddo Corporation, Saratoga Springs, NY.
114. O'Malley to Strand, 13 July 1932, Strand Papers, Centre for Creative Photography, University of Arizona, Tucson.
115. O'Malley to Strand, 19 Aug. 1932, Cormac O'Malley Papers, PP.
116. O'Malley to Hooker, 9 July 1933, Etáin O'Malley Papers, PP.
117. O'Malley to Golden, 21 Jan. 1934, Sax Papers, PP.
118. O'Malley to Hooker, 17 Dec. 1933, Etáin O'Malley Papers, PP.
119. O'Malley to Golden, 21 Jan. 1934, Sax Papers, PP.
120. O'Malley to (Helen Merriam) Golden, 9 Apr. 1935, Sax Papers, PP.
121. O'Malley to Strand, 28 Dec. 1934, Strand Papers, Centre for Creative Photography, University of Arizona, Tucson.

122. *Poetry*: published in Chicago by the Modern Poetry Association; founded and edited 1912–36 by Harriet Monroe.

123. Aiken to O'Malley, 4 Feb. 1935, Cormac O'Malley Papers, PP.

124. O'Malley to Hooker, 23 Apr. 1935, Etáin O'Malley Papers, PP.

125. O'Malley to Hooker, 8 May (1935?), Etáin O'Malley Papers, PP.

126. O'Malley to Hooker, 1 July 1935, Etáin O'Malley Papers, PP.

127. O'Malley to O'Malley, 30 May 1938, Cormac O'Malley Papers, PP.

128. O'Malley/Hooker Marriage Certificate, 27 Sept. 1935, Westminster Register Office, London.

129. O'Malley to Raleigh, 4 June 1935, Cormac O'Malley Papers, PP.

130. M. Ó hAodha, 'A Recollection of Ernie O'Malley', Cormac O'Malley Papers, PP.

131. John Fleetwood to the author, 5 Dec. 1990.

132. John Fleetwood, interview with the author, Dublin, 22 Nov. 1991.

133. O'Malley to Comer, 18 Dec. 1936, Cormac O'Malley Papers, PP.

134. O'Malley to Hooker, 30 Aug. 1937, Cormac O'Malley Papers, PP.

135. O'Malley to O'Malley, 20 June 1938, Cormac O'Malley Papers, PP.

136. *New York Times*, 28 Feb. 1937.

137. F. O'Connor, *My Father's Son* (London: Pan, 1971; 1st edn. 1968), 99. Yeats was, in fact, supportive of the idea that O'Malley should become a member of the Academy.

138. O'Malley to Ryan, 22 Dec. 1936; Ryan had apologized to O'Malley for having described him—in *Remembering Sion*—as a gunman, Ryan to O'Malley, 14 Dec. 1936, Cormac O'Malley Papers.

139. O'Malley, Autobiographical Notes (*c*.1950), Cormac O'Malley Papers, PP.

140. O'Malley to Golden, 13 Dec. 1937, Cormac O'Malley Papers, PP.

141. O'Malley, Autobiographical Notes (*c*.1950), Cormac O'Malley Papers, PP.

142. Citkovitz to O'Malley, Oct. 1936, Cormac O'Malley Papers, PP; cf. O'Malley's own comment that his handwriting was 'distinctive in its illegibility' (O'Malley, draft manuscript of *On Another Man's Wound* (1933?), Ernie O'Malley Papers, ADUCD P17b/147).

143. O'Malley, Autobiographical Notes (*c*.1950), Cormac O'Malley Papers, PP.

144. Metzner to Knapp, 29 Mar. 1983, Cormac O'Malley Papers, PP.

145. O'Malley, Autobiographical Notes (*c*.1950), Cormac O'Malley Papers, PP.

146. O'Malley, 'Farming' notebook (n.d.), Cormac O'Malley Papers, PP.

147. O'Malley, Autobiographical Notes (*c*.1950), Cormac O'Malley Papers, PP.

148. O'Malley to Laithwaite, Dec. 1941, Cormac O'Malley Papers, PP.

149. O'Malley, Autobiographical Notes (*c*.1950), Cormac O'Malley Papers, PP.

150. O'Malley to Sheehy, 11 Dec. 1955, Cormac O'Malley Papers, PP.
151. J. B. Yeats Sketch Book, Cormac O'Malley Papers, PP.
152. Marquand to O'Malley, 28 Aug. 1945, Cormac O'Malley Papers, PP.
153. Cormac O'Malley Notes (1960), Cormac O'Malley Papers.
154. *The Bell*, 1/3 (Dec. 1940), 5–6.
155. O'Malley to Childers, 5–7 Dec. 1923, in English and O'Malley (eds.), *Prisoners*, 110.
156. E. O'Malley, 'The Traditions of Mexican Painting' (2 Jan. 1947), BBC Written Archives Centre, Reading.
157. Cable, 28 Jan. 1949, O'Malley to Hooker, Etáin O'Malley Papers, PP.
158. O'Malley to Hooker, Jan. 1949, Etáin O'Malley Papers, PP.
159. O'Malley to Kelleher, Feb. 1950, Cormac O'Malley Papers, PP.
160. O'Malley to McGrail, 27 May 1956, Cormac O'Malley Papers, PP. Cf. Maureen O'Hara's comment on Ford as director: 'He was a tyrant' (Maureen O'Hara Blair, interview with the author, New York, 10 Apr. 1995).
161. Ford 'retained a love of Ireland and hatred of British rule that he was to seek with considerable tenacity to translate into film' (J. Richards, 'Ireland, the Empire, and Film', in K. Jeffery (ed.), *'An Irish Empire'? Aspects of Ireland and the British Empire* (Manchester: Manchester University Press, 1996), 38).
162. Maureen O'Hara Blair, interview with the author, New York, 10 Apr. 1995.
163. O'Malley to Hooker, 12 July 1952, Etáin O'Malley Papers, PP.
164. O'Malley to Golden, 10 July 1955, Sax Papers, PP.
165. O'Malley to Strand, 3 Aug. 1955, Strand Papers, Centre for Creative Photography, University of Arizona, Tucson.
166. O'Malley to MacManus, 16 Apr. 1953, Cormac O'Malley Papers, PP.
167. O'Malley to Strand, 19 July 1953, Cormac O'Malley Papers, PP.
168. O'Malley to Strand, 8 Dec. 1954, Cormac O'Malley Papers, PP.
169. O'Malley to McGrail, 20 Feb. 1955, Cormac O'Malley Papers, PP.
170. Beckett to O'Malley, 26 Mar. 1955, Cormac O'Malley Papers, PP.
171. There was much that O'Malley and Beckett shared: a passionate enthusiasm for painting, sculpture, and architecture; a love of reading (including Chaucer, Shakespeare, Dante, and Milton) and of theatre; loyalty to a select group of intimate friends; and tendencies towards stubbornness, independence of mind, moodiness, shyness, and introspection (J. Knowlson, *Damned to Fame: The Life of Samuel Beckett* (London: Bloomsbury, 1996)).
172. O'Malley to Sheehy, 11 Dec. 1955, Cormac O'Malley Papers, PP.
173. O'Malley to McGrail, 10 Apr. 1955, Cormac O'Malley Papers, PP.
174. O'Malley to McGrail, 16–17 Mar. 1955, Cormac O'Malley Papers, PP.
175. O'Malley to McGrail, 9 May 1955, Cormac O'Malley Papers, PP.
176. More specifically: aortic stenosis, sub-acute bacterial endocarditis, and left ventricular failure.

177. *Irish Press*, 26 Mar. 1957.
178. *Sunday Press*, 31 Mar. 1957.
179. *Irish Times*, 26 Mar. 1957.
180. *New York Times*, 27 Mar. 1957.

2 THE REVOLUTIONARY

1. O'Malley to Lynch, 9 Jan. 1923, in English and O'Malley (eds.), *Prisoners*, 25.
2. Liber to O'Malley, 24 Jan., 5 Mar. 1951, Cormac O'Malley Papers, PP.
3. O'Malley, *The Singing Flame*, 214.
4. O'Malley notebook (1931), Cormac O'Malley Papers, PP.
5. Francis Stuart, interview with the author, Dublin, 24 Feb. 1987.
6. Sheila Humphreys, interview with the author, Dublin, 26 Feb. 1987.
7. C. Dalton, *With the Dublin Brigade 1917–1921* (London: Peter Davies, 1929), 95.
8. Breen, *My Fight for Irish Freedom*, 174.
9. O'Malley to FitzGerald, 25 Aug. 1921, FitzGerald Papers, ADUCD P80.
10. O'Malley notebook, Ernie O'Malley Papers, NLI MS 10,973.
11. Sean Lemass, interview with Cormac O'Malley, Oct. 1970, Cormac O'Malley Papers, PP.
12. *An t-Óglách*, 15 Aug. 1918, 30 Sept. 1918, 15 Dec. 1919.
13. M. Ryan, *Liam Lynch: The Real Chief* (Cork: Mercier, 1986), 9.
14. O'Malley, *On Another Man's Wound*, 201.
15. S. O'Faoláin, *King of the Beggars: A Life of Daniel O'Connell* (Dublin: Poolbeg, 1986; 1st edn. 1938), 107.
16. O'Malley to O'Malley, 7 June 1938, Cormac O'Malley Papers, PP.
17. For extended discussion of O'Donnell's political thinking, see R. English, *Radicals and the Republic: Socialist Republicanism in the Irish Free State 1925–1937* (Oxford: Oxford University Press, 1994).
18. O'Malley to FitzGerald, 25 Aug. 1921, FitzGerald Papers, ADUCD P80.
19. O'Malley, *The Singing Flame*, 25.
20. O'Malley, *On Another Man's Wound*, 213.
21. O'Malley to Childers, c.27 Nov. 1923, in English and O'Malley (eds.), *Prisoners*, 94.
22. O'Malley to Childers, 29 Dec. 1923, ibid. 130.
23. O'Malley to Childers, 24 Nov. 1923, ibid. 63.
24. O'Malley to Childers, 17 Dec. 1923, ibid. 123–4.
25. L. Deasy, *Brother Against Brother* (Cork: Mercier, 1982), 32, 43.
26. O'Malley to Gallagher, 31 Dec. 1948, Cormac O'Malley Papers, PP.
27. O'Malley manuscript, 'Sean Connolly', Cormac O'Malley Papers, PP.
28. The Fenians were a conspiratorial, Republican, Irish revolutionary body which emerged in the mid-19th century.

29. O'Malley, manuscript draft of *On Another Man's Wound* (n.d.), Cormac O'Malley Papers, PP.

30. C. S. Andrews, *Dublin Made Me: An Autobiography* (Cork: Mercier, 1979), 101. This attitude even involved disdain towards sympathetic politicians; one Republican (Bob Brennan) later informed O'Malley that in the early phase of the 1917–21 struggle, 'Men around [Michael] Collins were on the defensive about the constitutional wing, sneering at them' (O'Malley interview with Brennan, Ernie O'Malley Papers, ADUCD P17b/88).

31. O'Malley, *The Singing Flame*, 11.

32. O'Malley to O'Malley, 30 May 1938, Cormac O'Malley Papers, PP.

33. L. O'Flaherty, *Thy Neighbour's Wife* (Dublin: Wolfhound, 1992; 1st edn. 1923), 122.

34. O'Malley, *On Another Man's Wound*, 317.

35. O'Malley, *The Singing Flame*, 132.

36. O'Malley interview with Maguire, Ernie O'Malley Papers, ADUCD P17b/100.

37. O'Malley manuscript, 'Sean Connolly', Cormac O'Malley Papers, PP.

38. O'Malley to Childers, 26 Nov.–1 Dec. 1923, in English and O'Malley (eds.), *Prisoners*, 80.

39. See e.g. O'Malley's notes on the movements of RIC men, and on the pressure exerted on publicans, in 1921 (O'Malley notebook, Ernie O'Malley Papers, NLI MS 10,973).

40. RIC Summary of Police Reports for 2 May 1920, PRO CO 904/139.

41. *Irish Times*, 5 May, 11 May 1920.

42. IRA Operation Order No. 7, 7 Aug. 1922, Ernie O'Malley Papers, ADUCD P17a/16.

43. O'Malley to Healy, 21 Sept. 1922, Ernie O'Malley Papers, ADUCD P17a/57.

44. C. Campbell, *Emergency Law in Ireland 1918–1925* (Oxford: Oxford University Press, 1994), 19–20.

45. O'Malley, *On Another Man's Wound*, 326.

46. M. Brennan, *The War in Clare 1911–1921: Personal Memoirs of the Irish War of Independence* (Dublin: Four Courts Press, 1980), 80–1.

47. O'Malley manuscript, 'Sean Connolly', Cormac O'Malley Papers, PP.

48. C. Townshend, *The British Campaign in Ireland 1919–1921: The Development of Political and Military Policies* (Oxford: Oxford University Press, 1975), 206; Campbell, *Emergency Law*, 345.

49. 'Guerrilla . . . 1. An irregular war carried on by small bodies of men acting independently . . . 2. One engaged in such warfare' (*Shorter Oxford English Dictionary*, i (Oxford: Oxford University Press, 1980; 1st edn. 1933), 900). This definition fits O'Malley perfectly.

50. C. von Clausewitz, *On War* (Harmondsworth: Penguin, 1968; 1st edn. 1832), 104.

51. O'Malley to Humphreys, 25 Dec. 1923, in English and O'Malley (eds.), *Prisoners*, 129.

52. O'Malley, *On Another Man's Wound*, 85.

53. O'Flaherty, *The Assassin*, 76.

54. T. Garvin, *1922: The Birth of Irish Democracy* (Dublin: Gill and Macmillan, 1996), 44.

55. Minutes of General Army Convention, 17 Mar. 1934, MacEntee Papers, ADUCD P67/525.

56. O'Malley manuscript, 'Sean Connolly', Cormac O'Malley Papers, PP.

57. See e.g. the very different passions respectively expressed in articles by John Waters and Kevin Myers in the *Irish Times*, 23 Apr. 1996.

58. M. G. Valiulis, *Portrait of a Revolutionary: General Richard Mulcahy and the Founding of the Irish Free State* (Blackrock: Irish Academic Press, 1992), 26.

59. See e.g. Bew, *Ideology and the Irish Question*.

60. M. Comerford, *The First Dáil: January 21 1919* (Dublin: Joe Clarke, 1969), 38.

61. D. G. Boyce, Review of English and O'Malley (eds.), *Prisoners*, in *Irish Political Studies*, 7 (1992), 125.

62. See, in particular, T. Garvin, 'Unenthusiastic Democrats: The Emergence of Irish Democracy', in R. J. Hill and M. Marsh (eds.), *Modern Irish Democracy* (Blackrock: Irish Academic Press, 1993).

63. O'Malley, *The Singing Flame*, 285.

64. Breen, *My Fight for Irish Freedom*, 29.

65. O'Malley to Childers, 5–7 Dec. 1923, in English and O'Malley (eds.), *Prisoners*, 110.

66. O'Donnell, quoted in M. McInerney, *Peadar O'Donnell: Irish Social Rebel* (Dublin: O'Brien Press, 1974), 219.

67. O'Malley, *On Another Man's Wound*, 24.

68. O'Malley, draft manuscript of *On Another Man's Wound* (1933?), Ernie O'Malley Papers, ADUCD P17b/147.

69. Brennan, *War in Clare 1911–1921*, 81.

70. O'Malley to Childers, 8 Dec. 1923, in English and O'Malley (eds.), *Prisoners*, 117.

71. O'Malley, *The Singing Flame*, 213.

72. J. H. Whyte, *Church and State in Modern Ireland 1923–1979* (Dublin: Gill and Macmillan, 1984).

73. O'Malley to Childers, 7 Nov. 1923, in English and O'Malley (eds.), *Prisoners*, 42.

74. Ernie O'Malley Papers, ADUCD P17a/43.

75. O'Malley, *The Singing Flame*, 252–3.

76. O'Malley to Childers, 12 Nov. 1923, in English and O'Malley (eds.), *Prisoners*, 48.

77. Aiken to all Volunteers on hunger strike, 30 Oct. 1923, Ernie O'Malley Papers, ADUCD P17a/43.

78. Aiken to all Volunteers on hunger strike, 5 Nov. 1923, Ernie O'Malley Papers, ADUCD P17a/43.

79. See e.g. the memoirs of O'Malley's colleague Frank Gallagher: F. Gallagher, *Days of Fear* (London, John Murray, 1928).

80. D. Macardle, *The Irish Republic: A Documented Chronicle of the Anglo-Irish Conflict and the Partitioning of Ireland, with a Detailed Account of the Period 1916–1923* (London: Corgi, 1968; 1st edn. 1937).

81. D. Macardle, *Tragedies of Kerry 1922–1923* (Dublin: Irish Freedom Press, 1988; 1st edn. 1924), 63.

82. O'Malley to Childers, 5–7 Dec. 1923, in English and O'Malley (eds.), *Prisoners*, 110.

83. Dalton, *With the Dublin Brigade*, 41.

84. T. MacSwiney, *Principles of Freedom* (Dublin: Talbot, 1921), 25.

85. P. H. Pearse, *Ghosts* (1915), in *Political Writings and Speeches* (Dublin: Phoenix, n.d.), 224–5.

86. O'Malley to Humphreys, 5 Jan. 1928, Humphreys Papers, ADUCD P106/755.

87. Pearse, *The Spiritual Nation* (1916), in *Political Writings and Speeches*, 299.

88. O'Malley, *On Another Man's Wound*, 61.

89. O'Malley, *The Singing Flame*, 279.

90. O'Malley, *On Another Man's Wound*, 317.

91. O'Malley, *The Singing Flame*, 214.

92. Ibid. 12.

93. See e.g. M. Collins, *The Path to Freedom* (Cork: Mercier, 1968; 1st edn. 1922), 47.

94. F. Gallagher, *The Indivisible Island: The History of the Partition of Ireland* (Westport: Greenwood Press, 1974; 1st edn. 1957), 16.

95. O'Malley manuscript, 'Sean Connolly', Cormac O'Malley Papers, PP.

96. O'Malley, untitled manuscript (n.d.), Cormac O'Malley Papers, PP.

97. Collins, *Path to Freedom*, 27.

98. Aiken to all ranks, 12 Nov. 1923, Ernie O'Malley Papers, ADUCD P17a/43.

99. Breen, *My Fight for Irish Freedom*, 30.

100. O'Malley to Hooper, 24 Aug. 1922, FitzGerald Papers, ADUCD P80/311.

101. *Poblacht na h-Eireann*, 28 Oct. 1922.

102. O'Faoláin, *De Valera*, 37.

103. O'Malley, *Raids and Rallies*, 158.

104. O'Malley, *On Another Man's Wound*, 332.

105. C. C. O'Brien, *Ancestral Voices: Religion and Nationalism in Ireland* (Dublin: Poolbeg Press, 1994), 152.

106. Gallagher, *The Indivisible Island*, 300; on Gallagher, see Graham Walker's excellent article, '"The Irish Dr Goebbels": Frank Gallagher and Irish Republican Propaganda', *Journal of Contemporary History*, 27 (1992).

107. O'Faoláin, *De Valera*, 155–6.

108. George Gilmore, interview with Jennifer FitzGerald, 27 May 1985. I am
most grateful to Dr FitzGerald for providing me with access to the
recording of this interview.

109. Valiulis, *Portrait of a Revolutionary*, 2, 239.

110. C. Ó Gráda, *Ireland: A New Economic History 1780–1939* (Oxford:
Oxford University Press, 1994), 242, 250, 307.

111. P. Hart, 'The Protestant Experience of Revolution in Southern Ireland',
in R. English and G. Walker (eds.), *Unionism in Modern Ireland:
New Perspectives on Politics and Culture* (Basingstoke: Macmillan,
1996), 94. Hart documents instances of sectarian murder and arson,
and of attacks on churches and cemeteries by the IRA; and he
demonstrates that the number of Protestant victims was disproportion-
ately large when compared either with their share of the population or
with any anti-Republican assistance which they provided to the
authorities.

112. O'Malley, untitled manuscript (n.d.), Cormac O'Malley Papers, PP.

113. O'Malley, 'Contemporary Mexican Influences in the Arts' (n.d.),
Cormac O'Malley Papers, PP.

114. O'Malley, *The Singing Flame*, 86.

115. R. F. Foster, *Modern Ireland 1600–1972* (London: Allen Lane, 1988), 596.

116. O'Malley, *On Another Man's Wound*, 126.

117. As argued powerfully in L. Colley, *Britons: Forging the Nation 1707–1837*
(London: Pimlico, 1994; 1st edn. 1992).

118. Andrews, *Dublin Made Me*, 118.

119. Ibid. 10.

120. Ó Gráda, *Ireland: A New Economic History*, ch. 13.

121. M. E. Daly, *Industrial Development and Irish National Identity
1922–1939* (Dublin: Gill and Macmillan, 1992), 3.

122. D. Fitzpatrick, 'The Logic of Collective Sacrifice: Ireland and the
British Army 1914–1918', *Historical Journal*, 38/4 (Dec. 1995);
T. Denman, *Ireland's Unknown Soldiers: The 16th (Irish) Division
in the Great War* (Blackrock: Irish Academic Press, 1992), 130–5.

123. O'Malley, *The Singing Flame*, 220.

124. R. D. Edwards, *Patrick Pearse: The Triumph of Failure* (Dublin:
Poolbeg, 1990; 1st edn. 1977), 70.

125. Pearse, 'Why We Want Recruits' (1915), in *Political Writings and
Speeches*, 121.

126. Valiulis, *Portrait of a Revolutionary*, 8.

127. *An t-Óglach*, 1 May 1920.

128. Thomas Malone, interview with Cormac O'Malley, Oct. 1970, Cormac
O'Malley Papers, PP.

129. J. J. Comerford, *My Kilkenny IRA Days*, 279, 284.

130. O'Malley's approach prompted a rather sniping response from some

quarters. See e.g. Tom Barry's comment that O'Malley's language 'and his constant use of long military words and phrases left no doubt in the minds of his listeners that he had read a military book of some sort' (T. Barry, *Guerilla Days in Ireland* (Dublin: Anvil, 1989; 1st edn. 1949), 158).

131. O'Malley to Plunkett, 5 Dec. 1919, Ernie O'Malley Papers, ADUCD P17a/158.
132. English and O'Malley (eds.), *Prisoners*, 27–8.
133. Madge Clifford, interviewed by Cormac O'Malley (n.d.), Cormac O'Malley Papers, PP.
134. See Tom Garvin's excellent *Nationalist Revolutionaries in Ireland 1858–1928* (Oxford: Oxford University Press, 1987).
135. Ibid. 49–53.
136. Ernie O'Malley birth certificate (26 May 1897), Office of the Register General, Dublin.
137. O'Malley, *On Another Man's Wound*, 27. A number of O'Malley's brothers also followed either soldierly or medical careers. Their mother was particularly ambitious for her sons, and prized education as a means of social advancement.
138. For a critique of such arguments, see English, *Radicals and the Republic*.
139. O'Malley to Humphreys, 12 Apr. 1923, Humphreys Papers, ADUCD P106/754.
140. A. Bunting, 'The American Molly Childers and the Irish Question', *Éire-Ireland*, 23/2 (Summer 1988), 92.
141. O'Malley to Childers, 26 Nov.–1 Dec. 1923, in English and O'Malley (eds.), *Prisoners*, 73; cf. O'Malley, *On Another Man's Wound*, 58–9.
142. O'Malley to Lynch, 9 Jan. 1923, English and O'Malley (eds.), *Prisoners*, 26.
143. C. S. Andrews, *Man of No Property: An Autobiography*, ii (Cork: Mercier, 1982), 9–10.
144. Breen, *My Fight for Irish Freedom*, 34.
145. O'Malley, *On Another Man's Wound*, 126.
146. O'Malley to Childers, 26 Nov.–1 Dec. 1923, in English and O'Malley (eds.), *Prisoners*, 72, 74, 77.
147. O'Malley, *Raids and Rallies*, 65.
148. O'Malley, *On Another Man's Wound*, 132.
149. See e.g. the work of D. G. Boyce, 'Brahmins and Carnivores: The Irish Historian in Great Britain', *Irish Historical Studies*, 25/99 (May 1987), and of Foster, *Paddy and Mr Punch*.
150. N. J. Curtin, *The United Irishmen: Popular Politics in Ulster and Dublin 1791–1798* (Oxford: Oxford University Press, 1994); A. T. Q. Stewart, *A Deeper Silence: The Hidden Origins of the United Irishmen* (London: Faber and Faber, 1993); J. Smyth, *The Men of No Property: Irish Radicals and Popular Politics in the Late Eighteenth Century* (Dublin: Gill and

Macmillan, 1992); I. McBride, 'The School of Virtue: Francis Hutcheson, Irish Presbyterians, and the Scottish Enlightenment', in D. G. Boyce, R. Eccleshall, and V. Geoghegan (eds.), *Political Thought in Ireland since the Seventeenth Century* (London: Routledge, 1993).

151. Cf. David Fitzpatrick's broader observation with regard to First World War recruitment in Ireland: 'Family precedent undoubtedly provided a strong impulse, and those having fathers or brothers with military experience often emulated them as a matter of course' (Fitzpatrick, 'The Logic of Collective Sacrifice', 1025).

152. O'Malley, *On Another Man's Wound*, 53.

153. G. Adams, *The Politics of Irish Freedom* (Dingle: Brandon, 1986), 39.

154. O'Malley, *On Another Man's Wound*, 59.

155. C. Foley, *Legion of the Rearguard: The IRA and the Modern Irish State* (London, Pluto, 1992), 54.

156. O'Malley to Gallagher, 12 Nov. 1926, Cormac O'Malley Papers, PP.

157. E. Hobsbawm, *Age of Extremes: The Short Twentieth Century 1914–1991* (Harmondsworth: Penguin, 1994), 24.

158. O'Malley to Childers, 11 Nov. 1923, in English and O'Malley (eds.), *Prisoners*, 44.

159. O'Malley to Golden, 4 Oct. 1936, Sax Papers, PP.

160. O'Malley to Childers, 16 Jul. 1923, in English and O'Malley (eds.), *Prisoners*, 37.

161. O'Malley to Humphreys, 12 Apr. 1923, Humphreys Papers, ADUCD P106/754.

162. English and O'Malley (eds.), *Prisoners*, 42–4, 46, 49, 60–1, 88–92, 114, 116, 118–19, 130; O'Malley, *The Singing Flame*, 105, 192–3, 256, 275.

163. R. F. Foster, *The Story of Ireland* (Oxford: Oxford University Press, 1995), 15.

164. O'Donnell, *The Gates Flew Open*, 147–51, 169–70; S. Cronin, *Frank Ryan: The Search for the Republic* (Dublin: Repsol, 1980), 19, 153; M. Harmon, *Seán O'Faoláin: A Life* (London: Constable, 1994), 46–7.

165. P. Golden, *Impressions of Ireland* (New York: Irish Industries Depot, n.d.), 61.

166. M. H. De Witt, *Taos: A Memory* (Albuquerque: University of New Mexico Press, 1992), 27.

167. O'Connor, *An Only Child*, 253–4.

168. Andrews, *Dublin Made Me*, 7.

169. See e.g. Seán O'Faoláin's reflection: 'one begins to wonder if revolutionary movements ever move towards defined ends, whether all such movements are not in the main movements of emotion rather than of thought, movements arising out of a dissatisfaction with things as they are but without any clear or detailed notion as to what will produce satisfaction in the end' (O'Faoláin, *Constance Markievicz*, 74).

170. L. O'Flaherty, *Insurrection* (Dublin: Wolfhound, 1993; 1st edn. 1950), 83.

171. O'Malley, *The Singing Flame*, 190.

172. D. G. Boyce, *The Sure Confusing Drum: Ireland and the First World War* (Swansea: University College of Swansea, 1993), 23.

173. See R. English, '"The Inborn Hate of Things English": Ernie O'Malley and the Irish Revolution 1916–1923', *Past and Present*, 151 (May 1996).

174. O'Malley to Humphreys, 21 Feb. 1923, in English and O'Malley (eds.), *Prisoners*, 32.

175. K. Grieves, 'Early Historical Responses to the Great War: Fortescue, Conan Doyle, and Buchan', in B. Bond (ed.), *The First World War and British Military History* (Oxford: Oxford University Press, 1991), 16.

176. J. A. Smith, *John Buchan: A Biography* (London: Rupert Hart-Davis, 1965), 89. See also A. Lownie, *John Buchan: The Presbyterian Cavalier* (London: Constable, 1995), 31, 35–6, 38.

177. See e.g. his comments in English and O'Malley (eds.), *Prisoners*, 46, 90–1; cf. R. L. Stevenson, *The Master of Ballantrae* (Oxford: Oxford University Press, 1983; 1st edn. 1889), 12, 38, 40, 87, 102.

178. O'Malley to Childers, 26 Nov.–1 Dec. 1923, in English and O'Malley (eds.), *Prisoners*, 89; J. Buchan, *Comments and Characters* (London: Thomas Nelson, 1940), 203.

179. A. C. Bradley, *Shakespearean Tragedy: Lectures on Hamlet, Othello, King Lear, Macbeth* (London: Macmillan, 1951; 1st edn. 1904), 2.

180. O'Malley to Childers, 26 Nov.–1 Dec. 1923, in English and O'Malley (eds.), *Prisoners*, 88.

181. O'Malley, *On Another Man's Wound*, 50–1.

182. O'Malley, *The Singing Flame*, 276.

183. Buchan, quoted in K. Grieves, '*Nelson's History of the War*: John Buchan as a Contemporary Military Historian 1915–1922', *Journal of Contemporary History*, 28 (1993), 538.

184. D. Cannadine, G. M. Trevelyan: *A Life in History* (London: HarperCollins, 1992), 33–4.

185. Childers, *The Riddle of the Sands*.

186. O'Malley to Childers, 26 Nov.–1 Dec. 1923, in English and O'Malley (eds.), *Prisoners*, 69.

187. O'Malley, *On Another Man's Wound*, 58.

188. E. O'Malley, untitled notebook, Cormac O'Malley Papers; cf. B. O'Connor, *With Michael Collins in the Fight for Irish Independence* (London: Peter Davies, 1929), 19.

189. O'Malley, *The Singing Flame*, 161.

190. O'Malley to Lynch, 12 Jan. 1923, in English and O'Malley (eds.), *Prisoners*, 26.

191. Cormac O'Malley, interview with the author, London, 30 Nov. 1991.

192. O'Malley to Solomons, 21 Dec. 1923, Sullivan/Solomons Papers, TCD 4632/584a.

193. See e.g. W. F. Mandle, *The Gaelic Athletic Association and Irish Nationalist Politics 1884–1924* (London: Christopher Helm, 1987).

194. O'Malley, *Raids and Rallies*, 40.
195. O'Malley, untitled manuscript (1928), Cormac O'Malley Papers, PP.
196. B. M. Coldrey, *Faith and Fatherland: The Christian Brothers and the Development of Irish Nationalism 1838–1921* (Dublin: Gill and Macmillan, 1988).
197. O'Malley, manuscript draft of *On Another Man's Wound* (n.d.), Cormac O'Malley Papers, PP.
198. Ibid.
199. On the enormous, and far from uniformly negative, legacy of Britain to the independent Irish state, see J. Coakley and M. Gallagher (eds.), *Politics in the Republic of Ireland* (Dublin: Folens, 1993; 1st edn. 1992), chs. 1 and 2.
200. O'Malley, *On Another Man's Wound*, 42.
201. O'Malley notebook, Ernie O'Malley Papers, ADUCD P17b/145.
202. A. J. Jordan, *Major John MacBride 1865–1916* (Westport: Westport Historical Society, 1991), 110.

3 THE INTELLECTUAL

1. O'Malley to Golden, 7 Mar.–4 July 1940, Sax Papers, PP.
2. O'Malley, Autobiographical Notes (*c*.1950), Cormac O'Malley Papers, PP.
3. O'Malley, 'The County of Mayo' (1946), Cormac O'Malley Papers, PP.
4. O'Malley to McGrail, 6 June 1955, Cormac O'Malley Papers, PP.
5. O'Malley to Strand, 8 Dec. 1955, Cormac O'Malley Papers, PP.
6. O'Malley to Golden, 7 Mar.–4 July 1940, Sax Papers, PP.
7. O'Malley, untitled manuscript (n.d.), Cormac O'Malley Papers, PP.
8. O'Malley to O'Malley, 20 Mar. 1937, Cormac O'Malley Papers, PP.
9. B. Behan, *Confessions of an Irish Rebel* (London: Arrow Books, 1991; 1st edn. 1965), 134.
10. See e.g. F. S. L. Lyons, *Culture and Anarchy in Ireland 1890–1939* (Oxford: Oxford University Press, 1982; 1st edn. 1979), 170.
11. O'Malley to Strand, 26 Sept. 1956, Cormac O'Malley Papers, PP.
12. S. Beckett, *Murphy* (London: Picador, 1973; 1st edn. 1938), 22, 28–9, 47, 75.
13. O'Malley to McGrail, 12 Feb. 1956, Cormac O'Malley Papers, PP.
14. O'Malley, Autobiographical Notes (*c*.1950), Cormac O'Malley Papers, PP.
15. O'Malley to Gallagher, 31 Dec. 1948, Cormac O'Malley Papers, PP.
16. O'Malley, untitled manuscript (n.d.), Cormac O'Malley Papers, PP.
17. See e.g. P. Maume, *D. P. Moran* (Dundalk: Historical Association of Ireland, 1995), 31.
18. J. V. Kelleher, 'Irish Literature Today', *The Bell*, 10/4 (July 1945), 344–5.
19. O'Malley to McGrail, 16–17 Mar. 1955, Cormac O'Malley Papers, PP.
20. O'Malley to Kelleher, 9 Mar. 1948, Cormac O'Malley Papers, PP.

21. P. O'Donnell, 'Suggestion for a Fighting Wake', *The Bell*, 14/4 (July 1947), 2.
22. P. O'Donnell, 'A Recognizable Gait of Going', *The Bell*, 16/2 (Nov. 1950), 6.
23. S. O'Faoláin, *The Irish* (Harmondsworth: Penguin, 1980; 1st edn. 1947), 130.
24. P. O'Donnell, 'Teachers Vote Strike', *The Bell*, 11/2 (Nov. 1945), 671.
25. P. O'Donnell, 'Facts and Fairies', *The Bell*, 13/1 (Oct. 1946), 2.
26. O'Malley to Kelleher, 9 Mar. 1948, Cormac O'Malley Papers, PP.
27. L. O'Flaherty, *The Informer* (London: Four Square Books, 1958; 1st edn. 1925); L. O'Flaherty, *Mr Gilhooley* (Dublin: Wolfhound, 1991; 1st edn. 1926); L. O'Flaherty, *The Assassin* (Dublin: Wolfhound, 1988; 1st edn. 1928); P. O'Donnell, *The Knife* (Dublin: Irish Humanities Centre, 1980; 1st edn. 1930); L. O'Flaherty, *The Mountain Tavern and Other Stories* (Leipzig: Tauchnitz, 1929); P. O'Donnell, *The Gates Flew Open* (London: Jonathan Cape, 1932); L. O'Flaherty, *Famine* (London: Four Square Books, 1959; 1st edn. 1937).
28. O'Flaherty to O'Malley, 16 July [1939?], Cormac O'Malley Papers, PP.
29. O'Flaherty to Cape, n.d. [1939?], Jonathan Cape Archives, University of Reading.
30. O'Malley to Golden, 28 Mar. 1935, Sax Papers, PP.
31. O'Malley, *On Another Man's Wound*, 269.
32. O'Malley notebook (Jan. 1931), Cormac O'Malley Papers, PP.
33. O'Malley, manuscript draft of *On Another Man's Wound* (n.d.), Cormac O'Malley Papers, PP.
34. J. Stallworthy, *Louis MacNeice* (London: Faber and Faber, 1995), 262.
35. L. MacNeice, 'Autumn Journal' in *Collected Poems* (London: Faber and Faber, 1979; 1st edn. 1966), 131.
36. Eliot wrote to Crane's mother after her son's death: 'There are very few living poets in America of equal interest to me' (Eliot to Crane, 29 June 1932, Crane Papers, Box 6, Rare Book and Manuscript Library, Columbia University, New York).
37. Rereadings of Crane have on occasions stressed other focal points in his work. See e.g. Thomas Yingling's attempt to read the poet's work within a 'sexual-cultural' rather than a 'national-cultural' matrix, with a view to highlighting the problem of sexual identity and practice (T. E. Yingling, *Hart Crane and the Homosexual Text: New Thresholds, New Anatomies* (Chicago: University of Chicago Press, 1990), 13). None the less, national-spiritual themes persist—and remain crucial—in Crane's poetry.
38. O'Malley to Monroe, 10 Jan. 1935, Cormac O'Malley Papers, PP.
39. B. Weber (ed.), *The Complete Poems and Selected Letters and Prose of Hart Crane* (New York: Liveright Publishing Corp., 1966), 247.
40. Ibid. 262.

41. Jeffers to Lehman, 31 Aug. 1929; Jeffers to Stookey, 8 Dec. 1929; Jeffers to Bender, 31 Aug. 1929, in A. N. Ridgeway (ed.), *The Selected Letters of Robinson Jeffers 1897–1962* (Baltimore: Johns Hopkins Press, 1968), 153, 155, 160.

42. Notes by Jeffers, 31 July 1937, in Ridgeway (ed.), *Selected Letters of Robinson Jeffers*, 247.

43. Strand to O'Malley, 1 July 1953, Cormac O'Malley Papers, PP.

44. P. O'Donnell, 'Liberty Ltd', *The Bell*, 12/4 (July 1946), 277.

45. Sean Lemass, interviewed by Cormac O'Malley, Oct. 1970, Cormac O'Malley Papers, PP.

46. O'Malley to Ames, Summer 1932, Cormac O'Malley Papers, PP.

47. R. Welch (ed.), *The Oxford Companion to Irish Literature* (Oxford: Oxford University Press, 1996), 445.

48. O'Malley to Golden, 30 June 1934, Sax Papers, PP.

49. O'Malley, manuscript draft of *On Another Man's Wound* (n.d.), Cormac O'Malley Papers, PP.

50. I. A. Richards, *Practical Criticism: A Study of Literary Judgment* (London: Routledge, 1964; 1st edn. 1929), 181–3.

51. O'Malley, *Raids and Rallies*, 24.

52. O'Malley, 'Tradition in European Painting' (n.d.), Cormac O'Malley Papers, PP.

53. *Irish Press*, 4 Sept. 1936.

54. *New York Herald Tribune*, 7 Mar. 1937.

55. *Boston Sunday Globe*, 14 Mar. 1937.

56. *Irish Times*, 17 Feb. 1996.

57. See e.g. *Sunday Press*, 16 Jan. 1983.

58. Francis Stuart, interview with the author, Dublin, 24 Feb. 1987.

59. See e.g. his scepticism regarding the people's political reliability, regarding the achievements of militant Irish nationalism, and regarding his own popularity (O'Malley to FitzGerald, 25 Aug. 1921, FitzGerald Papers, ADUCD P80; O'Malley to Humphreys, 10 Apr. 1923, O'Malley to Childers, 26 Nov.–1 Dec. 1923, in English and O'Malley (eds.), *Prisoners*, 36–7, 85).

60. O'Malley to Humphreys, 5 Jan. 1928, Humphreys Papers, ADUCD P106/755.

61. O'Malley, *The Singing Flame*, 274–5.

62. O'Malley to Monroe, 10 Jan. 1935, Cormac O'Malley Papers, PP.

63. O'Malley to Hooker, 1 July 1935, Etáin O'Malley Papers, PP.

64. O'Malley to Golden, n.d. (1933), Cormac O'Malley Papers, PP.

65. Recent scholarship on Irish emigration has rightly counteracted some of the more casual, simplistic, and self-serving features of popular assumption; see e.g. D. H. Akenson, *The Irish Diaspora: A Primer* (Belfast: Institute of Irish Studies, 1993). Scrutiny of O'Malley's American experience—especially his hostility towards sentimental or negative approaches to emigration—reinforces this trend.

66. O'Malley notebook (1929), Cormac O'Malley Papers, PP.
67. O'Malley essay, Ernie O'Malley Papers, ADUCD P17b/169.
68. Eithne Sax, interview with the author, New York, 22 Mar. 1995.
69. M. D. Luhan, *Lorenzo in Taos* (New York: Kraus, 1969; 1st edn. 1932), 3–4, 43. It is interesting also to reflect on the echoes between some of Lawrence's own writings on Mexico and the style of writing which O'Malley adopted during this period. Lawrence's *The Plumed Serpent*, which O'Malley read during his stay in New Mexico, contains passages of lyrical depiction of Mexico which pre-echo some of the distinctive passages of Irish description in O'Malley's *On Another Man's Wound* (D. H. Lawrence, *The Plumed Serpent* (Ware: Wordsworth, 1995; 1st edn. 1926), 83).
70. Plainly, refugee artists were not the only inhabitants. As well as attracting writers and artists from elsewhere, Taos represented the intersection of numerous other cultures, including the Indian and the Mexican. Farmers formed a substantial section of the New Mexican population in the 1920s and 1930s, and the depressed condition of contemporary US farming led to considerable hardship in the region during both decades.
71. M. H. de Witt, *Taos: A Memory* (Albuquerque: University of New Mexico Press, 1992).
72. Dorothy Eugenie Brett: London-born daughter of Reginald Brett, the second Viscount Esher; a painter, trained at London's Slade School of Art; came to know figures such as the influential photographer Alfred Stieglitz and painter Georgia O'Keeffe in New York during the late 1920s; something of a worshipper of Stieglitz and O'Keeffe, as of D. H. Lawrence (whom she had known in New Mexico in the mid 1920s); absorption in Taos culture reflected her rebellion against her aristocratic background.
73. Walter Willard ('Spud') Johnson (1897–1968) in significant ways typified the Taos culture in which O'Malley lived. Disaffected from aspects of mainstream, middle-class America, he began to spend time at Taos from 1924 onwards. Born in the same year as O'Malley, he had—like the Irishman—failed to complete his university studies (at the University of California at Berkeley) and had devoted himself to writing and to literary projects. He worked for the *New Yorker* magazine, wrote and published poetry, and thrived amid the other artists who visited or stayed in Taos (including the novelist D. H. Lawrence, the conductor Leopold Stokowski, and the writer Thornton Wilder). The magazine for which Johnson is known, *Laughing Horse*, appeared first in 1922 and reflected his impudent and iconoclastic outlook regarding aesthetic and political matters. The editors—Johnson and some fellow Berkeley students— declared at the outset that they intended 'to take nothing too seriously, to hold nothing sacred, to subject anything or everything which seems to us to affect too pontifical an air, too solemn an attitude, to ribald ridicule'

(S. R. Udall, *Spud Johnson and Laughing Horse* (Albuquerque: University of New Mexico Press, 1994), 97–8).

74. E. Young, *Flowering Dusk: Things Remembered Accurately and Inaccurately* (London: Dennis Dobson, 1947; 1st edn. 1945), 131.

75. Ibid. 41.

76. Young to O'Malley, n.d. (1930?), Cormac O'Malley Papers, PP.

77. Young, *Flowering Dusk*, 257.

78. O'Malley notebook (1929?), Cormac O'Malley Papers, PP.

79. O'Malley, *On Another Man's Wound*, 135.

80. As has recently been argued by Zachary Leader, the process of revision should not be seen as contradicting or detracting from the imaginative creativity of an author's original work; this is true even in the case of Romantic authors such as Wordsworth, Byron, and Coleridge (Z. Leader, *Revision and Romantic Authorship* (Oxford: Oxford University Press, 1996)), and it is certainly the case that O'Malley's repeated revisions strengthened rather than weakened his work's imaginative power.

81. O'Malley notebook (Feb. 1931), Cormac O'Malley Papers, PP.

82. O'Malley notebook (Sept. 1930), Cormac O'Malley Papers, PP.

83. O'Malley notebook (1931), Cormac O'Malley Papers, PP.

84. E. O'Malley, 'The Traditions of Mexican Painting', 2 Jan. 1947, BBC Written Archives Centre, Reading.

85. O'Malley notebook (Mar. 1931), Cormac O'Malley Papers, PP.

86. O'Malley to Childers, 12 Nov. 1923, in English and O'Malley (eds.), *Prisoners*, 48.

87. O'Malley, *The Singing Flame*, 214.

88. Ibid. 191.

89. E. O'Malley, 'The Background of the Arts in Mexico', *The Bell*, 14/5 (Aug. 1947), 59, 68.

90. O'Malley, *The Singing Flame*, 289.

91. Foster, *Modern Ireland*, 500.

92. O'Malley, *On Another Man's Wound*, 66.

93. *Irish Times*, 26 Oct. 1917.

94. O'Malley, *The Singing Flame*, 238.

95. Gallagher (ed.), *Irish Elections 1922–1944*, 31.

96. O'Malley, *On Another Man's Wound*, 10.

97. O'Malley, manuscript draft of *On Another Man's Wound* (n.d.), Cormac O'Malley Papers, PP.

98. *Irish Historical Studies*, 1/1 (Mar. 1938), 1–2.

99. O'Malley to Golden, 10 July 1955, Sax Papers, PP.

100. O'Malley manuscript, 'Sean Connolly', Cormac O'Malley Papers, PP.

101. O'Malley, untitled manuscript (n.d.), Cormac O'Malley Papers, PP.

102. E. O'Malley, 'Beauty's Pilgrim' (Jan. 1928), O'Malley poetry notebook, Cormac O'Malley Papers, PP.

103. O'Malley notebook, 'Poems' (1930), Cormac O'Malley Papers, PP.

104. O'Malley, *On Another Man's Wound*, 21.
105. Cormac O'Malley Papers, PP.
106. Ibid.
107. Ibid.
108. Ibid.
109. Ibid.
110. O'Malley poetry notebook (Jan. 1928), Cormac O'Malley Papers, PP.
111. O'Malley, *The Singing Flame*, 285.
112. O'Malley poetry notebook (Jan. 1928), Cormac O'Malley Papers, PP.
113. Ibid.
114. Ibid.
115. Cormac O'Malley Papers, PP.
116. O'Malley poetry notebook, Cormac O'Malley Papers, PP.
117. O'Malley to O'Malley, 6 Apr. 1938, Etáin O'Malley Papers, PP.
118. E. O'Malley, 'Renaissance', *La France Libre*, 13/74 (Dec. 1946–Jan. 1947), 138.
119. Ibid. 141.
120. O'Malley, 'Tradition in European Painting' (n.d.), Cormac O'Malley Papers, PP.
121. O'Malley to Solomons, 27 Nov. 1923, Solomons Papers, TCD MS 4632/581a.
122. O'Malley to MacGreevy, 6 Mar. 1939, MacGreevy Papers, TCD MS 8117/1.
123. O'Malley, 'Francisco Goya y Lucientes, *Portrait of a Woman*' (n.d.), Cormac O'Malley Papers, PP.
124. O'Malley, untitled manuscript (1947), Cormac O'Malley Papers, PP.
125. O'Malley to McGrail, 16–17 Mar. 1955, Cormac O'Malley Papers, PP.
126. O'Malley to MacGreevy, 5 Apr. 1939, MacGreevy Papers, TCD MS 8117/1.
127. O'Malley to McGrail, 16–17 Mar. 1955, Cormac O'Malley Papers, PP.
128. O'Malley, notebook (n.d.), Cormac O'Malley Papers, PP.
129. E. O'Malley, 'A Painter of his People', *The Bell*, 11/4 (Jan. 1946), 914.
130. Ibid. 915–16.
131. Le Brocquy to O'Malley, 22 Oct. 1989, Cormac O'Malley Papers, PP.
132. Le Brocquy to the author, 31 Mar. 1996.
133. E. O'Malley, 'Louis le Brocquy', *Horizon*, 14/79 (July 1946).
134. O'Malley, 'A Painter of his People', 915.
135. E. O'Malley, 'Painting: "The School of London"', *The Bell*, 14/3 (June 1947), 1, 4.
136. O'Malley to McGrail, 16–17 Mar. 1955, Cormac O'Malley Papers, PP.
137. See e.g. the collection of her work held at the University of Limerick.
138. O'Malley, 'The Background of the Arts in Mexico', 69.
139. O'Malley to Kelleher, 7 Apr. 1948, Cormac O'Malley Papers, PP.
140. O'Malley diary (12 Oct. 1928), Cormac O'Malley Papers, PP.

141. O'Malley diary (15 Oct. 1928), Cormac O'Malley Papers, PP.
142. O'Malley to Golden, 28 Mar. 1935, Sax Papers, PP.
143. See e.g. E. Nolan, *James Joyce and Nationalism* (London: Routledge, 1995).
144. A. Fernihough, *D. H. Lawrence: Aesthetics and Ideology* (Oxford: Oxford University Press, 1993).
145. L. MacNeice, 'Autumn Journal', in *Collected Poems*, 133.
146. R. Fisk, *In Time of War: Ireland, Ulster, and the Price of Neutrality 1939–1945* (London: Paladin, 1985; 1st edn. 1983), 420.
147. It is also interesting to compare here the attitude of another of O'Malley's Irish literary friends, Samuel Beckett, who was sustainedly anti-Nazi before and during the Second World War; see Knowlson, *Damned to Fame*, 237–8, 297–318. Indeed, Beckett joined the Resistance movement in France during the war: 'you simply couldn't stand by with your arms folded' (Beckett, quoted ibid. 304).
148. It should be remembered that severe censorship in Ireland restricted the amount of information which could be obtained about the war; see D. Ó Drisceoil, *Censorship in Ireland 1939–1945: Neutrality, Politics, and Society* (Cork: Cork University Press, 1996).
149. O'Malley notebook (n.d.), Cormac O'Malley Papers, PP.
150. O'Malley, untitled manuscript (n.d.), Cormac O'Malley Papers, PP.
151. O'Malley to O'Malley, 22 July 1940, Etáin O'Malley Papers, PP.
152. O'Malley notebook (1941), Cormac O'Malley Papers, PP.
153. *Irish Independent*, 6 Nov. 1936.
154. Irish Republican pronouncements during the war evinced, on occasions, both anti-Jewishness and pro-Germanism. See e.g. Copy of IRA Radio Broadcast, Dec. 1939, Files of the Dept. of the Taoiseach, NA S 11564 A, and *War News* (22 Mar. 1940), MacEntee Papers, ADUCD P67/532 (1).
155. O'Malley to McGrail, 20 Feb. 1955, Cormac O'Malley Papers, PP.
156. A useful comparison might also be made here in relation to another of O'Malley's artistic heroes, William Shakespeare. As one scholarly authority has recently suggested, the definition of Englishness as distinct from—indeed, free of—Jewishness formed a crucial informative background to Shakespeare's work (J. Shapiro, *Shakespeare and the Jews* (New York: Columbia University Press, 1996)). Again, Irish echoes are clear, with the official Republican view seeking to define Irishness as distinct from, even purged of, Englishness.
157. E. Said, *Musical Elaborations* (London: Vintage, 1992; 1st edn. 1991); see also M. Stokes (ed.), *Ethnicity, Identity, and Music: The Musical Construction of Place* (Oxford: Berg, 1994).
158. E. Said, *Representations of the Intellectual* (London: Vintage, 1994), 61.
159. 'Being separate from and critical of established institutions carries costs and annoyances, but also joys and opportunities, not least the contacts that develop with people of a similar cast of mind and with similar inter-

ests and concerns, many of whom have to work under conditions of considerable adversity, a not infrequent concomitant of dissidence and intellectual independence' (N. Chomsky, 'Preface' to *World Orders, Old and
New* (London: Pluto, 1994)).

160. E. Said, *Culture and Imperialism* (London: Vintage, 1994; 1st edn. 1993),
pp. xi–xii, 8; for an exploration of the full range of Irish responses to the
British connection, see Foster, *Paddy and Mr Punch*. Note also the
important point recently stressed by Professor David Cannadine, that
Irish people played an important role in the very creation and sustenance of the British Empire (D. Cannadine, 'The Empire Strikes Back',
Past and Present, 147 (May 1995), 191); this latter question is ably discussed in ch. 6 of Akenson's *The Irish Diaspora*.

161. Said, *Culture and Imperialism*, 266, 275.

162. Simple binary formulations similarly fail to convince in non-Irish cases.
As Gyan Prakash has recently observed, even anti-colonial nationalists
have tended to move beyond the simple polarities of 'colonizer' and 'col-
onized' (G. Prakash (ed.), *After Colonialism: Imperial Histories and Post-
Colonial Displacements* (Princeton: Princeton University Press, 1995),
9).

163. L. Kennedy, 'Modern Ireland: Post-Colonial Society or Post-Colonial
Pretensions?', *Irish Review*, 13 (Winter 1992–3).

164. D. Lloyd, *Anomalous States: Irish Writing and the Post-Colonial Moment*
(Dublin: Lilliput, 1993), 18.

4 THE COMPANION

1. O'Malley to Childers, 26 Nov.–1 Dec. 1923, in English and O'Malley
(eds.), *Prisoners*, 71–2.

2. Ibid. 71.

3. Cormac O'Malley, interview with the author, London, 30 Nov. 1991.

4. Liber (Citkovitz) to Malley, 19 Sept. 1949, Cormac O'Malley Papers, PP.

5. See e.g. O'Malley to Childers, 26 Nov.–1 Dec. 1923, in English and
O'Malley (eds.), *Prisoners*, 72.

6. Eithne Sax, interview with the author, New York, 22 Mar. 1995.

7. O'Malley to Humphreys, 12 Apr. 1923, Humphreys Papers, ADUCD
P106/754.

8. O'Malley to Gallagher, 27 May–6 June 1930, Cormac O'Malley Papers,
PP.

9. O'Malley, Autobiographical Notes (c.1950), Cormac O'Malley Papers,
PP.

10. Etáin O'Malley, interview with the author, Dublin, 22 June 1992.

11. Etáin O'Malley, interview with the author, Belfast, 8 Feb. 1996.

12. Jean McGrail, interview with the author, New York, 7 Apr. 1995.

13. O'Malley to Childers, 26 Nov.–1 Dec. 1923, in English and O'Malley (eds.), *Prisoners*, 70.
14. O'Malley, *On Another Man's Wound*, 74.
15. Aiken to OCs Divisions and Independent Brigades, 4 Aug. 1923, O'Malley Papers, ADUCD P17a/37.
16. Eithne Sax, interview with the author, New York, 22 Mar. 1995.
17. O'Malley to Golden (1933), Cormac O'Malley Papers, PP.
18. O'Malley, untitled manuscript (n.d.), Cormac O'Malley Papers, PP.
19. De Valera to O'Malley, 30 Nov. 1928, Cormac O'Malley Papers, PP.
20. For thoughtful reflections on Ireland and the First World War, see K. Jeffery, 'The Great War in Modern Irish Memory', in K. Jeffery and T. G. Fraser (eds.), *Men, Women, and War* (Dublin: Lilliput, 1993).
21. Ulick O'Connor, interview with the author, Dublin, 22 Nov. 1991.
22. Herbert to O'Malley, 21 Feb. 1956, Cormac O'Malley Papers, PP.
23. O'Malley to Golden, 7 Mar. 1940, Sax Papers, PP.
24. Kennedy to the author, 4 May 1992.
25. I am grateful to Mr Anthony P. Behan, who worked for Michael Noyk at the time of O'Malley's legal battle against Helen, for providing me with access to the menu for this meal.
26. D. H. Lawrence, *Mornings in Mexico* (London: Martin Secker, 1930; 1st edn. 1927), 43.
27. O'Malley notebook (Feb. 1931), Cormac O'Malley Papers, PP.
28. O'Malley notebook (Dec. 1930), Cormac O'Malley Papers, PP.
29. O'Malley notebook (Jan. 1931), Cormac O'Malley Papers, PP.
30. Peadar O'Donnell, interviewed by Cormac O'Malley, Oct. 1970, Cormac O'Malley Papers, PP.
31. Etáin O'Malley, interview with the author, New York, 24 Mar. 1995.
32. H. Melville, *Moby-Dick* (Harmondsworth: Penguin, 1972; 1st edn. 1851), 123.
33. O'Malley, 'Painting: "The School of London"', 6.
34. Maureen O'Hara Blair, interview with the author, New York, 10 Apr. 1995.
35. O'Malley to Hooker, 18 Apr. 1935, Etáin O'Malley Papers, PP.
36. Anon., *Elon Huntington Hooker 1869–1938* (n. d.), 8, 30.
37. Revd Thomas Hooker (1586–1647): English-born, Cambridge-educated itinerant Puritan preacher who clashed with Laudian authoritarianism; left England for Holland (1631) where he was engaged in further controversies; then, after briefly and secretly returning to England, he departed in 1633 for America; became a major figure—with religious and political influence—in New England; founded Hartford, Connecticut; a significant leader of the Puritan cause in England and New England. Elon was Thomas Hooker's great-great-great-great-great-grandson.
38. O'Malley to Hooker, 13 Oct. 1935, Cormac O'Malley Papers, PP.
39. Hooker to O'Malley, 24 Dec. 1935, Cormac O'Malley Papers, PP.

40. A. Hooker and H. Hooker, 'A High Time in Red Russia', *Good Housekeeping* (July 1930).

41. Marquand to O'Malley, 14 May 1948, Cormac O'Malley Papers, PP.

42. O'Malley, Autobiographical Notes (*c*.1950), Cormac O'Malley Papers, PP.

43. Hooker to Hooker, 21 Feb. 1934, Cormac O'Malley Papers, PP.

44. Helen O'Malley, interview with the author, Greenwich, Connecticut, 7 Apr. 1992.

45. Cable, 27 Sept. 1935, Hooker to Hookers, Etáin O'Malley Papers, PP.

46. O'Malley to Hooker, 18 Apr. 1935, Etáin O'Malley Papers, PP.

47. O'Malley to Hooker, n.d., Etáin O'Malley Papers, PP.

48. O'Malley to Kelleher, 8 Mar. 1947, Cormac O'Malley Papers, PP.

49. O'Malley to O'Malley, 20 Mar. 1937, Cormac O'Malley Papers, PP.

50. *Irish Times*, 22 Apr. 1993.

51. O'Malley to Hooker, 12 June 1936, Cormac O'Malley Papers, PP.

52. O'Malley to Walston, 19 July 1946, Cormac O'Malley Papers, PP.

53. O'Malley to Hooker, Dec. 1943, Etáin O'Malley Papers, PP.

54. O'Malley to O'Malley, 29 Aug. 1943, Etáin O'Malley Papers, PP.

55. See e.g. H. M. *Pulham Esquire* (Harmondsworth: Penguin, 1951; 1st edn. 1941), and *Point of No Return* (Boston: Little, Brown, and Co., 1949).

56. Etáin O'Malley, interview with the author, New York, 24 Mar. 1995.

57. O'Malley, Autobiographical Notes (*c*.1950), Cormac O'Malley Papers, PP.

58. O'Malley, handwritten notes (n.d.), Cormac O'Malley Papers, PP.

59. O'Malley to O'Malley, 7 Sept. 1943, Etáin O'Malley Papers, PP.

60. O'Malley, Autobiographical Notes (*c*.1950), Cormac O'Malley Papers, PP.

61. O'Malley to O'Malley, 22 Oct. 1946, Cormac O'Malley Papers, PP.

62. Etáin O'Malley, interview with the author, New York, 26 Mar. 1995.

63. Etáin O'Malley, interview with the author, New York, 24 Mar. 1995.

64. C. O'Malley, 'A Tribute to Helen Hooker O'Malley Roelofs' (5 Apr. 1993), Cormac O'Malley Papers, PP.

65. O'Malley to Hooker, 19 Feb. 1947, Etáin O'Malley Papers, PP.

66. O'Malley, Autobiographical Notes (*c*.1950), Cormac O'Malley Papers, PP.

67. O'Malley to Malley, 7 July 1948, Cormac O'Malley Papers, PP.

68. O'Malley, Autobiographical Notes (*c*.1950), Cormac O'Malley Papers, PP.

69. Hooker to O'Malley, 11 Dec. 1946, Cormac O'Malley Papers, PP.

70. Walston to O'Malley, 14 Oct. 1946, Cormac O'Malley Papers, PP.

71. Cormac O'Malley, interview with the author, New York, 24 Apr. 1994.

72. O'Malley, Autobiographical Notes (*c*.1950), Cormac O'Malley Papers, PP.

73. O'Malley, handwritten notes (n.d.), Cormac O'Malley Papers, PP.

74. O'Malley to Hooker, 26 Aug. 1948, Etáin O'Malley Papers, PP.
75. Cahal O'Malley, interview with the author, New York, 12 Apr. 1995.
76. O'Malley to Strand, 7 Nov. 1953, Cormac O'Malley Papers, PP.
77. In typically meticulous fashion O'Malley, in the mid-1940s, detailed on paper some reading material relevant for each of the children: for Cahal and Etáin, *Don Quixote* and the *Arabian Nights*; for Cormac, *Gulliver's Travels* and the Cuchulain saga; for all three, *The Odyssey* and *Moby-Dick*.
78. Etáin O'Malley, interview with the author, New York, 24 Mar. 1995.
79. Etáin O'Malley, interview with the author, New York, 24 Mar. 1995.
80. Etáin O'Malley, interview with the author, New York, 26 Mar. 1995.
81. Cahal O'Malley, interview with the author, New York, 12 Apr. 1995.
82. O'Malley to Golden, 10 July 1955, Sax Papers, PP.
83. O'Malley to O'Malley, 30 June 1952, Cormac O'Malley Papers, PP. The personal legacy of both parents is something stressed by Etáin O'Malley: her own acting career in part had its origins in an enthusiasm for theatre derived from her mother's theatrical involvement; and her attachment to Ernie was also very marked ('I loved father, missed him, was deeply influenced by him, and yet had little chance to be with him after I was nine except in my memory and heart. I have clung to these memories and the few visits I had with him tenaciously' (Etáin O'Malley to the author, 17 Sept. 1996)).

5 THE LEGACIES

1. O'Faoláin, *The Irish*, 7.
2. MacNeice, 'Autumn Journal', in *Collected Poems*, 105–6.
3. O'Malley to Childers, 5–7 Dec. 1923, in English and O'Malley (eds.), *Prisoners*, 108–10.
4. O'Malley notebook (Mar. 1931), Cormac O'Malley Papers, PP.
5. Cf. Eithne Sax's recollection that he was emphatically an 'intellectual snob' (interview with the author, New York, 26 Apr. 1994).
6. See e.g. O'Malley to Childers, 26 Nov.–1 Dec. 1923, in English and O'Malley (eds.), *Prisoners*, 78–9.
7. A. Bloom, *The Closing of the American Mind: How Higher Education has Failed Democracy and Impoverished the Souls of Today's Students* (New York: Simon and Schuster, 1987), 58, 62, 64.
8. Hobsbawm, *Age of Extremes*, 5.
9. Some evidence exists of tentative moves in this direction. See e.g. the way in which a leading author sympathetic to Irish Republican culture — J. Bowyer Bell — has recently acknowledged the importance of treating unionism with greater seriousness (J. Bowyer Bell, *Back to the Future: The Protestants and a United Ireland* (Dublin: Poolbeg, 1996)).
10. O'Malley to McHugh, 23 Apr. 1945, Cormac O'Malley Papers, PP.

11. J. Ring, *Erskine Childers* (London: John Murray, 1996), 293.

12. O'Malley, untitled manuscript (n.d.), Cormac O'Malley Papers, PP.

13. O'Malley to Kelleher, 9 Mar. 1948, Cormac O'Malley Papers, PP.

14. P. Mayhew, *Culture and Identity* (16 Dec. 1992), 15–16.

15. It has been suggested that O'Malley's participation in the UCD Literary and Historical Society debates during the 1920s introduced him—and other Republicans—to differing perspectives in a constructively friendly atmosphere and that, without relinquishing their own Republicanism, people like O'Malley did as a consequence become more willing to see the other person's viewpoint (J. Meenan (ed.), *Centenary History of the Literary and Historical Society of University College Dublin 1855–1955* (Tralee: The Kerryman, n.d.), 200).

16. Foster, *Modern Ireland*, 596.

17. D. G. Boyce, 'Past and Present: Revisionism and the Northern Ireland Troubles' in D. G. Boyce and A. O'Day (eds.), *The Making of Modern Irish History: Revisionism and the Revisionist Controversy* (London: Routledge, 1996), 229.

18. J. Augusteijn, 'From Public Defiance to Guerrilla Warfare: The Radicalization of the Irish Republican Army—A Comparative Analysis 1916–1921', Doctoral thesis (University of Amsterdam, 1994), 311.

19. O'Malley notes, Ernie O'Malley Papers, ADUCD P17b/143.

20. Bew, *Ideology and the Irish Question*, 20.

21. O'Malley, draft manuscript of *On Another Man's Wound* (1933?), Ernie O'Malley Papers, ADUCD P17b/147.

22. L. Greenfeld, *Nationalism: Five Roads to Modernity* (Cambridge, Mass.: Harvard University Press, 1992).

23. Consider the Gaelic Athletic Association (GAA) which, though hostile to Anglicization, actually echoed English Victorian sport (regarding, for example, attitudes towards health, morality, organization, competition, and indeed towards the importance of sport itself). Cf. Mandle: 'Much of what the GAA regarded as distinctive about the meaning of its games was merely the result of the substitution of the word "Ireland" for "Britain" or "England"' (Mandle, *The Gaelic Athletic Association*, 14). Consider also the irony that Greenfeld identifies, as crucial to the development of English nationalism, authors over whom Ernie O'Malley particularly enthused during his Irish Revolutionary years: Chaucer, Shakespeare, Milton (Greenfeld, *Nationalism*, 67–9, 76–7).

24. O'Malley to Humphreys, 10 Apr. 1923, in English and O'Malley (eds.), *Prisoners*, 36.

25. Greenfeld, *Nationalism*, 31.

26. As Benedict Anderson has observed, 'Nation, nationality, nationalism— all have proved notoriously difficult to define, let alone to analyse' (B. Anderson, *Imagined Communities: Reflections on the Origin and Spread of Nationalism* (London: Verso, 1983), 12).

27. E. J. Hobsbawm, *Nations and Nationalism since 1780: Programme, Myth, Reality* (Cambridge: Cambridge University Press, 1990), 8.

28. E. Kedourie, *Nationalism* (Oxford: Blackwell, 1993; 1st edn. 1960), p. xvi.

29. E. Gellner, *Nations and Nationalism* (Oxford: Basil Blackwell, 1983), 86.

30. E. Gellner, *Conditions of Liberty: Civil Society and its Rivals* (London: Hamish Hamilton, 1994), 22.

31. Gellner's arguments concerning the importance of education to nationalism are lucidly restated in E. Gellner, 'Nations, States, and Religions', in R. English and C. Townshend (eds.), *The State: Historical and Political Dimensions* (London: Routledge, forthcoming).

32. Hobsbawm, *Nations and Nationalism*, 43; J. Hutchinson and A. D. Smith (eds.), *Nationalism* (Oxford: Oxford University Press, 1994), 7.

33. Cf. also Anthony Smith, asking 'Under what conditions and by what mechanisms do nationalist movements arise?' (A. D. Smith, *Theories of Nationalism* (London: Duckworth, 1971), 6).

34. For one from the multitude of possible examples, see the arguments of Anthony Smith: A. D. Smith, *National Identity* (Harmondsworth: Penguin, 1991), ch. 4.

35. 'No model of social change will ever satisfy historians completely because of their professional interest in variety and difference' (P. Burke, *History and Social Theory* (Cambridge: Polity, 1992), 147).

36. The late-twentieth-century IRA have been the focus of many studies, but the kind of archival riches relating to Ernie O'Malley's generation are not available for scholars studying modern-day Republicans. It might, of course, be considered that what this biography has said about early-twentieth-century Republican physical force could, in places, have relevance to the latter-day IRA.

37. M. Hopkinson, 'Biography of the Revolutionary Period: Michael Collins and Kevin Barry', *Irish Historical Studies*, 28/111 (May 1993), 316.

38. O'Malley to Gallagher, 31 Dec. 1948, Cormac O'Malley Papers, PP.

39. F. O'Connor, *The Big Fellow: A Life of Michael Collins* (London: Thomas Nelson, 1937), pp. vii, x, 82.

40. Ulick O'Connor, interview with the author, Dublin, 22 Nov. 1991.

41. O'Malley, notebook (n.d.), Cormac O'Malley Papers, PP; cf. R. Graves, *Lawrence and the Arabs* (London: Jonathan Cape, 1927), 54.

42. C. Ricks, *Beckett's Dying Words* (Oxford: Oxford University Press, 1993), 78.

43. O'Malley, *The Singing Flame*, 214.

44. O'Malley, *On Another Man's Wound*, 323 (in reference to May 1921).

Bibliography

MANUSCRIPTS

Anthony P. Behan Papers, PP
Jonathan Cape Archives, University of Reading
Robert Erskine Childers Papers, TCD
Michael Collins Papers, NLI
Hart Crane Papers, Columbia University Library (New York)
Desmond FitzGerald Papers, ADUCD
Mabel FitzGerald Papers, ADUCD
Frank Gallagher Papers, NLI
Sheila Humphreys Papers, ADUCD
Andrew Bonar Law Papers, HLRO
Sean MacEntee Papers, ADUCD
Joseph McGarrity Papers, NLI
Thomas MacGreevy Papers, TCD
Mary MacSwiney Papers, ADUCD
Terence MacSwiney Papers, ADUCD
Richard Mulcahy Papers, ADUCD
National Archives, Dublin:
   Files of the Dept. of the Taoiseach
   Files of the Dept. of Foreign Affairs
New Yorker Papers, NYPL
Cormac O'Malley Papers, PP
Ernie O'Malley Papers, ADUCD
Ernie O'Malley Papers, NLI
Etáin O'Malley Papers, PP
Seumas O'Sullivan Papers, TCD
Public Record Office, Kew:
   Colonial Office Files
Eithne Sax Papers, PP
Estella Frances Solomons Papers, TCD
Paul Strand Papers, Centre for Creative Photography, University of Arizona
Sean Sweeney Papers, PP
Moss Twomey Papers, ADUCD
Frank Walsh Papers, NYPL
Edward Weston Papers, Centre for Creative Photography, University of
   Arizona
Yaddo Corporation Papers, Saratoga Springs, NY

NEWSPAPERS AND PERIODICALS

An Phoblacht
An t-Óglách
Bell
Irish Independent
Irish Press
Irish Times
New York Herald Tribune
New York Times
New Yorker
Poblacht na h-Eireann
Sunday Press

BOOKS, ARTICLES, ESSAYS, AND THESES

Adams, G., *Falls Memories* (Dingle: Brandon, 1983; 1st edn. 1982).
—— *The Politics of Irish Freedom* (Dingle: Brandon, 1986).
Adams, M., *Censorship: The Irish Experience* (Dublin: Scepter, 1968).
Akenson, D. H., *The Irish Diaspora: A Primer* (Belfast: Institute of Irish Studies, 1993).
Anderson, B., *Imagined Communities: Reflections on the Origin and Spread of Nationalism* (London: Verso, 1983).
Andrews, C. S., *Dublin Made Me: An Autobiography* (Cork: Mercier, 1979).
—— *Man of No Property: An Autobiography*, ii (Cork: Mercier, 1982).
Arnold, B., *A Concise History of Irish Art* (London: Thames and Hudson, 1969).
Augusteijn, J., 'From Public Defiance to Guerrilla Warfare: The Radicalization of the Irish Republican Army—A Comparative Analysis 1916–1921', Doctoral thesis (University of Amsterdam, 1994).
Bair, D., *Samuel Beckett: A Biography* (London: Jonathan Cape, 1978).
Balliett, C. A., 'The Lives—and Lies—of Maud Gonne', *Éire-Ireland*, 14/3 (Autumn 1979).
Banville, J., 'The Ireland of de Valera and O'Faoláin', *Irish Review*, 17–18 (Winter 1995).
Bardon, J., *A History of Ulster* (Belfast: Blackstaff, 1992).
Barnett, G. A., *Denis Johnston* (New York: Twayne, 1978).
Barrett, G., 'Disrobing in the Vestry: Autobiographical Writing in the Thirties', *Irish Review*, 13 (Winter 1992–3).
Barry, T., *Guerrilla Days in Ireland* (Dublin: Anvil, 1989; 1st edn. 1949).
Bartlett, T., and Jeffery, K. (eds.), *A Military History of Ireland* (Cambridge: Cambridge University Press, 1996).
Barton, B., 'Relations between Westminster and Stormont during the Attlee Premiership', *Irish Political Studies*, 7 (1992).

Baxter, J., *The Cinema of John Ford* (London: Zwemmer, 1971).

Beaslai, P., *Michael Collins: Soldier and Statesman* (Dublin: Talbot, 1937).

Beckett, S., *Murphy* (London: Picador, 1973; 1st edn. 1938).

—— *The Beckett Trilogy: Molloy, Malone Dies, The Unnamable* (London: Picador, 1979).

Behan, B., *Borstal Boy* (London: Arrow, 1990; 1st edn. 1958).

—— *Confessions of an Irish Rebel* (London: Arrow, 1991; 1st edn. 1965).

Bell, J. B., *The Secret Army: The IRA 1916–1979* (Dublin: Poolbeg, 1989; 1st edn. 1970).

—— *The Gun in Politics: An Analysis of Irish Political Conflict 1916–1986* (New Brunswick: Transaction, 1991; 1st edn. 1987).

—— *The Irish Troubles: A Generation of Violence 1967–1992* (Dublin: Gill and Macmillan, 1993).

—— *Back to the Future: The Protestants and a United Ireland* (Dublin: Poolbeg, 1996).

Bell, M., *Marquand: An American Life* (Boston: Little, Brown, and Co., 1979).

Bew, P., *Conflict and Conciliation in Ireland 1890–1910: Parnellites and Radical Agrarians* (Oxford: Oxford University Press, 1987).

—— *Ideology and the Irish Question: Ulster Unionism and Irish Nationalism 1912–1916* (Oxford: Oxford University Press, 1994).

Bishop, P., and Mallie, E., *The Provisional IRA* (London: Corgi, 1988; 1st edn. 1987).

Bloom, A., *The Closing of the American Mind: How Higher Education has Failed Democracy and Impoverished the Souls of Today's Students* (New York: Simon and Schuster, 1987).

Bond, B. (ed.), *The First World War and British Military History* (Oxford: Oxford University Press, 1991).

Bowman, J., *De Valera and the Ulster Question 1917–1973* (Oxford: Oxford University Press, 1982).

Boyce, D. G., *Englishmen and Irish Troubles: British Public Opinion and the Making of Irish Policy 1918–1922* (London: Cape, 1972).

—— 'Brahmins and Carnivores: The Irish Historian in Great Britain', *Irish Historical Studies*, 25/99 (May 1987).

—— *The Irish Question and British Politics 1868–1986* (Basingstoke: Macmillan, 1988).

—— *Nineteenth Century Ireland: The Search for Stability* (Dublin: Gill and Macmillan, 1990).

—— *The Sure Confusing Drum: Ireland and the First World War* (Swansea: University College of Swansea, 1993).

—— *Nationalism in Ireland* (London: Routledge, 1995; 1st edn. 1982).

—— (ed.), *The Revolution in Ireland 1879–1923* (Basingstoke: Macmillan, 1988).

—— and O'Day, A. (eds.), *The Making of Modern Irish History: Revisionism and the Revisionist Controversy* (London: Routledge, 1996).

Boyce, D. G., Eccleshall, R., and Geoghegan, V. (eds.), *Political Thought in Ireland since the Seventeenth Century* (London: Routledge, 1993).

Boyle, A., *The Riddle of Erskine Childers* (London: Hutchinson, 1977).

Bradley, A. C., *Shakespearean Tragedy: Lectures on Hamlet, Othello, King Lear, Macbeth* (London: Macmillan, 1951; 1st edn. 1904).

Bradshaw, B., 'Nationalism and Historical Scholarship in Modern Ireland', *Irish Historical Studies*, 26/104 (Nov. 1989).

Brady, Ciaran (ed.), *Interpreting Irish History: The Debate on Historical Revisionism 1938–1994* (Blackrock: Irish Academic Press, 1994).

Brady, Conor, *Guardians of the Peace* (Dublin: Gill and Macmillan, 1974).

Breen, D., *My Fight for Irish Freedom* (Dublin: Anvil, 1989; 1st edn. 1924).

Brennan, M., *The War in Clare 1911–1921: Personal Memoirs of the Irish War of Independence* (Dublin: Four Courts Press, 1980).

Brett, D., *Lawrence and Brett: A Friendship* (Santa Fé: Sunstone Press, 1974; 1st edn. 1933).

Breuilly, J., *Nationalism and the State* (Manchester: Manchester University Press, 1993; 1st edn. 1982).

Brody, H., *Inishkillane: Change and Decline in the West of Ireland* (London: Faber and Faber, 1986; 1st edn. 1973).

Brooke, R., *Rupert Brooke: The Collected Poems* (London: Papermac, 1992; 1st edn. 1918).

Brown, S. J. (ed.), *Robber Rocks: Letters and Memories of Hart Crane 1923–1932* (Middletown, Conn.: Wesleyan University Press, 1969).

Brown, T., *Ireland: A Social and Cultural History 1922–1985* (London: Fontana, 1985; 1st edn. 1981).

Buchan, J., *The Thirty-nine Steps* (London: Hodder and Stoughton, 1926; 1st edn. 1915).

—— *Greenmantle* (Harmondsworth: Penguin, 1956; 1st edn. 1916).

—— *The Power-House* (Edinburgh: B. and W. Publishing, 1993; 1st edn. 1916).

—— *Mr Standfast* (Edinburgh: Thomas Nelson, 1923; 1st edn. 1919).

—— *The Three Hostages* (Harmondsworth: Penguin, 1953; 1st edn. 1924).

—— *Nelson's History of the War* (London: Thomas Nelson, n.d.).

—— *The Island of Sheep* (Harmondsworth: Penguin, 1956; 1st edn. 1936).

—— *Comments and Characters* (London: Thomas Nelson, 1940).

Buchan, W., *John Buchan: A Memoir* (London: Buchan and Enright, 1982).

Buckland, P., *James Craig, Lord Craigavon* (Dublin: Gill and Macmillan, 1980).

Bunting, A., 'The American Molly Childers and the Irish Question', *Éire-Ireland*, 23/2 (Summer 1988).

Burke, P., *New Perspectives on Historical Writing* (Cambridge: Polity, 1992; 1st edn. 1991).

—— *History and Social Theory* (Cambridge: Polity, 1992).

Burnett, M. T., ' "Fill Gut and Pinch Belly": Writing Famine in the English Renaissance', *Explorations in Renaissance Culture*, 21 (1995).

Bush, S., *The Writings of Thomas Hooker: Spiritual Adventure in Two Worlds* (Madison: University of Wisconsin Press, 1980).

Butler, S., *Erewhon* (Harmondsworth: Penguin, 1935; 1st edn. 1872).

Callan, P., 'Recruiting for the British Army in Ireland during the First World War', *Irish Sword*, 17/66 (1987).

Campbell, C., *Emergency Law in Ireland 1918–1925* (Oxford: Oxford University Press, 1994).

Cannadine, D., *G. M. Trevelyan: A Life in History* (London: HarperCollins, 1992).

—— 'The Empire Strikes Back', *Past and Present*, 147 (May 1995).

Carlson, J. (ed.), *Banned in Ireland: Censorship and the Irish Writer* (London: Routledge, 1990).

Chavasse, M., *Terence MacSwiney* (Dublin: Clonmore and Reynolds, 1961).

Childers, R. E., *The Riddle of the Sands* (Harmondsworth: Penguin, 1978; 1st edn. 1903).

Chomsky, N., *For Reasons of State* (London: Fontana, 1973; 1st edn. 1970).

—— *World Orders, Old and New* (London: Pluto, 1994).

Clarke, K., *Revolutionary Woman: Kathleen Clarke 1878–1972: An Autobiography* (Dublin: O'Brien, 1991).

Clausewitz, C. von, *On War* (Harmondsworth: Penguin, 1968; 1st edn. 1832).

Clurman, H., *The Fervent Years: The Story of the Group Theatre and the Thirties* (New York: Hill and Wang, 1957; 1st edn. 1945).

Coakley, J., and Gallagher, M. (eds.), *Politics in the Republic of Ireland* (Dublin: Folens, 1993; 1st edn. 1992).

Coldrey, B. M., *Faith and Fatherland: The Christian Brothers and the Development of Irish Nationalism 1838–1921* (Dublin: Gill and Macmillan, 1988).

Colley, L., *Britons: Forging the Nation 1707–1837* (London: Pimlico, 1994; 1st edn. 1992).

Collini, S., *Matthew Arnold: A Critical Portrait* (Oxford: Oxford University Press, 1994; 1st edn. 1988).

Collins, M., *The Path to Freedom* (Cork: Mercier, 1968; 1st edn. 1922).

Comerford, J. J., *My Kilkenny IRA Days 1916–1922* (Kilkenny: privately published, 1980; 1st edn. 1978).

Comerford, M., *The First Dáil: January 21 1919* (Dublin: Joe Clarke, 1969).

Comerford, R. V., *The Fenians in Context: Irish Politics and Society 1848–1882* (Dublin: Wolfhound, 1985).

—— 'Comprehending the Fenians', *Saothar*, 17 (1992).

Connolly, J., *Collected Works*, i and ii (Dublin: New Books, 1987 and 1988).

Coogan, T. P., *The IRA* (London: Fontana, 1987; 1st edn. 1970).

—— *Michael Collins: A Biography* (London, Hutchinson, 1990).

—— *De Valera: Long Fellow, Long Shadow* (London: Hutchinson, 1993).

Costello, F. J., *Enduring the Most: The Life and Death of Terence MacSwiney* (Dingle: Brandon, 1995).

Crane, H., *Complete Poems of Hart Crane* (New York: Liveright, 1993).

Cranston, M., *The Romantic Movement* (Oxford: Blackwell, 1994).

Cronin, S., *Frank Ryan: The Search for the Republic* (Dublin: Repsol, 1980).

—— *Irish Nationalism: A History of its Roots and Ideology* (Dublin: Academy Press, 1980).

Curtin, N., *The United Irishmen: Popular Politics in Ulster and Dublin 1791–1798* (Oxford: Oxford University Press, 1994).

Dalton, C., *With the Dublin Brigade 1917–1921* (London: Peter Davies, 1929).

Daly, M. E., *Industrial Development and Irish National Identity 1922–1939* (Dublin: Gill and Macmillan, 1992).

Davis, R., *Arthur Griffith and Non-violent Sinn Fein* (Dublin: Anvil, 1974).

—— *The Young Ireland Movement* (Dublin: Gill and Macmillan, 1987).

Davis, T., *Literary and Historical Essays* (Dublin: James Duffy, 1854).

Dawson, R., *Red Terror and Green* (London: New English Library, 1972; 1st edn. 1920).

Deasy, L., *Towards Ireland Free: The West Cork Brigade in the War of Independence 1917–1921* (Cork: Mercier, 1977).

—— *Brother Against Brother* (Cork: Mercier, 1982).

Denman, T., *Ireland's Unknown Soldiers: The 16th (Irish) Division in the Great War* (Blackrock: Irish Academic Press, 1992).

De Witt, M. H., *Taos: A Memory* (Albuquerque: University of New Mexico Press, 1992).

Dickson, D., Keogh, D., and Whelan, K. (eds.), *The United Irishmen: Republicanism, Radicalism, and Rebellion* (Dublin: Lilliput, 1993).

Doherty, F., *Samuel Beckett* (London: Hutchinson, 1971).

Donnelly, J., *Charlie Donnelly: The Life and Poems* (Dublin: Dedalus, 1987).

Dostoyevsky, F., *Crime and Punishment* (Harmondsworth: Penguin, 1951; 1st edn 1866).

—— *The Idiot* (Harmondsworth: Penguin, 1955; 1st edn 1869).

—— *The Brothers Karamazov* (New York: Bantam, 1981; 1st edn 1880).

Doyle, D. N., 'The Irish in Chicago', *Irish Historical Studies*, 26/103 (May 1989).

Drudy, P. J. (ed.), *The Irish in America: Emigration, Assimilation, and Impact* (Cambridge: Cambridge Univesity Press, 1985).

Dunne, T., 'New Histories: Beyond "Revisionism" ', *Irish Review*, 12 (Spring/Summer 1992).

Dunphy, R., *The Making of Fianna Fail Power in Ireland 1923–1948* (Oxford: Oxford University Press, 1995).

Dwyer, T. R., *Eamon de Valera* (Dublin: Gill and Macmillan, 1980).

Eagleton, T., *Nationalism: Irony and Commitment* (Derry: Field Day, 1988).

—— *Heathcliff and the Great Hunger: Studies in Irish Culture* (London: Verso, 1995).

Eastwood, D., 'E. P. Thompson, Britain, and the French Revolution', *History Workshop Journal*, 39 (1995).

Edwards, O. D., *Eamon de Valera* (Cardiff: University of Wales Press, 1987).

Edwards, R. D., *Patrick Pearse: The Triumph of Failure* (Dublin: Poolbeg, 1990; 1st edn. 1977).

—— *James Connolly* (Dublin: Gill and Macmillan, 1981).

Eisler, B., *O'Keeffe and Stieglitz: An American Romance* (Harmondsworth: Penguin, 1991).

Elborn, G., *Francis Stuart: A Life* (Dublin: Raven Arts, 1990).

Elliott, M., *Wolfe Tone: Prophet of Irish Independence* (New Haven: Yale University Press, 1989).

Ellis, S. G., 'Nationalist Historiography and the English and Gaelic Worlds in the Late Middle Ages', *Irish Historical Studies*, 25/97 (May 1986).

—— 'Historiographical Debate: Representations of the Past in Ireland: Whose Past and Whose Present?', *Irish Historical Studies*, 27/108 (Nov. 1991).

Ellmann, R., *Oscar Wilde* (London: Penguin, 1988; 1st edn. 1987).

Elton, G. R., *The Practice of History* (Glasgow: Fontana, 1969; 1st edn. 1967).

—— *Return to Essentials: Some Reflections on the Present State of Historical Study* (Cambridge: Cambridge University Press, 1991).

English, R., 'Green on Red: Two Case Studies in Early Twentieth Century Irish Republican Thought', in D. G. Boyce, R. Eccleshall, and V. Geoghegan (eds.), *Political Thought in Ireland since the Seventeenth Century* (London: Routledge, 1993).

—— *Radicals and the Republic: Socialist Republicanism in the Irish Free State 1925–1937* (Oxford: Oxford University Press, 1994).

—— 'Defining the Nation: Recent Historiography and Irish Nationalism', *European Review of History*, 2/2 (1995).

—— ' "The Inborn Hate of Things English": Ernie O'Malley and the Irish Revolution 1916–1923', *Past and Present*, 151 (May 1996).

—— and O'Malley, C. (eds.), *Prisoners: The Civil War Letters of Ernie O'Malley* (Dublin: Poolbeg, 1991).

—— and Walker, G. (eds.), *Unionism in Modern Ireland: New Perspectives on Politics and Culture* (Basingstoke: Macmillan, 1996).

Fallon, C., 'The Civil War Hungerstrikes: Women and Men', *Éire-Ireland*, 22/3 (Autumn 1987).

Fanning, R., *Independent Ireland* (Dublin: Helicon, 1983).

Farrell, M., 'The Extraordinary Life and Times of Sean MacBride', *Magill*, 6/3 (Christmas 1982), 6/4 (Jan. 1983).

Fernihough, A., *D. H. Lawrence: Aesthetics and Ideology* (Oxford: Oxford University Press, 1993).

Fisk, R., *In Time of War: Ireland, Ulster, and the Price of Neutrality 1939–1945* (London: Paladin, 1985; 1st edn. 1983).

FitzGerald, D., *Memoirs of Desmond FitzGerald 1913–1916* (London: Routledge and Kegan Paul, 1968).

FitzGerald, G., *Towards a New Ireland* (Dublin: Torc, 1973; 1st edn. 1972).

Fitzpatrick, D., *Politics and Irish Life 1913–1921: Provincial Experience of War and Revolution* (Dublin: Gill and Macmillan, 1977).

Fitzpatrick, D., 'The Geography of Irish Nationalism 1910–1921', *Past and Present*, 78 (Feb. 1978).
—— 'Women, Gender, and the Writing of Irish History', *Irish Historical Studies*, 27/107 (May 1991).
—— 'The Logic of Collective Sacrifice: Ireland and the British Army 1914–1918', *Historical Journal*, 38/4 (Dec. 1995).
—— 'Militarism in Ireland 1900–1922', in T. Bartlett and K. Jeffery (eds.), *A Military History of Ireland* (Cambridge: Cambridge University Press, 1996).
—— (ed.), *Ireland and the First World War* (Mullingar: Lilliput, 1988).
—— (ed.), *Revolution? Ireland 1917–1923* (Dublin: Trinity College, 1990).
Foley, C., *Legion of the Rearguard: The IRA and the Modern Irish State* (London: Pluto, 1992).
Follis, B. A., *A State under Siege: The Establishment of Northern Ireland 1920–1925* (Oxford: Oxford University Press, 1995).
Foster, J. W. (ed.), *The Idea of the Union: Statements and Critiques in Support of the Union of Great Britain and Northern Ireland* (Vancouver: Belcouver Press, 1995).
Foster, R. F., *Charles Stewart Parnell: The Man and his Family* (Hassocks: Harvester, 1976).
—— *Lord Randolph Churchill: A Political Life* (Oxford: Oxford University Press, 1981).
—— 'We are all Revisionists Now', *Irish Review*, 1 (1986).
—— *Modern Ireland 1600–1972* (London: Allen Lane, 1988).
—— 'A Patriot for Whom? Erskine Childers, A Very English Irishman', *History Today*, 38 (Oct. 1988).
—— *Paddy and Mr Punch: Connections in Irish and English History* (London: Allen Lane, 1993).
—— *The Story of Ireland* (Oxford: Oxford University Press, 1995).
—— (ed.), *The Oxford Illustrated History of Ireland* (Oxford: Oxford University Press, 1989).
Freyer, G., *Peadar O'Donnell* (Lewisburg, W. Vir.: Bucknell University Press, 1973).
Gallagher, F., *Days of Fear* (London: John Murray, 1928).
—— *The Anglo-Irish Treaty* (London: Hutchinson, 1965).
—— *The Indivisible Island: The History of the Partition of Ireland* (Westport: Greenwood Press, 1974; 1st edn. 1957).
Gallagher, M., 'Do Ulster Unionists have a Right to Self-determination?', *Irish Political Studies*, 5 (1990).
—— (ed.), *Irish Elections 1922–1944: Results and Analysis* (Limerick: PSAI Press, 1993).
Garvin, T., *The Evolution of Irish Nationalist Politics* (Dublin: Gill and Macmillan, 1981).
—— 'Priests and Patriots: Irish Separatism and Fear of the Modern 1890–1914', *Irish Historical Studies*, 25/97 (May 1986).

—— *Nationalist Revolutionaries in Ireland 1858–1928* (Oxford: Oxford University Press, 1987).

—— 'The Politics of Language and Literature in Pre-Independence Ireland', *Irish Political Studies*, 2 (1987).

—— 'Unenthusiastic Democrats: The Emergence of Irish Democracy', in R. J. Hill and M. Marsh (eds.), *Modern Irish Democracy* (Blackrock: Irish Academic Press, 1993).

—— *1922: The Birth of Irish Democracy* (Dublin: Gill and Macmillan, 1996).

Gellner, E., *Nations and Nationalism* (Oxford: Basil Blackwell, 1983).

—— *Conditions of Liberty: Civil Society and its Rivals* (London: Hamish Hamilton, 1994).

—— 'Nations, States, and Religions', in R. English and C. Townshend (eds.), *The State: Historical and Political Dimensions* (London: Routledge, forthcoming).

Gillespie, R., 'Historical Revisit: T. W. Moody, *The Londonderry Plantation 1609–1641* (1939)', *Irish Historical Studies*, 29/113 (May 1994).

Golden, P., *Impressions of Ireland* (New York: Irish Industries Depot, n.d.).

Goldring, M., *Pleasant the Scholar's Life: Irish Intellectuals and the Construction of the Nation State* (London: Serif, 1993).

Graham, C., ' "Liminal Spaces": Post-Colonial Theories and Irish Culture', *Irish Review*, 16 (Autumn/Winter 1994).

Graves, R., *Lawrence and the Arabs* (London: Jonathan Cape, 1927).

Greenfeld, L., *Nationalism: Five Roads to Modernity* (Cambridge, Mass.: Harvard University Press, 1992).

Grieves, K., 'Early Historical Responses to the Great War: Fortescue, Conan Doyle, and Buchan', in B. Bond (ed.), *The First World War and British Military History* (Oxford: Oxford University Press, 1991).

—— '*Nelson's History of the War*: John Buchan as a Contemporary Military Historian 1915–1922', *Journal of Contemporary History*, 28 (1993).

Harkness, D., *Northern Ireland since 1920* (Dublin: Helicon, 1983).

—— *Ireland in the Twentieth Century* (Basingstoke: Macmillan, 1996).

Harmon, M., *Seán O'Faoláin: A Life* (London: Constable, 1994).

Hart, P., 'Michael Collins and the Assassination of Sir Henry Wilson', *Irish Historical Studies*, 28/110 (Nov. 1992).

—— 'Class, Community, and the Irish Republican Army in Cork 1917–1923', in P. O'Flanagan and C. G. Buttimer (eds.), *Cork: History and Society — Interdisciplinary Essays on the History of an Irish County* (Dublin: Geography Publications, 1993).

—— 'The Protestant Experience of Revolution in Southern Ireland', in R. English and G. Walker (eds.), *Unionism in Modern Ireland: New Perspectives on Politics and Culture* (Basingstoke: Macmillan, 1996).

Harvey, A. D., 'Who were the Auxiliaries?', *Historical Journal*, 35/3 (1992).

Harvie, C., *The Centre of Things: Political Fiction in Britain from Disraeli to the Present* (London: Unwin Hyman, 1991).

Harvie, C., 'Second Thoughts of a Scotsman on the Make: Politics, Nationalism, and Myth in John Buchan', *Scottish Historical Review*, 70/188 (Apr.
1991).

Herlihy, J., *Peter Golden: The Voice of Ireland* (Cork: Peter Golden
Commemoration Committee, 1994).

Higgins, M. D., 'Liam O'Flaherty and Peadar O'Donnell: Images of Rural
Community', *Crane Bag*, 9/1 (1985).

Hill, R. J., and Marsh, M. (eds.), *Modern Irish Democracy: Essays in Honour
of Basil Chubb* (Blackrock: Irish Academic Press, 1993).

Himmelfarb, G., *Victorian Minds* (London: Weidenfeld and Nicolson, 1968).

Hobsbawm, E. J., *Nations and Nationalism since 1780: Programme, Myth,
Reality* (Cambridge: Cambridge University Press, 1990).

—— *Age of Extremes: The Short Twentieth Century 1914–1991*
(Harmondsworth: Penguin, 1994).

Holmes, C., 'The British Government and Brendan Behan 1941–1954: The
Persistence of the Prevention of Violence Act', *Saothar*, 14 (1989).

Hooker, A., and Hooker, H., 'A High Time in Red Russia', *Good
Housekeeping* (July 1930).

Hopkinson, M., *Green Against Green: The Irish Civil War* (Dublin: Gill and
Macmillan, 1988).

—— 'Biography of the Revolutionary Period: Michael Collins and Kevin
Barry', *Irish Historical Studies*, 28/111 (May 1993).

Hoppen, K. T., *Ireland since 1800: Conflict and Conformity* (London:
Longman, 1989).

Howell, D., *A Lost Left: Three Studies in Socialism and Nationalism*
(Manchester: Manchester University Press, 1986).

Hutchinson, J., *The Dynamics of Cultural Nationalism: The Gaelic Revival
and the Creation of the Irish Nation State* (London: Allen and Unwin, 1987).

—— and Smith, A. D. (eds.), *Nationalism* (Oxford: Oxford University Press,
1994).

Inglis, B., *Roger Casement* (Belfast: Blackstaff, 1993; 1st edn. 1973).

Jackson, A., *The Ulster Party: Irish Unionists in the House of Commons
1884–1911* (Oxford: Oxford University Press, 1989).

—— 'Unionist History' (i and ii), *Irish Review*, 7 (Autumn 1989) and 8 (Spring
1990).

—— 'Unionist Myths 1912–1985', *Past and Present*, 136 (Aug. 1992).

—— *Sir Edward Carson* (Dundalk: Dundalgan Press, 1993).

—— *Colonel Edward Saunderson: Land and Loyalty in Victorian Ireland*
(Oxford: Oxford University Press, 1995).

Janaway, C., *Schopenhauer* (Oxford: Oxford University Press, 1994).

Jeffers, R., *Roan Stallion, Tamar, and Other Poems* (London: Hogarth, 1928).

Jeffery, K., 'Irish Culture and the Great War', *Bullán*, 1, 2 (Autumn 1994).

—— (ed.), *'An Irish Empire'? Aspects of Ireland and the British Empire*
(Manchester: Manchester University Press, 1996).

—— and Fraser, T. G. (eds.), *Men, Women, and War* (Dublin: Lilliput, 1993).

Joannon, P., 'Graham Greene's Other Island', *Études Irlandaises*, 6 (1981).

Jordan, A. J., *Major John MacBride 1865–1916* (Westport: Westport Historical Society, 1991).

Joyce, P., 'History and Postmodernism', *Past and Present*, 133 (Nov. 1991).

Judge, P. M. (ed.), *O'Connell School: 150 Years 1828–1978* (Dublin: O'Connell School, 1978).

Kafka, F., *The Castle* (Harmondsworth: Penguin, 1957; 1st edn. 1926).

—— *America* (London: Minerva, 1992; 1st edn. 1927).

Karsten, P., 'Irish Soldiers in the British Army 1792–1922: Suborned or Subordinate', *Journal of Social History*, 17 (1983).

Kearney, R. (ed.), *The Irish Mind: Exploring Intellectual Traditions* (Dublin: Wolfhound, 1985).

Kedourie, E., *Nationalism* (Oxford: Blackwell, 1993; 1st edn. 1960).

Keena, C., *Gerry Adams: A Biography* (Cork: Mercier, 1990).

Kelleher, J. V., 'Irish Literature Today', *The Bell*, 10/4 (July 1945).

Kelley, K. J., *The Longest War: Northern Ireland and the IRA* (London: Zed, 1988; 1st edn. 1982).

Kelly, A. A., *Liam O'Flaherty: The Storyteller* (London: Macmillan, 1976).

—— and Saunders, N., *Joseph Campbell: Poet and Nationalist 1879–1944: A Critical Biography* (Dublin: Wolfhound, 1988).

Kennedy, D., *The Widening Gulf: Northern Attitudes to the Independent Irish State 1919–1949* (Belfast: Blackstaff, 1988).

Kennedy, L., 'Modern Ireland: Post-Colonial Society or Post-Colonial Pretensions?', *Irish Review*, 13 (Winter 1992–3).

Kennedy, S. B., *Irish Art and Modernism 1880–1950* (Belfast: Institute of Irish Studies, 1991).

Kenny, M., *The First New Left: British Intellectuals after Stalin* (London: Lawrence and Wishart, 1995).

Keogh, D., *Twentieth Century Ireland: Nation and State* (Dublin: Gill and Macmillan, 1994).

Khilnani, S., *Arguing Revolution: The Intellectual Left in Postwar France* (New Haven: Yale University Press, 1993).

Kiberd, D., 'Wilde and the English Question', *Times Literary Supplement* (16 Dec. 1994).

Knowlson, J., *Damned to Fame: The Life of Samuel Beckett* (London: Bloomsbury, 1996).

Komesu, O., and Sekine, M. (eds.), *Irish Writers and Politics* (Gerrards Cross: Colin Smythe, 1990).

Kotsonouris, M., *Retreat from Revolution: The Dáil Courts 1920–1924* (Blackrock: Irish Academic Press, 1994).

Laffan, M., *The Partition of Ireland 1911–1925* (Dundalk: Dundalgan, 1983).

Lawrence, D. H., *The Plumed Serpent* (Ware: Wordsworth, 1995; 1st edn. 1926).

Lawrence, D. H., *Mornings in Mexico* (London: Martin Secker, 1930; 1st edn. 1927).
—— *Movements in European History* (Oxford: Oxford University Press, 1971; 1st edn. 1921).
—— *Selected Poems* (Harmondsworth: Penguin, 1972).
Lawrence, T. E., *Revolt in the Desert* (London: Cape, 1927).
—— *Seven Pillars of Wisdom: A Triumph* (Harmondsworth: Penguin, 1962; 1st edn. 1926).
Leader, Z., *Revision and Romantic Authorship* (Oxford: Oxford University Press, 1996).
Le Brocquy, A. M., *Louis le Brocquy: A Painter, Seeing His Way* (Dublin: Gill and Macmillan, 1994).
Lecky, W. E. H., *A History of Ireland in the Eighteenth Century* (London: Longmans, Green, and Co., 1913; 1st edn. 1892).
Lee, J. J., *Ireland 1912–1985: Politics and Society* (Cambridge: Cambridge University Press, 1989).
Lewis, R. W. B., *The Poetry of Hart Crane: A Critical Study* (Princeton: Princeton University Press, 1967).
Lloyd, D., *Anomalous States: Irish Writing and the Post-Colonial Moment* (Dublin: Lilliput, 1993).
Longley, E., *Louis MacNeice: A Study* (London: Faber, 1988).
—— *The Living Stream: Literature and Revisionism in Ireland* (Newcastle: Bloodaxe, 1994).
Lownie, A., *John Buchan: The Presbyterian Cavalier* (London: Constable, 1995).
Luhan, M. D., *Lorenzo in Taos* (New York: Kraus, 1969; 1st edn. 1932).
—— *Intimate Memories: Background* (New York: Kraus, 1971; 1st edn. 1933).
—— *European Experiences* (New York: Harcourt, Brace and Co., 1935).
Lyman, W. W., 'Ella Young: A Memoir', *Eire-Ireland*, 8/3 (Autumn 1973).
Lyons, F. S. L., *Culture and Anarchy in Ireland 1890–1939* (Oxford: Oxford University Press, 1982; 1st edn. 1979).
Macardle, D., *The Irish Republic: A Documented Chronicle of the Anglo-Irish Conflict and the Partitioning of Ireland, with a Detailed Account of the Period 1916–1923* (London: Corgi, 1968; 1st edn. 1937).
—— *Tragedies of Kerry 1922–1923* (Dublin: Irish Freedom Press, 1988; 1st edn. 1924).
MacBride, I. 'The School of Virtue: Francis Hutcheson, Irish Presbyterians, and the Scottish Enlightenment', in D. G. Boyce, R. Eccleshall, and V. Geoghegan (eds.), *Political Thought in Ireland since the Seventeenth Century* (London: Routledge, 1993).
MacBride, M. G., *A Servant of the Queen: Reminiscences* (London: Victor Gollancz, 1974; 1st edn. 1938).
McCabe, A., ' "The Stormy Petrel of the Transport Workers": Peadar O'Donnell, Trade Unionist 1917–1920', *Saothar*, 19 (1994).

McCartney, D., *W. E. H. Lecky: Historian and Politician 1838–1903* (Dublin: Lilliput, 1994).

MacDonagh, O., *States of Mind: A Study of Anglo-Irish Conflict 1780–1980* (London: Allen and Unwin, 1983).

—— *O'Connell: The Life of Daniel O'Connell 1775–1847* (London: Weidenfeld and Nicolson, 1991).

McDonald, P., *Louis MacNeice: The Poet in his Contexts* (Oxford: Oxford University Press, 1991).

MacEoin, U. (ed.), *Survivors* (Dublin: Argenta, 1987; 1st edn. 1980).

MacEvilly, M., 'Sean MacBride and the Republican Motor Launch *St. George*', *Irish Sword*, 16/62 (1984).

McHugh, J. P., 'Voices of the Rearguard: A Study of *An Phoblacht*: Irish Republican Thought in the Post-Revolutionary Era 1923–1937', MA thesis (University College, Dublin, 1983).

McInerney, M., *Peadar O'Donnell: Irish Social Rebel* (Dublin: O'Brien, 1974).

Macintyre, A., *The Liberator: Daniel O'Connell and the Irish Party 1830–1847* (London: Hamish Hamilton, 1965).

McIntyre, A., 'Modern Irish Republicanism: The Product of British State Strategies', *Irish Political Studies*, 10 (1995).

McKenzie, F. A., *The Irish Rebellion: What Happened—and Why* (London: C. Arthur Pearson, 1916).

McMahon, D., *Republicans and Imperialists: Anglo-Irish Relations in the 1930s* (New Haven: Yale University Press, 1984).

MacMillan, G. M., *State, Society, and Authority in Ireland: The Foundations of the Modern State* (Dublin: Gill and Macmillan, 1993).

MacNeice, L., *Collected Poems* (London, Faber and Faber, 1979; 1st edn. 1966).

MacSwiney, T., *Principles of Freedom* (Dublin: Talbot, 1921).

Maher, J., *The Flying Column: West Kilkenny 1916–1921* (Dublin: Geography Publications, 1987).

Mair, P., *The Changing Irish Party System: Organizations, Ideology, and Electoral Competition* (London: Pinter, 1987).

Mandle, W. F., *The Gaelic Athletic Association and Irish Nationalist Politics 1884–1924* (London: Christopher Helm, 1987).

Markievicz, C., *Prison Letters of Countess Markievicz* (London: Virago, 1987; 1st edn. 1934).

Marquand, J. P., *So Little Time* (Gateshead: Robert Hale, 1944; 1st edn. 1943).

—— *Point of No Return* (Boston: Little, Brown, and Co., 1949).

—— *H. M. Pulham Esquire* (Harmondsworth: Penguin, 1951; 1st edn. 1941).

—— *Women and Thomas Harrow* (London: Collins, 1959; 1st edn. 1958).

Matthews, J., *Frank O'Connor* (Lewisburg, W. Vir.: Bucknell University Press, 1976).

Maume, P., *'Life That is Exile': Daniel Corkery and the Search for Irish Ireland* (Belfast: Institute of Irish Studies, 1993).

Maume, P., *D. P. Moran* (Dundalk: Historical Association of Ireland, 1995).
—— 'The Ancient Constitution: Arthur Griffith and his Intellectual Legacy to Sinn Féin', *Irish Political Studies*, 10 (1995).
Meenan, F. O. C., *Cecilia Street: The Catholic University School of Medicine 1855–1931* (Dublin: Gill and Macmillan, 1987).
Meenan, J. (ed.), *Centenary History of the Literary and Historical Society of University College Dublin 1855–1955* (Tralee: The Kerryman, n. d.).
Melville, H., *Moby-Dick* (Harmondsworth: Penguin, 1972; 1st edn. 1851).
Miller, K., *Emigrants and Exiles: Ireland and the Irish Exodus to North America* (Oxford: Oxford University Press, 1985).
Mitchell, A., *Revolutionary Government in Ireland: Dail Eireann 1919–1922* (Dublin: Gill and Macmillan, 1995).
Moody, T. W., *The Londonderry Plantation 1609–1641: The City of London and the Plantation of Ulster* (Belfast: William Mullan, 1939).
—— (ed.), *The Fenian Movement* (Cork: Mercier, 1978; 1st edn. 1968).
Moran, S. F., *Patrick Pearse and the Politics of Redemption: The Mind of the Easter Rising 1916* (Washington: Catholic University of America Press, 1994).
Morgan, A., *James Connolly: A Political Biography* (Manchester: Manchester University Press, 1988).
Muenger, E., *The British Military Dilemma in Ireland: Occupation Politics 1886–1914* (Dublin: Gill and Macmillan, 1991).
Murphy, B. P., *Patrick Pearse and the Lost Republican Ideal* (Dublin: James Duffy, 1991).
Murphy, B. S., 'Politics and Ideology: Mary MacSwiney and Irish Republicanism 1872–1942', Ph.D. thesis (National University of Ireland, 1994).
Murphy, J. A., *Ireland in the Twentieth Century* (Dublin: Gill and Macmillan, 1975).
Newey, V., and Thompson, A. (eds.), *Literature and Nationalism* (Liverpool: Liverpool University Press, 1991).
Newsinger, J., 'Fenianism Revisited: Pastime or Revolutionary Movement?', *Saothar*, 17 (1992).
Ni Dhonnchadha, M., and Dorgan, T. (eds.), *Revising the Rising* (Derry: Field Day, 1991).
Nolan, E., *James Joyce and Nationalism* (London: Routledge, 1995).
Norton, C., 'The Left in Northern Ireland 1921–1932', *Labour History Review*, 60/1 (Spring 1995).
Nutt, K., 'Irish Identity and the Writing of History', *Éire-Ireland*, 29/2 (Summer 1994).
O'Brien, B., *The Long War: The IRA and Sinn Fein 1985 to Today* (Dublin: O'Brien, 1993).
O'Brien, C. C., *States of Ireland* (St Albans: Panther, 1974; 1st edn. 1972).
—— *Passion and Cunning: Essays on Nationalism, Terrorism, and Revolution* (New York: Simon and Schuster, 1988).

—— *Ancestral Voices: Religion and Nationalism in Ireland* (Dublin: Poolbeg Press, 1994).

O Broin, L., *W. E. Wylie and the Irish Revolution 1916–1921* (Dublin: Gill and Macmillan, 1989).

O'Callaghan, M., 'Language, Nationality, and Cultural Identity in the Irish Free State 1922–1927: The *Irish Statesman* and the *Catholic Bulletin* Reappraised', *Irish Historical Studies*, 24/94 (Nov. 1984).

O'Carroll, J. P., and Murphy, J. A. (eds.), *De Valera and his Times* (Cork: Cork University Press, 1986; 1st edn. 1983).

O'Connell, M. R., *Daniel O'Connell: The Man and his Politics* (Blackrock: Irish Academic Press, 1990).

O'Connor, B., *With Michael Collins in the Fight for Irish Independence* (London: Peter Davies, 1929).

O'Connor, F., *The Big Fellow: A Life of Michael Collins* (London: Thomas Nelson, 1937).

—— *An Only Child* (Belfast: Blackstaff, 1993; 1st edn. 1961).

—— *My Father's Son* (London: Pan, 1971; 1st edn. 1968).

—— *Collected Stories* (2 vols.; London: Pan, 1990).

Odets, C., *Six Plays of Clifford Odets* (New York: Random House, 1939).

O'Donnell, P., *Storm: A Story of the Irish War* (Dublin: Talbot, n. d. (1926?)).

—— *Islanders* (Cork: Mercier, 1963; 1st edn. 1927).

—— *Adrigoole* (London: Jonathan Cape, 1929).

—— *The Knife* (Dublin: Irish Humanities Centre, 1980; 1st edn. 1930).

—— *The Gates Flew Open* (London: Jonathan Cape, 1932).

—— *Wrack: A Play in Six Scenes* (London: Jonathan Cape, 1933).

—— *On the Edge of the Stream* (London: Jonathan Cape, 1934).

—— *Salud! An Irishman in Spain* (London: Methuen, 1937).

—— *The Big Windows* (Dublin: O'Brien, 1983; 1st edn. 1955).

—— *There Will be Another Day* (Dublin: Dolmen, 1963).

—— *Proud Island* (Dublin: O'Brien, 1977; 1st edn. 1975).

—— 'Teachers Vote Strike', *The Bell*, 11/2 (Nov. 1945).

—— 'Liberty Ltd.', *The Bell*, 12/4 (July 1946).

—— 'Facts and Fairies', *The Bell*, 13/1 (Oct. 1946).

—— 'Suggestion for a Fighting Wake', *The Bell*, 14/4 (July 1947).

—— 'A Recognizable Gait of Going', *The Bell*, 16/2 (Nov. 1950).

O'Donovan, D., *Kevin Barry and his Time* (Sandycove: Glendale, 1989).

O Drisceoil, D., *Censorship in Ireland 1939–1945: Neutrality, Politics, and Society* (Cork: Cork University Press, 1996).

O Duibhir, C., *Sinn Fein: The First Election 1908* (Manorhamilton: Drumlin, 1993).

O'Faoláin, S., *De Valera* (Harmondsworth: Penguin, 1939).

—— *Constance Markievicz* (London: Sphere, 1967; 1st edn. 1934).

—— *The Heat of the Sun* (London: Pan, 1969; 1st edn. 1963).

O'Faoláin, *The Great O'Neill: A Biography of Hugh O'Neill Earl of Tyrone 1550–1616* (Cork: Mercier, 1970; 1st edn. 1942).

—— *The Irish* (West Drayton: Penguin, 1947).

—— *The Irish* (Harmondsworth: Penguin, 1980; 1st edn. 1947).

—— *King of the Beggars: A Life of Daniel O'Connell* (Dublin: Poolbeg, 1986; 1st edn. 1938).

O'Farrell, P., *The Ernie O'Malley Story* (Cork: Mercier, 1983).

O'Flaherty, L., *The Informer* (London: Four Square Books, 1958; 1st edn. 1925).

—— *Insurrection* (Dublin: Wolfhound, 1993; 1st edn. 1950).

—— *The Assassin* (Dublin: Wolfhound, 1988; 1st edn. 1928).

—— *Thy Neighbour's Wife* (Dublin: Wolfhound, 1992; 1st edn. 1923).

—— *Famine* (London: Four Square Books, 1959; 1st edn. 1937).

—— *Mr Gilhooley* (Dublin: Wolfhound, 1991; 1st edn. 1926).

—— *The Mountain Tavern and Other Stories* (Leipzig: Tauchnitz, 1929).

—— *Irish Portraits: Fourteen Short Stories* (London: Sphere, 1970).

O'Flanagan, P., and Buttimer, C. G. (eds.), *Cork: History and Society— Interdisciplinary Essays on the History of an Irish County* (Dublin: Geography Publications, 1993).

Ó Gráda, C., *Ireland: A New Economic History 1780–1939* (Oxford: Oxford University Press, 1994).

O'Halloran, C., *Partition and the Limits of Irish Nationalism: An Ideology under Stress* (Dublin: Gill and Macmillan, 1987).

O'Halpin, E., *The Decline of the Union: British Government in Ireland 1892–1920* (Dublin: Gill and Macmillan, 1987).

O'Hara, M., *The Scent of the Roses* (Glasgow: Fontana, 1981; 1st edn. 1980).

O'Malley, E., *On Another Man's Wound* (Dublin: Anvil, 1979; 1st edn. 1936).

—— *The Singing Flame* (Dublin: Anvil, 1978).

—— *Raids and Rallies* (Dublin: Anvil, 1982).

—— 'Renaissance', *La France Libre*, 13/74 (Dec. 1946–Jan. 1947).

—— 'Louis le Brocquy', *Horizon*, 14/79 (July 1946).

—— 'A Painter of his People', *The Bell*, 11/4 (Jan. 1946).

—— 'Painting: "The School of London" ', *The Bell*, 14/3 (June 1947).

—— 'The Background of the Arts in Mexico', *The Bell*, 14/5 (Aug. 1947).

O'Toole, F., *A Mass for Jesse James: A Journey through 1980s Ireland* (Dublin: Raven Arts Press, 1990).

Parekh, B., 'Discourses on National Identity', *Political Studies*, 42/3 (Sept. 1994).

Paret, P., *Understanding War: Essays on Clausewitz and the History of Military Power* (Princeton: Princeton University Press, 1992).

Pearse, P. H., *Political Writings and Speeches* (Dublin: Phoenix, n.d.).

Philpin, C. H. E. (ed.), *Nationalism and Popular Protest in Ireland* (Cambridge: Cambridge University Press, 1987).

Phoenix, E., *Northern Nationalism: Nationalist Politics, Partition, and the*

Catholic Minority in Northern Ireland 1890–1940 (Belfast: Ulster Historical Foundation, 1994).

Prager, J., *Building Democracy in Ireland: Political Order and Cultural Integration in a Newly Independent Nation* (Cambridge: Cambridge University Press, 1986).

Prakash, G. (ed.), *After Colonialism: Imperial Histories and Post-Colonial Displacements* (Princeton: Princeton University Press, 1995).

Quinn, V., *Hart Crane* (New York: Twayne Publishers, 1963).

Raine, K., *William Blake* (London: Thames and Hudson, 1970).

Richards, I. A., *Practical Criticism: A Study of Literary Judgment* (London: Routledge, 1964; 1st edn. 1929).

Richards, J., 'Ireland, the Empire, and Film', in K. Jeffery (ed.), '*An Irish Empire*'? *Aspects of Ireland and the British Empire* (Manchester: Manchester University Press, 1996).

Ricks, C., *Beckett's Dying Words* (Oxford: Oxford University Press, 1993).

Ridgeway, A. N. (ed.), *The Selected Letters of Robinson Jeffers 1897–1962* (Baltimore: Johns Hopkins Press, 1968).

Ring, J., *Erskine Childers* (London: John Murray, 1996).

Robbins, K., *The First World War* (Oxford: Oxford University Press, 1984).

Roe, N., *Wordsworth and Coleridge: The Radical Years* (Oxford: Oxford University Press, 1990; 1st edn. 1988).

Roelofs, H. H. O., *The Irish Sculptures of Helen Hooker O'Malley Roelofs 1905–1993* (Limerick: University of Limerick, 1993).

Rose, P. L., *Wagner: Race and Revolution* (London: Faber and Faber, 1992).

Rumpf, E., and Hepburn, A. C., *Nationalism and Socialism in Twentieth Century Ireland* (Liverpool: Liverpool University Press, 1977).

Ryan, M., *The Tom Barry Story* (Cork: Mercier, 1982).

—— *Liam Lynch: The Real Chief* (Cork: Mercier, 1986).

Said, E. W., *Yeats and Decolonization* (Derry: Field Day, 1988).

—— *Musical Elaborations* (London: Vintage, 1992; 1st edn. 1991).

—— *Culture and Imperialism* (London: Vintage, 1994; 1st edn. 1993).

—— *Representations of the Intellectual: The 1993 Reith Lectures* (London: Vintage, 1994).

Sarbaugh, T. J., 'Eamon de Valera and the *Irish Press* in California 1928–1931', *Eire-Ireland*, 20/4 (Winter 1985).

Schmitt, D. E., *The Irony of Irish Democracy: The Impact of Political Culture on Administrative and Democratic Political Development in Ireland* (London: Heath, 1973).

Shannon, C. B., *Arthur J. Balfour and Ireland 1874–1922* (Washington: Catholic University of America Press, 1988).

Shapiro, J., *Shakespeare and the Jews* (New York: Columbia University Press, 1996).

Shaw, F., 'The Canon of Irish History: A Challenge', *Studies*, 61/242 (Summer 1972).

Sheeran, P. F., *The Novels of Liam O'Flaherty: A Study in Romantic Realism* (Dublin: Wolfhound, 1976).

Shirakawa, S. H., *The Devil's Music Master: The Controversial Life and Career of Wilhelm Furtwängler* (Oxford: Oxford University Press, 1992).

Siedentop, L., *Tocqueville* (Oxford: Oxford University Press, 1994).

Sinnott, R., *Irish Voters Decide: Voting Behaviour in Elections and Referendums since 1918* (Manchester: Manchester University Press, 1995).

Smith, A. D., *Theories of Nationalism* (London: Duckworth, 1971).

—— *The Ethnic Origins of Nations* (Oxford: Basil Blackwell, 1986).

—— *National Identity* (London, Penguin, 1991).

Smith, J. A., *John Buchan: A Biography* (London: Rupert Hart-Davis, 1965).

Smith, M. L. R., *Fighting for Ireland? The Military Strategy of the Irish Republican Movement* (London: Routledge, 1995).

Smith, W., *Real Life: The Group Theatre and America 1931–1940* (New York: Knopf, 1990).

Smout, T. C. (ed.), *Victorian Values: A Joint Symposium of the Royal Society of Edinburgh and the British Academy* (Oxford: Oxford University Press, 1992).

Smyth, D., 'Democratic Vistas', *Fortnight*, 336 (Feb. 1995).

Smyth, J., *The Men of No Property: Irish Radicals and Popular Politics in the Late Eighteenth Century* (Dublin: Gill and Macmillan, 1992).

Stallworthy, J., *Louis MacNeice* (London: Faber and Faber, 1995).

Stevenson, R. L., *The Master of Ballantrae* (Oxford: Oxford University Press, 1983; 1st edn. 1889).

—— *Kidnapped* (OUP, 1969).

Stewart, A. T. Q., *A Deeper Silence: The Hidden Origins of the United Irishmen* (London: Faber and Faber, 1993).

Stokes, M. (ed.), *Ethnicity, Identity, and Music: The Musical Construction of Place* (Oxford: Berg, 1994).

Stuart, F., *Black List: Section H* (Harmondsworth: Penguin, 1982; 1st edn. 1971).

Tarpey, M. V., 'Joseph McGarrity, Fighter for Irish Freedom', *Studia Hibernica*, 11 (1971).

Taylor, R., *Michael Collins* (London: Four Square, 1961; 1st edn. 1958).

Thompson, W. I., *The Imagination of an Insurrection: Dublin, Easter 1916: A Study of an Ideological Movement* (West Stockbridge: Lindisfarne, 1982; 1st edn. 1967).

Tierney, M., *Eoin MacNeill* (Oxford: Oxford University Press, 1980).

Tóibín, C., *The South* (London: Picador, 1992; 1st edn. 1990).

—— *The Heather Blazing* (London: Pan, 1993; 1st edn. 1992).

—— 'New Ways of Killing Your Father', *London Review of Books*, 15/22 (18 Nov. 1993).

Tone, T. W., *The Autobiography of Theobald Wolfe Tone 1763–1798* (2 vols.; London: T. Fisher Unwin, 1893).

Toolis, K., *Rebel Hearts: Journeys within the IRA's Soul* (London: Picador, 1995).

Townshend, C., *The British Campaign in Ireland 1919–1921: The Development of Political and Military Policies* (Oxford: Oxford University Press, 1975).

—— 'The Irish Railway Strike of 1920: Industrial Action and Civil Resistance in the Struggle for Independence', *Irish Historical Studies*, 21/83 (Mar. 1979).

—— 'The Irish Republican Army and the Development of Guerrilla Warfare 1916–1921', *English Historical Review*, 94 (1979).

—— 'Bloody Sunday: Michael Collins Speaks', *European Studies Review*, 9 (1979).

—— *Political Violence in Ireland: Government and Resistance since 1848* (Oxford: Oxford University Press, 1983).

—— *Britain's Civil Wars: Counterinsurgency in the Twentieth Century* (London: Faber and Faber, 1986).

—— 'British Policy in Ireland 1906–1921', in D. G. Boyce (ed.), *The Revolution in Ireland 1879–1923* (Basingstoke: Macmillan, 1988).

—— (ed.), *Consensus in Ireland: Approaches and Recessions* (Oxford: Oxford University Press, 1988).

—— *Making the Peace: Public Order and Public Security in Modern Britain* (Oxford: Oxford University Press, 1993).

—— 'The Suppression of the Easter Rising', *Bullan*, 1/1 (Spring 1994).

Turner, J., *British Politics and the Great War: Coalition and Conflict 1915–1918* (New Haven: Yale University Press, 1992).

Udall, S. R., *Spud Johnson and Laughing Horse* (Albuquerque: University of New Mexico Press, 1994).

Unterecker, J., *Voyager: A Life of Hart Crane* (New York: Farrar, Straus, and Giroux, 1969).

Valiulis, M. G., *Almost a Rebellion: The Irish Army Mutiny of 1924* (Cork: Tower Books, 1985).

—— *Portrait of a Revolutionary: General Richard Mulcahy and the Founding of the Irish Free State* (Blackrock: Irish Academic Press, 1992).

Vance, N., *Irish Literature: A Social History—Tradition, Identity, and Difference* (Oxford: Blackwell, 1990).

Walker, D., *Louis le Brocquy* (Dublin: Ward River Press, 1981).

Walker, G., *The Politics of Frustration: Harry Midgley and the Failure of Labour in Northern Ireland* (Manchester: Manchester University Press, 1985).

—— 'Propaganda and Conservative Nationalism during the Irish Civil War 1922–1923', *Éire-Ireland*, 22/4 (Winter 1987).

—— 'Old History: Protestant Ulster in Lee's *Ireland*', *Irish Review*, 12 (Spring/Summer 1992).

—— ' "The Irish Dr Goebbels": Frank Gallagher and Irish Republican Propaganda', *Journal of Contemporary History*, 27 (1992).

Walsh, M., *The Quiet Man and Other Stories* (Belfast: Appletree, 1992).

Ward, A. J., *The Irish Constitutional Tradition: Responsible Government and Modern Ireland 1782–1992* (Washington: Catholic University of America Press, 1994).

Ward, M., *Unmanageable Revolutionaries: Women and Irish Nationalism* (London: Pluto, 1983).

Weber, B. (ed.), *The Letters of Hart Crane 1916–1932* (New York: Hermitage House, 1952).

—— *The Complete Poems and Selected Letters and Prose of Hart Crane* (New York: Liveright Publishing Corp., 1966).

Welch, R. (ed.), *The Oxford Companion to Irish Literature* (Oxford: Oxford University Press, 1996).

White, T. de V., *Kevin O'Higgins* (Dublin: Anvil, 1986; 1st edn. 1948).

Whitehouse, H., *Inside the Cult: Religious Innovation and Transmission in Papua New Guinea* (Oxford: Oxford University Press, 1995).

Whyte, J. H., *Church and State in Modern Ireland 1923–1979* (Dublin: Gill and Macmillan, 1984; 1st edn. 1971).

—— *Interpreting Northern Ireland* (Oxford: Oxford University Press, 1990).

Wilde, O., *Complete Works of Oscar Wilde* (3 vols.; London: Heron, 1966).

Williams, T. D. (ed.), *The Irish Struggle 1916–1926* (London: Routledge and Kegan Paul, 1966).

—— (ed.), *Secret Societies in Ireland* (Dublin: Gill and Macmillan, 1973).

Wilmer, S. E. (ed.), *Beckett in Dublin* (Dublin: Lilliput, 1992).

Wu, D. (ed.), *Romanticism: An Anthology* (Oxford: Blackwell, 1994).

Yeats, J. B., *The Charmed Life* (London: Routledge and Kegan Paul, 1974; 1st edn. 1938).

Yeats, W. B., *Yeats's Poems* (Dublin: Gill and Macmillan, 1989).

Yingling, T. E., *Hart Crane and the Homosexual Text: New Thresholds, New Anatomies* (Chicago: University of Chicago Press, 1990).

Young, E., *Flowering Dusk: Things Remembered Accurately and Inaccurately* (London: Dennis Dobson, 1947; 1st edn. 1945).

Younger, C., *Ireland's Civil War* (Glasgow: Fontana, 1979; 1st edn. 1968).

—— *Arthur Griffith* (Dublin: Gill and Macmillan, 1981).

Zaller, R. (ed.), *Centennial Essays for Robinson Jeffers* (Newark: University of Delaware Press, 1991).

Zneimer, J., *The Literary Vision of Liam O'Flaherty* (Syracuse: Syracuse University Press, 1970).

Index